Changing Urban Education

STUDIES IN GOVERNMENT AND PUBLIC POLICY

Changing Urban Education

Edited by Clarence N. Stone

 University Press of Kansas

Published by the University Press of Kansas (Lawrence, Kansas 66049), which was
organized by the Kansas Board of Regents and is operated and funded by Emporia State
University, Fort Hays State University, Kansas State University, Pittsburg State
University, the University of Kansas, and Wichita State University

Library of Congress Cataloging-in-Publication Data

Changing urban education / edited by Clarence N. Stone.
p. cm. — (Studies in government and public policy)
Includes bibliographical references and index.
ISBN 0-7006-0901-6 (cloth : alk. paper). — ISBN 0-7006-0902-4 (pbk. : alk. paper)
1. Education, Urban—Political aspects—United States—Case studies. 2. Education and
state—United States—Case studies. 3. Educational change—United States—Case
studies. I. Stone, Clarence N. (Clarence Nathan), 1935– . II. Series.
LC5131.C39 1998
370′.9173′2—dc21
                                                                            98-10098

British Library Cataloguing in Publication Data is available.

Printed in the United States of America

10 9 8 7 6 5 4 3 2 1

To the memory of
Byran O. Jackson
scholar and colleague

Table of Contents

Preface

The origins of this book trace to fall 1989. At that time I had just published *Regime Politics,* my study of the biracial coalition that governs Atlanta. Thanks to the College of Urban, Labor, and Metropolitan Affairs of Wayne State University, I had the luxury of a semester as a visiting research scholar in "Motor City." As I thought about the urban condition broadly, the question that joined the Atlanta and Detroit experiences for me was this: Why, in their search for strategies of revitalization, have American cities given so little sustained attention to social reconstruction and intertwined issues of human capital development? Later, in collaboration with others, I narrowed the issue of social reconstruction and human capital to an inquiry into the politics of urban school improvement. But from the start, this inquiry was part of a larger issue about social reconstruction and what it would take politically to put and keep such a concern on the action agenda of the nation's cities.

In the sweep of urban history, social reconstruction is not an unthought-of consideration. After all, it has been around for a long time. It was part of the progressive agenda in an earlier era, and it reemerged briefly in the 1950s when big-city school superintendents were among the first to report signs of a new rise in social distress. The Ford Foundation's "gray areas" project, followed by a nationally funded skirmish with poverty, represented one wave of problem recognition. But social reform faded, and mayors, along with business leaders, continued to occupy themselves mainly with physical renewal and economic development.

A new era emerged in 1983, when *A Nation at Risk* directed attention to the broad question of the quality of American schools. Even so, several more years passed before *urban* education received special recognition among city political and business leaders as a problem in need of their attention. With mounting concern, finally in fall 1997, under the joint auspices of the U.S. Conference of Mayors and the Council of Great City Schools, a summit meeting brought together mayors and urban school officials, signaling that top-level discussion now includes urban schools and their performance. A related concern about community building has also made its way into the discourse about the urban condition.

On the surface, a corner appears to have been turned. But what we can realistically expect is hard to predict. A single summit does not make a new policy direction. *Regime Politics* suggested that a sustained policy effort must rest on a stable set of political arrangements. Public recognition of a problem is not enough, even when top officials acknowledge a need for action. Attention soon ebbs if there is no structured basis for policy cooperation between key actors. Who are the key actors? The answer suggested by regime analysis is "those who can contribute useful resources." Thus it depends on the nature of the policy problem. Here we begin to see why decision makers might be reluctant to take on an issue like school improvement; to succeed may mean assuming a responsibility to mobilize "the whole village." Because education entails a broad array of resources, school reform potentially brings into play parents and a variety of community and voluntary groups. Business also figures prominently in efforts to change the practice of public education. Nevertheless, because the mobilization of resources is crucial, what will be regularized and how remains to be seen. The school reform script for the years ahead is thus not easy to read at this stage.

Though regime analysis does not enable us to make firm predictions, it does indicate where we should look to understand the process of change. It tells us that verbal endorsement of a new policy direction is only a weak sign that change is in the making. A much stronger sign is a commitment of resources. Without that commitment, a reform may have limited staying power.

The general model of social reform suggested here thus runs: problem recognition—attempts to rearrange political and other relationships, including the mobilization of efforts and resources—policy response. In short, we do not simply move from problem recognition to durable policy response. We do not even move from problem recognition to dissemination of new ideas to durable policy response. Some institutionalization of effort, some rearranging of relationships forms an essential step in the reform process.

Many would-be reformers skip this intermediate, political step and go directly to the question of whether various initiatives improve test scores and enhance the academic performance of students from poverty backgrounds. Questions about outcomes undoubtedly need to be asked at some stage, but first it must be established that reform initiatives can be put into place and kept there—not just in name but in reality. It is this issue that makes the political context of reform a matter of central concern. *Talk* about reform or about what is desirable is not the same as a *politically secured* program of action.

Some readers may be uneasy about the word "politics" because it is often understood in strictly negative terms as the pursuit of personal or group advantage narrowly conceived. I see a more open-ended definition of politics: the ways in which we cope with our interdependence and differences as we pursue collective aims. We can have healthier and more constructive forms of politics or forms that are less so; we are unable, however, to avoid politics. Apolitical reform is simply talk, not action.

This book, then, is an unapologetic look at the political context of efforts to change urban education. The contributors to this collection take us through sundry issues in a variety of settings, and they show us how hard it is to rearrange political relationships so they will be conducive to school reform. If we return, then, to the broad question of why social reconstruction has not been a central concern of city officials and other local leadership figures, one answer, suggested by the issue of school reform, is the severity of the challenge.

Fundamental school reform is not only hard to organize, but the politics of the process are also little understood. Over the years urban political science has paid more heed to the physical redevelopment of cities than to education and related policy areas. This was certainly true of my own research career up until my conscious redirection began at Wayne State, a redirection that made me aware that some social analysts on the left are wary of terms like "human capital," fearing that they focus attention on individual deficits ("blaming the victim") rather than on the structure of opportunity in society.

I have come to see the issue somewhat differently. To me, human capital is about the investment that *society* makes in people, especially in children and youth. That class is such a strong predictor of scholastic performance is evidence that the *informal* processes by which society fosters the development of children leads to inequalities of opportunity. If the pattern is to be altered, we need conscious efforts to go beyond the informal process and promote human capital development more systematically.

Some on the political right may wish to downplay a social responsibility to deal with the structure of opportunity, and for partisan reasons they may bristle at the African saying that "it takes a whole village to raise a child." But social science research is heavily on the side of African wisdom in this case. One might debate the balance between governmental and nongovernmental efforts to invest in human capital development for children who are disadvantaged. But in today's complex world, if one is genuinely committed to the idea of equal opportunity, only a shallow and legalistic understanding of human capital development can stand in the way of acknowledging a responsibility to take actions.

In quest of a way to identify purposeful actions, I settled on the term "civic capacity" to highlight the different degrees to which cities are able to bring various sectors of the community together in efforts to improve educational opportunity for children in urban schools. Because half of the nation's children below the poverty line are in big-city school districts, urban education is the major testing ground for civic capacity. The need is great; delivery is a different matter.

On my return from Detroit to Maryland in 1990, Civic Capacity and Urban Education became the focal topic for bringing together a small number of urban political scientists to talk about a multicity study. The initial effort, supported by the College of Behavioral and Social Sciences at the University of Maryland, culminated in a grant from the Education and Human Resources Directorate of the National Science Foundation. Much of this collection stems directly from that project, and it has also been the Civic Capacity and Urban Education project that provided a basis for a dialogue with still other scholars, some of whom are also contributors to the volume. A report on the Civic Capacity and Urban Education project is being prepared separately, but I wish to acknowledge here its major role as a catalyst for *Changing Urban Education*.

Civic capacity is a term intended to convey the idea that education depends on activities broader than what happens inside the classroom. Some reformers will argue that a skillful and dedicated corps of teachers is the only real answer to the problems of urban education. In no way do I wish to suggest that classroom teaching is unimportant. But, at the same time, I hope that the focus in this book on political context and the term "civic capacity" will serve as reminders that classroom teaching is embedded in a larger context. The ability to recruit and retain a capable faculty for children from poor neighborhoods rests partly on providing supports that enable teachers and prospective teachers to see that they do not face an overwhelming task. The resource needs of schools are not exhausted by skilled and trained faculty. Meeting those needs is a civic process, a political process that warrants greater understanding.

Clarence N. Stone

Acknowledgments

This book represents both a personal odyssey and a collective journey. The two are inseparably joined and have received support from a variety of sources. For crucial institutional encouragement and support, I am indebted to Jonathan Wilkenfeld, my departmental chair, Dean Irwin Goldstein, and the General Research Board of the University of Maryland, and to Dean Sue Smock of Wayne State University. Because this book is in good measure an outgrowth of the Civic Capacity and Urban Education project funded by the Education and Human Resources Directorate of the National Science Foundation (Grant no. RED 9350139), I wish also to express appreciation to then program officers David Jenness and Iris Rotberg and to Larry Suter, deputy director of the Division of Research, Evaluation, and Communication.

The Civic Capacity and Urban Education study involved a collective effort, sustained over a period of years, beginning with a lengthy exercise in research design, then covering two or more years of field research, and finally encompassing an ongoing period of analysis and writing. The Civic Capacity and Urban Education project is the direct source of several chapters in this book, one of which is chapter 12. Though authored by me, this chapter is thoroughly the product of a collective research effort.

I want to acknowledge the significant contributions of that project team, for which I was principal investigator. Jeffrey Henig and Bryan Jones, coprincipal investigators, were full partners in every step of this project, from the original design through the preparation of the grant proposal to the execution of the study itself. They showed throughout that the highest intellectual rigor can be combined with warm colleagueship.

Several people provided the field research for the project as well as extensive discussion of its implications:

- Atlanta——Carol Pierannunzi, Desiree Pedescleaux, and John Hutcheson;
- Baltimore——Marion Orr;
- Boston——John Portz;
- Denver——Susan Clarke, Rodney Hero, and Mara Sidney;
- Detroit——Richard Hula, Richard Jelier, and Mark Schauer;
- Houston——Thomas Longoria;
- Los Angeles——Fernando Guerra and Mara Cohen;
- Pittsburgh——Robin Jones;
- St. Louis——Lana Stein;
- San Francisco——Luis Fraga and Bari Anhalt;
- Washington, DC——Jeffrey Henig.

Bryan Jones, Whitney Grace, and Heather Strickland are responsible for all steps in the coding of the 516 interviews across eleven cities. Jeffrey Henig and Mark Kugler, assisted by Cheryl Jones, Connie Hill, and Kathryn Doherty, collected and analyzed a large body of demographic, program, and financial data.

In addition to these contributors to the project, several other individuals also helped shape the research design and the field research protocol itself. These include the late Byran Jackson, Alan DiGaetano, Barbara Ferman, Valerie Johnson, Katherine McFate, Timothy Ross, Jorge Ruiz de la Vasco, and Marta Tellado.

Presentations from the Civic Capacity and Urban Education project brought me into contact with still other scholars conducting research in the area of education politics, some of whom are also contributors to *Changing Urban Education*. I want to offer deep thanks to the contributors to this volume, not only for their substantive contributions but also for their willingness to meet together, confer, exchange comments, and studiously adhere to deadlines.

Jennifer Hochschild merits special thanks. In addition to being a contributing author, she has been my dialogue partner on numerous ideas and issues related to this volume, dating back to the earliest days of the Civic Capacity and Urban Education project. Whether we agreed or disagreed about particulars mattered not at all; I always came away from our conversations with better understanding. She is a paragon of clear thinking.

I would be remiss if I neglected to express my appreciation to my colleagues in the College of Education at the University of Maryland: Edward Andrews, Betty Malen, and Sylvia Rosenfield for their strong support, advice, and encouragement. Similar support, advice, and encouragement have come from two fellow political scientists, Marilyn Gittell and Fredrick Wirt. Though I have learned a great deal from many people, these five particularly have drawn on their keen observations to tutor me in divers subtleties in the politics of education.

For extraordinarily helpful comments and suggestions on the manuscript, I wish to thank Mary Stone, Kenneth Wong, and Margaret Weir. Kathryn Doherty and Cheryl Jones are not only contributors to the volume, but they have also been exceptionally helpful workmates, facilitating the development of this book at several stages while shouldering numerous other responsibilities. They have been generous with their time to a fault.

Major thanks go to Fred Woodward, Susan Schott, and Rebecca Knight Giusti of the University Press of Kansas for shepherding the publication of this book. They have offered steady encouragement, sage advice, and unfailing assistance. Their professionalism and their friendship are both deeply appreciated.

1

Introduction: Urban Education in Political Context

Clarence N. Stone

One knows the world by seeking to change it.
Jean-Paul Sartre

PROLOGUE

Education, like other areas of policy action, is mediated through local politics. The stimulus to act may come from elsewhere—the changing world economy, the ongoing struggle for equal opportunity, or the venerable belief that education should be a means to realize human potential and to equip citizens for self-governance. Yet, regardless of the source of a policy issue, the local community is a place where the response is carried out, and that response involves some form of accommodation between governmental and nongovernmental sectors. This accommodation is a political arrangement. Hence it is important to know what possibilities and constraints inhere in various forms of accommodation. *How community players are related to one another* (the short definition of an urban regime) is not the whole policy story, but it is an important part of it. Real policy innovation comes about less by simple enactment than by changing relationships. This process is one version of what it means to say "politics matters." Of course, political arrangements don't explain everything, but they do mediate responses to policy problems.

1

The old saw "all politics is local" may be an overstatement, but it applies with considerable force to the education arena. Education politics has a stubbornly local dimension, notwithstanding Supreme Court decisions, the global economic order, national and state legislation, societywide battles over ideology, and much more. Structurally, despite the fact that local school districts are legal creatures of the state, local autonomy in education is "deeply rooted" in the American tradition.[1] Sustained effort for change rests ultimately on some form of local support. The local political context is thus a matter of utmost importance. It is at the local level that crucial support for reform is built, resistance mounted, and conflicts over education worked out. Major corporate executives, federal lawmakers, officers in major foundations, education scholars, and state officials play a part in proposing change, and states especially can change the rules under which local actors play. But local players give the final imprint to change, and how they do that is part of the process of change. The local political context is the central concern in this book, not because it is all that matters but because it is a significant though largely unexplored part of the story of educational reform.

CHANGE IN URBAN EDUCATION

Urban education seems ready for change. Continuing reports of poor performance and highly publicized accounts of mismanagement generate a sense of a system in crisis, of an old order in decline and disarray.[2] By all accounts, public concern is growing. Schools are widely seen as in need of reform, and a drive for increased academic performance has gained standing on the action agenda in many communities.

With economic strength and social stability both tied to the performance of urban school systems, many segments of the community justifiably see themselves as stakeholders in education. Moreover, schools are costly and education expenditures continue to rise. In most places, education costs about as much as all other local services combined, and in several large systems the school budget exceeds $1 billion annually. The taxpayers' stake in schools is, then, itself no small matter. With so much at issue socially, economically, and financially, it is especially unsettling for stakeholders when urban school officials appear not to have a firm grip on their enormously important enterprises.

A call for increased accountability is loud and clear,[3] but the specifics of how to achieve it are in question. Although new ideas and a host of current initiatives abound, what will prove to be lasting and how the demand for greater accountability will be given a durable political foundation are uncertain. A major purpose of this book is to examine both the sources of support for reform and the forces that resist various attempts at it. The contributors examine the experiences of several localities, with particular attention to what happens as efforts are made to change urban education.

No matter how intellectually appealing the argument for reform, it will happen only if a political foundation for change can be built and solidified. But what is it that makes for a durable foundation? Much, of course, depends on the particulars of each proposal and the scope of change involved. For the kinds of far-reaching reforms being advocated currently, our knowledge of the political forces at work is limited. It is thus important to examine these forces in a variety of settings, and that is another aim of this book. This is therefore not a book that advocates a particular initiative or that assesses the test-score impacts of the latest pedagogical innovations. It is a book about political processes, as they operate in urban communities, and about how these processes variously shape, reinforce, or undermine efforts to bring about change in education.

THE TERM "URBAN"

The term "urban" has many meanings. It is used here to refer to jurisdictions that are large and old enough to include socially and economically diverse populations. Typically these are central cities and mature suburbs. Within the broad category of urban communities recent trends show a greater concentration of poverty and of people of color. American cities have always thronged with recent migrants, minorities, and poor people; but patterns of metropolitan growth now assign their urban cores a greater concentration of such residents than in the past. This trend gives contemporary urban politics, and contemporary urban education in particular, a different dynamic from that of earlier times.

Of course, urban communities are not identical. Further, they connect to other jurisdictions and other populations in various ways. Particularly is this so with urban school districts. Consider the individual cases in this book. They range from Baltimore, with its preponderantly African American enrollment, to San Francisco, with its complex, multiracial student body. Chicago, Houston, and New York also have their own version of social complexity. Included as well is Charlotte-Mecklenburg, a consolidated city-county school district that contains both an inner-city enrollment and a suburban fringe. By contrast, the Houston school district is significantly smaller than the city of Houston. The New Haven case is not about the city itself but about a regional planning process in which the city and its suburbs were involved. Yonkers provides a case of an older suburban municipality, bordering New York City. Montgomery County, Maryland, a very large suburban jurisdiction, adjoins Washington, DC, and it contains both an inner urban corridor and an outer belt of ongoing growth.

Within these communities, concentrated poverty is a particularly pressing issue, but its urgency varies from jurisdiction to jurisdiction. Consider these data. Over half (53.9 percent) of the schools in Baltimore City have three-quarters or more of their students below the poverty level. In suburban Montgomery County —a school system of comparable size—only three schools (less than 2 percent) have such a concentration. If we take a different cut-off point, more than four-fifths of the Baltimore schools (82.2 percent) have at least half of their students below the poverty level. In Montgomery County, the figure is significant but still less than one-tenth (9.4 percent).

As we turn to the politics of education, it is more fitting to talk about urban contexts (plural) than about a single urban context. Nevertheless, there is an over-all trend toward greater concentration of the poor, evident even in older suburbs like the inner corridor of Montgomery County.

URBAN EDUCATION THEN AND NOW

Understanding variations from place to place within a given time period is impor-tant, but change over time also offers a useful perspective. Around the mid-1900s, several big-city school systems were regarded as among the best in the nation. Although conflict was never totally absent, these systems enjoyed substantial support. They had a solid tax base, their top officials operated under an aura of professional authority, and they possessed a diverse student body with heavy rep-resentation of the middle class. It would perhaps be an overstatement to call the political climate of that period indulgent, but urban school superintendents typi-cally had long tenure and substantial resources with which to work.[4] Teachers' organizations had yet to make themselves a major political presence, and a norm of professional autonomy provided school administrators with considerable lati-tude in making decisions.

That time has passed, and today many city school systems, along with an in-creasing number located in inner suburbs, face a different situation. A tax base no longer robust, the exodus of much of the middle class, large minority enroll-ments, and declining deference to professional expertise—these circumstances add up to a political context radically different from that of mid-century.

This contrast is by no means intended to glorify urban schools of yesteryear. They were far from problem-free. Class and racial segregation were rampant. Teachers' pay was often shockingly low, and expenditures tended to lag behind needs. Moreover, it is far from clear that their overall academic standards were rigorous.[5] The glitter of big-city systems as academic gems in this earlier period may have come more from the middle-class aspirations of their students than from the instructional skills of the schools themselves. So one should not leap to the conclusion that mid-century was "the good old days" when schools were better. Their political and demographic context was different, and the challenges they faced were less onerous. More than that should not be claimed. After all, most coped poorly with change as urban conditions became more problem-laden.

Although mid-century provides an instructive contrast with the present scene in urban education, the 1960s and 1970s are significant in a different way for current understanding. These were years of great turmoil, and they set in motion changes that are very much part of the contemporary situation. Battles over desegregation and teacher unionization left their mark and put claims for professional autonomy in a different light from that of mid-century. With greater political turbulence, the tenure of school superintendents shortened and a concern grew that administrators be able "to obtain the respect of the community," that they have "a record of involvement with minorities," and in short that they bring to the position something more than a technical aptitude for school management.[6] In many cities euphemistic phrases soon gave way to direct claims about the need for racial succession, in particular for black administrators to run preponderantly black schools. In the meantime, collective bargaining provided an alternative voice in determining working conditions and in setting resource priorities.[7]

How, then, does the current era—the period that emerged in the 1980s and continues to the present—differ from the decades of the 1960s and 1970s? Two conditions have merged that put educators under enormous pressure and that give contemporary urban education a distinctive twist. As the 1960s and 1970s gave way to the 1980s and 1990s, the concentration of lower-socioeconomic status (SES) students in urban school districts grew. And at the same time, the expectation that *all* students learn and achieve at an academically higher level has become explicit. For urban schools, this is an unsettling combination. Lower-SES students, despite many significant exceptions, have generally been low academic achievers. Now educators are asked to turn that around, not just in selected instances, but en masse.

The point cannot be overemphasized. Urban educators have a disproportionately large share of lower-SES students; they are asked to bring these students to a high level of academic achievement and to do so at a time when the tax base and other resources are, in many places, diminishing and when federal funds have become more scarce. Furthermore, the deference accorded professional educators is perhaps more limited today than at any other time in the past 100 years. The contrast with mid-century could hardly be more striking.

CHANGING EXPECTATIONS

At mid-century there were, of course, expectations that schools would advance academic achievement, but there was also a view that some proportion of students lacked the aptitude or appetite for advanced learning. With industrial work widely available, however, such students could go through an undemanding course of study or simply drop out of school and still land blue-collar jobs that required no advanced academic skills. The international economy and a changed labor market have altered that reality, as low-skill jobs with decent pay have virtually disappeared.

Worry about the phenomenon we now know as deindustrialization was already evident as early as the 1950s, but it was the publication in 1984 of *A Nation at Risk* that framed much of the debate about schools.[8] In directing attention to the global economy, the report framed a growing set of concerns and heightened the interest of America's business leaders in education as a policy issue.

Important as these events are, they are not the full story behind the initiation of education reform and the current push for higher academic standards. Part of the reform movement rests on a long-standing humanistic and democratic foundation. Critics of schooling at least as far back as John Dewey have talked about the intrinsic worth of education, its value to citizenship, and how practice failed to serve these ends. Thus over the years, many observers have seen American education as falling far short of its potential. As one writer put it, he was "indignant" at the extent to which schools were "intellectually sterile."[9] In this tradition a number of foundation-funded studies of the 1980s offered a wide-ranging critique of school performance and called for greater intellectual rigor.[10] These writers emphasized the need and the potential for academic achievement *for all students.* The "standards" movement, as it is sometimes called, thus is not about excellence for a talented few but an expectation that *all* or certainly most students learn at a high level.

The proposition that all or most students can learn at a high level poses a particularly acute challenge for contemporary urban schools. By socioeconomic background, their students start with an enormous disadvantage. The matter, moreover, does not end with typical urban schools. With attention directed toward the performance of all students, even those systems with small enrollments of the poor are subject to questions about how well their lower-SES students are performing and why. Demonstrated academic performance, then, is an issue to a greater degree than in the past, encompassing the performance of all students, not just those who are clearly college-bound.[11]

REFORM AS A POLITICAL ACTIVITY

> *Nothing is more difficult to handle, more doubtful of success, nor more danger-ous to manage, than to put oneself at the head of introducing new orders. For the introducer has all those who benefit from the old order as enemies, and he has lukewarm defenders in all those who might benefit from new orders. This lukewarmness arises partly from fear of adversaries . . . and partly from the incredulity of men, who do not truly believe in new things unless they come to have a firm experience of them.*
>
> Machiavelli

Reformers often believe that a proposed ideal order will have such intrinsic appeal that it will override the ever-present potential for conflict and noncoopera-tion.[12] Not so, Machiavelli reminds us—not only does the status quo always have its defenders, but the future beneficiaries of change are an undependable body of supporters. For most people who might benefit from reform, a changed order

is a distant and uncertain possibility; more immediate concerns occupy their attention. Moreover, in today's climate, reforms run up against a high degree of
skepticism about whether planned change can actually work. Indifference and
disbelief are formidable barriers, and small but determined opposition can feed
both. Thus a reform idea never holds the stage alone but must contend with a
variety of considerations.

Some reform efforts may shape up as broad confrontations between supporters and opponents. This has often been the case with desegregation, a high
visibility action that centers on a relatively straightforward issue of who will be
sitting in the classroom with whom. What is at issue is highly conspicuous. The
standards movement involves a more diffuse set of activities, and what is at issue
is less overt. Conflict is only one peril and not necessarily the greatest one. Indifference to the larger picture and failure to embrace the possibility of acting
collectively are perhaps more serious threats.

Reform also lags because there is no clear and simple proposal around which
to rally support. As survey data will show in a later chapter, wide support exists
for the idea that change is needed but not much agreement on the particulars of
what should be done. Different reformers have a varied mix of proposals to make.
Some emphasize outcome accountability, others look to greater parental participation. To some a pedagogy of active learning is the central issue; others look to
partnership with business or other forms of community involvement. Site-based
management has enjoyed a prominent place as a way of decentralizing operations
and altering governance. Some reformers are mainly concerned to give educators a set of coherent directives and hold them accountable to these directives.[13]
Others would rely on a market approach,[14] and still others would call for programs to create a more supportive environment for learning.[15]

The contemporary reform movement thus not only has to contend with
opposition, but it also has to overcome the dispersion of effort around a loosely
defined agenda. And the dispersion of effort can be heightened by a tendency
for stakeholders to gravitate to different directions. Parents, particularly Latino
and African American parents, have displayed great concern about the quality
of schooling for their children. As NAACP president Kweisi Mfume has said,
"People are increasingly frustrated that their children are not getting the kind of
education they want."[16] Yet concerned parents do not automatically rally behind
the reform *principle* that all children can and should have the opportunity to learn.
They largely focus on their own children, not necessarily on the fate of children
collectively.

Educators are another key group in the furtherance of reform. Educators,
one might assume, favor the principle that all children can achieve academically.
But in reality, teachers and administrators are a varied lot and have different ways
of coming to terms with a host of practical considerations, including job security
and pursuit of career advancement. Many are either ambivalent about or indifferent toward—and in some cases hostile to—the call for reform.[17]

Business executives have been key players in the current reform movement;

however, they too are a varied lot. Some see that a community's social well-being, its economic health, and the strength of its school system interconnect. Others have a less encompassing set of concerns, and some, no doubt, share the view of a suburban official who said, "The more the country moves toward the concept of school choice, . . . the more likely [public] schools are going to be seen as schools of last resort. People no longer believe that the community will go to hell if the public schools are not strong."[18] Potential business support is thus easily deflected or channeled toward alternative considerations.

Reform, then, is unlikely to gather active and cohesive support just because there is a widely shared sense that change is needed. Bringing together disparate sources of support and amplifying that support while responding to various misgivings are political acts that are executed with varying degrees of skill and that occur under varying conditions to be explored in the chapters that follow. Readers will see that the forces of reform in some communities are a small and insufficiently equipped army, badly in need of allies and reinforcements. In others they are in a stronger position. But in all of them, they face significant obstacles—if not active opponents of reform itself, players who are oriented toward an alternative set of concerns.

SCHOOL REFORM AND EMPLOYMENT REGIMES

In the chapters that follow we see the politics of school reform from a variety of angles, starting in part 1 with desegregation as a beleaguered means for bringing about equitable educational opportunity for the urban poor. In parts 2 and 3 the contributors detail various settings within which reform has been attempted, the nature of the reform efforts made, and the obstacles these efforts have encountered. Part 4 contains first an analysis of survey research, showing that support for change is widespread but that there is no unified understanding of the nature of the problem. In part 4 the authors also report on an eleven-city study and probe the pattern of limited and piecemeal change, giving particular attention to why it is so difficult to bring together a coalition of the major stakeholders around a program of broad-gauge reform. Part 5 is an overview. Collectively the different parts of the book give a clear message that education politics is not readily organized around the aim of improved school performance in educating children from lower-SES backgrounds.

Why? Two answers emerge. One is that middle-class parents are often able to shape educational arrangements to accord with their preferences, but lower-SES parents often lack that capacity. This is partly because middle-class parents have more clout than their lower-SES counterparts. But it is also because lower-class parents face a tougher challenge; they have to bring about more change. The reader is directed to the desegregation chapters on Yonkers, New York, and the New Haven region of Connecticut, and to the later chapters on Montgomery

County, Maryland, and on the Charlotte-Mecklenburg system in North Carolina to see clear class differences at work. Only in San Francisco, under the aegis of the U.S. District Court, are there arrangements strongly oriented toward improved achievement for lower-SES students.

A second explanation focuses on the difficulty in organizing education politics around improved school performance for lower-SES children. If we want to understand a core part of school politics, then we need to see that education is not simply a service over which users struggle. Education is also about jobs, contracts, career tracks, and employment opportunities. What Wilbur Rich calls the "education cartel" is, in a sense, an "employment regime."[19] In short, the protection of jobs and career ladders is often at the heart of how education politics is organized. The chapters on Baltimore and on the East Brooklyn area of New York City make it abundantly clear that education politics organized around employment and related issues is a formidable obstacle to change.

Reformers can thus never write on a blank slate. They must overcome an entrenched form of politics. Nevertheless, in urban education, groundwork exists for bringing about change. The standards movement poses a challenge for established practices, and the overall weak level of academic achievement in lower-SES schools has eroded the legitimacy of long-standing arrangements. Yet it is uncertain how much change will take place.

The goal is clear enough—schools that are oriented toward seeing that their students perform well in pursuit of academic achievement. But change does not occur by simply endorsing a new policy and calling for it to be carried out through existing arrangements.[20] This is a point where thinking in regime terms can be instructive. Urban regime theory posits that *policy change comes about only if reformers establish a new set of political arrangements commensurate with the policy being advocated.* Promoting stronger academic achievement means, then, building support for schools that are driven by a performance imperative. This might be called putting into place a "performance regime." But how do we achieve such schools and enable them to institutionalize practices that will sustain an effective performance level? That is no easy matter. Even though the legitimacy of the old system has weakened, a new regime has yet to form in more than a rudimentary way. It is not enough to destabilize the old order. The political challenge is to build a new set of arrangements in which *academic performance is a focal concern.* The question is one of how to motivate stakeholders, including professional educators, to make the academic performance of students a matter of central concern.

There is no clear answer to this question, but we can use past experience to explore patterns of change. Consider the case of Atlanta.[21] If we go back several decades to the early part of the twentieth century, we find the following situation. With growing middle-class support for public education, Atlanta business shifted from its minimum-taxation/minimum-expenditure position to the endorsement of more generous spending on the public school system. By the 1940s the business elite was a mainstay of support for quality schools and a close ally of the superintendent.[22] At this point the Atlanta system resembled those in other, larger cities. Later, with Atlanta's business leadership playing a strategic role, the proeducation coalition turned around the state's policy of massive resistance to *Brown v. Board of Education* and created a favorable climate for peaceful school desegregation.

Demographic change altered the situation, however. Over time a continuing white exodus to the suburbs left the city school system with a predominantly and growing African American enrollment (and concurrently fewer and fewer middle-class students). Litigation over busing and racial balance threatened to spill over into the metropolitan area and fuel resistance to business-backed initiatives, particularly the building of a regional mass-transit system. At this point, a federal judge set in motion a negotiated settlement that came to be known as the Atlanta Compromise. Essentially the agreement ended litigation by providing for a transition to political and administrative control of the Atlanta school system by the African American community.[23] However, parental participation diminished as the middle class became a decreasing source of school enrollment, and, with a shift in racial control, business involvement in education also receded.

Initially, hopes within the African American community ran high that "black administrators would understand the needs of black children and would *find* ways to make segregated, low-income inner-city schools equal to middle-class white schools."[24] Some positive changes were achieved,[25] but weak test scores proved intractable. And as schools came increasingly to have a concentration of low-income students, opportunism and cynicism grew.[26] The school system became a poaching ground for those concerned with garnering immediate benefits. One observer referred to the school board as "an employment agency of last resort."[27]

This employment-centered politics of education took shape in a context of limited parental and business participation along with vigorously defended professional prerogatives.[28] Nevertheless, education enjoyed significant public support. Per pupil expenditure was relatively high, and Atlanta currently pays its teachers salaries comparable to and even slightly higher than those in surrounding suburbs.[29] However, low performance and high expenditures proved to be an unstable compound. Performance concerns became a key element in the mobilization of a new coalition, including parents, Concerned Black Clergy, and the Atlanta Chamber of Commerce. Still, the reform effort has thus far resulted mostly in economy and efficiency initiatives. Academic achievement has not to date proved to be a goal around which a supportive politics of education could be organized *and maintained.*

Two different patterns can be found in the Atlanta experience. One is for education politics to be organized around distributive benefits, especially job and career matters but also including school board members performing constituency service roles.[30] Thus some of the time education politics can be understood as an employment regime. But that is not the entire story. In a second pattern, at various stages, alliances form around collective goals. Early on a broad coalition was effective in replacing a minimum-taxation/caretaker regime with a "modern city" regime of quality services and an active public sector. Later this same coalition repelled the effort of die-hard segregationists to close down public schools in the state. Many years later, after the system slipped into an employment regime, a coalition came together to end abuses of that system but has yet to prove itself as a foundation for a performance regime.

The Atlanta experience tells us that, though a performance regime is hard to establish, it is possible to mobilize a broad coalition around collective goals. Distributive benefits do not necessarily carry the day. But what does it take to create an alternative set of political arrangements, namely a durable performance regime?

Consider the change from the earlier period to the present. At mid-century, with a largely middle-class enrollment, performance was not an issue. But as the middle-class exodus took its toll, the ability of the schools to provide a quality education for a growing number of lower-income black students became a salient issue. Shifting racial control of the school system, however, did not solve the performance problem (and neither did it generate the problem). As improved performance became a receding hope, lax oversight from the limited involvement of parents and business provided the context within which distributive politics gained full sway. As abuses grew, the resulting employment regime proved vulnerable to a new broad-based coalition. Lacking for a performance regime, however, are the informal supports that middle-class families are well-positioned to provide but that poor families often are not. Elements of a support system are present in the work of organizations like 100 Black Men, but the city's poverty creates needs that are greater than what the voluntary sector can meet. In short, the current reform coalition seems unable to bring resources to bear that are able to turn around the disadvantage of many of the students in the city's educational system.

Thus it seems that a restructuring of control at the top is not enough to establish a performance regime. Electoral change, standardized measures of outcome, or new directives by themselves do not meet the needs of a school system with a high concentration of poverty among its student body. Reformers, it seems, have not only to gain popular support, but they also need to be able to bring enough resources to bear in a sustained way in order to make headway in achieving an improved academic performance. It is by no means apparent that classroom technique alone can yield the desired results.

The reform task, then, is not only to rally support for an idea; it is also to garner resources. This means a struggle with competing demands for those resources, and it also means overcoming skepticism about past uses of resources. Although educators working with the poor argue that they need more resources to be successful, potential supporters respond that they want to see effective use of the resources already available before more are provided. An impasse over this issue would pose an insurmountable barrier to the establishment of a performance regime. The potential for this impasse, however, is at the heart of the politics of urban education.

Atlanta illustrates how concentrated poverty can aggravate the problem. With a predominantly lower-SES student body, effective academic performance is difficult,[31] and a high academic performance seems to be an elusive goal for most actors unless they are part of a broad and encompassing movement to transform the old order into a new one. Lacking such a movement, the education arena provides fertile ground for narrow and opportunistic considerations to expand.[32] Given a normal tendency for centrifugal forces to prevail, distributive benefits may be the easiest way to organize education politics in the short run. But it is not necessarily a stable form of politics over the long haul.

The Atlanta experience also points to coalition building as crucial in bringing about change. The issue is whether various stakeholders go their separate ways, following a narrow understanding of their stake in the education system, or whether they come together around a larger vision of what is at issue. Operating alone, business, for example, is likely to be either indifferent or concerned mainly about keeping taxes down. Individual educators may have high aspirations, but teachers' unions tend to concentrate on bread and butter issues. In the absence of a broadly defined coalition, discontented parents concentrate on concessions for their own children and make targeted efforts on behalf of a particular neighborhood or category of users (such as gifted and talented or special education parents). The concerns of parents and other stakeholders tend to be highly fragmented. The challenge, then, is how to fold the particular and lasting concerns of diverse stakeholders into a general effort to make a strong education performance an ongoing reality.

ELEMENTS OF A PERFORMANCE REGIME

A performance regime, i.e., one constructed to further the goal of academic achievement for all students, rests on a different kind of political foundation from an employment regime. The latter is a form of distributive politics, but the former involves what might be called social-purpose politics. If advancement of a social purpose is the defining feature of a regime, then its advocates must in some way displace "politics as usual." Key actors also must motivate others to do more than passively endorse high-sounding proposals; they must play an active and particular part in furthering a social purpose.

In distributive politics, asymmetrical incentives separate individuals who are effective players from those who are not. Those with the greatest immediate stake mobilize to advance or protect their interests, and they tend to carry the day. By contrast, those "with broad objectives, [who] attempt to appeal to widely diffused sentiments are infrequent, ineffective political participants."[33] They have difficulty mobilizing and sustaining support.

Social-purpose politics is less well understood and rests on a different body of motives.[34] The task is to overcome asymmetrical incentives and enlist a diverse set of players to support and contribute to a general goal. The challenge lies first in the fact that potential players vary in the degree to which the social purpose has immediacy to them. In education, for example, improved schooling is of immediate concern to teachers and administrators, who work in the school system, and to parents. To members of the business sector, however, the quality of schooling is a matter of much less immediacy. The same may be the case with various community groups.

A second element of the challenge is to persuade various players to hold steady in their support for a general goal even though competing considerations are present. Business executives, for example, may favor a strong-performance school system, but they may also want low taxes or a spending priority for a new convention center. Active support is thus more than vague rhetoric; it means taking *concrete* steps in the service of the general goal and avoiding being pulled away by alternative priorities. For teachers and administrators the test is whether work is to be driven mainly by the rewards of salary and job security or by the rewards of professional accomplishment and the intrinsic satisfaction of doing social good. To forsake professional accomplishment and pursuit of intrinsic rewards would be to follow a path that makes attainment of social purpose difficult.

A third element of the challenge is the collective-action problem. The issue is how to motivate individuals to contribute to a shared purpose even though the effort of any single actor does not determine the outcome; yet without the contributions of many, the efforts of a few are wasted.[35] Orchestrating the *active* support of a diverse group of players in the face of such potent centrifugal forces, then, is no easy matter. The workability of a social-purpose effort thus rides on how tasks and responsibilities are allocated, the availability of psychic and social benefits, reassurances that others are meeting their obligations, and the perceived likelihood of success. Putting together a durable coalition of this kind is always more challenging than building a distributive coalition.

Framing change in terms of different kinds of coalitions enables us to see more clearly what education reform entails. Reform (i.e., establishing a performance regime) requires more than the discrediting of the old ways in favor of a fresh idea. It involves the difficult shift from a coalition built around distributive benefits to one built on a more complex set of factors.

What does the advancement of a social purpose within the education arena entail? The Atlanta experience suggests some important considerations. One is that professional educators must be a core group in a reform coalition even if they were an integral part of the old arrangements. The formation of a new education regime comes about through a fresh set of relationships, even though some of the players remain the same. Typically it is not a matter of completely replacing an in-group with what had been an out-group, nor is it simply a matter of pressuring an in-group to enact new policies. Instead, how various players are related and what motivates them are the key. Hence the emergence of a new group can be important but only if its presence alters a previous set of relationships and the expectations that go with them.

For educators in particular, it appears crucial that they see themselves as having a reasonable chance to succeed in furthering a high level of academic achievement. Only then is the goal of professional accomplishment available as the motivator. Only then is the satisfaction of doing social good able to come into play. Though teachers work alone in the classroom, their ability to succeed depends on what is happening in other classrooms and on what supports are available through family and community.[36] Administrators have more capacity to shape their work environment than do individual teachers, but that capacity can be strengthened or weakened by the actions and inactions of others. The argument can be extended to noneducators as well. Each has a limited capacity to contribute to improved academic performance, but that capacity depends on others. A performance regime thus rests on the successful orchestration of diverse efforts and the motivation that comes from being part of such an orchestration.

Thus the essential point is whether or not relationships change. Hence it is important to remember first that formal structures can be rearranged without altering basic relationships and second that even if formal relationships remain the same, the appearance of new players can alter how the formal structures actually function. In regime analysis, then, informal understandings are potentially important complements to arrangements that are formally institutionalized, and nongovernmental actors are treated as potentially as important as their governmental cohorts. The regime concept thus is a way of focusing attention on *how* various players are related to one another. The key question, then, is not simply one of who makes up the governing coalition in a policy arena (or interconnected set of policy arenas), but one of how various players relate to one another, including the resources and efforts they bring to the task of educating children.

CIVIC CAPACITY

Focusing on coalitions seems particularly appropriate in the study of school politics today because education practitioners and scholars have come to use the term "stakeholders" to describe the array of actors with an interest in improved education. Stakeholders are thus a broader category than professional educators and officials such as school board members with a formal responsibility for education. The term includes parents, of course, but, given the intertwining of community well-being with local school systems, stakeholder also encompasses the business sector, city hall, and a variety of community-based actors.

The term "stakeholder," though useful in bringing attention to the question of what is at issue for various sectors of the community, still raises a question about what parents, community members, businesses, and other employers can contribute to the education of children. In short, we need to see that an education coalition is not simply an arrangement for holding educators accountable for the academic achievements of their students; it is also about providing resources and other supports to educators and students so that a high level of academic performance is more achievable.

To bring this more complex issue of active involvement into the spotlight, I have used the term "civic capacity."[37] Civic capacity refers to the mobilization of varied stakeholders in support of a communitywide cause. Two elements enter the picture.[38] One is participation or involvement, especially as it includes *contributing* in some way to the cause. The more each sector participates, the greater the civic capacity. The other element is understanding. Civic capacity comes into play when people see an issue as a community problem, one that therefore calls for a collective (that is to say, civic) response. In short, civic capacity builds when actors see an issue as more than a matter of individual concern or an opportunity to further particular interests. As different actors become aware of a shared concern, they have an opportunity to engage in a deliberation that broadens their grasp of the issue and enlarges their understanding of what is at stake. Though they may continue to differ in some particulars, ideally they are able to come together in a coalition with a shared responsibility to act on their common concern. Civic capacity, then, is presumed to be manifest in a cross-sector mobilization (a coalition that encompasses multiple categories of actors) around a community issue.

In school improvement it is imperative that the coalition include educators. Their know-how and their control over operational detail make them essential partners in efforts to improve school performance. Any attempt to organize educational activity around increased academic achievement is unlikely, then, to be sustained without enlisting substantial cooperation from teachers and administrators.[39] Thus civic capacity in education should never be thought of as a coalition of outsiders exerting pressure on the school system.

In an interesting three-city comparison, Robin Jones, John Portz, and Lana Stein highlight the complexity of coalition building in education and thus call attention to a crucial need for leadership.[40] Citing an important Rand study,[41] they discuss the double helix of reform—the outside loop of support by noneducators and the inside loop of professional educators oriented toward broad concerns of educational performance. Leadership involves the ability to make that important connection. Without the connection, external actors are only sporadically concerned with education and insiders tend to be narrowly focused. The connection provides civic capacity for educational improvement, and only an act of leadership seems to be able to bring it about. The normal course of events is for the disparate elements to operate alone and thus not to be drawn into the broader potential to which they could contribute.

Civic capacity is not an all-or-nothing matter. Groups can vary in the levels of participation and in the terms on which they are involved. Business, for example, can be an on-again, off-again player, as in Atlanta, or a strong and consistent player, as in Charlotte. Because each group has its own particular set of concerns, terms of involvement can also vary. Writing about Houston, Thomas Longoria in chapter 9 shows that business can play a significant partnership role, particularly in expanding the social supports available to students and their families. But the Houston case also illustrates that business involvement may carry with it a tendency to limit public spending and therefore to narrow the scope of the public effort. In a somewhat similar vein, the Chicago case shows business leaders in that city to be heavily focused on management processes to the neglect of wider concerns.

In the chapters that follow, we will mainly see the forces that distract from or weaken civic capacity. In the cases where there is a double helix—Charlotte-Mecklenburg and San Francisco, for example—arrangements are tenuous. Demographic change puts civic capacity in Charlotte at risk, especially because the current focus on performance puts the system under strong demands. In San Francisco, the double helix operates in a limited number of schools and does so under the protective cover of a consent decree in the federal court. However, that legal arrangement has been challenged by the Chinese American community, which is outside its operation; and further, the teachers' union is pressing for greater protection of job security.

At least two factors influence civic capacity. One is the ability of players within the local community to overcome their divisions. The black and white racial divide is especially important, as the Baltimore case illustrates; civic capacity depends on the ability of players to bridge that divide. In some localities group rivalries also produce tensions among minority groups, as in Houston and San Francisco. In these cases, civic capacity is weakened to the extent that competition over distributive benefits eclipses a concern with general education goals.

A second significant factor is an external stimulus to which local actors must respond. Local communities do not operate in isolation. Thus federal court orders have provided especially important stimuli to local coalitions between blacks and white business leaders in Charlotte-Mecklenburg and between the NAACP and school administrators in San Francisco.

Although a general condition such as global economic competition does not in itself have much direct impact, worries about the community's ability to attract outside investment have helped to stimulate business involvement and a search for allies in such cities as Charlotte, Chicago, and Houston. In general, though, the more focused the external stimulus, the more likely it is to generate local cooperation. For example, a diffuse effort, such as the Connecticut approach to regional education planning, has limited impact. And the Yonkers case reminds us that external initiatives can be resisted and are subject to locally based counterattacks.

In Baltimore, state-mandated tests of student achievement are a crucial factor in moving the city, however haltingly, toward the building of a performance regime. The force of the state tests is increased by the authority of the state to mandate the restructuring of low-performance schools. At the same time, state testing has come under criticism from various sources, ranging from the political right to local branches of the NAACP.[42] The state program is thus a less-than-secure cornerstone for performance assessment. Overall, then, building civic capacity around the issue of school performance is a task encumbered by formidable obstacles.

IN SUM

Urban education is awash in moves toward change and crosscurrents of resistance. Yet there is no doubt that the forces of change are strong, perhaps strong enough to make previous patterns of education politics an unreliable predictor of the future. The past, in which schools were guided by large, central offices of autonomously operating professional educators, is unlikely to be recaptured. Still, the pattern for the future is unclear.

Though many reform advocates have embraced broad programs of systemic change, political reality may lie elsewhere. It is hard to mount and sustain a broad effort. Discontented parents and community representatives usually concentrate on concessions for their specific group, not on the big picture. Citywide coalitions seeking systemic change, then, are likely to be less common than targeted efforts on behalf of a particular neighborhood or category of users. Resistance, too, is often well organized and durable and may narrow the scope of change.

Reformers have a strong tendency to focus on what should be, and they often have great skill in showing why an alternative set of practices would be better than what is in place. But they frequently fail to pay attention to political context—to the relationships that are necessary to establish and sustain a body of practices. Accountability, for example, is a widely appealing principle. It seems unlikely to operate in practice, however, unless educators come to internalize it as part of how they go about their work. This internalization seems most likely if a diverse body of stakeholders plays an active and at least partly informal role of oversight and if educators believe that they are receiving the kind of support that will enable them to succeed. Accountability, then, is less a mechanical process that can be imposed on unwilling subjects than a frame of mind to be shared by practitioners and by an attentive and involved set of stakeholders. That sharing, in short, manifests a performance regime in operation.

That such regimes now exist only in embryonic form is a sign that politically they are hard to bring about. In education, centrifugal forces are especially strong. The concerns of parents and other stakeholders are highly fragmented; the occupational and career concerns of educators themselves sometimes loom larger than concern about academic achievement for children. The sheer difficulty of breaking the connection between a low-SES background for students and weak academic achievement makes it hard to enlist the needed troops for a long-term effort. The political test of reform, then, lies not in accumulating endorsements for an appealing idea. Rather, it is the challenge of how to fold the particular and lasting concerns of diverse stakeholders into a general effort to bring about change. Because narrow concerns often hold sway, there is much in our experience to render us pessimistic about the viability of general efforts. Yet there are experiences that hold promise. With the future uncertain, the chapters that follow identify significant benchmarks well worth watching closely. The turbulent change enveloping today's schools gives us a chance to understand the politics of urban education in a way that a more settled period would not provide.

NOTES

1. Gary Orfield and Susan Eaton, *Dismantling Desegregation* (New York: New Press, 1996), p. 11.

2. A distinction should be made between the performance of public education generally and urban school systems specifically. A case can be made that schools in general are performing at least as well as they have in the past (see Jeffrey R. Henig, *Rethinking School Choice* (Princeton: Princeton University Press, 1994), and David C. Berliner and Bruce J. Biddle, *The Manufactured Crisis* (Reading, MA: Addison-Wesley, 1995), though the important point may be that our needs are greater today than in past times. Urban systems are, however, a different matter; see, for example, Jeffrey Mirel, *The Rise and Fall of an Urban School System: Detroit 1907–81* (Ann Arbor: University of Michigan Press, 1993). See also Maribeth Vander Weele, *Reclaiming Our Schools* (Chicago: Loyola University Press, 1994).

3. Three diverse examples are Susan H. Fuhrman, ed., *Designing Coherent Education Policy* (San Francisco: Jossey-Bass, 1993); Chester E. Finn Jr., *We Must Take Charge* (New York: Free Press, 1991); and Ted Kolderie, "How the State Should 'Break Up' the Big-City District," in *Politics of Education Association Yearbook, 1995* (Washington, DC: Falmer Press, 1996), pp. 127–33.

4. Charles Bidwell, "Toward Improved Knowledge and Policy on Urban Education," in *Politics of Education Association Yearbook, 1991,* pp. 193–99.

5. Mirel, *Rise and Fall of an Urban School System,* and John L. Rury and Frank A. Cassell, eds., *Seeds of Crisis* (Madison: University of Wisconsin Press, 1993).

6. Jesse J. McCorry, *Marcus Foster and the Oakland Public Schools* (Berkeley: University of California Press, 1978), pp. 19–20.

7. William J. Grimshaw, *Union Rule in the Schools* (Lexington, MA: Lexington Books, 1979).

8. National Commission on Excellence in Education, *A Nation at Risk* (Washington, DC: GPO, 1983). The earlier period is discussed in Peter Marris and Martin Rein, *Dilemmas of Social Reform,* 2d ed. (Chicago: University of Chicago Press, 1982).

9. Charles Silberman, *Crisis in the Classroom* (New York: Random House, 1970), p. 10.

10. John Goodlad, *A Place Called School* (New York: McGraw Hill, 1983); Theodore R. Sizer, *Horace's Compromise* (Boston: Houghton Mifflin 1985); and Arthur G. Powell, Eleanor Farrar, and David K. Cohen, *The Shopping Mall High School* (Boston: Houghton Mifflin, 1985).

11. For a recent overview, see Consortium for Political Research in Education, *Public Policy and School Reform: A Research Summary* (Philadelphia: CPRE, Graduate School of Education, University of Pennsylvania, 1996), and Dianne Massell, Michael Kirst, and Margaret Hoppe, *Persistence and Change* (Philadelphia: CPRE, Graduate School of Education, University of Pennsylvania, 1997).

12. On the pervasive character of conflict in education and the "apolitical myth," see Frederick M. Wirt and Michael W. Kirst, *The Political Dynamics of American Education* (Berkeley, CA: McCutchan, 1997).

13. Fuhrman, ed., *Designing Coherent Education Policy,* p. 1.

14. John E. Chubb and Terry M. Moe, *Politics, Markets, and America's Schools* (Washington, DC: Brookings Institution, 1990).

15. See, for example, Jeannie Oakes, *Improving Inner-City Schools* (Santa Monica, CA: Rand Corporation and Center for Policy Research in Education, 1987), and Mary Haywood Metz, "How Social Class Differences Shape Teachers' Work," in *The Context of Teaching in Secondary Schools,* ed. Milbrey W. McLaughlin, Joan E. Talbert, and Nina Bascia (New York: Teachers' College Press, 1990), pp. 40–107.

16. *Washington Post,* July 15, 1997.

17. See, for example, David Tyack and Larry Cuban, *Tinkering Toward Utopia* (Cambridge: Harvard University Press, 1995); Dianna Tittle, *Welcome to Heights High* (Columbus: Ohio State University Press, 1995); Tony Wagner, *How Schools Change* (Boston: Beacon Press, 1994).

18. Tittle, *Welcome to Heights High,* p. 261.

19. Wilbur C. Rich, *Black Mayors and School Politics* (New York: Garland, 1996).

20. Tyack and Cuban, *Tinkering Toward Utopia.*

21. Atlanta is one of the cities in the eleven-city study (see chapter 12).

22. Paul E. Peterson, *The Politics of School Reform* (Chicago: University of Chicago Press, 1985).

23. Clarence N. Stone, *Regime Politics* (Lawrence: University Press of Kansas, 1989), pp. 103–6. For details on the compromise itself, see Barbara L. Jackson, "Desegregation: Atlanta Style," *Theory into Practice* 17, no. 1 (1978): 43–53; and Joel L. Fleishman, "The Real Against the Ideal—Making the Solution Fit the Problem," in *Roundtable Justice,* ed. Robert B. Goldman (Boulder, CO: Westview Press, 1980).

24. Gary Orfield and Carole Ashkinaze, *The Closing Door* (Chicago: University of Chicago Press, 1991), p. 109.

25. See, for example, Sarah Lawrence Lightfoot, *The Good High School* (New York: Basic Books, 1983), pp. 29–55.

26. Robert Holmes, *The Status of Black Atlanta, 1993* (Atlanta: Southern Center for Studies in Public Policy, Clark Atlanta University, 1993). For accounts of Atlanta's education politics, see Carol Pierannunzi, Desiree Pedescleaux, and John D. Hutcheson Jr., "From Conflict to Coalition: The Education of Educational Reform in Atlanta," report for Civic Capacity and Urban Education Project, 1994, and Clarence Stone and Carole Pierannunzi, "Atlanta and the Limited Reach of Electoral Control," in *Racial Politics in American Cities,* ed. Rufus P. Browning, Dale R. Marshall, and David H. Tabb (New York: Longman, 1997), pp. 171–74.

27. Cynthia Tucker, "Ousting School Board May Not Be So Simple," *Atlanta Journal and Constitution,* January 20, 1993, p. A13.

28. Marilyn Gittell, *Limits to Citizen Participation* (Beverly Hills, CA: Sage, 1980), p. 187.

29. Orfield and Ashkinaze, *The Closing Door,* and Pierannunzi, Pedescleaux, and Hutcheson, "From Conflict to Coalition."

30. On local school boards generally, see Jacqueline Danzberger, Michael Kirst, and Michael Usdan, *Governing Public Schools* (Washington, DC: Institute for Educational Leadership, 1992); *School Boards* (Washington, DC: Institute for Educational Leadership,

1986); *Facing the Challenge* (New York: Twentieth Century Fund Press, 1992); and Wirt and Kirst, *Political Dynamics of American Education.*

31. Oakes, *Improving Inner-City Schools,* and David Cohen, "What Is the System in Systemic Reform?" *Educational Researcher* 24 (December 1995): 11–17.

32. Cf. Mirel, *Rise and Fall of an Urban School System.*

33. Paul Peterson, *School Politics Chicago Style* (Chicago: University of Chicago Press, 1976), p. 44.

34. Clarence N. Stone et al., "Schools and Disadvantaged Neighborhoods," in *The Future of Community Development,* ed. Ronald Ferguson and William Dickens (Washington, DC: Brookings Institution, forthcoming).

35. Cf. Dennis Chong, *Collective Action and the Civil Rights Movement* (Chicago: University of Chicago Press, 1991).

36. Cohen, "What Is the System in Systemic Reform?" and William H. Clune, "Systemic Educational Policy," in Furhman, ed., *Designing Coherent Education Policy.*

37. This concept was devised as part of the project, "Civic Capacity and Urban Education," funded by the Education and Human Resources Directorate of the National Science Foundation, grant no. RED 9350139.

38. I am indebted to Luis Fraga for framing the concept in this particular way.

39. Goodlad, *A Place Called School.*

40. Robin Jones, John Portz, and Lana Stein, "The Nature of Civic Involvement and Educational Change in Pittsburgh, Boston, and St. Louis," *Urban Affairs Review* 32 (July 1997): 871–91.

41. Paul Hill et al., *Educational Progress* (Santa Monica, CA: Rand Corporation, 1989).

42. *Montgomery Journal,* July 17, 1997, and *Washington Post,* July 19, 1997.

PART I

Desegregation

The bedrock of the education problem in the United States remains the concentration of poor children, preponderantly Latino and African American, in central cities and in some older suburbs. One policy response to this situation has been a call for desegregation. But that response, as Jennifer Hochschild and Michael Danielson show in their study of Yonkers, has met with intense resistance. Even where desegregation could have been achieved *within* a single local jurisdiction and state agencies were positioned to further that goal, opposition prevailed.

Kathryn McDermott moves the story to the metropolitan level in considering the experience in New Haven with regional educational planning. She shows that the existing system of autonomous local districts is so deeply embedded that it becomes difficult to view poverty and disadvantage as problems stemming from economic and social changes that transcend local boundaries. Rather than perceiving it as a shared problem, suburban actors tend to see educational disadvantage as a city condition to be contained. The state of Connecticut, by defining desegregation goals in vague terms and giving local officials the prime responsibility to pursue these goals, reinforced a provincial outlook and provided individuals with broader concerns no meaningful arena in which to build support for an alternative agenda.

In both Yonkers and the New Haven region, the strength of localism in education is a major factor, particularly as manifested in resistance to desegregation. Of the three experiences examined here, only in San Francisco, with its high degree of social diversity and a direct role for the federal judiciary, has racial concentration been held in check. And even in this instance, if the current consent decree were ended, no one can be sure what would result. Further, as the Charlotte case, in part 3, shows, even a success story of desegregation can encounter renewed resistance as demography changes and new participants enter the picture.

That desegregation has remained an elusive goal under many different conditions might be explained in various ways. Perhaps the simplest is that the white majority, despite lip service to the principle, is opposed in practice. And, indeed, even support for desegregation in minority communities is not especially strong. It is not surprising, then, that in both Yonkers and the New Haven region, elected officials are key forces of resistance. (Nor have they been a positive force in San Francisco's desegregation experience.) They speak for majority sentiments, and no mere change of approach, Hochschild and Danielson show, can alter that fact. Yet a careful reading of the cases in part 1 suggests that the story is not a simple one of pervasive white bigotry. Support for a desegregated society exists to a significant degree, but giving it effective institutional expression is difficult and likely to be achieved only to a limited degree.

What, then, are the alternatives for dealing with concentrated disadvantage in urban schools? Can the school situation for disadvantaged students be changed without massive desegregation? Is significant reform possible? Does it have political feasibility? These are questions explored from various perspectives in the remainder of this book. The San Francisco case is thus a particularly appropriate bridge between desegregation policy and the current movement for school reform. As Luis Fraga, Bari Anhalt Erlichson, and Sandy Lee show in their study, improved educational achievement for minorities can be a goal of desegregation and indeed was embodied in the consent decree issued by the federal court for San Francisco. Yet constitutional law on this point is uncertain. Federal courts have generally taken the position that their primary concern is enrollment desegregation, not parity in educational achievement. Nevertheless, the effort to make schools effective that historically have performed poorly is one way to try to integrate the disadvantaged into the mainstream of American life. San Francisco has made this effort by targeting a set of high minority schools for reconstitution. The political challenge of pursuing that goal is different from the challenge of desegregation, but it is not apparent that it is less difficult. And it involves more than gathering popular support. The experience in San Francisco underscores the importance of enlisting not just the school superintendent but also the education foot soldiers—the teachers and principals—in bringing about change.

Thus, although San Francisco's experience may have limited significance as a legal precedent, it may nevertheless be important as a demonstration that, under favorable conditions, school reform can be accomplished. Even so, lessons from the San Francisco case can be read in different ways. One way is that favorable conditions for reform require some form of external intervention to override contending local forces. Another way is that the maintenance of favorable conditions requires skill in broadening the base of support among local forces that are potentially contentious. There is an ongoing strategy debate. Must accord be imposed or is consensus building possible? Is it better to proceed from the top down and enforce direction on unruly local forces or to build from the bottom up and bring potentially conflicting elements into a broad coalition? Hochschild and Danielson show that there is no simple answer to that question, and it may be that only a carefully blended mix of the two can work.

2

Can We Desegregate Public Schools and Subsidized Housing? Lessons from the Sorry History of Yonkers, New York

Jennifer Hochschild and Michael N. Danielson

The history of efforts to desegregate public schools and public housing in Yonkers, New York, is full of ironies that tell us much about the role of race in American politics and policymaking and that bode ill for the future of racial equality in our schools. First, although Americans generally endorse the principles of equal opportunity and racial integration, most white Americans resist making the changes in their lives and communities that would be necessary for those principles to be implemented. Even African and Latino Americans are sufficiently ambivalent about those changes that they too do not insist upon the implementation of principles to which most are committed. Second, although the state government of New York was powerful, determined upon racial desegregation, and active on its behalf for more than two decades, it was unable to overcome the obstacles of local opposition, electoral politics, agency priorities, and structural complexity in order to achieve meaningful amounts or forms of desegregation. Racial hostility was neither unimportant nor all-important in explaining the failure to desegregate Yonkers. Instead, it worked as a catalyst to alter the nature of conventional political obstacles to substantial change so that desegregation became almost impossible to achieve.

Yonkers is a microcosm of the United States on these issues. Its history demonstrates that, even with the best intentions and a lot of power, political actors as currently constituted cannot or will not face down public opposition to desegregated public schools and subsidized housing. If Americans are serious about implementing the principles of equal opportunity and racial integration, they must find other means than the forms of desegregation with which our nation has been preoccupied since the 1960s. In this chapter we begin the search for those other means, first by drawing lessons from the history of school and housing desegregation in Yonkers and then by suggesting general principles for policy change that emerge from these lessons.

WHY YONKERS?

Yonkers provides an excellent case for examining the politics of school and housing desegregation for several reasons. First, it is the site of an important series of judicial decisions, which may ultimately set precedents for other school districts, cities, and states. In 1985 a federal district court found the Yonkers school board and city officials guilty of de jure segregation in public schools and subsidized housing.[1] This was one of the first cases to draw an explicit causal link between the two arenas of public activity—and *the* first case connecting schools and housing to be upheld by the U.S. Supreme Court. It was also the first sustained case to require a remedy to ameliorate segregation in both schools and housing. In September 1996 the U.S. Court of Appeals for the Second Circuit found the state of New York liable, along with the Yonkers school district, for that de jure segregation. It required the state to enter into negotiations with the district over funding the remedies needed to eliminate vestiges of segregation—negotiations that began in 1997.[2] The *New York Times* called the decision "groundbreaking" since "the ruling means that a state government can be held responsible for the acts of cities that have historically maintained segregated systems."[3]

Yonkers is also an important case for reasons that have more to do with academic analysis than public importance. In many ways Yonkers is a typical—and thus potentially generalizable—community. It includes both a poor urban center whose residents are disproportionately people of color and relatively wealthy surrounding suburban neighborhoods whose residents are disproportionately white. Yonkers developed around the Hudson River and the New York Central Railroad, with a classic downtown, adjacent industrial areas, and a mix of residential neighborhoods fanning out from the center. In 1990 Yonkers was the fourth largest city in the state, with a population of 188,000 within its eighteen square miles. Physical separation of the old and the new is particularly sharp in Yonkers; with older commercial, industrial, and residential sections concentrated along the river in the southwestern part of the city and separated from the newer and more attractive areas in the east by natural features and transportation corridors. Sectional interests have been vigorously represented in the Yonkers political system, with a ward-based city council that is highly responsive to neighborhood and local constituent interests. No Latino has been elected to the council, and the first African American was elected in 1985, after twenty years of substantial population.

In other ways Yonkers is not a typical community, but its very dissimilarity to other cities offers additional grounds for thinking it a good test case for studying school and housing desegregation policy. Because a mix of racial and economic groups is contained within one school district, the possibility of desegregation is not confounded by the problem of having to cross school district and jurisdictional boundaries, as was the case in *Milliken v. Bradley,* and as remains the case in most major urban centers. Yonkers, however, is not a free-standing small city

politan area. Yonkers is bordered by New
n communities of Westchester County on
pulation and neighborhoods, auto-oriented
and location in a sea of largely residential
version of what we are now coming to call
ontain within their boundaries a microcosm

tive because, during the period of our study,
y powerful, activist, wealthy, and seemingly
segregation. Thus Yonkers offers a best case
-mandated racial change and for change that
n in both school and housing policies. State
ea of racial policies need more attention than
re, especially as more and more responsibili-
ties for social policies are being devolved from Washington to the state capitals.

Finally, Yonkers is an excellent case to analyze because the combined histories of efforts at school and housing desegregation make it clear that the desegregative failure was not a result of bad strategy, poor timing, insufficient attention,
inept leadership, institutional weakness, lack of resources, or most other typical explanations for implementation failure. To put the point most aphoristically,
the State Education Department (SED) followed a path of persuasion, incentives,
and efforts to increase pressure on local districts to devise their own desegregation plans—and failed, not only in Yonkers but also across the state of New
York. The Urban Development Corporation (UDC) followed the opposite path;
the state created an extraordinarily powerful agency that proposed top-down, authoritative imposition of desegregated and dispersed housing projects along with
financial incentives and the promise of economic benefits. It too failed to advance
its racial goals, most spectacularly in Yonkers but more generally across the state.
Bottom-up inducement and top-down requirements were both foiled by the intransigence—even though it was amateurish and parochial—of local officials and
their supporters, by the responsiveness of state legislators to their constituents,
and by the inability of the SED and the unwillingness of the UDC to pursue
racially inclusionary goals in the face of unremitting political hostility to desegregated schools and dispersed housing projects.

Putting these trajectories together yields a more powerful conclusion than
is possible from examining either one alone. Each in isolation suggests that the
opposite strategy could have worked—the case of the SED allows the claim that
failure resulted from too much passivity and deference to local concerns, whereas
the case of the UDC allows the claim that failure resulted from too much rapid
and heavy-handed intervention from above. But if both strategies failed, as they
did, albeit in different policy areas, then we are left with the conclusion that poor
strategic choices probably do not explain the failure to desegregate schools or

housing. Something else is to blame, and some other policy lever than "better strategy" is necessary. Let us turn, then, to our explanations for the failure and to the policy levers that grow from those explanations.

NEW YORK STATE AND SCHOOL DESEGREGATION

The State Education Department of New York was established over a century ago in order to foster the image and practice of public education as a professional rather than as a political activity. When our story started, the Board of Regents held staggered fifteen-year terms. Regents were appointed by the governor, often on the advice of a legislator representing the district from which the appointee was to come, but without explicit (or usually implicit) political considerations. The commissioner of education was appointed by the regents and was responsible only to them. He had the responsibility of carrying out the regents' broad policy mandates and had investigatory and quasi-judicial powers as well as standard administrative ones. The SED dealt with all aspects of education, ranging from universities to museums to local school districts.

Following the findings in *Brown v. Board of Education,* the regents concluded in 1960 that segregated schools "damage the personality of minority group children" and "decrease their motivation and thus impair their ability to learn."[5] Such schools therefore must be eliminated in the name of good educational practice. In response, Commissioner James Allen Jr. asked each district to begin eliminating segregation in its schools and over the next few years put pressure on schools to collect racial data and to develop desegregation plans. He also responded to a "310 petition"[6] by requiring the Malverne School District to desegregate a predominantly black elementary school.[7]

(Mainly white) citizens and school boards were appalled with both the 310 order and the commissioner's directives on racially imbalanced schools. Parents formed protest groups; school boards refused to implement Allen's orders; lawsuits were filed. The press covered extensively the politics of desegregation and resistance to it. State legislators began to react by introducing dozens of bills in opposition to busing and any other compulsory measure to effect racial balance. One such bill passed in 1969 (a federal court later found the law unconstitutional).[8] Legislators also sponsored bills to limit the scope of, or even abolish, the commissioner's powers, to create an Office of Inspector General to review the commissioner's 310 decisions, to cut the terms of members of the Board of Regents, to eliminate funding for the desegregative units and activities of the SED, and so on.[9]

Lacking sufficient funds and the capacity to claim that "the State" was behind his policies, Allen's successor, Ewald Nyquist, could by 1970 no longer battle effectively for statewide desegregation. He instead pursued integration in a few districts through his 310 power and even limited its use to responses to official complaints. Legislators and local officials and citizens, however, kept up the pressure. Some legislators sought to intervene in rulings for particular districts. Others called on the regents to fire Nyquist. Legislators began to use an antibusing litmus test in the appointment of regents, thereby politicizing a process that had previously been prized as nonpartisan and professionally oriented.[10]

Throughout this activity, the SED continued to try to encourage or even mandate desegregation in local districts. Its efforts included setting up new divisions within the SED, developing several master plans, producing numerous research reports, working closely with a gubernatorial commission on public schooling, writing a handbook on desegregation for local districts, and meeting with local educators and parents.[11] Similarly, the Board of Regents stood firm behind its commitment to desegregation for a while. Starting in 1960, and four times thereafter through 1972 (an unprecedented repetition), the regents issued policy statements mandating desegregation as essential to good education for all of New York's students. The 1968 statement called for "more determined, more powerful, more energetic pursuit of the objectives set forth therein" by local districts and the state and claimed that "where the solution to the problem [of racial integration of the schools] is beyond the capability of the local school districts, or where a district fails or refuses to act, then the responsibility for corrective action is clearly and inescapably that of the state."[12]

By the 1970s, however, the legislature's efforts succeeded in checking the SED's initiatives. Regents who supported active policies to mandate desegregation were replaced with strong opponents of busing and other mandatory measures.[13] The legislature halved the terms of office of the regents and passed a law to provide for stricter judicial review of the commissioner's 310 orders. The regents themselves eventually revised their strong policy statements on school desegregation, starting in 1974 and culminating in 1976 with inclusion of the dictum that desegregation did not necessarily include any arithmetic count of students by race. After all, as one regent observed, "Education thinking is one thing and political thinking is another."[14] After Nyquist persisted in issuing desegregative 310 orders throughout the first half of 1976, a majority of the regents voted to fire him. The next commissioner, Gordon Ambach, no longer pursued the goal of integrated schools and issued no 310 rulings ordering schools to desegregate.[15]

At the time the state was becoming less willing and able to help or to require local districts to achieve racial balance, Yonkers was becoming more segregated. Although some of its schools were racially distinct by 1961, racial balance was not much of an issue until the late 1960s when whites began to move out of the city and were replaced by growing numbers of African Americans and Latinos. Because the new residents settled in racially secluded neighborhoods (partly because of the location of subsidized housing), these demographic changes reinforced the racial separation already present in Yonkers's schools.

By the late 1960s, SED officials had targeted Yonkers as one of the school districts most in need of prodding, or even of a plan written by the state, to deal with increasingly severe racial imbalance. And at two points local educational leaders were demonstrably willing to cooperate with the state to desegregate Yonkers's schools. In the late 1960s, Superintendent Paul Mitchell took steps toward improving the racial balance among students and faculty and changing the racial atmosphere in the schools. He sought technical aid from the SED and money from the Racial Balance Fund (some of which he received). A state education official came to Yonkers and spoke to the PTA about the need for the district to desegregate its schools, but he returned to Albany, wrote a memo about "rather heated" mothers with the "express intention of 'not letting my child be bused for 45 minutes . . . all the way across town,' " and did nothing more.[16]

Then Superintendent Mitchell died suddenly. Lacking both his dedication to integration and any commitment from the state for supplemental funding, aid, or regulation, local school officials' efforts to desegregate Yonkers ceased. Almost a decade later, Superintendent Joseph Robitaille made the next major effort to desegregate Yonkers's schools in conjunction with school closings forced by severe budget cuts. Despite opposition from the mayor and many white citizens, the superintendent issued his Phase II reorganization plan in August 1977.

Yonkers, however, was in the midst of a citywide financial crisis and could not pay for desegregation on its own. SED officials promised technical assistance and came close to promising state funds to help develop and implement Phase II. But the now deeply weakened SED provided no aid, and opponents to desegregation became increasingly well organized and energetic. Mayor Angelo Martinelli replaced liberal, activist school board members with conservatives who rejected programs that would destroy "the tradition of neighborhood schools." [17] No one in Yonkers perceived any state pressure to behave otherwise; as one neighborhood organization observed, "It is clear that busing for integration purposes is out of favor even at the state level, and that there is very little likelihood that the commissioner [Ambach] would mandate a forced busing program on the city of Yonkers. . . . [We] therefore again recommend . . . that the Board of Education reject Robitaille's plan without being intimidate[d] by fear of federal or state agency sanctions." [18] When the state did not provide the money or technical assistance it had offered, the board felt as though the SED had "literally abandoned us and we found ourselves in the soup," according to one former school board member.[19] Desegregative efforts were abandoned, and Superintendent Robitaille soon resigned.

In 1980 the U.S. Department of Justice (DOJ) and the federal Office for Civil Rights (OCR) filed charges of racial discrimination against the board of education. Although, for example, the SED had a year earlier found that Yonkers had made "considerable progress" in resolving problems in the special education program and was almost within compliance of state regulations, the OCR found that Yonkers had overincluded minorities in special education and was thus in violation of Title VI of the Civil Rights Act. SED officials even offered to help Yonkers develop a voluntary desegregation plan and provided funds for consultants for this purpose, but it withdrew when Yonkers decided to fight the DOJ order to develop such a plan. The federal government, joined by the NAACP, took the school board and the city to court. Five years later, Judge Leonard B. Sand found intentional segregation by the city and school board of Yonkers in the location of school boundaries, the siting of new schools, and the running of vocational and special education programs, in an extensive opinion that provided exquisite detail about the development of separate and unequal schools in the city.

Since 1985 Yonkers's schools have embarked on an ambitious, but only partly successful, effort to desegregate the schools through voluntary means. The district built several magnet schools on the west side of town, both to lure affluent or white students or both away from east-side schools and to provide better facilities and more innovative curricula to poor students of color who predominate on the west side. Simultaneously, the schools began a concerted effort to attract minority students to east-side schools. The schools became much more attentive to the racial implications of placement in special education classes, upper and lower tracks, and vocational educational classes. These efforts, in combination with the new administration's clear desire to overcome the past, sufficed to persuade Judge Sand that no mandatory desegregative measures were needed.

However, the educational consequences of the physical desegregation have not met the hopes of the judge or the educators. Black and Latino children still achieve at substantially lower levels than do white children, and the racial gap in achievement continues to grow as students move through the grade structure. African American and Latino children still disproportionately drop out of high school, experience more disciplinary measures, and are seldom in the highest tracks. Both white and black families are increasingly discouraged about the benefits of desegregation, and school officials worry that the district will slip back into separate schools as whites leave the magnets and blacks return to schools within the city proper. At this writing, the school district is engaged in court-ordered negotiations with the state of New York, with the goal of attaining up to $500 million of state funds to enable the district to overcome the vestiges of the previously segregated system.

The story of school desegregation before the involvement of the federal judiciary, in short, is one of slow but steady growth in commitment and effort by one part of the state, combined with correspondingly increasing effort to reject that commitment by another part of the state. The legislature's control over budgets, lawmaking, and appointments eventually intimidated, hampered, and halted the cautious efforts of the SED to desegregate Yonkers's schools. The SED moved from a master plan to encourage or even require desegregation to a position on the opposite side of the table from the NAACP and the Justice Department in the eventual desegregation suit.

NEW YORK STATE AND SUBSIDIZED HOUSING

The story of subsidized housing desegregation has the same outcome but follows a different path. New York was a leader among the states in housing as well as in education, with pioneering efforts in public housing, middle-income projects, and fair-housing laws. By the late 1960s the state had financed, built directly, or authorized through local agencies a number of housing projects in Yonkers. All but one (for senior citizens) had been located in increasingly or predominantly black areas of the city, as had similar projects in other cities in New York and the vast majority of federal public housing across the nation.

A dramatic change in state policy occurred in 1968 when Gov. Nelson Rockefeller forged an instrument to provide stronger state leadership in housing development, economic revitalization of cities, and reduction of racial separation. Capitalizing on the assassination of the Reverend Martin Luther King Jr., Rockefeller induced the legislature to approve creation of the New York State Urban Development Corporation (UDC), "perhaps the most powerful state housing and development agency ever created."[20] The UDC combined the functions of several agencies in its marriage of housing finance and project development and management. It was also given unprecedented authority to override local building and land-use controls and to exercise powers of eminent domain. In defense of the UDC's powers, Rockefeller argued that "sovereignty or home rule rights are a privilege" and that the state was responsible for intervening in any arena in which local governments were doing a poor job.[21] The UDC's designer and first president, Edward Logue, specifically insisted on these sweeping powers in order to achieve bargaining leverage with local officials, an ability to avoid local vetoes, and the capacity to override race-based opposition.

Rockefeller and Logue explicitly intended to empower the state's new agency to mandate racial desegregation. Rockefeller presented the UDC bill to the legislature with the words, "We cannot live as a segregated people. The American dream is not divisible."[22] Logue concurred, claiming that "the noble tool of zoning has been perverted to maintaining the character of affluent, lily-white suburbs."[23] The legislature initially agreed with these goals; the mandate of the UDC, according to the law that created it, was to "enable the State, in cooperation with private enterprise, to attack the root causes of poverty and slums."[24]

Once the UDC began its work, however, opposition within the legislature grew. Resistance centered on the desire to strip the UDC's power to override local authorities and was fueled by the UDC's plans to build subsidized housing in the suburbs of Westchester. In 1973, after the legislature threatened to deny the UDC additional borrowing authority, Rockefeller reluctantly signed a bill giving villages and towns the right to veto proposed UDC projects. Legislation to extend the override ban to cities followed but did not pass. The UDC then withdrew from projects in Westchester County and Long Island. By 1975 the UDC was bankrupt, and its role as an instrument for reducing racial separation was abandoned in its reincarnation as an economic development agency.

Shortly before the UDC was created, the director of urban renewal in Yonkers notified the governor that a new agency with considerable power might aid in overcoming local "political and social prejudices" that produced "the inability of local and other agencies to execute urban renewal."[25] Because of these "prejudices," Yonkers had been unable to devise a relocation plan for displaced minority families that was acceptable to the U.S. Department of Housing and Urban Development (HUD), which had halted urban renewal in the city. As soon as the UDC was established, officials in Yonkers urgently requested its help in relocating residents in response to demands for space from a major employer. The UDC responded to Yonkers in part because one of the state agency's missions was to rescue stalled urban renewal programs in the state's cities.

The UDC's initial plan called for scattered-site housing for 1,000 mostly black families, targeted for locations throughout the city selected in consultation with local officials. Logue's hope, expressed to Yonkers's mayor, that the recommended sites "would have some hope of not meeting overwhelming opposition in your city" were quickly dashed.[26] Publication of the list of proposed housing sites in the local press produced a tumultuous reaction against the UDC and its supporters in Yonkers. White residents protested vociferously; the city council held raucous public meetings; the Westchester County Board of Supervisors passed a resolution condemning the UDC for proposing subsidized housing that would "completely destroy the residential character of the adjacent neighborhoods";[27] and the UDC-friendly mayor and a supportive council member lost their next elections.

Despite the UDC's formidable powers and its control over access to federal urban renewal money that Yonkers desperately needed, Logue chose not to bargain or to maintain pressure on the city. Of ninety-eight original proposed sites, seventy-six of which were outside Yonkers's urban core, the UDC accepted the four sites chosen by the city council—all within the inner city—for its first housing projects. The UDC was more interested in getting on with its primary goals in Yonkers—rescuing urban renewal and building projects—than in taking on the impassioned foes of scattered-site housing in Yonkers and throughout the state. The UDC largely dropped its concern for spatial desegregation in Yonkers and focused only on its concern for "rapid development [of housing] . . . in sufficient quantity to meet the needs of both the state arterial program [and] the city's . . . redevelopment program" with "minimal disruption of community life."[28] That shift implied building projects where there would be the least political opposition—that is, in the urban core. The UDC wanted to show results, it wanted to develop a constituency, and it wanted to house people in better conditions. To these goals desegregation gave way.

As had almost happened with the SED, the UDC ended up supporting the city of Yonkers against efforts by the federal government to insist on greater desegregative effort in policy choices. In the late 1960s, HUD had conditioned urban renewal funding on the building of scattered-site housing for families displaced from the inner neighborhoods of Yonkers. Once the UDC agreed to the city council's choice of sites, its very powerfulness, ironically, relieved Yonkers of concern about HUD pressure. Because of the broad leeway HUD accorded the UDC, Yonkers was able to proceed with a racially segregative program of UDC relocation housing in Southwest Yonkers larger than the relocation housing plans HUD previously had forbidden the city to undertake on its own because of their probable segregative impact. By 1972, the UDC was successfully lobbying HUD to relax its rules conditioning further urban renewal funds on dispersal of new subsidized housing.

In the end, the UDC sponsored 1,800 out of a total of 2,600 units of family-oriented public housing built in Yonkers from 1968 to 1972. All its projects were located in Southwest Yonkers, the section of the city that is overwhelmingly poor, crowded, and peopled by African Americans and Latinos. As Judge Sand wrote in 1985, "It is . . . difficult to discern any plan at work in the . . . site selection process during these years, except for an apparent determination to avoid, at virtually any cost, a confrontation with community opponents of public housing."[29] Mayor Albert DelBello, elected in the wake of the initial uproar over the UDC's scattered-site plan, was more partisan but did not disagree: "The big threat had been . . . adequately controlled. The methods that the city administration used to produce housing . . . reflected a consideration for neighborhoods, induced public participation in the process. I believe the public in Yonkers was no longer offended, as they were in prior years, by illogical approaches as to where housing should be built and where housing should not be built."[30]

EXPLAINING THE FAILURE OF DESEGREGATION IN YONKERS

In explaining the failure of both the SED and the UDC to desegregate public agencies in Yonkers despite their commitment, ostensible power, strong leaders, and considerable resources, we emphasize three phenomena that deserve more attention in discussions of school and housing desegregation.

First, these agencies were operating in a system of separated and shared powers. The American political system does not create hierarchies of power. Instead it delegates and interweaves authority among levels of government, executive and legislative branches, and elected and appointed officials. Players at different levels and in different branches of government have distinctive roles, perspectives, agendas, and resources; they respond to particular stimuli and constituencies; and they must cope with particular constraints that are shaped by their place in the system.[31]

Consider the difference between the form and the reality of the power of state government over its local subdivisions. New York's formal authority and legal supremacy meant that the state could in principle order the desegregation of public schools and subsidized housing, in Yonkers and anywhere else in the state. But in reality the state was severely constrained by the diffusion of political power. No matter how much authority or autonomy were assigned to the SED or the UDC, their formal powers could at any point be modified by the state legislature, as were the UDC's as a result in part of opposition to scatter-site housing. Similarly, their policies could be changed by personnel changes at the top, as when the legislature ensured that opponents of busing were appointed to the state Board of Regents. Moreover, both state agencies preferred cooperative to hostile relations with their local counterparts. The SED, after all, educated no children; it depended heavily on local school systems for information and for carrying out state programs and was expected to be partners with rather than adversaries of local school officials and their communities. The UDC had considerably more freedom of action with regard to housing. But Logue, who had made his mark as a local urban renewal official, understood that the agency could not survive without forging close ties with its local constituents, particularly in cities like Yonkers that needed the UDC's money and power to implement local programs. Both state agencies were powerful, but using that power effectively meant operating within the web of shared and delegated power and being sensitive to legislative and local concerns. Thus employing the power of the SED or the UDC was difficult when the issue was school or housing desegregation.

A second cluster of explanations for the failure of the SED and the UDC to desegregate focuses more on internal dynamics within each agency rather than on relations across agencies and levels of government. Neither agency had racial desegregation as its primary mission, and in each racial goals were secondary to the primary functional concerns. The SED's mission encompassed every aspect of public education, a task involving it with hundreds of school boards, thousands of public officials, and millions of children. The UDC was created to build subsidized housing, renew New York's faltering cities, and stimulate economic development.[32] Whatever the commitment of these agencies to racial integration, and it was substantial among some key officials in both agencies, promoting racial inclusion was a secondary objective. Both the SED and the UDC committed relatively meager financial and staff resources to racial goals, even in comparison with investments in other secondary agency missions. And this particular subsidiary objective was highly controversial and thus a threat to the more central goals of each agency. Pressing for racial integration provoked political retribution by legislators, jeopardized the local cooperation that was essential to carrying out core education and housing programs, and risked contaminating other programs with the contagion of race-based controversy. For both agencies, the response to the dilemma was to de-emphasize racial objectives; they revised priorities, shelved controversial proposals, abandoned activist policies, and accepted local preferences for racial separation.[33]

Third, ultimately the state agencies failed to desegregate Yonkers because a majority of citizens, certainly in Yonkers and probably in the state as a whole, did not want them to do so and were able to use the democratic process to achieve their preferences. Democracy—in the basic sense of government responsiveness to the desires of a majority—worked in both cases, at the expense of the rights of some citizens and perhaps the long-term strength of democracy itself. Elected officials at the local and state level were responsive to opponents of desegregated schools and dispersed subsidized housing, and their responses imposed constraints on the SED and the UDC that foreclosed policies and plans promising less racial separation. As a result, in the sensitive policy areas of schools and housing, especially when the issue was race, the most powerful players in New York were democratically elected officials rather than strong, independent agencies, flamboyant public entrepreneurs, policy wonks, faceless bureaucrats, committed advocates, or economic elites. Two formidable agencies—the SED with its wide powers and apolitical expertise, the UDC with its expansive powers and skilled leadership—were no match for elected officials responding to citizens who did not want desegregated schools or scattered subsidized housing.

LESSONS FROM THE YONKERS FIASCO ABOUT THE CONTENT OF RACIAL POLICY

We draw two sets of lessons from this history of Yonkers. The first has to do with the nature of possible policies to promote racial equality and the second with the requirements of the policymaking process. That is, the first lesson is that policymakers need an implementable policy. To be implementable, a policy needs to have at least one of four characteristics.[34]

An implementable policy may offset market distortions created by "inefficient" tastes such as that for racial discrimination. The best example here is public accommodations, or the sports and entertainment industries. Once policy changes forced the market to open up to all potential consumers or producers, the desire for profits from new customers, a winning team, or a popular show took over as the "enforcement" mechanism.

An implementable policy may instead be a single-stage policy, that is, one with "no intermediate steps between adoption of the policy and production of the effects."[35] A good example here is the right to vote; once an end to discrimination against black would-be voters is required, it is relatively easy to figure out how to stop intimidation and discrimination in registration and voting procedures.

To be implementable, a policy should accord with or be necessary to some other goal of the implementing institution. The best example here is desegregation of the armed forces. Once the military realized that it needed black soldiers to fill out the ranks and that those soldiers had to be able to win battles, the various branches took the necessary steps to achieve that goal. The process included

ensuring that black soldiers were trained as well as white ones, that morale remained high and racial tensions low, and that "the leaders look . . . like the led."[36]

Finally, an implementable policy creates positive-sum rather than zero-sum
or negative-sum games. Employment discrimination declined less as a result of
external enforcement than as a result of personnel officers realizing that procedures for guaranteeing equal opportunity helped them to do their jobs better.
Such procedures gave them grounds for rejecting pressures of nepotism, for enhancing their own professional standing and importance within their firms, and
for reinforcing their self-perception as fair and equitable.[37] Personnel officers were
reinforced by managers of sales forces, who realized that people were more likely
to buy goods and services when offered by salespersons who looked like them.
Thus everyone—or at least enough people—"won" within corporations to make
reducing job discrimination worthwhile from their perspective.

School and housing desegregation enjoy none of these characteristics. School
desegregation is either outside the reach of market forces, or market incentives
work against desegregating schools (since schools with relatively high proportions of African American students are typically assumed to be less good and
therefore a handicap to the housing market). Desegregation of subsidized housing
is more within the reach of market forces, but there are typically more applicants
than there are units, and residents of subsidized housing are usually seen as more
of a disadvantage than a boon to private housing markets. We can see both of
these phenomena at work in Yonkers—the strongest opponents of both school
and housing desegregation were the neighborhood organizations in the wealthier
suburban sections of the city whose members voiced fears about the adverse consequences of school and housing desegregation for property values.

Furthermore, neither housing nor school desegregation is a single-stage
policy. A huge array of features of a school and school system must change for
desegregation to be implemented, and an even larger array must be changed for
that desegregation to succeed and persist.[38] Scatter-site housing is equally complicated, and maintaining a desegregated neighborhood is even more difficult.[39]
In both cases, implementation must persist over a very long period of time, with
changing and complicated circumstances and the need for constant repetition of
policy interventions.

Similarly, educators or housing authorities seldom see desegregation as essential to their key mission; they are more likely, in fact, to see it as an impedi-
ment. Educators' goal is to teach the children they confront every day, and they
seldom feel a lack of a sufficient number of students to reach their goals (as is
the case in the armed forces). Housing agencies seek to build, rent, and maintain
as much housing as possible, and political controversy over its location or racial
mix simply gets in the way of this goal. The school superintendents in Yonkers
who expressed interest in desegregation did so as a sidelight to their more central concerns—reducing racial tension and occasional violence in the schools for
Paul Mitchell, and closing schools and reorganizing grade structures for Joseph

Robitaille. Logue's commitment to dispersing subsidized housing gave way to his stronger commitment to the construction of new housing, which was most expeditiously accomplished by locating projects where they were locally acceptable.

Moreover, neither school nor housing desegregation is typically construed as benefiting all participants, so it does not look like a positive-sum game. White citizens have almost always seen school desegregation as imposing direct and severe costs on themselves and their children without any compensating benefits. Many black citizens have come reluctantly to the view that the potential benefits of desegregated schools do not outweigh the certain costs of trying to achieve them; a small but important proportion have moved beyond that view to a principled rejection of publicly mandated integration. Most white families are no more eager to live in desegregated housing than they are to send their children to desegregated schools. Some black families are indifferent to the racial composition of neighborhoods compared with their desire to live somewhere decent at prices they can afford; others see efforts to desegregate neighborhoods as a source of further tension in already difficult lives. A few are principled nationalists, and another few remain principled integrationists.

In Yonkers, whites consistently opposed school and housing desegregation. Many blacks supported desegregation efforts but for instrumental more than intrinsic reasons. They saw that schools and neighborhoods were much better in white than in black Yonkers and that a racial divide blocked black access to newer schools, better teachers, and attractive neighborhoods. Once school and housing desegregation seemed to offer more problems than benefits even to black residents of Yonkers. However, their support faded.

The second lesson of the history of school and housing policies in Yonkers is that policymakers need not only an implementable set of policies but also the incentive and opportunity to carry out the goal of fostering racial equality. More particularly, they need to have at least one of four characteristics:

Policymakers need a strong institutional structure on which to build, or the tools with which to build a strong new institution. The transformation of the right to vote and seek office nicely illustrates the value of institutions. During the 1960s a new federal law and regulations, and newly appointed agents of the Justice Department, shifted the ground from futile individual efforts to exercise the right to vote into legal wrangles over district boundaries and routines for policing voting rules and practices. African Americans increasingly voted and attained elective office, thereby securing the status of incumbents and the financial, organizational, and personal resources attached to public offices and party organizations. They, in turn, moved to higher offices and promoted the prospects of other African American political hopefuls.[40] The DOJ continues to monitor voting rights, and the Voting Rights Act was continually strengthened, even through the Reagan presidency.

Alternatively, policymakers need the ability to require another political actor to change his behavior and to bear the costs of doing so. President Truman in Executive Order 9981 told the armed forces to desegregate; the Supreme Court in

Brown v. Board of Education told southern educators and judges to desegregate the schools; northern members of Congress told southern election officials to desegregate the voting booth. They succeeded, in part because they sustained their resolution through not having to change themselves in order to invoke change by others.

Policymakers can succeed if they are able to issue a mandate to an organization that is tightly hierarchical rather than loosely coupled. One can be relatively confident that an order will be obeyed in the army, in a courtroom, or on a sports team, at least compared with the expectations one has when issuing a mandate to homeowners or schoolteachers.

They also succeed if they demonstrate the commitment and capacity to stick with a problem as long as is necessary to overcome the inevitable obstacles to success. Elected officials seldom dare to commit themselves to a program with a good chance of success in the long run but with little immediate payoff. Nor can they afford to devote much of their energy to a program with a lot of complications and opponents. Thus the most effective policy entrepreneurs are often agency officials or private actors with long tenure in their position, deep conviction about the importance and ultimate success of their cause, relative insulation from outside forces, and a touch of fanaticism.

School and housing desegregation have seldom, if ever, enjoyed a policy context with some or all of these four characteristics. The state of New York did not build a strong institutional base under its efforts to desegregate schools and subsidized housing in Yonkers (or elsewhere). The Division of Intercultural Relations (DIR) was the desegregative unit of the SED; it was always underfunded, its positions were never completely filled, and many members of its staff were personally and professionally weak. It simply did not exude institutional authority or strength, and it certainly did not inspire respect or awe. In the UDC, desegregation never had a separate institutional base. So when desegregation came into conflict with other agency goals, its advocates had no independent grounds on which to take a stand. Contrast this situation to HUD, which had a formal site-selection review process undertaken by a civil rights office to ensure that federally aided projects did not increase racial concentration.[41]

The history of Yonkers also demonstrates clearly that school and housing officials cannot issue orders to other actors and expect them to bear the costs of carrying out those orders. The desegregative elements of the SED survived fifteen years, but eventually the mounting political pressure of opposition to desegregation cost the department so much that it halted any further effort to desegregate schools. The desegregative elements of the UDC started out by seeking to impose much higher costs on Yonkers's officials and residents than the SED had ever dared to contemplate; the political costs redounded quickly enough to destroy the UDC's scatter-site venture in less than a year and ensured that the UDC would build future projects in locations that did not impose unwanted costs on Yonkers's dominant majority.

In addition to these problems of policymakers' incentives and opportunities, schools are the quintessential loosely coupled organization.[42] Housing is even less hierarchically structured, with scores of developers and lenders, hundreds of Realtors, and thousands of buyers and sellers in the smallest metropolitan area as well as dozens of public agencies involved in planning, zoning, building codes, and subsidized housing, and a growing phalanx of nonprofits concerned with everything from halfway houses to the homeless. Thus school administrators and housing officials could expect very little direct responsiveness even if they were to issue orders mandating racial equality or integration in classrooms, real estate firms, and rental offices.

Finally, all responsible analysts agree that it takes years if not decades for reforms in education or the housing market to show substantial impact, and then it is possible only if reforms are sustained and deepened. And this is in a context in which the core reforms may be highly controversial themselves (as with school and housing desegregation) or may simply be competing against other plausible reforms for scarce time, money, and commitment. In these circumstances, policy entrepreneurs with many resources and much commitment and staying power are essential. School desegregation has been unusually blessed with such policy entrepreneurs, but they have more often advocated from outside the schools than made and implemented decisions from within. Housing desegregation has lagged behind education in these terms; organized interests generally have been weak, underfinanced, unable to penetrate the decision-making process, and discouraged by the tedious necessity to deal with individual cases and the marginalized public agencies responsible for housing discrimination.[43]

In short, if one were to search for two policies that are maximally difficult to promulgate and implement, one could not do much better than to choose school and housing desegregation in an electoral context.

But even this characterization of the obstacles facing the state of New York is incomplete. We must consider two additional features of the policymaking process before turning from the nature of the problems to an outline of the solutions.

The likelihood of attaining a policy goal depends in part on resources. Agencies seeking to implement a substantial policy change need a fairly high level of resources, flexibility in deploying them, and appropriate substantive content. Money is the most fungible resource; it offers the greatest flexibility in deployment and the best means for attaining appropriate substantive resources. But it is not the only resource and cannot even buy some of the most essential ones. An agency needs systematic and neutrally gathered information about the problem it is addressing in order to plan and evaluate. It needs responsible and knowledgeable experts—on its staff, as advisers and consultants, and as part of an informed and supportive policy subcommunity that can enhance the agency's efforts and legitimacy. It needs support from strong political figures, a firm legal or legislative mandate, a powerful and effective constituency, or some other tool for withstanding opposition. The level and kind of resources available for reform are not, of course, independent of the characteristics of policies and policymakers that we have described. But control over resources is as critical to a policy's success or failure as are the policy's characteristics or champions.

The final feature of the policymaking context is public opinion. An agency needs a decent fabric of public opinion—that is, a workable mix of visibility, saliency, and intensity—in order to accomplish its reforms. By *visibility,* we mean how aware the public is of policies and policy changes. Most citizens are unaware, for example, of banking rules that effectively deny the possibility of loans to homeowners in some predominantly black neighborhoods in their community. Citizens are more aware of proposals to build subsidized housing, and they are vividly aware of proposals to desegregate schools.

By *saliency,* we mean how much people care about policy changes. The general softening of whites' racial attitudes over the past forty years has allowed for major policy changes in some arenas, such as participation in professional sports and entertainment, voting rights, and public accommodations. In other arenas, either there has been less softening of white racial attitudes (e.g., with regard to interracial marriage, perhaps until recently), or there is too big a gap between a general softening of racial attitudes and a willingness to acquiesce in a particular policy change (such as school or housing desegregation). There is simply too much at stake—emotionally, socially, culturally, financially—for whites to see schools and neighborhoods as only occasionally salient.

By *intensity,* we mean the depth of people's passion about the arena in which policy changes are proposed. Low levels of intensity permit policy change—think of sports, entertainment, or public accommodations. But public opinion is likely to become intense, and therefore policy change is likely to be difficult, when the site of a policy change is tied to a particular space or set of daily practices, as are schools and homes; when the new policy will affect people over a long duration, as do changes in schools and neighborhoods; and when there is no exit option, or exit is very costly. Again, contrast schools and housing with hotels or a baseball game. One can readily avoid the latter if the imposition of desegregation is intensely distasteful, but it is difficult to leave a home or an assigned public school, particularly for people who lack the means to exercise the exit option.

Thus citizens' concerns over issues that are visible, salient, and intense will produce a break between their general support for principles of racial desegregation and their particular behaviors. The dominant opinion of local publics is likely to become amplified and effective in these circumstances because its continuance provides enough time for elected officials to be roused into defensive action, which often means retaliation against agency officials who took the actions that so alarmed the public to begin with. Moreover, a policy intervention can set up sympathetic vibrations among citizens who perceive that the threat will reach them next—thus making the issue highly visible, salient, and intense even for people not currently affected by it.[44]

WHAT IS THERE TO DO?

Given this context—a policy whose nature is intrinsically difficult to implement, policymakers who lack the characteristics that lead to success, insufficient resources, and a hostile or skeptical public opinion—is there any chance for achieving racial equality through schools and housing? To put the question more programmatically, what would it take to make a public agency take responsibility and succeed in desegregating schools and housing?

We do not have a complete answer at this point (perhaps we never shall). But we can offer three rules that the history of Yonkers suggests are necessary if not sufficient for success.

First, begin where the public is—individual racism is wrong, and institutional racial discrimination is wrong. Most white Americans do not want (or are unwilling to admit that they want) to see themselves as prejudiced and do not want to act in a way that denies opportunities to black Americans. Similarly, most white Americans do not want their political and economic institutions and practices to discriminate against black Americans. This is a real and important change over the past forty years, and it is the essential starting point for any policy designed to promote racial inclusiveness. At a minimum, leaders need to remind citizens endlessly that racial discrimination is bad for all Americans, that all Americans will gain from its demise, and that policies can be designed to ensure that improving the life chances of African Americans need not harm the life chances of white Americans.

Second, give focused responsibility to a single agency, so that ameliorating racial discrimination is the central, if not the sole, agenda of that agency. The history of Yonkers, and many other places, shows that if an agency has other mission(s), they will take precedence over desegregation, given how hard it is to do and how much public opposition it arouses. Most civil rights agencies have been weak components (offices for civil rights, the DIR) of weak functional departments (Departments of Education, Labor, HUD, SED), a reflection of weak commitment to civil rights and the primacy of core functional responsibilities. Thus it is hardly surprising that such agencies rarely have prevailed. Officials of a new civil rights enforcement agency must be committed to the success of its central mission—whether for reasons of ideological belief, political ambition, or material gain—for that agency to have any chance of thriving in a dense political environment.[45]

Third, ensure that the agency responsible for promoting racial equality has substantial resources and sufficient authority to carry out its mandate. It should be constituted as a law enforcement agency, analogous to the specialized agencies within the DOJ that oversee voting rights and investigate civil rights violations. It needs an authoritative legal mandate, an independent funding source, the ability to streamline procedures, the capacity to cut across functional categories that

most other agencies focus on, insulation from short-term political punishment—
and a passion for racial justice.[46]

We are under no illusions about the political feasibility of these proposals—
how could we be after analyzing Yonkers and its stark teachings about civil rights
and political realities? But one of the key lessons of this case is that our nation
must find better means for ensuring racial justice than those now established.
Those means will begin with current laws and the post-1960s consensus that publicly endorsed racism and discrimination are unacceptable. But they must build
more powerfully than heretofore upon that legal and normative base if civil rights
guarantees are ever to be more than haphazardly enforced. And after all, almost
nothing that has advanced the rights and broadened the opportunities of people
of color in the United States seemed politically feasible a decade before change
came. We would like to believe that creative thinking and bold political claims,
whether ours or others', will once again create a way out of no way, perhaps for
the kind of approaches that we suggest here.[47]

NOTES

1. *U.S. v. Yonkers Board of Education* (1985) 624 F. Supp. 1276 (S.D.N.Y.)

2. *U.S. v. City of Yonkers* (1996) 96 F. 3d 600 (2d Cir.)

3. Joseph Berger, "State Faulted in Segregation in Yonkers," *New York Times,* September 25, 1996, p. B1. Both of us worked as expert witnesses in the case leading to the
1995 decision by the federal district court, which was reversed upon appeal to the U.S.
Court of Appeals for the Second Circuit. The 1995 district court ruling was by Judge
Leonard B. Sand, who presided over the entire Yonkers litigation. He held that the state
was morally culpable but could not be found legally liable for segregation in Yonkers because it had been a passive bystander rather than an active fomenter of segregation (*U.S. v.
City of Yonkers* [1995], 880 F. Supp. 212 [S.D.N.Y.]). In July 1997 the U.S. Supreme Court
declined to review the 1996 appeals court ruling.

4. Joel Garreau, *Edge City: Life on the New Frontier* (New York: Doubleday, 1991).

5. University of the State of New York Regents' statement on intercultural relations
in education, *Journal of Regents Meeting* (New York: University of the State of New York),
January 27–28, 1960.

6. A 310 petition is an official complaint to which the commissioner must respond
with "quasi-judicial proceedings designed to enforce state education policies" (*Yonkers
Board of Education v. New York State* [1995], p. 13). The commissioner may also initiate 310
actions on his own behest. (The term comes from Section 310 of the New York Education
Law, which spells out the commissioner's responsibility and authority for these proceedings.) During the period of our study, substantive decisions could not be appealed; the only
possible appeal to the courts was the procedural claim that the commissioner's decision was
"arbitrary and capricious." The courts traditionally interpreted this standard very narrowly.

7. *Matter of Mitchell* (June 17, 1963), Decision no. 7240, Ed. Dept. Rep. 501.

8. *Lee v. Nyquist* (1970) 318 F. Supp. 710. The law did not prohibit elected school

boards from reassigning students for desegregative purposes; its strictures reached only to the SED and appointed boards of education. Thus it can be described, and was so described by its supporters, as an endorsement of democratic reform. Even after the provision was struck down by the courts, the legislature continued to debate and occasionally to pass antibusing bills for the next few years.

9. As early as 1963, the regents requested funds from the legislature to address "urgent problems of racial imbalance" (State Education Department of New York [1963], the Regents Major Legislative Proposals for December 1964), and the plea continued through the 1970s. The SED generally requested $10 to $15 million annually; the legislature allocated $3 million in 1968, $1 million each of the succeeding two years, and nothing after that.

10. Kenneth Clark [deposition], *Yonkers Board of Education v. New York State* (1988) 60 Civ. 6761 (LBS), S.D.N.Y., 14.

11. The SED did not take other possible steps. Among the steps not taken that Judge Sand identified in his 1995 ruling were removing school officials who failed to comply with the commissioner's orders, withholding state funds under the same circumstance, initiating 310 investigations and rulings without waiting for a citizen's petition, issuing regulations for desegregation and following them with inspection and enforcement procedures, and denying approval for the construction of new schools in sites that would exacerbate segregation (*Yonkers Board of Education v. New York State* [1995], pp. 12–14). The state did take some of these steps, especially that of strict regulation and detailed compliance reviews, to implement other controversial policies such as special education, bilingual education, and vocational education. As a former Yonkers school board member put it, "On everything else the state followed through except on racial balance" (interview with Robert Jacobson, November 26, 1990, by Jennifer Hochschild, Steven Routh, and Monica Herk).

12. State Education Department of New York, *Integration and the Schools: A Statement of Policy and Recommendations by the Regents of the University of the State of New York,* Position Paper no. 3 (Albany), January 1968, pp. 7, 12.

13. Observed one new regent, "It breaks my heart to see those little bitsy things standing on the corner in ice, snow, and wind waiting for the bus" (Mike Gershowitz, "New Regents Board Member Will Make Waves," *Long Island Press,* April 7, 1974, p. 22).

14. Carl Pforzheimer, Regents Minutes, June 27, 1969. Chancellor McGovern (head of the Board of Regents) made the same observation regretfully rather than pugnaciously: "Recent events . . . turn away the Regents from a position of leadership which they have long maintained" (Joseph McGovern, letter to Bishop Paul Moore, March 3, 1975).

15. In fact, he delayed or watered down several of Commissioner Nyquist's remaining 310 orders. As an assistant commissioner concluded in 1985, "Our mission is limited, our purview is limited. We are a wonderful department, but we can't solve all of the problems of society."

16. Morton Sobel, Memorandum to Yonkers File Regarding Title IV Technical Assistance, October 29, 1970. Inaction followed, despite the fact that Sobel had noted in the same memo that "we would not be faced with insurmountable [*sic*] difficulties in assisting Yonkers to desegregate."

17. Joseph Guerney, interview by Beth Lorenz, Steven Routh, and Monica Herk, November 1, 1990.

18. TONEY (Taxpayers Organization of North East Yonkers Education Committee), *Report on School Reorganization Phase no. 2* (printed in the *Herald Statesman,* March 5,

1978, pp. 1–1d); see also Lincoln Park Taxpayers Association Education Committee, *Report,* March 1977.

19. Jacobson interview, November 26, 1990.

20. *U.S. v. Yonkers Board of Education* (1995), p. 32.

21. Steven V. Roberts, "Governor Insists City Must Yield," *New York Times,* March 8, 1968, p. 28.

22. In *Public Papers of Nelson A. Rockefeller,* state of New York (Albany, New York), 1968, p. 204.

23. "A Superagency for Urban Superproblems," *Business Week,* March 7, 1970, p. 98.

24. New York, Urban Development Act of 1968.

25. Walter Webdale to Gov. Nelson Rockefeller, plaintiff, exhibit in *United States v. City of Yonkers* (1995).

26. Ibid., Edward Logue to Mayor James O'Rourke.

27. *U.S. v. Yonkers Board of Education* (1985), p. 1319.

28. UDC document in plaintiff's brief, *U.S. v. City of Yonkers* (1985).

29. *U.S. v. Yonkers Board of Education* (1985), p. 1310.

30. Deposition of Albert DelBello in *U.S. v. Yonkers Board of Education* (1995), p. 95.

31. Michael Danielson, *The Politics of Exclusion* (New York: Columbia University Press, 1976); Judy Failer, Anna Harvey, and Jennifer Hochschild, "Only One Oar in the Water: The Political Failure of School Desegregation in Yonkers, New York," *Educational Policy* 7, no. 3 (1993): 276–96.

32. Similarly, HUD was willing to overlook the UDC's locational policies in Yonkers because the federal housing agency was interested in production, and the UDC was the largest single developer of federally subsidized dwellings in the early 1970s.

33. As one SED official pointed out as early as 1968, Commissioner Allen should take strong desegregative actions, but he must also "recognize the political . . . ramifications." Civil rights activists must in turn understand the "political realities faced by the commissioner and his concern to protect the powers of his office" (Wilbur Nordos, memorandum to Ewald Nyquist, April 2, 1968).

34. For a more detailed exposition of the next few paragraphs and fuller citations, see Jennifer Hochschild, "You Win Some, You Lose Some . . . Explaining the Pattern of Success and Failure in the Second Reconstruction," in *Taking Stock: Policy and Governance in the Twentieth Century,* ed. Morton Keller and R. Shep Melnick (New York: Oxford University Press, forthcoming 1998).

35. Douglas Arnold, *The Logic of Congressional Action* (New Haven: Yale University Press, 1990), pp. 19–20.

36. Edwin Dorn, "Helping All of Us Become All We Can Be," *Los Angeles Times,* August 9, 1995, p. B9; Charles Moskos and John Butler, *All That We Can Be* (New York: Basic Books, 1996).

37. Frank Dobbin, "Equal Opportunity Law and the Construction of Internal Labor Markets," *American Journal of Sociology* 99, no. 2 (1993): 396–427; James Heckman and Brook Payner, "Determining the Impact of Federal Antidiscrimination Policy on the Economic Status of Blacks," *American Economic Review* 79 (1989): 138–77.

38. Jennifer Hochschild, *The New American Dilemma: Liberal Democracy and School Desegregation* (New Haven: Yale University Press, 1984).

39. Danielson, *Politics of Exclusion,* and W. Dennis Keating, *The Suburban Racial Dilemma* (Philadelphia: Temple University Press, 1994).

40. This sequence, of course, was reinforced by the political advantages that resulted from the concentration of blacks in particular districts and jurisdictions—a product of historic settlement patterns, housing discrimination, segregated schools, and racial gerrymandering. Thus one institutionalized success (voting and officeholding) worked against creating another (desegregated schools and neighborhoods).

41. Of course, such formal institutionalization did not ensure desegregative results. But the existence of the process in HUD made race an explicit factor in site selection, which was not the case at the UDC.

42. Karl E. Weick, "The Twigging of Overload," in *People and Information,* ed. H. B. Pepinsky (New York: Pergamon, 1970), pp. 67–129.

43. See Michael N. Danielson, "Open Housing in America: Promises, Performance, and Prospects," Report to Ford Foundation, March 1979.

44. These vibrations are amplified by the publicity given to particularly vivid instances by the media, particularly local television, which crave the dramatic images of chanting opponents of busing and clamorous meetings to protest scattered-site housing. And for those on the other side of the racial divide, attitudes about desegregation inevitably are shaped by television cameras that capture the frightened faces of black children on beleaguered school buses or the anger and fear of African Americans whose dream house has been vandalized.

45. In this chapter we do not address the myriad other proposals for systemic reform in public education or housing that are currently under serious consideration. They are beyond our scope here, and in any case most do not have as a central goal the enhancement of racial equality and equal opportunity. Our general stance is that of cautious enthusiasm; after all, some school systems and housing environments could hardly be worse, so almost any change is bound to be an improvement. Most relevant here is our claim that all of these reforms should be carefully vetted by a strong civil rights enforcement agency to ensure that at least they did not violate civil rights and that at most they helped to foster them.

46. Those few agencies that *have* been dedicated to civil rights enforcement (Office of Equal Opportunity [OEO], Office for Federal Contract Compliance and Procurement [OFCCP]) have not had the resources or legislative backing they needed to do their job.

47. We are working on a book that will develop these policy proposals in more detail, focusing particularly on what this new law enforcement agency should do, if it were ever brought into being. We acknowledge with thanks the support of the Spencer Foundation in this larger project as well as in the preparation of this chapter.

3

Regionalism Forestalled: Metropolitan Fragmentation and Desegregation Planning in Greater New Haven, Connecticut

Kathryn A. McDermott

The structure of metropolitan political institutions and the intervention of state or federal authorities in local politics decisively influence the success of efforts to desegregate public schools. Desegregation of school districts that include both city and suburbs, such as Charlotte-Mecklenburg County, North Carolina, has been more thorough and more lasting than that of city-only school systems. However, even in school districts like Charlotte-Mecklenburg, where geography is conducive to desegregation, the catalyst for and sustaining force behind integration has generally come from actors outside local districts, generally but not always the federal courts. Neither geography (see chapter 10 on Charlotte) nor outside political and legal pressure (see chapters 2 and 4 on Yonkers and San Francisco) is sufficient by itself to produce desegregation, but in the absence of one or both elements it is exceedingly unlikely to occur.

Unfavorable geography or the absence of a court order does not make equal educational opportunity a less important goal. How, then, should efforts to achieve integration and justice proceed when conditions are not ideal? Such was the case in Connecticut in 1993, when the state General Assembly passed the Act Improving Educational Quality and Diversity (EQD), a law requiring the state's 169 fiercely independent municipalities to engage in regional planning of programs to enhance educational quality and diversity and to combat racial and socioeconomic isolation. Measures such as this one could conceivably be a viable means of creating institutional change conducive to desegregation and of exercising state authority in a political culture that enshrines home rule as one of its highest values. In practice, however, the legislation was fatally weakened by deference to local prerogatives and by a definition of the problem that obscured the links between metropolitan fragmentation and educational inequality. A challenge to the autonomy of local school districts was necessary if racial and socioeconomic isolation was to be reversed, but the larger political culture of local control led the state legislature and local actors to shy away from such a challenge. In its failure to challenge prevailing power structures and understandings of the issue, Connecticut's Act Improving Educational Quality and Diversity provides an example of how *not* to exercise outside political power to change local institutions. The Yonkers case discussed in chapter 2 demonstrates that even well-planned outside intervention may not succeed in desegregating schools; the Connecticut case is a worst-case example of poorly conceived outside intervention.

THE "TWO CONNECTICUTS" AND THE ACT IMPROVING EDUCATIONAL QUALITY AND DIVERSITY

The state of Connecticut contains some of the country's most affluent communities as well as some of its poorest. Connecticut's public schools span the full range between abundance and inadequacy. In the 1990s, the gap between public schools in overwhelmingly white suburbs and mostly nonwhite cities has been the target of both a desegregation lawsuit and a state law billed as an alternative to court-ordered integration measures. Efforts to address the problems of urban education often run afoul of the widespread belief that local communities should take care of their own and the state should interfere as little as possible in local affairs.

Racial and Socioeconomic Segregation in Connecticut

Connecticut's political culture emphasizes home rule and local autonomy. Most of the state's 169 towns run their own school districts, although a few regional districts serve rural areas. Since 1960, the state has had no county government. Until 1991, there was no state income tax, and Gov. John Rowland won his office in 1994 on a platform that included a pledge to eliminate it.

The Connecticut Supreme Court ruled in *Horton v. Meskill* (1977) that disparities in funding between wealthy and poor school districts violated the state's constitutional guarantees of free public education and equal rights. Legislation passed in response to the *Horton* verdict has moved the state's school districts quite close to fiscal parity. Indeed, in some cases, urban schools spend more money per student than suburban ones. According to 1994–1995 figures, average per-pupil expenditure was $8,649 in the New Haven Public Schools and $8,243 in ten nearby suburban districts.[1] Nonetheless, stark differences between urban and suburban public schools remain, particularly in racial composition and student achievement on standardized tests. Former governor Lowell Weicker, in his 1993 State of the State address, proclaimed, "Despite all good intentions, there are two Connecticuts when it comes to the education of our children."

The New Haven metropolitan population is 80 percent white, 15 percent black, 2 percent Asian, and 3 percent other races. Self-identified Hispanics, who can be of any race, made up 5 percent of the population. Three out of four black residents of the New Haven metropolitan area live in the city of New Haven, and three out of four whites live in the suburbs. The population of New Haven itself is 54 percent white, 36 percent black, and 10 percent other, with 13 percent additionally identified as Hispanic. The region is also economically segregated: 73 percent of children in the New Haven public schools are eligible for free or reduced-price meals, compared with 15 percent in the suburbs. Students in the suburbs outscore New Haven students on statewide achievement tests. About two-thirds of suburban eighth-graders scored at or above the state goal on the 1994 Connecticut Mastery Test of reading, compared with about one-fifth of their city counterparts. The proportion of suburban students at or above the goal on the eighth-grade writing test was about half as opposed to 6 percent in New Haven. Over half of suburban students and less than one-fifth of city students were above the goal score on the eighth-grade mathematics test.[2] Similar disparities exist between Connecticut's other major cities and their suburbs.

Prevailing Definitions and Understanding of Problems in Urban Schools

In Connecticut, town lines have political as well as jurisdictional significance. William Dyson, a powerful African American state legislator, aptly characterized the situation: "The issue with local control, it's like how people feel about their own household—this is my house, I decide what goes on here." To many suburbanites, the links between social disadvantage and educational disadvantage appear to be the responsibility (both in terms of causation and policy remedies) of the city. Dyson identified "the myth" of Connecticut politics as "somebody else has the problems. The problems are over there. Just keep things separate. That way we can protect ourselves." During the EQD planning process, at least two of New Haven's suburbs were struggling with new demands placed on their schools by increasing levels of poverty. Close observation of school politics in these two towns suggested that officials there viewed poverty and its associated problems as "spillover" from New Haven, spread by city residents fleeing to the suburbs.[3]

For example, when asked whether his community had "more of its share of challenges, and dysfunctional families," one suburban board of education member responded, "Well, sure, because we're nearer New Haven. We're getting the immigration from New Haven."[4] Another board member in the same community said, "We get hit from New Haven and Bridgeport, and they're looking to Mill Harbor [pseudonym] as a safe haven." In another community, one board of education member cited the "failure of the New Haven school system" as the biggest problem facing her own school system because of the resulting influx of children from New Haven:

A disproportionate number of these children enter school not knowing how to count to ten and name the parts of their body and tell what the primary colors are. Some of them are coming to us as fifth and sixth graders. Physically overly large, and maybe a bit over age. They haven't learned how to behave. They haven't learned how to go to school. . . . We have a challenge . . . providing the education that those parents are striving for on a decreasing budget.

The suburban town officials were not necessarily unsympathetic to the newcomers. They simply assumed, however, that their problems were due to migration from New Haven or other cities because children in New Haven had problems. Suburban officials perceived that they were inheriting New Haven's problems, not that they and New Haven were both dealing with shared regional problems.

The Act Improving Educational Quality and Diversity

In 1989 a group of residents of Hartford and its suburbs filed a lawsuit claiming that racial and economic segregation, coupled with local control of the public schools, violated the state constitution. Hartford Superior Court judge Harry Hammer began hearing testimony in the case, *Sheff v. O'Neill,* late in 1992. Shortly thereafter, Governor Weicker proposed a legislative and community-based response to the issues raised by the plaintiffs. In his 1993 State of the State address, Weicker called upon the Connecticut General Assembly to pass legislation that would create regional committees of elected officials, parents, and teachers charged with producing regional plans for voluntary programs to improve educational quality and diversity. In June 1993, the General Assembly passed PA 93-263, the Act Improving Educational Quality and Diversity, which divided the state into eleven regions and set guidelines for membership and duties of the Regional Forums that would do the planning.

The legislation established a complicated, three-stage process by which the Regional Forums would gather information and recommendations, produce a plan, and present the plan to citizens for their approval (see Fig. 3.1). The first stage of the process took place in cities and towns rather than at the regional level. Between February and April 1994, Local Advisory Committees appointed by each town's board of education produced reports on their towns' and school districts' needs for, and possible contributions to, a regional quality and diversity program.

The second stage, which began in April and continued through the summer, involved the eleven Regional Forums, each composed of the chief elected official and board of education chairperson of each town in the region plus four parent and two teacher representatives. The Regional Forums appointed Regional Advisory Committees, intended to bring a wide range of community viewpoints to bear in synthesizing findings and proposals from the local committees. In the New Haven region, the forum received the advisory committee's reports in June 1994 and deliberated on its own recommendations through October.

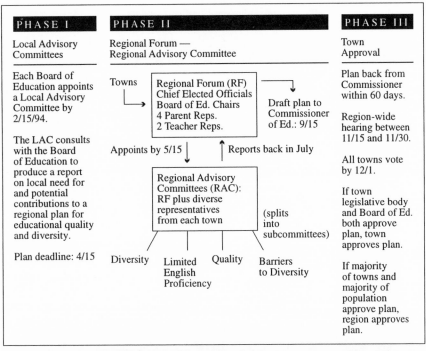

PHASE I	PHASE II	PHASE III
Local Advisory Committees	Regional Forum — Regional Advisory Committee	Town Approval
Each Board of Education appoints a Local Advisory Committee by 2/15/94. The LAC consults with the Board of Education to produce a report on local need for and potential contributions to a regional plan for educational quality and diversity. Plan deadline: 4/15	Towns → Regional Forum (RF) Chief Elected Officials Board of Ed. Chairs 4 Parent Reps. 2 Teacher Reps. — Draft plan to Commissioner of Ed.: 9/15 Appoints by 5/15 ↓ ↑ Reports back in July Regional Advisory Committees (RAC): RF plus diverse representatives from each town (splits into subcommittees) Diversity Limited English Proficiency Quality Barriers to Diversity	Plan back from Commissioner within 60 days. Region-wide hearing between 11/15 and 11/30. All towns vote by 12/1. If town legislative body and Board of Ed. both approve plan, town approves plan. If majority of towns and majority of population approve plan, region approves plan.

TIMETABLE

Local Advisory Committees Named by Boards of Education	2/15/94
Local Advisory Committee Reports	4/15/94
Regional Forum Appoints Regional Advisory Committee	5/15/94
Regional Advisory Committee Collation of LAC Reports	7/94
Regional Forum Draft Plan to State Commissioner of Education	9/15/94
Regional Hearing	11/30/94
Town and School District Approval Votes	12/1/94

Figure 3.1. The educational quality and diversity planning process.

The plan produced by the New Haven Regional Forum emphasized incremental change, which some participants hoped would lay groundwork for bolder action later and others understood as the maximum that would occur. Proposals included expanding urban-suburban exchanges and cross-district magnet schools, creating a regional parent organization, regionalizing recreation programs, linking state funds for school construction to the construction of affordable housing, establishing a regional computer network, and beginning regional coordination of staff development (particularly on multicultural education), minority staff recruitment, and the school calendar.

The final stage of the regional process returned to the local level, where each town and board of education could vote to approve or reject the Regional Forum plan. In order for a town to be counted as having approved the plan, both the board of education serving the town and the town's legislative body had to pass the plan by majority vote. A regional plan would go into effect if the majority of towns in a region, containing the majority of the region's population, approved it. Thus, a coalition of small towns could not impose a plan on a city whose population exceeded their combined total, and a small number of large municipalities could not force a plan on a larger number of small towns.

Eight of eleven regional plans, including the New Haven area's, failed to survive the approval process that concluded on December 1, 1994. None of the plans, including the ones that were approved, included substantial mixing of students across town, racial, or class lines. Instead, like the New Haven plan, they focused on expanding existing inter-town magnet schools or on encouraging more limited exchanges.

HOW THE GENERAL ASSEMBLY DESIGNED A WEAK PROCESS

In the United States, improving educational opportunities for poor children and for children of color has generally required countermajoritarian exercises of state or federal power. According to Jennifer Hochschild, "Success for popular control means little change in racial isolation and racial injustice."[5] At the same time, a second problem in achieving educational equity arises from these solutions to the first. Hochschild insists that "citizens' preferences for incremental changes (at most) must be ignored if desegregation is to succeed," but Christine Rossell claims to the contrary that "more incremental policymaking works better than less incremental policymaking to desegregate schools because it causes less white flight and less citizen resentment."[6] Achieving educational equity is such a complex political process that both Hochschild and Rossell are right in part. The impetus for integration has nearly always come from legal mandates. However, coercion by the courts, though generally necessary, has only sometimes been effective. For every Charlotte-Mecklenburg, where early resistance gave way to eventual desegregation, there is a Richmond or a Boston, harmed both by intense (and occasionally violent) opposition to busing and by the persistence of segregation in their now overwhelmingly nonwhite public school systems.

The declared goal of Governor Weicker's original proposal for regional planning was to strike a compromise between the necessity for outside pressure to incite action and the likelihood that localities and citizens would resist court-ordered solutions. As the Connecticut General Assembly considered regionalization legislation, however, it moved in a direction that shifted the balance too much in the direction of local discretion. The legislature gave excessive deference to existing definitions of the issues, themselves shaped fundamentally by local control, and to town officials' desire for autonomy.

Although a better-designed process would not necessarily have yielded more significant results, decisions made by the General Assembly in its deliberations on the Act Improving Educational Quality and Diversity made weak plans the likeliest outcome. Rather than attempting to shift the terms of the debate or to reshape public consensus about the causes of urban schools' problems, the legislature accepted the same definition of the problem as local officeholders and designed a planning process that local officials would control.

Governor Weicker's original proposal unambiguously set regional desegregation as the goal. Weicker had proposed dividing the state into six regions, based on the regions the state already used for human services. Within each region, a representative committee would prepare a five-year plan "to reduce racial isolation in the region's schools and to provide students with a quality, integrated learning experience." Although decisions would be made locally and communities would have what Weicker called "a voice and a choice" in program design, the goal of the process would be mandated by the state: "Within five years of the implementation of the plans, local school districts in the region will reflect the racial mixture of the region within limits to be established during the planning process."[7]

Unlike Weicker's proposal, the EQD enacted neither mandatory programs nor desegregation. The only mandate in the law was for towns to participate "in good faith" in the planning process.[8] The state provided grants as incentives to participate in whatever programs came out of the planning process, but there were no sanctions against towns that opted out of regional programs. Second, the legislature rejected the goal of numerical racial balance and substituted language requiring Regional Forums to "improve the quality of school performance and student outcomes," "reduce barriers to opportunity," "enhance student diversity and awareness of diversity," and "address the programmatic needs of limited English proficient students."[9] Because it perceived race and educational issues as politically volatile, the legislature did not define "good faith," "quality," or "diversity."

According to Rep. Cameron Staples (D-New Haven), who was then vice-chair of the legislature's joint education committee, many legislators presumed Weicker's proposal to be "dead on arrival" in the committee. Even among Democrats, who were Weicker's usual allies (he was a liberal Republican turned Independent), there was "incredible resistance to mandating anything." Representative Dyson said that the General Assembly did not want to "tamper with the issue" and that some legislators who supported the goals of the legislation did not want to push for a stronger law because of "their perception of what the public response would be." He himself had been reluctant to "[put] people's feet to the fire" on the issue because he believed that doing so would jeopardize his chances of cooperating with them on subsequent issues.

Furthermore, both Weicker's original proposal and the legislation as passed by the General Assembly made towns, rather than citizens, the principal actors in the regional planning process. The proposal and the legislation did so by giving local elected officials control over the process. Regional Forums were to include the chief elected official and board of education chair from each town and school district in a region, in addition to two teacher representatives and four parent representatives. A process that had been promoted as "grassroots democracy" was in practice a conclave of elected officials. The Local Advisory Committees and Regional Advisory Committee involved a broader cross-section of the regional population; but as their names suggest, they served only in an advisory capacity.

State officials had deferred to local authorities because they did not want to appear overbearing and make the outcome of the process seem like a state program rather than a locally produced plan. According to Dyson, the legislation allowed local elected officials to "walk away from [regional planning] any time they chose," but at the same time, "you could say that you had been involved, you could say that you'd participated, you could say that you'd tried." Town representatives could (and in some cases probably did) participate in the planning process without taking any responsibility for whether its outcomes would confront educational inequalities. Taking part in the process did not necessarily indicate an intention to support or participate in the initiatives that did result.

CONSEQUENCES OF WEAK DESIGN AT THE REGIONAL LEVEL

By failing to provide clear definitions of the goals of the process and by giving local elected officials most of the power on the Regional Forums, the General Assembly reduced the likelihood that regional planning would address or redress segregation in the public schools.

What Constituted a Good Faith Effort and a Voluntary Plan?

The state's deference to localities and adherence to the idea of voluntary participation created great uncertainty about what it meant for programs to be voluntary. Even though the legislature never defined "good faith," everybody agreed that the law required towns to designate representatives to the Regional Forum and to refrain from actually obstructing the regional planning process. Beyond that, the situation was less clear.

It is possible for desegregation plans to have significant voluntary components, such as individual choice among public schools controlled for racial balance. The proposals discussed by the Regional Forum went one step further in the direction of voluntarism. Not only individual families but also whole towns could opt in or out of programs. Although municipalities were required to participate in planning, they would not be required to participate in the programs that resulted. Some Regional Forum participants seemed to be under the impression that "voluntary" meant there should be no negative consequences at all for towns that did not support the Regional Forum's plan or that chose not to participate in some part of it. At one Regional Forum meeting, a suburban first selectman asked how he was supposed to tell people in his town that the plan was voluntary if it linked state aid for school construction to towns' decisions to build affordable housing. He believed that if the state did so, it would be "taking money from the town's pockets." Even if it was clear that the state aid was meant as an incentive for certain behavior, said the representative, "it's still not voluntary." He finally compromised and allowed the provision to be left in the report so long as it was made clear that no town could lose state aid it was already receiving.

Like this Regional Forum member, a significant proportion of elected officials interviewed in the New Haven region believed that no program originating in a state mandate and tied to state funding could really be "voluntary." Although one was a Democrat and the other a Republican, two suburban board of education members agreed on this point. The Republican said that the program had been "basically forced down everybody's throat. There's just too many ramifications that the state has just come in and mandated, look at this program, do this, try and find something out. And instead of having any real answers, they're just throwing out like, try to do it, or, but nothing's been solved." And "If we did not comply with all of [Weicker's] wishes, then you could face stiff penalties." The Democrat agreed; "It was like, come up with a plan or else. Like everything else the governor does." When advocates for the regional plan told town officials (particularly town council members) that they should support what was entirely voluntary and "a plan to plan," skeptics replied that sooner or later something would be mandated: "At what point does this stop being voluntary?"[10]

Many New Haven residents and officials perceived as feeble half-measures the same provisions that struck suburbanites as coercive. One New Haven Board of Education member insisted that the suburbs held the majority of votes in the state legislature and could enact true regional cooperation any time they wanted; therefore, the intricate process in the regional planning law had been intended to allow the suburbs to duck any real sacrifices. New Haven superintendent Reginald Mayo said that no massive changes would happen without court orders and that unless his school system received more resources, nobody would attend city schools voluntarily: "I can't even keep the white population in *New Haven* in New Haven," to say nothing of attracting suburban whites.

The divergence between urban and suburban understandings of voluntary programs fueled conflict on the Regional Forum over whether or not its recommendations should include forming a committee to oversee program implementation. Representatives from New Haven wanted the forum's recommendations to include such an oversight committee, but suburban representatives strongly believed that doing so would undermine the plan's voluntary nature. As one suburban first selectman insisted, "This is voluntary! If you decide to go along with it, you'll go along with it! We don't need oversight!" The initial draft of the regional plan did not provide for oversight. However, after speakers at public hear-ings had criticized the omission, the New Haven representatives again raised the issue during revision of the plan, this time successfully. (Ultimately, of course, this was a moot point because the plan did not survive the local approval process.)

The lack of statutory clarity about what communities were required to do also produced confusion over what it meant for a particular town to vote for or against the plan once the Regional Forum had approved it (see Phase III of Fig. 3.1). Did a "yes" vote mean agreeing to participate in, and perhaps take financial responsibility for, everything the plan proposed? Was it, as the New Haven Forum's report claimed, merely assent to a "plan to plan"? It was clear that voting "no" meant that a town would be unable to qualify for competitive state grants for implementing EQD programs, but did it also mean that individual children from the town would be unable to attend voluntary regional programs or magnet schools? On the Regional Forum itself, it was never clear whether representatives' voting for the plan also entailed a commitment to support it politically during the local approval process. Defenders of the status quo continued to see the plan's voluntary nature as cover for coercion in the future, and advocates of desegregation and regionalization saw the same provisions as evidence that the Regional Forum had not taken the issues sufficiently seriously.

Educational Quality and Diversity versus Desegregation

As a policy objective, "enhanced quality and diversity" is both narrower and broader than "desegregation and distributive justice." It is narrower in the sense that a single magnet school can provide individual children with a quality education in a diverse environment without affecting overall patterns of justice. It is broader, in that it opens debate to almost all school-related issues. As with the term "voluntary," the vague meanings of "quality" and particularly "diversity" appear to have hindered both attention to socioeconomic/racial justice and ratification of any plan at all.

Ironically, given the state's fear of putting pressure on the regions to arrive at preordained conclusions, members of the New Haven Regional Forum complained much more about how *little* guidance they were getting than about overweening state power. Only one state official, Jack Hasegawa, had full-time responsibility for the regional process. As a result, town and regional participants often faced delays in having questions answered. Often, the answers were necessarily vague. Hasegawa recalls being told, " 'You can't [direct the Regional Forums toward particular interpretations of the statute] because the regions have to work it out for themselves' . . . but at the same time receiving from the Regional Forums this overwhelming request, 'please tell us what we're supposed to do here.' "

Because the legislature had removed specific references to racial and socioeconomic segregation, discussions of diversity tended to lose focus. Hasegawa recalled,

I found myself, when I was out then giving technical assistance to districts, when they would say, "well, do you mean children with disabilities?" You'd say, "yes, but that's addressed under special ed, so—" the only thing that we were left with was saying, "well, but that's got its own stuff, so maybe you don't need to consider that as much." "Well, what about kids who smoke?" "Well, that's definitely not." But then you'd have to have this long debate about why smoking was different from skin color.

In Hasegawa's (and other state officials') understanding of the terms, a racially diverse experience was a crucial component of a quality education in the late-twentieth-century United States. This definition differed from the most familiar one—a quality education is one that enables children to reach high-level academic outcomes—and thus required a case to be made on its behalf before the public would accept it. State officials made no such case, because according to Connecticut state-government norms, if a statute is silent on a definitional question, the bureaucracy must not advance one interpretation over others. According to Hasegawa, "As much as the [bureaucracy's] impulse was to go in and say, 'this is what it means,' which would be the historic and I think honorable task of a bureaucracy, we were told over and over again administratively, 'you can't do that; what you can do is quote the statute to people and allow them to work out their own application.' "

Because there was never a moment at which a facilitator or state official set a specific goal for the process, the field was left open for any number of proposals without direct connections to desegregation and equal opportunity. Examples included "non-face-to-face interaction" through distance learning, cooperative projects, and visits involving urban and suburban schools.[11] Many of these ideas were well intentioned, but on the whole they avoided the central questions behind *Sheff* and the legislation. Furthermore, they reflected activities that were already occurring and would continue with or without a regional plan, rather than movement beyond the status quo.

The New Haven Regional Forum explicitly rejected the idea that diversity was integral to quality education. One of the most heated debates in the New Haven Regional Forum occurred during its second-to-last meeting, when the group discussed proposed changes to the draft Education and Community Improvement Plan. The draft plan had advanced the idea of a quality-diversity link by stating, "An education that lacks diversity is *not* a quality education." Representatives of one suburban town proposed changing that statement to "diversity enhances the quality of education" and submitted a detailed rationale for the change to the group.

According to the advocates of the changed language, the revision made a "positive assertion" rather than drawing attention to a "deficit" and "offer[ed] a persuasive rationale for improving both quality and diversity without making one dependent on the other." Also, they said, they wanted to ensure "that all diversity enrichment programs add to and enhance the excellent quality of education offered in the [town's] school system today." Furthermore, according to the document outlining reasons for the change, the original "stark, strong, unproven statement usually provokes more arguement [*sic*] than constructive solutions because there are many examples of non-diverse quality education systems (e.g. Japan, Europe, etc.) and many examples of greater diversity correlating with lower quality education (e.g. many U.S. urban schools)." The statement equated "diversity" with larger numbers of black and Hispanic students, not recognizing that the urban schools ostensibly targeted for improvement in the EQD process were and are not "diverse," in the sense of a cross-section or microcosm of society, but instead overwhelmingly nonwhite and poor. Supporters of the change also believed that the original language could have given leverage to opponents of the status quo: "With a narrow (legislative/judicial) definition, this statement [the original] could be used to prove in court that the majority of school districts in Connecticut do not provide a 'quality education.' " The forum accepted these arguments and agreed to drop the original language.

Both of the major changes the General Assembly made to the goals stated in Weicker's proposal reduced the likelihood that the regional planning process would address or redress segregation in the public schools. The assembly's decision to broaden the mandate of the planning process to take in all issues related to quality and diversity reduced the Regional Forums' ability to focus on the problem of segregation. The decision that all programs resulting from EQD planning would be voluntary for individuals and municipalities greatly reduced the likelihood that they would substantially alter institutions of school governance.[12]

How Local Officials' Power Affected the Regional Process

The Act Improving Educational Quality and Diversity, as well as the original Weicker proposal, had given local elected officials most of the power over regional planning because state lawmakers believed that the process would not work without local officeholders' involvement. Yet local elected officials mainly seem to have perceived planning for educational quality and diversity as either irrelevant or inimical to their interests. Some were reluctant to expend time or political capital on a program identified with a lame-duck, Independent governor rather than with either party's overall policy goals. In the middle of the Regional Forum's planning process, one suburban mayor said that he had decided not to continue his personal involvement in it because the program was unlikely to continue under a new governor: "The guy that's governor is not gonna be there now. The guys that are running for governor aren't supporting, or even saying anything about the goddamn plan, so I'm gonna spend all of my time working on this damn plan that nobody's going to pay attention to? I don't think so." It was probably easier for suburban leaders to imagine being hurt by support for

Table 3.1. Regional Forum Attendance, New Haven Region

Meeting Date	Officials Present	Parents/Teachers Present
3/2/94	18	6
3/30/94	23	5
4/27/94	16	6
5/4/94	16	6
6/1/94	12	4
6/29/94	12	3
7/20/94	7	4
7/27/94	12	4
8/10/94	8	4
9/8/94 [a]	breakdown n/a; 22 attended	
9/27/94	9	3
10/24/94	17	5

Source: Unless otherwise noted, Regional Forum no. 2 official meeting summaries prepared by Area Cooperative Educational Services, Hamden, CT.

Note: Thirty-seven members total: thirty-one local officials and six parent/teacher representatives.

[a] Meeting at which final plan was approved. Attendance figure is from author's notes.

regionalization than for them to imagine regionalization advocates forming the core of their reelection coalition. Officials also did not trust the state to follow through financially, given continuing economic recession and budget difficulties. Not surprisingly, in the New Haven region, the teacher and parent representatives who had volunteered for their positions had much more regular attendance at the meetings than did the elected officials (see Table 3.1).

New Haven Board of Education members' comments on regional planning included that the process had been flawed from the beginning, that there was "not much behind it, necessarily"; "I don't know that everybody is giving it full, undivided attention"; and "I don't think it's going to amount to a hill of beans." New Haven mayor John DeStefano, who was officially a Regional Forum member, said, "I've made choices about where I can spend my time, and so have representatives and I'm relying on the school district to represent the city's interests there. . . . I've not been able to make a commitment." DeStefano was concentrating on efforts to achieve regional property tax equity because "people will sacrifice their pocketbooks before they sacrifice their prejudices."

Although DeStefano said he was "relying on the school district" to represent city interests, the school district did not take an active role. During an interview before the EQD process began, New Haven Board of Education chairwoman Patricia McCann-Vissepó was much more interested in addressing New Haven's problems with curriculum and dropout prevention than in regionalization. In

October 1994 she told a newspaper reporter, "It's the same as always: 'We have to learn to live together' but nobody is talking about moving people of color to the suburbs.' "[13]

Suburban elected officials also gave the process a low priority. One mayor complained about the time commitment expected by the organizers of the regional meetings, who scheduled at least one two-and-a-half-hour meeting per month and spent time at the beginning of the process doing icebreaker games and team-building exercises: "There's enormous numbers of meetings that they scheduled. And the few that I've gone to, so much of the time was spent on, like, seventies fishbowl techniques and methods of discussion. I don't find them particularly productive." One mayor said, "Let me know when everybody's ready to work and take part, but to have roundtable discussions with a bunch of educators with pie in the sky ideas is not my idea of being productive." Making a bad situation worse, the process overlapped and conflicted with towns' budget deliberations, which usually run from January through June but can extend through the summer. The voluntary nature of the process reinforced the incentives for elected officials not to take an interest. Jack Hasegawa recalled, "Everybody who read [the law] carefully realized that what came out of the local process was not mandatory. They didn't have to do anything with it. And so, ranging from just a total ignorance of process to a very cynical understanding of what really would happen meant that there wasn't much motivation for the people who'd be making decisions down the way."

In addition to assigning responsibility for the process to local officials, some of whom were disinclined to participate and many of whom were already overburdened with local budget responsibilities, the decision to represent towns had three significant consequences for the quality of representation on the Regional Forum.

First, the fact that all towns had at least two representatives (the chief elected official and board of education chairperson) meant that the suburbs were over-represented relative to their share of the region's total population. The only way in which larger communities gained a greater voice on the Regional Forum was through a provision specifying that each forum should include four parent representatives, one from each of the four largest towns, and two teacher representatives, one from each of the largest bargaining units in the region.

On the New Haven Regional Forum, twenty-seven of thirty-three members represented the suburbs. New Haven's teacher representative was not even a city resident, although he was nonetheless a forceful advocate for urban education. Small towns (two of which had populations under 10,000) had disproportionate power on the forum. According to the 1990 U.S. Census, the total population of the thirteen towns in the New Haven area planning region was 401,716. The city of New Haven had 130,474 inhabitants, or about one-quarter of the region's population. Of the thirty-three members of the Regional Forum, four were from New Haven. A strict "one person, one vote" rule would have given New Haven eight forum members. Through another institutional quirk, three of the region's smallest towns in effect had an extra representative on the Regional Forum because they combine their secondary-school students into a regional district, whose board of education chairman sat on the Regional Forum.

Voters in the smaller suburbs also had a greater opportunity to influence the process than voters in the cities and larger towns, once the regional plan came back to the towns for approval. For reasons unrelated to school regionalization, the classic, deliberative forms of New England local government have been retained only in the smallest communities. Many suburban residents had an opportunity to vote directly on the plan through a town meeting or a referendum; in New Haven and its larger suburbs, the vote was at a routine city council or board of aldermen meeting. Because New Haven's board of education is appointed, rather than elected like all the others, only one of its four representatives on the forum was directly accountable to voters. These variations in the institutions of town government compounded overrepresentation of suburban interests in regional planning.

The second problematic dimension of representing towns rather than populations was that most members of the Regional Forum were elected officials, and most of the area's elected officials are white. Because of the resulting overwhelmingly white membership, observers often charged that the forum was not sufficiently inclusive or representative of minorities. However, the New Haven Regional Forum actually did roughly reflect the region's population of various races, according to the 1990 U.S. Census. There were thirty-three members: four black, one Puerto Rican, and twenty-eight non-Hispanic white.[14] Why, then, did forum members and outsiders repeatedly claim that the process did not sufficiently represent minorities?

In the first place, two New Haven members (an African American alderwoman who was Mayor DeStefano's delegate and board of education president Patricia McCann-Vissepó) did not attend many meetings. Some white members of the forum consequently became frustrated when their colleagues (black and white) spoke of the need to hear more from minorities. They had tried, they said, and minorities were not interested. If they were not represented, it was their own fault.[15] This answer does not go far enough, however, because it ignores the numerous substantive reasons for urban minority leaders not to take the process seriously.

The Regional Forum's efforts to bring in more minorities through its Regional Advisory Committee (RAC) were readily interpreted as tokenism by minority citizens, many of whom already mistrusted the motives behind the process. As on the forum, New Haven had a few extra seats on the RAC. However, the RAC shared the forum's emphases on involving elected officials and giving each town roughly equal representation, thus limiting the number of slots open to be filled by minorities and urban delegates. The RAC's division into four subcommittees spread the black and Hispanic members it did have quite thinly. Most tellingly, the RAC subcommittee charged with making recommendations about diversity had one black person attend one of its six meetings. Even he was officially a member of another subcommittee and had joined the diversity group for only one meeting. One of the forum's black members also organized an informational meeting to reach out to the black and Hispanic communities, but it was only sparsely attended.

The Census-data interpretation of sufficient minority representation makes sense only if strict numerical parity of races for its own sake is the goal—representing blacks and Hispanics as blacks and Hispanics in some general sense. People who criticized the Regional Forum for not being representative enough were most likely thinking not of statistical representativeness, however, but of political legitimacy and respect. At the most basic level, in a political climate that is especially sensitive to racial differences, having a discussion about increasing racial diversity in which at most five of thirty-three voting participants are black or Hispanic invites criticism and ridicule. African American and Latino New Haveners seem, quite understandably, to have read a message of indifference into the fact that suburban elected officials had a guaranteed voting majority on the forum while they were to be included in the RAC at the forum's discretion and in a purely advisory capacity. Representative Dyson also cited the voluntary nature of the final plans as a disincentive for blacks and Latinos to take the process seriously. He personally "really didn't think anything was going to happen—you know, talk about something, and then some town can decide 'I don't want to be involved.' "

Finally, the decision to represent towns and to have most members of the Regional Forum be elected officials meant that there was no significant role left to be played by citizens who took a particular interest in regionalization or desegregation. In the New Haven region, many such individuals had served on Local Advisory Committees. Their reports were collated and summarized by a staff member at the educational agency responsible for supporting the process, but there was no way for the people responsible for the ideas in the reports to continue articulating their positions and the reasoning behind them. Jack Hasegawa and many others observing the process thought that the local phase had been the best part of the process and regretted that local participants' ideas tended to get lost or diluted as they were passed along. One suburban board of education member who had served on her local committee but was not on the Regional Forum because she was not the board chairperson said of the forum, "I haven't been involved with the regional part of it at all, and I don't even know what's going on— I haven't even been informed of what's going on." At the public hearing on the New Haven regional plan, one member of a Local Advisory Committee stated, "I am truly disappointed that [the forum] did not have the courage to move further along in this process [desegregation]. I'm really upset because we were so enthusiastic in our planning and had so many good ideas that just aren't here." [16]

Hasegawa said, "One of the things I heard over and over again when I went out to the presentations by local groups was people would stand up and say, 'I was on the local committee, and I don't really understand where you got that,' and it was a devastating statement for people to hear. Even though the person would almost always, almost 100 percent of the time, come back and express their emotional commitment to the concept and to improving both quality and diversity and awareness of diversity. The initial statement that 'this isn't really what we sent in,' I think, was very damaging to the process of getting it through." Exclusion of the Local Advisory Committee members, many of whom were volunteers personally committed to educational equity, from the regional deliberations may have been the unkindest cut of all the ones the legislature made. With a few momentous exceptions, majoritarian political processes in the United States have not served the cause of justice for racial minorities. The legislature's choices compounded this problem by leaving the most sympathetic members of the general public out of the deliberative process.

Because local officials had power over the process but little interest in it, and others who were interested had little power, there was no natural constituency for regionalization. Such a constituency was necessary because each municipality's town meeting or legislative body had to be convinced to accept the regional plan. Members of the local committees would have been the obvious advocates for the plan when it came back to the towns for approval. Some did take on this role, but their effectiveness was limited because they had not been included in the regional planning. So little information came out of the Regional Forum during its deliberations that it was easy for local participants to lose interest in following unfolding developments.

Even if information had been available for LAC members to organize their communities around, many potential advocates seem to have had trouble getting excited about quality and diversity, as opposed to justice or desegregation. Quality had limited efficacy as an organizing issue or a reason for change in communities where many people already believed their schools were of high quality. Treated apart from quality or justice, diversity for its own sake is not a very compelling issue. A suburban board of education member who had also served on her local committee said, "We've been so careful not to give people an opportunity to, I mean, we didn't want to sensationalize it by saying we were going to do all these things like bus kids into New Haven, because we didn't want people coming out and just opposing that. We were trying to be very intelligent about it. But as a result, I guess, the people who usually come to that sort of thing were just bored and didn't see any reason to do it."

In the absence of a strong proregionalization force, fear and distrust of the state seem to have triumphed over the hope that the regional plan might be a start toward achieving desegregation or equal opportunity. Most statements in favor of the Regional Forum's plan were lukewarm. In New Haven, arguably the community with the most to gain from regionalization, some aldermen were rumored to be considering a vote against the plan because it did not address the economic and political causes of segregation and poor student performance in urban schools. Supporters of the plan argued that the plan ignored structural causes of inequality in education not because of bad faith but because the process had been focused on other issues. They were apologizing for the plan's inadequacies at least as much as they were advocating approval of it. Both the board of aldermen and the board of education ultimately approved the plan unanimously.

Advocates in two suburban towns presented similar arguments. They conceded that they had reservations, particularly about how programs would be funded, and that the plan was not perfect but that a "yes" vote was only a commitment to a "plan to plan." The towns made opposite decisions, however. In Newmarket, arguments about cost, impracticality, and excessive bureaucracy carried the day and the council rejected the plan. In Mill Harbor (both town names are pseudonyms), the only two people who spoke at a hearing the night of the vote were members of the Regional Forum who urged approval of the report, as a "plan to plan." Despite such weak support, and the efforts of one member who wondered in a long speech how it could be that "what we have before us this evening is the work of many months of meetings and discussions, yet we are told it is not a complete work," the council approved the plan. However, the regional plan for the New Haven area failed to win approval by enough towns for it to be enacted.

EVENTS AFTER REGIONAL PLANNING:
THE STATE'S CONTINUED CAUTION

In the view of many participants, the regional planning set in motion by the Act Improving Educational Quality and Diversity had the potential to replace the *Sheff v. O'Neill* litigation as the main response to problems in urban schools and to head off a court-ordered solution. Superior Court judge Harry Hammer went so far as to delay his ruling until the conclusion of the regional process. Despite the regional planning law, and in part because of its weaknesses, the litigation continued.

In April 1995, four months after the end of the EQD process, Judge Hammer announced his somewhat anticlimactic verdict. Relying on federal precedents, Hammer ruled that the plaintiffs had not proved that state action was the "direct and sufficient" cause of segregation in the schools. He therefore ruled in the state's favor without rendering a verdict on the plaintiffs' constitutional claims.[17]

In July 1996 the Connecticut Supreme Court overturned Hammer's decision by a 4 to 3 vote. Chief Justice Ellen Ash Peters, writing for the majority, declared that racial segregation between Hartford and suburban public schools, coupled with the concentration of poverty in the city, violated the state's constitutional guarantee of a free public education, its provision that no person is entitled to exclusive public emoluments or privileges, and its guarantee that no person in Connecticut would ever be subjected to segregation. Contrary to Hammer's judgment, the state was responsible for these violations because it had set school district boundaries at town lines and enforced a statute requiring each child to attend the public school "in which such child resides." Despite the unequivocal language of the majority opinion, the court did not dictate a remedy but directed the General Assembly to find a solution and remanded the case to the Hartford Superior Court.[18]

As of the one-year anniversary of the Connecticut Supreme Court verdict, the General Assembly's response had followed the same path as deliberation over the Act Improving Educational Quality and Diversity. The Education Improvement Panel charged with recommending a response to the supreme court decision removed the most controversial ideas, such as mandatory reassignment of students, from its agenda early in the process and concentrated on issues such as improving school readiness and parent involvement. Ultimately, two bills passed that were understood as partial responses to the *Sheff* verdict. One expanded access to early childhood education and school readiness programs in the cities, and the other enacted a variety of programs such as multidistrict charter schools and voluntary transfers from urban to suburban schools, which would affect only about 1,000 additional students.[19] Once again, the legislature deferred to local prerogatives and enacted laws that have generally laudable purposes but that fail to address the issue of segregation directly. Chief Justice Peters retired after the 1996 session and was replaced by a more conservative justice, which suggests that the 4 to 3 majority for the plaintiffs may have become a 4 to 3 majority for the state. Nonetheless, the plaintiffs announced in June 1997 that they intended to go back to court to challenge the legislative response as inadequate.[20]

Both in its drafting of the Act Improving Educational Quality and Diversity and in its reaction to the Supreme Court's *Sheff* verdict, the Connecticut General Assembly has demonstrated unwillingness to make fundamental changes in the structure of education governance. The legislature accepted the existing system of local control and autonomy as an exogenous constraint on policymaking rather than treating it as a circumstance that could be changed in the course of policymaking. It also accepted the public consensus that the causes of urban school problems are local, not regional, instead of advancing any alternate understanding of the problem.

Neither outcome is especially surprising, given that the General Assembly is a representative body whose members want to please their constituents. The majority of Connecticut residents are not black, Latino, or poor; thus, it would indicate unusually widespread altruism if the state's legislature undertook a major redistribution of resources (including scarce places in good schools) to poor and minority communities. The existing system of local control in education makes desegregation and other redistributive measures almost impossible, and the representation of those same local communities in the state legislature makes any change in the system equally unlikely. In circumstances such as these, minority advocates generally concentrate their efforts on the legal system, a strategy that sometimes succeeds (as in San Francisco and Charlotte-Mecklenburg) and sometimes fails (as in Yonkers, Boston, and any number of other places). Even in the presence of a court order or consent decree, an intimidating volume of political work remains to be done in order to build and maintain a consensus for change. The lesson of Connecticut's regional planning experience is that under unfavorable local conditions, half-hearted state intervention will not produce racial justice as a sort of happy accident. On this issue, as on other difficult ones, leaders must lead. This lesson seems unsatisfyingly banal, but many actors in Connecticut appear not yet to have learned it.

NOTES

1. The source for these figures is *Strategic School Profiles* (1995–1996) produced by the Connecticut Department of Education. The suburban average includes the Amity Regional School District and the towns of Bethany, Branford, Guilford, Hamden, Madison, North Branford, North Haven, Orange, West Haven, and Woodbridge.

2. All figures except for those on the school lunch program are my calculations from 1990 U.S. Census data, STF 3. The question about Hispanic ancestry is separate from the question about race. The school-lunch and achievement statistics are my calculations from *Strategic School Profiles* (1995–1996).

3. This research was done by the author and is reported in detail in "Decentralization, Distribution, and Democracy: Problems in Local Control of Public Education" (Ph.D. diss., Yale University, 1997), chap. 3. In some cases, names of towns and interviewees were changed to protect respondents' anonymity.

4. Unless otherwise noted, all quotations are from author's interviews.

5. Jennifer Hochschild, *The New American Dilemma: Liberal Democracy and School Desegregation* (New Haven: Yale University Press, 1984), p. 143.

6. Ibid., p. 192, and Christine H. Rossell, *The Carrot or the Stick for School Desegregation Policy: Magnet Schools or Forced Busing?* (Philadelphia: Temple University Press, 1990), p. 215. See also Gerald Rosenberg, *The Hollow Hope: Can Courts Bring About Social Change?* (Chicago: University of Chicago Press, 1991).

7. Press release of 1993 State of the State address, pp. 10–12.

8. PA 93-263, Section 4.

9. Ibid., Section 1, subsection 3, i–iv.

10. Author's notes from audiotape of city council meeting.

11. Regional Advisory Committee, Region 2, "Responding to the Challenge: A Voluntary Education and Community Improvement Plan from Regional Forum no. 2" (Hamden, CT: Area Cooperative Educational Services, 1994), mimeo.

12. On the links between voluntary compliance, unanimity, and preservation of the status quo, see James M. Buchanan and Gordon Tullock, *The Calculus of Consent: Logical Foundations of Constitutional Democracy* (Ann Arbor: University of Michigan Press, 1962), chap. 7. Buchanan and Tullock insist that although the unanimity rule imposes intolerably high costs of decision making, it should still occupy a "central place" in "any normative theory of government" (p. 96). Douglas Rae argues, to the contrary, that consensus is not only an impractical decision rule but also an undesirable one for many

reasons, including its bias toward the status quo ("The Limits of Consensual Decision," *American Political Science Review* 69 [1975]: 1270–94). The outcome of regional planning in Connecticut reinforces Rae's critique of Buchanan and Tullock.

13. Karla Schuster, "Report Points the Way to Integrate Schools," *New Haven Register,* October 5, 1994, p. A3.

14. According to the 1990 U.S. Census, the total population of the thirteen towns making up the New Haven planning region was 401,716; 80 percent were white, 15 percent black, 2 percent Asian, and 3 percent other races. Five percent of the population additionally identified themselves as Hispanic. Thus, for a Regional Forum of thirty-three people to be statistically representative of the general population, four or five members would have to be black and one or two Hispanic, ignoring overlap between the black and Hispanic population. By this standard, the total membership of the New Haven Regional Forum, counting the African American alderwoman who was Mayor DeStefano's delegate instead of DeStefano himself, was "racially balanced."

15. All meeting observations are from my field notes and official meeting minutes.

16. Karla Shuster, "Desegregation Plan Not 'Bold' Enough," *New Haven Register,* October 21, 1994, p. A3.

17. *Sheff v. O'Neill,* 1995 Conn. Sup. LEXIS 1148, p. 88. Several months later, Hammer also submitted a postdecision list of factual findings to the Connecticut Supreme Court, at that court's request.

18. *Sheff v. O'Neill,* 238 Conn. 1 (1996), pp. 5–6, 33, 38, and 47. The antisegregation guarantee, which only Connecticut, New Jersey, and Hawaii's constitutions contain, dates from the 1965 Constitutional Convention, called as a response to federal court decisions requiring legislative reapportionment. See *Sheff,* pp. 105–24, Borden, J., dissenting.

19. The laws described here are PA 97-259 and PA 97-290.

20. Anne M. Hamilton, "*Sheff* Plaintiffs to Take State Back to Court; Lawmakers Defend Their Effort to Meet Desegregation Order," *Hartford Courant,* June 18, 1997, p. A1.

4

Consensus Building and School Reform: The Role of the Courts in San Francisco

Luis Ricardo Fraga, Bari Anhalt Erlichson, and Sandy Lee

Attaining racial equality in American public education has not often been seen as consistent with efforts at systemic school reform. It seems ironic that the effort to desegregate public education that followed *Brown v. Board of Education*[1] could be understood as anything other than an attempt to change major aspects of public schooling to enhance the opportunities that African American children would have in order to achieve academically. However, the evolution of public school desegregation law and related public policy has focused primarily on attaining enrollment desegregation.[2] Rarely have desegregation goals been defined in ways that are fully consistent with systemwide efforts to reform public education to enhance achievement parity for all major racial and ethnic groups in a community.

Similarly, it is surprising that so many of the current strategies of systemic school reform have not directly addressed how a proposed reform will enhance the academic achievement of African American, Latino, and other racial and ethnic minority students who seem to have the greatest difficulty attaining success in public education. Proposed systemic reform programs such as school choice, site-based management, teacher testing, and graduation examinations often do not explicitly identify how these practices will enhance the performance of racial and ethnic minority students.[3] It is possible that some reforms might even exacerbate differences in achievement rates of ethnic and racial minority students as compared to whites, or that a reform might lead to further racial and ethnic enrollment segregation.

In the case of *NAACP v. San Francisco Unified School District*,[4] the federal court proved an exception to this disjunction between enrollment desegregation and systemic school reform. In the consent decree approved by the court in 1983, enrollment desegregation and enhanced academic achievement were seen as fully consistent with one another. In fact, the court stated that desegregation would not be attained until academic achievement of African Americans had been substantially improved. Moreover, the court accepted that the primary means to attain both desegregation and enhanced achievement would be the reform mechanism of school reconstitution.[5]

We argue that the history of race relations in San Francisco prevented any educational policymaker from successfully developing the consensus necessary to address the detrimental effects of racial segregation and differential academic achievement in public schools.[6] Although attempts had been made by some advocacy groups, superintendents, and even earlier federal courts to forge agreement and development of a coherent plan to address the issues of segregation and underachievement, none was successful. It was not until the federal district court became the primary mechanism through which a consensus on reform goals, including both desegregation and enhanced achievement, and a consensus on reform strategies, primarily school reconstitution, were effected that systemic school reform has been possible in San Francisco. In sum, court-induced consensus by simultaneously addressing desegregation and achievement has been the only way through which the San Francisco Unified School District (SFUSD) has been able to mount any sustained attempt to improve the educational attainment of all its students.

SCHOOL REFORM AND RACE IN SAN FRANCISCO: FIRST ATTEMPTS

San Francisco has been characterized as distinct from other major urban centers in the United States for many years.[7] It is known for the overwhelming beauty of its bay, hills, and mountains. It is a major center of commerce and tourism. It is home to a substantial number of gays and lesbians. It has a consolidated city-county government where the mayor is the chief executive officer, but the county board of supervisors, on which the mayor does not sit, is the legislative branch. According to the 1990 Census, it has one of the most ethnically and racially diverse populations in the country, yet non-Hispanic whites are the largest group at 45.6 percent; 29.1 percent are Asian, 13.9 percent are Hispanic, and African Americans constitute 10.9 percent of the population.[8] Nonetheless, San Francisco has two features of many cities in the United States: a longstanding pattern of racial segregation in residences and public schools and a history of unsuccessful efforts to try to overcome the consequences of that segregation.

The first call for the desegregation of schools came in 1962. Two civil rights groups, the local chapter of the Congress on Racial Equality (CORE) and the Council for Civic Unity, an aggregation of several local civil rights groups, asked the school board to correct levels of segregation of African American students in certain schools.[9] Superintendent Harold Spears issued a report later that year that rejected the need to reassign students, stating, "If we are preparing to ship these children to various schools, in predetermined racial allotments, then such brands would serve the purpose they have been put to in handling livestock. . . . I have no educationally sound program to suggest to the Board to eliminate the schools in which the children are predominantly of one race."[10] Nonetheless, later that year 1,400 San Franciscans went before the board to demonstrate their dissatisfaction with the superintendent's report. The board established an ad hoc committee to examine the issue further. Subsequently the NAACP filed suit against the district in *Brock v. Board of Education*.[11]

In April 1963 the board's ad hoc committee did recommend that race be taken into account in the determination of school assignment policies. Moreover, a black human relations officer was appointed and several hundred minority students were reassigned to schools with predominantly white student populations.[12] The NAACP allowed the *Brock* case to lapse and praised the board for taking action.

Under the leadership of new superintendent Robert Jenkins, in 1967 yet another committee recommended that the district desegregate, although again in a limited fashion. It recommended that the two neighborhoods of Richmond and Park South be targeted. These areas would be designated as School Complexes, and each had stable black and white populations where busing, if necessary, would occur only in short distances.[13] Although it was apparent that areas of considerable black population such as Bayview–Hunter's Point were not included in this design and that Latinos and Chinese were also not included in these desegregation plans, the prospects for building a working consensus both with substantial segments of the public and education professionals seemed favorable.

Yet the unexpected opposition of Mayor Joseph Alioto in 1970 even to this limited plan proved too much for desegregation proponents to overcome. Alioto decided that he would oppose any mandatory busing in the city, however limited. Together with conservative supervisor John Barbagelata, a ballot proposition was put before the voters against the busing or reassignment of elementary school children outside of their neighborhoods. By a margin of three to one, voters decided that the school board should not be allowed to bus or to reassign students without parental consent. Interestingly, the school board proceeded with its plans, nonetheless.[14]

Again under Mayor Alioto's urging, suit was filed by a group of parents to stop the implementation of the limited desegregation plan in June 1970.[15] The case *Nelson v. San Francisco Unified School District* was filed in California Superior Court.[16] In response the NAACP filed *Johnson v. San Francisco Unified School District* on June 24, 1970, in federal district court.[17] As David Kirp states, the NAACP "asked for complete student and faculty desegregation in the elementary schools."[18] Consensus regarding school desegregation was no longer possible through the efforts of San Francisco's own public officials and citizens; the courts would have the responsibility for structuring educational policy.

In May 1971, almost a decade after the first call to desegregate, Judge Stanley A. Weigel issued his order that the San Francisco Unified School District desegregate the students and staff in its 102 elementary schools by September

1971. Along with the order came a mandate to submit the desegregation plan by June 10. That the presiding judge gave the district only six weeks to come up with a plan revealed the court's impatience with past foot-dragging when desegregation was left in political hands. When he announced his decision, Judge Weigel added, "The court will approve no requests for continuance. . . . The time is long past for arguments."[19]

Ultimately the Horseshoe Plan for desegregation devised by the district was approved by the court. It was implemented on schedule in time for the 1971–1972 academic year. Under the plan, more than half of the 48,000 elementary students were reassigned. Though cross-city busing was avoided by limiting transfers within narrower zones, the new policy affected most students immediately, either requiring that they be bused or changing the racial composition of their schools. All students were to be bused for half of their elementary school years; they could attend neighborhood schools during the other half.

Kirp argues that neither the school board, nor school administration, nor relevant civil rights groups effectively tried to oversee desegregation efforts after 1971.[20] Mayor Alioto had been reelected, a referendum had been passed to make the school board elected rather than appointed, and much of the board electoral campaign centered on desegregation. Of the seven persons elected to the board, only two were strong supporters of desegregation.[21] Further, the lack of commitment to desegregation was evidenced by the fact that most Chinese students were subsequently exempted from participation in the desegregation plan,[22] other students were exempted from attending schools outside of their neighborhoods through the acquisition of optional enrollment requests (OERs) issued by the district for reasons such as motion sickness, foot ailments, and maternal attachments,[23] and three elementary schools in Bayview–Hunter's Point remained overwhelmingly black.[24]

Robert Alioto, the third superintendent to deal with desegregation, was appointed in 1975. He was no relation to the mayor. Superintendent Alioto soon developed an alternative to the Horseshoe Plan, which he referred to as the Educational Redesign Program. Under this plan desegregation would be pursued through a restructuring of grade levels, in which all students would spend four years in the same school, the maximum percentage of students of any one ethnic or racial group at a school was 45 percent, and each school had to have students from four ethnic groups within its enrollment. Fewer students were to be bused and fewer OERs were to be issued. Additionally, there was a new focus on enhancing the attractiveness of alternative, i.e., magnet, public schools.[25]

Ultimately, the NAACP challenged the plan for Educational Redesign in federal court, reopening the *Johnson* case. Unexpectedly, the local chapter of the NAACP favored the plan, but the national NAACP wanted it declared unconstitutional and did not want to risk losing one of its first major desegregation cases outside the South. Judge Weigel refused to rule on the constitutionality of the plan and decided to dismiss the suit instead, without prejudice, on June 22, 1978.[26]

Inaction on the part of both sides was the primary reason Weigel advanced for dismissal. As he noted, "Circumstances have changed significantly since this Court's judgment in 1971" with respect to "the racial mix of the district, the governance and administration of the schools, and the operant legal standard." For those reasons, dismissal seemed appropriate to the court.[27]

This history of school desegregation in San Francisco through 1978 demonstrates that the city mirrored the experiences of many other cities. There was strong and consistent public opposition to systemwide desegregation and especially to busing as a remedy. School officials demonstrated considerable hesitation in addressing desegregation in a comprehensive way. Some officials, particularly Mayor Joseph Alioto and members of the school board, seemed to demonstrate the strongest opposition to systematic efforts to desegregate. Although some of the superintendents during this period tried to be constructive in addressing what was clearly an important issue, they were constrained by the opposition they confronted. It is also important to note that desegregation in San Francisco was understood exclusively in black versus white terms. Although Chinese and Latino populations were also present in the city in considerable numbers during this period, they were not systematically included in either assessments of the detrimental consequences of segregation or in the possible impact that a desegregation plan would have on their communities. In sum, this history demonstrates that San Francisco was unable to attain necessary levels of consensus among major stakeholders to address public school segregation effectively.

SCHOOL REFORM AND RACE IN SAN FRANCISCO: THE 1983 CONSENT DECREE

Eight days after the dismissal of *Johnson,* the attorneys from the national office of the NAACP filed *NAACP v. San Francisco Unified School District* on behalf of three African American students residing in Bayview–Hunter's Point.[28] The California State Department of Education was named as a defendant in addition to the SFUSD. The case was assigned to Judge William Orrick. In the initial petition to the court, plaintiffs' attorneys argued that the district's school assignment policy that maintained segregated schools with poorer resources and less qualified teachers violated the equal protection rights of the African American children in Bayview–Hunter's Point. Although prior desegregation efforts had accomplished a measurable increase in the degree of desegregation in some schools, Bayview–Hunter's Point was a distinct exception to this progress. It remained highly segregated and retained the stigma and reputation for low achievement and for schools plagued by violence. The court agreed that the NAACP would be the sole representative of the plaintiffs.

It is likely that the previous difficulties San Francisco had faced in implementing an effective desegregation plan pushed all parties in the suit to accept resolution through a consent decree. The agreement was made in December 1982, and it was formally approved in May 1983. The court was explicit in specifying the advantages of settlement through a consent decree:

> The parties, as indicated by the signature of their counsel below, have determined to settle this action, with the Court's approval, through entry of this Consent Decree, which the parties believe will benefit the children of San Francisco, conserve the resources and time of the parties and the Court, permit educational authorities to devote their attention to sound educational planning and programming, maximize the amount of state and federal financial assistance available to assist S.F.U.S.D. to meet its constitutional and statutory obligations, and serve the best interests of the parties themselves.[29]

Further, the consent decree still held the SFUSD liable for the policies and practices that led to school segregation in the first place: "The parties stipulate and agree that, if proof were presented in formal proceedings, the Court would be justified in making factual findings and legal conclusions sufficient to require the systemwide remedies that are set forth in this Consent Decree."[30] Final agreement was facilitated by the presence of a court-appointed Settlement Team composed of two representatives from the court, two from the NAACP, two from the SFUSD, and two from the state's Department of Education.[31] These representatives had extensive experience as educators, administrators, and academics involved in desegregation or diversity issues.[32]

The consent decree designated roles for the official parties that established a system of checks and balances. The school district was charged with the direct task of implementing and assessing progress annually; the state would provide substantial financing and would conduct its own independent assessment; and the NAACP would be responsible for general oversight. Any changes to the stipulations in the decree had to be approved by the three parties as well as by the court.

The consent decree moved boldly forward with an innovative approach using some untried reform measures that seemed to overshadow the underlying comprehensiveness of the plan. Its primary goals, simply stated, indicated that the decree was rearticulating the ends that desegregation should accomplish. The consent decree had two primary objectives. First,

> A major goal of this Consent Decree shall be to eliminate racial/ethnic segregation or identifiability in any SFUSD school, program, or classroom and to achieve the broadest practicable distribution throughout the system of students from the racial and ethnic groups which comprise the student enrollment of the SFUSD.[33]

Second, "The parties agree that the overall goal of this Consent Decree will require continued and accelerated efforts to achieve academic excellence throughout the S.F.U.S.D." [34] The second goal implied a more specific aim: to improve academic achievement for all San Francisco students, particularly for African American students who had suffered previous discrimination and segregated school conditions and who continued to experience the most dismal academic outcomes. The two major goals of racial and ethnic desegregation of schools and academic excellence for all provided the framework for the intermediary objectives that involved a specific racial balance formula, philosophical tenets, and, ultimately, school reform. The specific inclusion of enhanced academic achievement as a critical part of San Francisco's desegregation efforts make the provisions of this decree unlike most other desegregation court orders and consent decrees issued in the history of the United States.[35]

The specific desegregation strategy required the classification of the population into nine categories, representing the most prominent groups in the city. The nine groups included "Spanish-surname, Other White, *African-American,* Chinese, Japanese, Korean, Filipino, American Indian, and Other Non-White."[36] Consistent with the numerical goals of the Educational Redesign plan, it was stipulated that each school must have students from four of the nine racial and ethnic groups; no school could have more than 45 percent representation in its student body from one group; and no alternative school could have more than 40 percent of one group.[37]

To achieve these ends, the district maintained a great deal of flexibility in the design, being able to draw on such options as magnet schools, redrawing or eliminating attendance boundaries, and busing. The consent decree gave the district six years to implement the plan, after which the progress would be reviewed and then modified as needed. The time frame was expected to allow sufficient time for all schools fully to desegregate enrollment to the required 40–45 percent, without moving students en masse out of the schools at which they had started. The multiple-year implementation was intended to allow a gradual desegregation that would correct existing imbalances primarily by adjusting the composition of the entering class at each school level. For example, if an elementary school could not immediately meet the required 45 percent cap for a certain group, then its student composition would be affected primarily by the entering class of kindergartners and would thus take six years to fully desegregate.

No matter how flexible and unintrusive, out of practicality a desegregation plan required some amount of busing to achieve elimination of racial isolation in certain schools, to say nothing of a semblance of racial/ethnic balance in schools throughout the district. The consent decree, however, did not explicitly mandate busing. Moreover, to defuse any potential controversy over the busing issue, Superintendent Robert Alioto promised that "there [would] be no mandatory busing to any of the schools," though in fact, busing was already practiced and would continue with the implementation of the consent decree.[38] Since the school district in 1983 was still engaged in a desegregation plan that required busing, of the 60,515 students in the district, 6,000 were already being bused for purposes of desegregation.[39] Thus, the busing question as it accompanied the consent decree was not particularly disruptive even though it irked some parents. In fact, it was reported, the "settlement, worked out by attorneys during more than seven months of negotiation, basically confirms the attendance pattern of the school system and does not require any additional student busing."[40] A fifteen-member district committee responsible for developing school assignment plans attempted to create a "minimum movement plan."[41] Beginning in fall 1983, nearly 1,000 elementary and middle school students—primarily black, Hispanic, and Chinese—were bused. Moreover, according to the committee's director, Don Barfield, to attenuate the sense of isolation, the plan attempted to bus groups of students who lived in the same neighborhoods to the same schools when it was possible.[42]

The focus on academic excellence was an explicit part of the consent decree. Section 7, Academic Excellence, not only specified this as a goal, it also indicated that the district was to "evaluate student academic progress for the purpose of determining the curricula and programs most responsible for any improved test scores and learning in the District and the extent to which these curricula and programs are available to students of all racial/ethnic groups . . . [and] adopt any additional curricula and programs necessary to promote equal educational opportunity."[43] Further, "The annual report . . . shall include a section on SFUSD's progress toward the goal of academic excellence, setting forth test scores and other evaluative data for each building and for the District as a whole."[44]

The precise strategies as to the attainment of academic achievement were not specified in this section, however. Indeed there is no specific guidance in the consent decree as to how it was to be attained for the district as a whole. The guidance that was provided was contained within the subsection, Special Plan for Bayview–Hunter's Point, the key principle of school reform noted being reconstitution.[45]

> The S.F.U.S.D. shall declare all staff and administrative positions in the Bayview–Hunter's Point schools open, and shall reconstitute the staff and administration of those schools on the basis of a desegregation plan developed by S.F.U.S.D. and submitted to the Court. The plan shall specify changes in attendance boundaries and methods for selecting staff and administrators appropriate to the new educational programs. The plan shall provide for the assignment of administrators who are strong instructional leaders, with sufficient administrative support.[46]

Reconstitution gave the district the capacity to vacate a school's administrators and teachers under the guidance of the central administration. Six schools in Bayview–Hunter's Point were targeted for this reform: Dr. Charles R. Drew, Sir Francis Drake, and George Washington Carver Elementaries; Dr. Martin Luther King Jr. and Horace Mann Middle Schools; and Philip Burton High School. Two of these schools, King and Burton, were to be newly established, and the four others were to be reconstituted.[47]

The idea for reconstitution in San Francisco has its origins in the frustrations of one of the attorneys of the NAACP who had been involved in arguing a number of desegregation cases. Thomas Atkins, the lead attorney for the NAACP in *NAACP v. SFUSD*[48] called for the "vacating" of schools to promote school improvement.[49] He acknowledged that having new administrators, faculty, and staff would not necessarily guarantee that new, more effective personnel would be chosen. It was critical that criteria be established that could guide district administrators in the selection of personnel and that would guide newly chosen school administrators and teachers in their work subsequently. Yet Atkins did not specify what those criteria should be.[50]

That responsibility would be accepted by several high-ranking school administrators, some of whom had extensive experience as school principals.[51] This group developed a set of eleven philosophical tenets that were intended to guide the district by embodying what they believed were the expectations of desegregation as far back as *Brown v. Board of Education*.[52] As such, these tenets were the backbone of the consent decree and were to convey its spirit:

> All individuals should learn to live and to work in a world that is characterized by interdependence and cultural diversity.
>
> All individuals are entitled to be treated with respect and dignity.
>
> All individuals want to learn and to be recognized for their achievements.
>
> All individuals can learn.
>
> All individuals learn in many different ways and at varying rates.
>
> Each individual learns *best* in a particular way.
>
> All individuals are both potential learners and potential teachers.
>
> If individuals do not learn, then those assigned to be their teachers should accept responsibility for this failure and should take appropriate remedial action.
>
> Learning has both cognitive and affective dimensions.
>
> Learning can be subdivided into a number of specific, concrete competencies that can be used as a focus for teaching.
>
> Parents want their children to attain their fullest potential as learners and to succeed academically.[53]

The process of articulating what they considered the essential components of effective desegregation at the school level was conducted fairly informally by the members of this small group. They drafted these principles in relative isolation without having to receive approval in the process and then presented them to Superintendent Robert Alioto.

Two ideas underlie the tenets: belief in the capability of all students to learn and a resistance to blame students for their failure. These ideas would provide the foundation for the seven primary components of school reconstitution that were to serve as specific guidelines for administrators and teachers in targeted schools:

The faculty would be vacated and staff hired who are committed to the consent decree vision, the Philosophical Tenets and this plan.

Commitment to the Philosophical Tenets that established expectations for learning and behavior would be required.

Specific and explicit student outcomes would be delineated for each subject at each grade level.

Technologically rich environments (computers, multimedia, and so on) would be available for instruction.

Flexibility in adult/student ratios would be encouraged: more adults would be available so that small group instruction at various times throughout the day would be possible.

Heavy staff development across the first three items would be provided. New staff would select a unique instructional focus for their school.[54]

Reconstitution was the primary innovative mechanism that was to demonstrate how school desegregation and academic achievement could be linked. The success of desegregation efforts in San Francisco would rely heavily therefore on the proven benefits of reconstitution.

It must also be noted that the decree was comprehensive in its understanding of the context within which these efforts to desegregate were to be made. The decree tried to anticipate major barriers to desegregation that had occurred in other communities and thus pushed the SFUSD and state of California to overcome them. Several examples are noteworthy. Provisions of the decree required state officials to prevent students from transferring to suburban schools as a way to avoid attending desegregated schools. If this practice was found, the court would require that the state withhold any funding to the suburban school district.[55] The Department of Defense was prohibited from providing transportation to the children of persons in the military to attend private schools.[56] Funding for staff development regarding "student discipline procedures and goals, academic achievement and performance goals, teaching in a diverse racial/ethnic environment, parental involvement, and the desegregation goals and provisions of [the] Consent Decree" was provided.[57] The decree required school district and state officials to spearhead efforts to promote the greater racial and ethnic integration of housing in San Francisco by making recommendations to "the Mayor of San Francisco, the San Francisco Public Housing Authority, the San Francisco Redevelopment Agency, and concerned state and Federal agencies."[58] The state was required to fund a substantial portion of costs associated with desegregation, including those related to reconstitution.[59] Finally, in retaining jurisdiction over the case, the court specified in the decree that "any party . . . may at any time propose modification of the Decree to the Court and the other parties."[60] In essence, constant review and critical reexamination of the continuing implementation of the decree was made possible.

The 1983 consent decree was innovative in addressing school desegregation in several respects. First, it had a dual focus on school desegregation regarding student attendance and academic achievement. Indeed, it ranked academic achievement as a critical and necessary component of school desegregation overall. The SFUSD was told that it would not be in compliance with the court's directives regarding desegregation unless it could demonstrate that it had been able systematically to enhance the performance of its African American students, especially those who attended schools in the most segregated part of San Francisco, Bayview–Hunter's Point. Second, the decree provided considerable guidance and direction as to how enrollment desegregation and academic achievement were to be enhanced. Precise formulas for enrollment were specified, and the concept of reconstitution was used to suggest how schools needed to be reformed. Yet it is perhaps the lack of specificity regarding how enrollment desegregation and reconstitution were to work in practice that made the decree's comprehensiveness unique. By not providing all the details for implementation, the court allowed senior personnel of the SFUSD to push their own creativity and innovative skills to make school reform work in Bayview–Hunter's Point. Ultimately, district personnel would decide on school assignment policies and mechanisms. They would also decide on the principals to lead the schools in Bayview–Hunter's Point; and it was these principals, working with central office personnel, who would choose teachers and develop curricula for reconstituted schools. Ultimately, considerable support from central office personnel and from many principals and teachers, the frontline service providers of education, was developed.

The decree established a set of conditions in San Francisco that facilitated the development of consensus necessary to support public school desegregation. By its nature the decree represented an agreement, and acceptance, by three major players in San Francisco educational politics, the NAACP, the SFUSD, and the state's Department of Education. Their efforts were explicitly supported by a Settlement Team organized by the court. The history of previous attempts to desegregate schools demonstrated that considerable opposition came from public officials, some school administrators, and large sections of the public. The consent decree sidestepped these sources of opposition through its authoritative position. Although some initial protest to the decree surfaced, interestingly enough from elements of the African American leadership concerned with the possibility of too many blacks being bused to other parts of town, levels of protest did not approach those that had occurred in the past. The explicit focus on academic achievement and the implementation mechanism of reconstitution in the decree provided the direction necessary to focus much action by school officials on all levels. It was difficult for anyone to question the goal of academic excellence, the philosophical tenets guiding the district, and the need for major reform in some schools. Although success at reconstitution was based on proven performance, which concerned a number of school officials, it was also difficult to question the need to try substantial innovation in certain city schools. Reconstitution was dramatic; its need was clear.

THE CHALLENGES OF MAINTAINING CONSENSUS

It has become apparent that the consensus attained initially for action was not necessarily long lasting. The implementation of a new policy in the context of a city can often generate unanticipated outcomes and create new issues. Consensus had to be maintained regarding the implementation of the consent decree; and, as with any policy issue of considerable complexity, the longer it was addressed, the more challenges previous agreements faced from actors, interests, and competing perspectives. As there is a difference between electoral coalitions and governing coalitions, a difference also exists between initial policy consensus regarding goals and implementation and the maintenance of this consensus over time. The persistent oversight of the federal district court and the continued willingness of major stakeholders to renegotiate details of the implementation of the decree, nevertheless, suggest a strong possibility that educational reform in San Francisco will continue.

Implementation and the Superintendent

Robert Alioto, superintendent from 1975 to 1985, was largely responsible for averting a long and drawn-out court battle over desegregation. His team of hand-picked advisers worked to develop the original consent decree. Superintendent Alioto and his team vigorously implemented Phase One of the decree in six schools in the Bayview–Hunter's Point area and, as the Expert's Report of 1992 later noted, they did so with some success.[61]

Part of Superintendent Alioto's plan was to place administrators and teachers who were deeply committed to the consent decree in Phase One schools. In effect, each principal in Phase One was chosen deliberately as part of a strategic plan. Overall, there was little turnover among this group of early administrators; thus, Alioto had succeeded in placing foot soldiers committed to the process of reconstitution in the schools. In 1985, however, Superintendent Alioto was fired by the school board. According to some observers, the reasons for his termination stemmed mainly from his vigorous enforcement of the consent decree. Many of the school board members represented constituencies, e.g., whites and students of Chinese descent, who thought that their interests were not being served by the decree.

The two superintendents who followed Alioto were mindful of this larger political consequence. Carlos Cornejo, the acting superintendent in 1985 during Phases Two and Three, was a district insider, having joined the district as an educator in the mid-1950s. During his short tenure, the implementation of the consent decree continued but with much less vigor and structured planning. In 1985, at the beginning of Cornejo's tenure, the implementation of the decree stood at a critical juncture. The reconstitution of Phase One schools and the desegregation plan carefully specified by the decree had largely been carried out. Thus, the next steps could secure the expansion of the decree beyond the small scope of the Bayview–Hunter's Point area. Unfortunately, Phases Two and Three merely identified twelve underperforming schools, which were not required to be reconstituted, as were Phase One schools. Acting Superintendent Cornejo chose to adhere to a much more traditional view of desegregation, and the next stages of implementation were much less forceful. As the Experts' Report of 1992 points out, they were also much less successful.

Ramon Cortines succeeded Cornejo in 1986 and served as superintendent until 1992, during what was considered Phase Four of the decree. Cortines's hostile attitude toward the consent decree was in dramatic contrast to Alioto's and even Cornejo's. Cortines, although rhetorically committed to it, believed that the decree and the involvement of the court effectively stripped him of the power to manage the district. He often referred to the decree as a "cookie-jar" that served special interests and attorneys better than the district's students. Under Cortines, the unraveling of the implementation and the movement away from the philosophical tenets occurred at a fast pace until the decree seemed all but discarded. Phase Four again identified a small number of schools, five to be exact, but did not pursue their reconstitution. Cortines retired in 1991, complaining of exhaustion. Soon thereafter, he assumed the position of chancellor of schools in New York City.

Waldemar "Bill" Rojas took the helm of the SFUSD just as the Committee of Experts submitted its ten-year review to the court in 1992. Largely buoyed by the experts' findings, Rojas has sought aggressively to return to the process of implementation of the decree and to its philosophical tenets. Rojas, unlike his immediate predecessors, seems personally committed to those tenets. Moreover, as did Alioto before him, Rojas has worked to spread commitment to the decree through all levels of the administration; principals in many schools now seem to have a more heightened commitment to it. In many of the reconstituted schools in the district, students, when prompted, can actually recite the tenets, which are posted in classrooms and hallways. Principals in these schools cite the ability to hire teachers and other administrators who are committed not only to the tenets but also to their particular vision of implementation and management as a crucial part of their success. In contrast, principals of nonreconstituted schools speak of the difficulty of persuading an already existing, if not immobile, staff of teachers and administrators of the value of their particular vision for the schools.

In 1992 a Committee of Experts, commissioned by the court to evaluate the impact of the consent decree with regard to its desegregation and academic achievement goals, found that the district had met the goals of the former but that the goals of the latter for all students were still unfulfilled.[62] More important, they found gains in achievement had occurred in the Phase One schools that had been fully reconstituted. Building on this finding, the SFUSD developed a plan in 1993 to expand the reconstitution efforts that had been successful in Phase One schools.

The 1993 plan, the Comprehensive School Improvement Program (CSIP), specified both qualitative and quantitative criteria to use in identifying low-performing schools. Some of the criteria included analysis of historical trends, review of writing samples, the number of student suspensions, the grades of students, the dropout rate, the transfer rate (both into and from the school), and a review of the school's Site Plan and Portfolio.[63] Nine schools were initially determined to be low achievers and were enrolled in the CSIP probation period, lasting for one year, during which time the school had the opportunity to demonstrate that it had improved. Failure to improve meant that the school would be reconstituted at the end of the probation period. Each year the court has required the district to reconstitute three of the low achieving schools. The district has chosen to implement this requirement by reconstituting two existing schools and by creating a third new one. To date, since 1983, twelve of the district's 100 schools have been reconstituted.[64]

Growing Ethnic and Racial Diversity

The desegregation law suit had been filed by the NAACP, and leaders of the Latino and Asian communities were not parties to the suit. The interests of African American students have therefore always been present in the court's thinking. The interests of Latino students were explicitly included in the 1993 Experts' Report, however, when it noted that African American and Latino students were being underserved by the SFUSD. In comparisons of achievement scores across all schools in the district, the mean academic achievement levels of these two groups of students were well below the districtwide average.

In 1993 advocates on behalf of Latino and Asian students attempted formally to intercede in the court's further considerations of the consent decree. Attorneys from the Chinese American Democratic Club and from Multicultural Education, Training, and Advocacy, Incorporated, a Latino educational advocacy group, made the request, arguing that representatives of the two largest ethnic groups in the district should justifiably be allowed to sit as part of the overseeing committee. At the time, Chinese students constituted 24.5 percent of the student body and Latino students accounted for 19.9 percent of those enrolled. Of particular concern to the parties filing the request was the treatment of Limited English Proficiency (LEP) students. They argued that the decree disproportionately affected the LEP students through the special enrollment practices. The effect, they argued, was to disperse LEP students throughout the district, fragmenting LEP programs, which led to the district's inability to retain many bilingual teachers.[65]

Judge Orrick considered the request and noted that substantial increases in the numbers of Latino and Asian students had occurred in the SFUSD in the eight years since the decree, with a related decline in the number of African American students.[66] In 1983–1984 the racial and ethnic enrollment percentages in the district were Chinese, 19.9; Latino, 17.3; African American, 22.5; other white, 17.0; other nonwhite, 11.9; Filipino, 8.7; Korean, 1.1; Japanese, 1.1; and American Indian, 0.6. In 1992–1993, enrollment percentages were Chinese, 24.5; Latino, 19.9; African American, 18.5; other white, 14.5; other nonwhite, 12.1; Filipino, 7.8; Korean, 1.1; Japanese, 1.0; and Native American, 0.6.[67] However, the judge denied the initial petition of these attorneys to intercede, and this decision was upheld on appeal. Judge Orrick did grant limited amicus status to the attorneys, but they were restricted to making recommendations as to who might serve on the panel of experts continuing to assist the court in its assessment of academic progress made by San Francisco students.[68]

Clearly, the consent decree has allowed an alliance to develop between certain external actors, including the court, its experts, the superintendent, and some African American leaders, to attempt to change broad patterns of the provision of educational services to African American students. The continuing mandate of the decree allows for a type of institutionalization of this alliance and its agenda. Through the exclusion of some groups and the inclusion of others as parties to the decree, the court has institutionalized a division between the parties who feel that their concerns are not addressed in the current implementation of the decree and those who do. This outsider versus insider dichotomy presents perhaps the greatest challenge to maintaining consensus. The situation at Lowell High School provides a particularly good example of this conflict.

Lowell High School

In the city of San Francisco, each high school was asked by Superintendent Rojas to develop a specific theme or mission.[69] Lowell High School has long been known as the college preparatory high school. The test scores of its students, for example, have always exceeded those in other high schools. Lowell's admissions process is not open. Instead, Lowell uses a modified college admissions process, admitting students based on a combination of grade point average in the seventh and eighth years, the content of their middle school curriculum, and their scores on the Comprehensive Test of Basic Skills (CTBS).

The consent decree restricts the percentage of students of any specified ethnic group attending a magnet school such as Lowell to 40 percent. If admission to Lowell were based solely on grade point average and examination scores, the percentage of students of Chinese descent who would attend Lowell would exceed that limit. In the past the district required that Chinese students score higher than other students to be admitted. For example, in 1993–1994, students could score a maximum of 69. Chinese students were required to score 61; whites, Japanese, Koreans, Filipinos, and American Indians were required to score 59; and blacks and Latinos were required to score 56.[70] This use of differential scores to admit students of racial and ethnic groups is alleged to discriminate against students of Chinese descent. The district continues to consider establishing another academically focused high school in hopes of constructively addressing this concern. Although such a school might allow more Chinese students to attend, it is not clear that sufficient numbers of students of other ethnic groups would qualify for enrollment at such a school.

A new admissions formula for Lowell was proposed and implemented in 1996. According to the plan, 80 percent of the incoming freshman class would be selected using the same formula of grade point average, middle school curriculum, and standardized test scores that had been used in the past. However, one single cut-off score would be specified for all groups in the district, regardless of race or ethnicity. This score would be adjusted from year to year, depending on the distribution of scores among racial and ethnic groups in the applicant pool.

The remaining 20 percent of the entering class would be admitted on a "value-added" diversity basis, open to all students, regardless of race or ethnicity, but based largely on low socioeconomic status. The criteria to determine low socioeconomic status include (1) free and reduced-price lunch eligibility; (2) receipt of Aid to Families with Dependent Children; (3) residence in public housing; (4) homelessness; and (5) national and state income poverty levels. Additional criteria that might be used in determining desirability of an applicant include (6) coursework completed in middle school; (7) participation in extracurricular activities; and (8) residence, in particular zip codes, to facilitate east/west integration in the city.[71]

The plan specified that a selection committee would be composed of faculty, parents, and administrators from Lowell; members of the superintendent's staff; designees from the Division for Integration, the Division of Planning and Research, and the Educational Placement Center; academic university representation; and representatives from the high- and middle-school operations' offices. This committee is charged with reviewing the applications and selecting the final 20 percent of the entering class.

The freshman class in the academic year 1996–1997 (the class of 2000) was the first to be selected using the new system. However, few differences actually emerged with regard to outcomes of the process. Chinese students still constitute approximately 38 percent of the class, followed by whites with 18 percent, Latinos with 14 percent, the category of other nonwhites with 13 percent, and African Americans with 7 percent. Thus, the process did result in an outcome in accord with the racial and ethnic guidelines in the consent decree.

Perhaps most troubling to some critics is that the new process seemed to function much as the old system had. In fact, as a feature of the new plan, every student who scored above 63 (out of 69 possible points) was automatically admitted, regardless of race or ethnicity. But, as the old system had also allowed, it is alleged that under the new system, blacks, Latinos, or Native Americans who scored as low as 50 were also automatically admitted.[72] The remaining slots in the freshman class were reportedly filled with students who were admitted under the value-added provision of the new plan. Although the new system was billed as a fairer and more equitable process in that it allowed for additional criteria besides race and ethnicity to be used, it has not had the effect of quieting the critics of the consent decree.

THE LIMITS OF COURT-INDUCED CONSENSUS

The history of consensus building and school reform in San Francisco demonstrates that, like many other urban communities in the United States, it has had great difficulty coming to terms with racial desegregation and its detrimental consequences for African Americans and Latinos in its public schools. At least since the mid-1970s, San Francisco has been characterized by progressive politics. Yet on many issues that progressive politics has been unable to establish its own course as to what the future of the city should be. This limited capacity to address a controversial and complex issue such as school desegregation through the forging of agreement among a diverse, sometimes competing, and perhaps even incompatible set of interests fits a broader pattern in San Francisco: i.e., there is a great deal of political action, a strong sense of political empowerment, and much community organization yet only limited success in the capacity of any one set of leaders to direct public policymaking.[73] Current mayor Willie Brown noted in his State of the City address on October 15, 1996: "One thing I have learned about San Francisco—this is a city committed religiously to process, very little to results. This must change. We have got to be prepared to listen and to act. Otherwise we will forfeit the opportunity for leadership."[74] In this environment, it was only through the intervention of the federal court that it was possible to establish structures of communication, interest reconciliation, identification of policy goals and means, and consistent funding to address school desegregation with an emphasis on enhancing academic achievement and to achieve the necessary levels of consensus.

Challenges to continued court-induced consensus are apparent, however. In 1995 the U.S. Supreme Court in *Missouri v. Jenkins* told the school district in Kansas City, Missouri, that it could no longer receive the protection and guidance of the local federal court in their efforts to promote school desegregation and academic achievement.[75] As part of the school desegregation order, the district court had required the state of Missouri to fund a comprehensive program of school construction, hiring of administrators and teachers, acquisition of computers and other state-of-the-art technological equipment, and innovative programs in teaching and learning that were designed to improve the educational attainment of Kansas City's African American students, limit the exit of white students from the city's schools, and encourage students living in suburban areas to attend Kansas

City schools. A 5-to-4 majority of the Supreme Court stated that the district court had exceeded its constitutional authority to require school desegregation by focusing so many of its efforts on establishing programs to enhance academic achievement. The Supreme Court stated: "Insistence upon academic goals unrelated to the effects of legal segregation unwarrantably postpones the day when the KCMSD will be able to operate on its own."[76] The Court also stated that the district court had been intervening in the affairs of the Kansas City School District for almost twenty years. This continued violation of local control was also beyond the constitutional authority of the district court. Local control was desirable except in the most egregious of circumstances.

Each of these main conclusions by the Court could apply to San Francisco. The district court in this city has expressed a clear expectation that all desegregation efforts be coupled with an explicit focus on academic achievement and that the court will continue to oversee all desegregation efforts. The case in San Francisco is different in that the district court oversees a consent decree, voluntarily agreed to by all parties to the suit, and is not intervening through a court order, as was the case in Kansas City. It is unclear as to whether this distinction would be significant if one of the parties to the suit chose to withdraw from participating in the consent decree under the new standards of judgment established by the Supreme Court in *Missouri v. Jenkins.*[77]

It was within this context that a group of Chinese parents and students filed a motion for summary judgment against the constitutionality of the consent decree on July 5, 1994, in *Ho v. SFUSD.*[78] The plaintiffs claimed that the 40 to 45 percent capping of Chinese enrollment at certain elementary, middle, and high schools, such as had occurred at Lowell High School, violated the Fourteenth Amendment rights of these students to be treated without regard to race. The motion made three primary claims. First, it argued that the court never made any formal findings of fact regarding the history of racial segregation in the San Francisco public schools. Second, it argued that the district and the Committee of Experts have agreed since 1993 that there is no longer any racial segregation in student enrollment. Third, as in *Missouri v. Jenkins,* it was argued that the district court had no constitutional authority to include academic achievement as a criterion in determining effective desegregation.[79]

On May 5, 1997, Judge Orrick denied the motion for summary judgment, basing his opinion on two main points. He wrote that it was inappropriate for the *Ho* plaintiffs to raise a constitutional challenge in this motion: "The record shows that the interests of the *Ho* plaintiffs were adequately represented at the time the Consent Decree was entered."[80] The NAACP, he continued, adequately represented their interests. Moreover, given that the plaintiffs "did not raise their constitutional challenge at the time the Consent Decree was entered, or subsequently on appeal, plaintiffs may not raise it now."[81] Second, he noted that the plaintiffs did not meet their burden of proof as to "the absence of a dispute of fact"[82] regarding the history of past discrimination and other related aspects of the case.[83] For example, Judge Orrick stated that although the "Court did not reach any conclusion on the issues of fact and law underlying the merits of the dispute . . . this does not mean, as a matter of law, that there was insufficient evidence to support a finding of past discrimination."[84] At this writing, the plaintiffs have appealed the case to the Ninth Circuit Court of Appeals and they are awaiting a date to present their oral arguments.[85]

The second major challenge to the maintenance of court-induced consensus derives from the focus of the consent decree on reconstitution as the means to attain both desegregation and enhanced academic achievement. Evidence of the effectiveness of reconstitution is limited. The only systematic evidence that reconstitution in Phase One was successful is presented in "Desegregation and Educational Change in San Francisco," the 1992 report of the Committee of Experts.[86] Although it is stated that "four independent analyses confirm the importance of the Bayview–Hunter's Point strategy in the Consent Decree's overall success,"[87] the only reported evidence of enhanced academic achievement is a comparison of the "average scores by race on the combined reading, language arts, and math scores on the California Test of Basic Skills for all 106 schools in the District in 1990–91."[88] African American, Hispanic, white, Chinese, and Korean students scored higher in Phase One schools than in schools in Phases Two through Five.[89] More specifically, it is stated that "African American students scored higher in Phase One even though free lunch statistics showed that they were as disadvantaged as African American students in other Phases."[90] It is only within the last year that the SFUSD has begun systematically to document both the nature of past reconstitution in the district and its more recent efforts. For example, no record was kept of the magnitude of changes that occurred in previously reconstituted schools. Questions need to be answered: How many teachers were hired? What was their training? How many new classes were established? Did parental involvement increase? Although students in Phase One schools performed better than students in schools in other phases, what occurred in the Phase One schools that directly contributed to this achievement has not been systematically examined. Stated differently, the major factors that have enhanced or inhibited academic achievement have not been determined.

This lack of information is a weakness that hits at the very heart of the consent decree. If the major mechanism to promote school reform, i.e., reconstitution, has had a largely uncharted existence and if it cannot be shown systematically to contribute to higher student academic achievement, then the purpose of the entire decree can be called into question. The Committee of Experts is only now undertaking a systematic study of reconstitution. The logic of its benefits is well articulated and sound. It is necessary to determine if this logic is reflected in the reality of school reform in the San Francisco public schools.

It is clear that the reason the court had to become involved in the pursuit of racial desegregation and school reform in San Francisco—that is, the inability of traditional policy leaders successfully to establish consensus on this issue—has meant that no leader has attempted to build this consensus subsequently. Superintendent Rojas has come close to doing it, and he does have a strong reputation among many segments of the San Francisco community.[91] However, his support of reconstitution can be perceived as enhancing his own power over the educational bureaucracy, especially administrators and teachers, who do not seem to serve students adequately. His embracing of reconstitution has also led to the district's receiving a substantial state supplement to the already-strained district budget, which again makes his position seem self-serving. In a school board election in San Francisco held November 5, 1996, the local teachers' union opposed candidates in part on the basis of their endorsement of reconstitution as a reform that should be implemented in the entire district.

Superintendent Rojas did sign a tentative agreement on May 1, 1997, with Joan-Marie Shelley, former president of the United Educators of San Francisco (UESF), to consider how the process of placing schools on the Comprehensive School Improvement Plan could include the participation of teachers generally, especially those at targeted schools. The primary purpose of the agreement was to "creat[e] alternatives which [were] intended to lead to the elimination of the need for reconstitution."[92] Among the principles of agreement were the use of "mutually agreed upon standards" and the need for "an appeal process" for staff who have been identified for "involuntary transfer."[93] It is clear that many details need to be specified before the principles are implemented. The UESF has already issued a memorandum outlining "a six stage cycle of improvement that [should occur] within CSIP schools."[94]

Any major change in the process of implementing reconstitution would of course have to be approved by all the parties to the consent decree as well as by Judge Orrick. Further, in June 1997 the superintendent established the CSIP/Reconstituted Schools Committee. It is composed of representatives of the district administration, school principals, teachers, the UESF, parents, and educational consultants. Its purpose is to help the administration further develop ways to promote the improvement of schools on the CSIP and those currently undergoing reconstitution. These recent developments indicate a willingness by the major player in the further implementation of the consent decree, Superintendent Rojas, to develop a broader consensus for reconstitution among major education stakeholders by involving them more in the details of assessing school performance, enhancing student achievement, and legitimizing the involuntary transfer of teachers and administrators.

It is evident that court-induced consensus has not led to the guarantee of a broad sentiment expressly in favor of the goals the court has endorsed. If the court chooses to withdraw from active participation in school reform, it may not leave behind a strong constituency in support of reform. It is possible that the pattern of educational policy decision making that existed prior to 1983—decision making in which difficult issues were avoided or the strongest opinions were those against school reform—will reappear. If this were to occur we know what the consequences would be for many of the city's African American and Latino students—more segregation than currently exists and continuing low levels of academic achievement.

The politics of race and of school reform in San Francisco are exemplary of the best of what Thurgood Marshall and others could have anticipated when they argued *Brown v. Board of Education of Topeka, Kansas* in 1954.[95] A federal district court intervened to promote consensus that the traditional political process could not produce, a consensus that would serve the long-term interests of African American students by promoting school reforms to enhance their educational achievement. It would be ironic if that same court chose to withdraw from further participation in school desegregation. Given recent U.S. Supreme Court decisions, it may have no other choice.

NOTES

This essay is based in part on the project "Civic Capacity and Urban Education," Clarence Stone, principal investigator, funded by the National Science Foundation, no. S134.331. The larger project compared educational reform in the cities of Atlanta, Baltimore, Boston, Denver, Detroit, Houston, Los Angeles, Pittsburgh, San Francisco, St. Louis, and Washington, DC.

1. *Brown v. Board of Education of Topeka,* 347 U.S. 483, 74 S. Ct. 686, 98 L. Ed. 873 (1954).

2. Ibid.; *Brown v. Board of Education of Topeka,* 349 U.S. 294, 75 S.Ct. 753, 99 L.Ed. 1083 (1955); *Milliken v. Bradley,* 418 U.S. 717 (1974); Jennifer L. Hochschild, *The New American Dilemma: Liberal Democracy and School Desegregation* (New Haven: Yale University Press, 1984).

3. See, for example, John E. Chubb and Terry M. Moe, *Politics, Markets, and America's Schools* (Washington, DC: Brookings Institution, 1990); Jeffrey R. Henig, *Rethinking School Choice: Limits of the Market Metaphor* (Princeton: Princeton University Press, 1994); Jeffrey R. Henig, Luis R. Fraga, Alan DiGaetano, and Bari E. Anhalt, "Restructuring School Governance: Reform Ideas and Their Implementation," paper presented at the Annual Meeting of the American Political Science Association, New York City, September 1994; David C. Berliner and Bruce J. Biddle, *The Manufactured Crisis: Myths, Fraud, and the Attack on America's Public Schools* (Reading, MA: Addison-Wesley, 1995).

4. C78-1445 WHO, Northern District, California (June 30, 1978).

5. School reconstitution, sometimes referred to as zero-based staffing, is the practice of replacing administrators and teachers in a school that has been identified as not serving its students properly. In the case of the SFUSD, schools have been targeted for reconstitution on the basis of having a substantial number of students who were achieving below districtwide norms on standardized tests.

6. Consensus refers to agreement on policy goals as well as agreement on the most effective programmatic means to achieve those goals. The agreement that is sought is among major stakeholders in the educational policy process, including school board members, the superintendent, principals, teachers, parents, and students. On the politics of con-

sensus as it relates to policymaking, see E. E. Schattschneider, *The Semisovereign People* (New York: Harcourt Brace Jovanovich College Publishers, 1960, 1988); John W. Kingdon, *Agendas, Alternatives, and Public Policies* (New York: HarperCollins, 1984); Frank R. Baumgartner and Bryan D. Jones, *Agendas and Instability in American Politics* (Chicago: University of Chicago Press, 1983).

7. This discussion relies heavily upon the work of David L. Kirp, *Just Schools: The Idea of Racial Equality in American Education* (Berkeley: University of California Press, 1982), and Doris Fine, *When Leadership Fails: Desegregation and Demoralization in the San Francisco Schools* (New Brunswick, NJ: Transaction Books, 1986).

8. Department of Commerce, *Statistical Abstract of the United States, 1992*, 112th ed. (Washington, DC: GPO, 1992), Table 38, pp. 35–37.

9. At this time school board members were initially appointed by the mayor and were subsequently ratified by voters (Kirp, *Just Schools*, p. 84).

10. As quoted in ibid., p. 86.

11. Ibid., p. 87; no. 71034, N.D. California (October 2, 1962).

12. Kirp, *Just Schools*, p. 87.

13. Ibid., p. 91.

14. Ibid., p. 93.

15. Ibid.

16. No. 618-643, San Francisco Superior Court, June 15, 1970.

17. 339 Federal Supplement 1315, 1325-27 (N.D. California 1970, 1971).

18. Kirp, *Just Schools*, p. 94. The focus was exclusive to elementary schools because levels of racial and ethnic integration were higher at middle and high schools.

19. Ron Moskowitz, "School Integration Delay to Be Asked," *San Francisco Chronicle*, June 27, 1971. This ruling came just one week after the Supreme Court's decision in *Swann v. Charlotte-Mecklenburg Board of Education*, 402 U.S. 1 (1971), where busing was approved as a remedy to public school segregation.

20. Kirp, *Just Schools*, p. 110.

21. Ibid.

22. Ibid., p. 108. When the Horseshoe Plan was first implemented, an estimated 76 percent of Chinese students boycotted the public schools and attended Chinese Freedom Schools instead. See SFUSD, "Active Fall Enrollment," October 1975, Table 4, p. 9. By 1974, white enrollment in the public schools dropped from 34.5 percent to 27 percent.

23. Kirp, p. 108.

24. Ibid., pp. 112–13.

25. Ibid., pp. 111–12.

26. Ibid., p. 113.

27. Ibid.

28. C78-1445 WHO, Northern District, California (June 30, 1978).

29. Consent Decree, San Francisco Unified School District, U.S. District Court for the Northern District of California, 1983 Consent Decree with Modifications Required by Court Approved Stipulations and Orders Through November 5, 1993, *San Francisco NAACP et al. v. San Francisco Unified School District et al.*, C78-1445 WHO, paragraph 7, p. 4.

30. Consent Decree, 1983, 1993, paragraph 8, p. 4.

31. The members of the Settlement Team were Harold Howe II and Gary A. Orfield for the court, Gordon Foster and Robert L. Green for the NAACP, Barbara Cohen and

Fred C. Leonard Jr. for the SFUSD, and Ples A. Griffin and Thomas M. Griffin for the state of California (Consent Decree, 1983, 1993, exhibit B, p. 5).

32. A criticism of this committee has been that its members as a whole operate on a higher policy level and do not have extensive experience working in public schools at the K through 12 level.

33. Consent Decree, 1983, 1993, paragraph 12, p. 5.

34. Ibid., paragraph 39, p. 27.

35. The other major city that linked academic achievement to racial desegregation in its public schools is Kansas City, Missouri. In this case, a court order required that the state of Missouri fund improvements in the academic attractiveness of central-city schools to minimize the extent of white flight that occurred and to encourage suburban residents to think of sending their children to public schools in Kansas City. Thus the academic opportunities provided to Kansas City's minority students would be enhanced as well. On June 12, 1995, the Supreme Court in *Missouri et al. v. Kalima Jenkins et al.,* U.S., S.C., 93-1823 (1995) decided that enhancing "suburban attractiveness" was not a sufficient justification to maintain court review. It also found that the continuous requirement of state funding unconstitutionally limited the local control of public education by the school board.

36. Consent Decree, 1983, 1993, paragraph 12, p. 5 (emphasis in original).

37. Ibid., paragraph 13, p. 6.

38. "San Francisco Settles Integration Dispute," *New York Times,* January 1, 1983, sec. 1, p. 5.

39. United Press International, AM cycle, Regional News, California, February 14, 1983.

40. Ibid.

41. Ibid., July 11, 1983.

42. Ibid.

43. Consent Decree, paragraph 39, pp. 27–28.

44. Ibid., paragraph 40, p. 28.

45. Ibid., pp. 14–24.

46. Ibid., paragraph 18, p. 17.

47. "Basic Information About School Reconstitution," San Francisco Unified School District, n.p., n.d.

48. C78-1445 WHO, Northern District, California (June 30, 1978).

49. Interview with an administrator for the SFUSD, March 25, 1996.

50. Ibid.

51. Interview with senior district administrators, March 25, 1996, and April 12, 1996.

52. *Brown v. Board of Education,* 347 U.S. 74 S. Ct. 686, 98 L.Ed. 873 (1954).

53. "The San Francisco Unified School District's Philosophical Tenets," Sir Francis Drake Press, n.d. (emphasis in original).

54. "Basic Information About School Reconstitution." In practice, an eighth component was found to be important: parent involvement.

55. Consent Decree, 1983, 1993, paragraph 32, pp. 24–25.

56. Ibid., paragraph 33, p. 25.

57. Ibid., paragraph 36, p. 26.

58. Ibid., pp. 29–31.

59. Ibid., pp. 32–33.

60. Ibid., paragraph 50, p. 33.

61. *Desegregation and Educational Change in San Francisco: Findings and Recommendations on Consent Decree Implementation* (1992), Gary Orfield, chair (hereafter the Experts' Report).

62. Ibid., p. 30.

63. *Annual Report by the Local School District Defendants, 1994–1995,* submitted to the Hon. William H. Orrick, 1994.

64. An important caveat to mention is the role of the desegregation funding provided to the district by the state of California as part of the decree. Given the relative dismal state of funding for education in California, the importance of the contributions that flow to the district from the state as a result of the desegregation plan cannot be overemphasized. In the years since the plan was instituted in San Francisco, the district has received over $400 million from the state. This amounts to $33 million annually or approximately 7 percent of the district's annual budget of $530 million. In the academic year 1995–1996, 31 percent of the desegregation money went to elementary schools, 16 percent to high schools, 12 percent to middle schools, 12 percent to the desegregation's program office, 8 percent to the busing program, 5 percent to planning, research, and program development, 5 percent to summer school programs, 4 percent to address the disproportionate assignment of blacks and Latinos to special education classes, 4 percent to mandated staff development, 1 percent to legal services, and a small amount (.5 percent) to parent/community relations (*San Francisco Chronicle,* October 10, 1996, p. B2).

65. No. C-78-1445 (Class Action), March 4, 1993.

66. *San Francisco Chronicle,* April 9, 1993, p. B4.

67. These figures are reported in San Francisco Unified School District, Grades K–12 Student Enrollment Percentages, 1967–1968 to 1995–1996, revised March 24, 1996.

68. Interview with one of the attorneys asking for amicus status, February 8, 1995.

69. This section draws heavily from the excellent work of Racy Ming, "Desegregation in a Diverse and Competitive Environment: Admissions at Lowell High School," Undergraduate Honors Program in Education, Stanford University, May 30, 1997.

70. *San Francisco Chronicle,* April 19, 1993, p. B2.

71. "Revised Admissions Process for Lowell High School," Office of Superintendent Bill Rojas, January 8, 1996.

72. *San Francisco Chronicle,* August 28, 1996, p. B4.

73. Richard E. DeLeon, *Left Coast City: Progressive Politics in San Francisco, 1975–1991* (Lawrence: University Press of Kansas, 1992). See also Frederick D. Wirt, *Power in the City: Decision Making in San Francisco* (Berkeley: University of California Press, 1974).

74. As quoted in "Brown's Vow—City Will Shine Again," *San Francisco Chronicle,* October 16, 1996, p. A1.

75. 115 S. Ct. 2038 (1995).

76. Ibid.

77. Ibid. This argument is made explicitly by plaintiffs' attorneys in *Ho v. San Francisco Unified School District,* C-94-2418-WHO.

78. Ibid.

79. 115 S. Ct. 2038 (1995).

80. *Brian Ho v. San Francisco Unified School District,* no. C-94-WHO Opinion, May 5, 1997, p. 10.

81. Ibid., p. 11.

82. Ibid., p. 18.

83. Ibid., p. 16.

84. Ibid., p. 15.

85. Both Gov. Pete Wilson and the California Board of Education have publicly stated their support of the plaintiffs in the *Ho* case. The Center for Individual Rights, a legal advocacy firm in Washington, DC, is now representing the state of California in this matter. The Center for Individual Rights represented the plaintiffs in the case of *Hopwood v. Texas* (Fifth Circuit Court of Appeals, 94-50664, March 18, 1996) in which the court declared unconstitutional the racial and ethnic affirmative action program used in admissions to the University of Texas Law School. Interestingly, the California Department of Education does not agree with the position taken by the governor and the state board of education. The American Civil Liberties Union has filed an amicus curae brief in favor of the San Francisco Unified School District. Information related to the status of the *Ho* case was obtained in an interview with Daniel Gerard, attorney for the *Ho* plaintiffs, November 17, 1997.

86. "Desegregation and Educational Change in San Francisco: Findings and Recommendations on Consent Decree Implementation," paper submitted to Judge William H. Orrick, U.S. District Court, San Francisco, California, Gary Orfield (chair), Barbara L. Cohen, Gordon Foster, Robert L. Green, Paul Lawrence, David S. Tatel, and Fred Tempes, July 1992.

87. "Desegregation and Educational Change," p. 33.

88. Ibid.

89. Ibid., Table 3, p. 34.

90. Ibid.

91. See the interview with Lulann McGriff, an intern at the NAACP during the late 1970s and president of the local chapter of the NAACP through the 1980s, in "Guardian at the School Gate," *San Francisco Chronicle,* November 3, 1996. In assessing Rojas, she states, "Well, I think Rojas is pretty much on the same wavelength we're on. He's an educator, and he's had some good ideas, and he's not afraid to implement them. . . . And, you know, Rojas stands on his own. He'll get out there and take the heat. I respect that."

92. "Outline of Tentative Agreement to Reduce the Need for Reconstitution," signed May 1, 1997, reprinted in *San Francisco Educator* 8, no. 17b (May 5, 1997): p. 1.

93. Ibid.

94. "Conceptual Framework for Developing an Alternative to Reconstitution: A proposal by UESF," memorandum drafted by the United Educators of San Francisco to Superintendent Waldemar Rojas, June 4, 1997.

95. 347 U.S. 483, 74 S. Ct. 686, 98 L.Ed. 873 (1954).

PART II
Obstacles to Reform

Because educators have an immediate stake in school performance, some observers might expect them to be in the forefront of the education reform movement. Not so, it turns out. Though there are individuals and even particular faculties deeply committed to reform, educators collectively are often a force for resistance. Accorded less status than many other professions, educators are thinly insulated from public criticism. Politically they are often in a defensive posture, and they have become one of the most unionized occupations in the United States.

Yet to talk in such general terms misses much of the contextual richness of education politics. Marion Orr shows how race, employment, and education are intricately intertwined in Baltimore in chapter 5. Indeed, they are intertwined in such a way that criticism of school performance is filtered through considerations of group power and control. Union influence is never an isolated force; in Baltimore it needs to be seen as part of a picture that includes black churches and a set of personal bonds rooted in shared racial experiences. Desegregation, Orr shows, is not a distant history unconnected to the present. The Baltimore case captures well the way in which a past experience of racial segregation and discord shapes the contemporary understanding of what is at stake.

Timothy Ross takes us to New York City in chapter 6 and offers a bottom-up view of the frustrations encountered by a grassroots organization, East Brooklyn Congregations (EBC). Patronage, entrenched privilege, and the cumbersome procedures of large and complex bureaucracies provide a formidable set of barriers. Even when some of these obstacles can be diminished by starting new schools, there are other hurdles, such as the need to recruit able teachers and to motivate students in an area beset by poverty and the cumulative consequences of social inequality.

What, then, does one find in a suburban jurisdiction, one not mired in poverty or entangled in patronage politics? Cheryl Jones and Connie Hill examine re-

91

form initiatives and the resistance they meet in Montgomery County, Maryland, a large suburban jurisdiction firmly imbued with a "good government" ethos. Traditionally, educators have enjoyed a high level of autonomy, especially in day-to-day operations. As Jones and Hill show, top-level administrators continue to be positioned to defend their voice in education decision making. They have the command of details, the immediate control of organizational action, and the claim of expertise to defend their prerogatives—even in the face of an educated and assertive constituency of parents. Moreover, they possess enough control over the distribution of site-level resources largely to set the terms on which the school-community dialogue takes place.

Often those individuals with the greatest immediate interest in a policy area have a preponderant influence in the decisions made. Yet, though education fits this pattern in a general way, it would be a mistake to see education politics as a matter of *pressure on* the school system. In each of the three communities examined in this section, schools are part of a complex set of relationships. To think of the reform as pressuring schools to improve performance misses an important point. Change requires altering significant relationships—whether they are about the connections between race and jobs in the school system, the role of patronage and union contracts in a big city, or the way in which good government procedures of a middle-class suburb hinder the development of various issues and concerns. Education reform, then, may be less a matter of bringing in a new superintendent or launching a catchy initiative than it is of restructuring school-community relations. That is why race is so fundamental in Baltimore. That is why overcoming bureaucratic inertia is only part of the battle in East Brooklyn. And that is why diffuse discontent in Montgomery County does not cumulate into real change.

5

The Challenge of School Reform in Baltimore: Race, Jobs, and Politics

Marion Orr

Over a decade ago, Kurt L. Schmoke, Baltimore's first elected African American mayor, took office and pledged to bring about "a renaissance in public education" to Maryland's largest city. In his first inaugural address, Mayor Schmoke vowed to make education a top priority of his administration, to make Baltimore "the city that reads."

> Of all the things I might be able to accomplish as mayor of our city, it would make me proudest if one day it could simply be said of Baltimore that, "this is the city that reads. . . . This is the city that waged war on illiteracy. . . . This is the city that recognized brainpower as its most precious resource . . . and this is the city whose citizens, businesses, industries and institutions joined together to make education work for all who were willing to work for an education.[1]

With the authority to appoint the nine-member board of school commissioners, Mayor Schmoke has the formal authority to change how the schools operate. He played a major role in the appointment of Baltimore's last two school superintendents. He supported efforts to decentralize the school system's bureaucracy and move more authority and decision making to principals, teachers, and parents. In 1991, with Mayor Schmoke's encouragement, the city gained national attention when it hired a private firm to manage nine of its public schools. Without question, Mayor Schmoke has devoted much of his energy toward public education.

Since the middle 1980s, Baltimore's business community, organized under the Greater Baltimore Committee (GBC), has become more active in school affairs. The GBC has testified before committees of the state legislature in support of increased state funding for Baltimore's schools, forged partnerships with numerous schools, and helped train principals to operate schools more like businesses. The Abell Foundation, one of Maryland's largest foundations, has contributed millions of dollars to support school reform efforts in Baltimore. Baltimoreans United in Leadership Development (BUILD), an influential organization made up of fifty-five black churches and three labor unions, has been very effective in mobilizing community-based support to improve the quality of public schooling. Moreover, state officials—especially the state board of education and the state superintendent of education—have pushed school reform initiatives in Baltimore and throughout Maryland.

Baltimore should be a city with significant capacity to carry out systemic school reform. However, school reform and improved student achievement remain elusive. Baltimore consistently performs far worse than Maryland's other school districts on the Maryland School Performance Program's tests of student achievement. In 1996 over 20 percent of Baltimore's schools were designated "reconstitution eligible" by state education officials, meaning that they were eligible for state intervention, such as taking over the school or turning it over to a private company to run. In 1997 the Maryland legislature—frustrated with the slow pace of school improvement—passed legislation that increased the role of state officials in the operation of the Baltimore City Public Schools (BCPS). Mayor Schmoke recently admitted that the public schools in his city "still have serious problems."[2]

Why has school improvement remained so elusive in Baltimore? To be sure, such factors as inadequate funding and low levels of parental involvement are part of the explanation. Moreover, Baltimore schools serve the largest population of students with special needs and impoverished backgrounds, making the challenge of improved education especially demanding. In this chapter, I contend that meaningful school reform in Baltimore is also hampered by three related factors: race, jobs, and politics. In Baltimore, improving education for children often competes with concerns about the viability of the school system as a source of wages and professional and economic advancement. Because a significant proportion of the school system's employment base is African American workers, the interplay between jobs and race hinders school reform efforts. The school bureaucracy is an employment regime for blacks, and school reformers have tried to improve the schools without destabilizing the historical and racial legacy of this employment base in the African American community.

RACE AND THE DEVELOPMENT OF A BLACK-LED SCHOOL SYSTEM

To suggest that race plays a significant role in school affairs and school reform in Baltimore requires setting the Baltimore school experience within historical context. The legacy of segregation and racial polarization helped shape the context of contemporary school affairs in Baltimore and is an important part of the school reform story today.

Racial Segregation

Baltimore's location makes it unique among other large northeastern industrial cities. Situated just below the Mason-Dixon line, Baltimore has many traditions that are characteristic of the Deep South. Historian Joseph Arnold describes Baltimore as a city with a "southern culture and a northern economy."[3] Like many Deep South cities, whites in Baltimore kept black residents firmly "in place" through a southern system of legal and social segregation. White citizens' desire to avoid racial mixing created two educational systems: one black, one white.[4] Schools for African American children were overcrowded. Textbooks and other educational materials for black schools were dated and typically secondhand. Discrepancies existed in the funds allocated per pupil for use in white and black schools. Despite excellence in some black classrooms (Frederick Douglass High School, for example), African American illiteracy was widespread when compared to that of whites.[5]

The 1954 *Brown* decision gave hope to African Americans across the nation that at last their quest for educational justice had the sanction of law. Officials in Baltimore desegregated fairly quickly.[6] The decision to desegregate was made without huge disruption. When the desegregation plan took effect in September 1954, board president Walter Sondheim said it operated "so smoothly there is no need for comment."[7] Beneath the surface, however, things were different. First, systemwide desegregation never occurred. The "freedom of choice" desegregation plan the board adopted "permitted any child to change schools for any reason, including race. Thus no child was required to attend a desegregated school against his will."[8] Second, Baltimore officials implemented a "tracking" plan modeled after the District of Columbia's "four-track" system, which grouped students according to their scores on standardized tests, effectively maintaining segregated schools and classrooms.[9]

By the 1960s, not much had changed. Faculty and staff in the BCPS remained racially segregated. In 1963, 53 of the city's 189 schools still had all-white faculties; 67 had all-black faculties. Discrimination continued in promotion and hiring practices. Complicating matters were demographic changes that were occurring in the Baltimore metropolitan region. Baltimore's population peaked in 1950, with 950,000 residents. Since 1950 the city's population has declined during each census count, down to 736,000 in 1990. Much of Baltimore's population loss can be explained by the exodus of whites from the city. The proportion of the Baltimore population that is African American rose from 24 percent in 1950 to 59 percent in 1990, and the white population declined from 76 percent to 39 percent.

Black Protest and Racial Politics: The 1960s and 1970s

The late 1960s and early 1970s were more than an era of demographic change; they were also a period of political change. Sharon P. Krefetz has observed that "blacks as political actors were virtually ignored by white Democratic party bosses" until the late 1960s.[10] The change, she notes, was due largely to a dramatic event in Baltimore's political history: the 1963 election of Theodore Roosevelt McKeldin to the office of mayor. McKeldin's election marked the first time a Republican had been elected to that office since 1943, when McKeldin himself had accomplished the feat. McKeldin attributed his 1963 victory to the "massive support he obtained in the black and to a lesser extent Jewish precincts."[11]

Mayor McKeldin took advantage of the considerable powers of the office to fulfill many of his campaign promises. For example, he used his appointive powers to put more African Americans into positions within many of the departments of city government. He adopted a policy of having roughly equal numbers of blacks and whites appointed to municipal jobs.[12] Moreover, McKeldin made sure that Baltimore was an "early enlistee" in the War on Poverty, establishing Baltimore's Community Action Program just six months after Pres. Lyndon B. Johnson signed the enabling legislation in February 1965.[13]

In the 1967 mayoral election, Baltimore's Democratic party leaders regrouped, and McKeldin was defeated. Although his successor, Thomas D'Alesandro III was considered a liberal and received overwhelming support from African American voters, black disenchantment grew. Mayor D'Alesandro, working closely with business leaders and leaders in the black community, wanted to avoid the racial conflict that afflicted Detroit, Los Angeles, Newark, and other cities. D'Alesandro, for example, continued McKeldin's policy of having roughly equal numbers of blacks and whites appointed to municipal jobs. By 1971, 46 percent of the 41,000 municipal jobs in Baltimore were held by African Americans. Mayor D'Alesandro also expressed concerns about the state of Baltimore's public schools, and in 1968 he launched a successful $80 million bond referendum to support school construction. The bonds were earmarked to address the black community's concerns that their children attended "ramshackle schools, many of them built in the nineteenth century."[14] Consistent with Baltimore's tradition of patronage politics, D'Alesandro also directed school officials to use funds from Title I of the Elementary and Secondary Act of 1965 to hire thousands of "neighborhood people" as teachers' aides.[15] Further, Mayor D'Alesandro appointed more blacks to the board of school commissioners so that by 1970 four blacks served on the nine-member board.

Like many major cities, Baltimore erupted in flames after the assassination of Dr. Martin Luther King. The riots of 1968 deeply wounded Baltimore. One local observer noted that "the riots only exacerbated racial divisions and assuaged any guilt that might have been felt by middle class parents fleeing the city or choosing private schools."[16] The racial tensions spilled over into the schools. "Board meetings were so raucous in those days that Mayor Thomas J. D'Alesandro III called the [school] commissioners to a private meeting and threatened to fire them all if the 'name calling, picayune bickering and discourtesies' didn't stop."[17]

As more whites left the city for the suburbs, the racial makeup of the schools

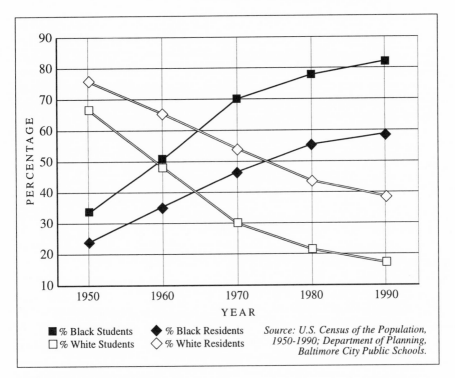

Figure 5.1. Racial composition of Baltimore residents and students in Baltimore city public schools, 1950–1990.

changed dramatically. In 1955, the year after the *Brown* decision, 60 percent of the students were white. By September 1960, 51 percent of the students in the BCPS were African American. For the first time in the city's history, more blacks than whites attended Baltimore's public schools. In 1966 the school superintendent warned that "unless the movement of the white population from the city is halted, the question of integration will no longer have meaning for the city school system."[18] By 1974, 70 percent of the students in the Baltimore schools were African American; the percentage of the black student population was close to 84 percent in 1995.

Enrollment trends in the schools and the racial composition of the city's total population since 1950 can be tracked (see Fig. 5.1). The lines for white students and white residents have similar slopes, revealing the racial dimensions of population shifts and student composition. The data also show a significant difference between the percentage of white students enrolled in the city's schools and the percentage of whites residing in the central city. For instance, in 1970, although the city was over 50 percent white, the school system's white student enrollment was just 30 percent. The gap between the percentage of whites living in the city and the percentage of whites attending the public schools widened during the 1980s and 1990s. Many African Americans viewed these differences as evidence that whites had abandoned the city's public schools.

As the percentage of African American students grew, leaders in Baltimore's black community wanted the proportion of school administrators, teachers, and other school personnel to reflect this shift. Fueled in part by research that showed that white middle-class teachers and administrators often had low expectations for minority youth and that this attitude contributed to poorer performance, community control of schools became the rallying cry of many blacks in Baltimore and other major cities.[19]

In January 1970 Superintendent Thomas D. Sheldon proposed a decentralization plan that, he emphasized, *did not* involve "community control" of the schools. The plan angered the four black school board members and a white liberal who sided with them. Sheldon's decentralization plan was rejected by the board. He eventually resigned after the liberal majority on the school board rejected his nominations for school principals and demanded that he submit a list that better reflected the racial composition of the student body. Sheldon would be the last white to lead the city's schools on a permanent basis.

In late 1970 Mayor D'Alesandro shocked the city when—at age forty-two— he declared that he would "retire" from politics at the end of his term. The racial strife had taken a toll on the young mayor. "One day it all turned sour," he told a reporter when he made his decision not to seek reelection.[20] As a city councilor recalled years later: "The school board was a battleground. I would go to the board meetings; they would put on a show each week. Tommy D'Alesandro really wanted justice for the school system. He wanted to help the system but couldn't because of the conflict."[21]

The First Black Superintendent: 1971–1975

In July 1971 (before Mayor D'Alesandro's term expired) the school board voted 8 to 1 to appoint Roland N. Patterson, an assistant superintendent from Seattle, to become the city's first black school superintendent.[22] And in December 1971, city council president William Donald Schaefer, after defeating two African American candidates, was sworn in as mayor.[23] Schaefer remained as mayor until trading that office for the governorship in 1986.

Superintendent Patterson and Mayor Schaefer clashed repeatedly. A reporter observed that city hall seemed to "scrutinize" Patterson "much more assiduously than it had his predecessors," and Patterson was aware of it.[24] Moreover, Patterson's willingness to develop close ties with former black mayoral candidates and militant black leaders did not endear him to the new mayor. Patterson's decentralization plan, which was designed to give community leaders a significant role in education decision making, antagonized Schaefer. And the superintendent's reorganization of the central administration further alarmed City Hall. Several high-ranking white administrators were reassigned; many were replaced by African Americans. The so-called "Patterson massacre" affected about 450 administrators.[25] As Kenneth K. Wong notes, it was hoped that Patterson's appointment would "quell racial tension in the school system."[26] Ironically, Patterson's tenure turned out to be the most racially acrimonious in the school system's modern history.[27]

Three major crises in 1974 kept the issue of race and the schools on the local agenda. First, the teachers went out on strike over salary in February 1974. Many Baltimore teachers complained about low salaries, poor working conditions, and crowded classrooms. They demanded an 11 percent increase in fringe benefits and salary. The strike lasted for over a month and literally closed the schools. Mayor Schaefer took a strong stance against the teachers. Giving in to the teachers, Schaefer calculated, would lead other municipal unions to seek similar raises, and the result would be a large increase in the tax rate. A higher tax rate, Schaefer argued, would only lead to more white flight and even higher tax rates. Edward Berkowitz has argued that the strike took on a racial aspect as it appeared that Mayor Schaefer feared alienating middle-class whites at the expense of a black school system:

> Indeed, the entire episode of the school strike could be read as a betrayal of the city's blacks by the white entrenched political leadership. The city hesitated to spend more money on the school system for fear of making the city, already on the verge of a black majority, even more black. Preservation of the property tax in an effort to maintain a good business climate triumphed over a proper concern for the education of the city's school children.[28]

The teachers eventually settled for a 6 percent salary increase. Although the teachers did not receive all they had demanded, the strike established the Baltimore Teachers Union (BTU) as a powerful player in city politics.

Next, as city leaders were dealing with the strike, word leaked that federal officials were mandating school officials to desegregate the students and faculties or risk losing approximately $23 million in federal grants. According to Berkowitz, the federal mandate "further exposed the many racial tensions within the school system."[29] The federal desegregation order, and the desegregation plan that the school board eventually adopted, led to massive demonstrations by white students and parents. A look at enrollment figures shows that thousands of whites left the system in 1974 and 1975.

If there were any doubts left that a racial crisis existed in the BCPS, they were squashed in August 1974 when hundreds of Patterson's supporters packed a school board meeting after it was learned that the white majority on the board was clandestinely planning the superintendent's dismissal. When a motion to fire Patterson was put to a vote, chaos erupted. "An angry crowd briefly surged onto the stage, ripping out microphone cords and slamming papers and books about the meeting table."[30] The *Sun* reported that one black board member "leapt from his seat" and "nose-to-nose" screamed at one of his white colleagues: "There ain't gonna be no vote. You don't get no vote tonight."[31] Congressman Parren Mitchell, an ardent supporter of Patterson and the first black to represent Maryland in the U.S. House of Representatives, angrily denounced the attempted move to oust him, saying, "Never have I seen the racist scum come through as it has tonight."[32] The city school crisis had become a clear-cut racial issue.

The board was unable to remove Patterson quickly. A black judge, Joseph C. Howard, ordered the board to grant Patterson a public hearing. But by January 1975 Mayor Schaefer had appointed new school board members to replace the expired terms of four members. Three of Schaefer's new appointees were black, giving blacks a majority on the school board for the first time in history. A white attorney was appointed president of the board. Acknowledging the racial tensions prevalent in the BCPS, the editors of the *Sun* observed that the appointment of a white board president, "should serve to allay white fears of a black-dominated School Board during the touchy period when a high school desegregation plan is imminent."[33] The *Sun*, an important molder of elite opinion, applauded the makeup of the new board: "It is obvious that . . . Mr. Schaefer has chosen Baltimoreans with solid community credentials who are not given to predetermined positions or readily identified with pressure groups and who are more likely to vote along educational lines than racial lines."[34] With the extension of Schaefer's authority into the school board, Patterson was removed in July 1975.

SCHOOLS AND JOBS: PATRONAGE POLITICS AND RACE

During the 1970s and 1980s, an enduring alignment and relationship developed between African American professional educators, city hall, and the school system. The department of education increasingly became identified as the black agency of city government. The public school system offered black professional educators control over substantial benefits in the form of jobs, fringe benefits, and various business and professional opportunities, opportunities that had been severely limited before 1970.

Mayor Schaefer and the BCPS

Determined to bring calm to the school system, Schaefer and other white elites reached an accommodation with black leaders about control of the school system. A tacit agreement was made that consolidated African American administrative control of the school system.[35] African Americans thus would control the key positions in the education arena. In July 1975 the school board named John L. Crew as the second black superintendent. Crew was an insider, a twenty-year veteran of the system who had taken pains to remain neutral in the controversy over Superintendent Patterson. In Crew, Mayor Schaefer had a "more cooperative black professional" who "accepted as legitimate strong mayoral leadership."[36] Alice Pinderhughes succeeded Crew in 1982 and retired in 1988 shortly after Schaefer was elected governor of Maryland. Pinderhughes gained the superintendent's position after a forty-five-year career in the BCPS and owed her appointment to Mayor Schaefer. He persuaded the school board to elevate her and then encouraged the state superintendent, David W. Hornbeck, to waive a state requirement that the city's school superintendent have a master's degree, which Pinderhughes had not earned.[37]

Mayor Schaefer's authority over the school system was key in prolonging his hold on the mayor's office as Baltimore's population became a black majority. His black supporters were appointed as school administrators and principals and were given other professional jobs as rewards for their political support. African Americans were also hired in lower level positions as janitors, secretaries, and teachers' aides. As Wong has described it:

> Increasingly, the school district resembled a patronage base. Personnel that orchestrated mayoral activities were put on the school system's pay-roll. Central office administrators critical of the administration were either demoted or transferred. Not infrequently school resources were allocated in a politicized manner to serve as warnings to dissenters at the school building level.[38]

African Americans gained administrative control over the schools but became more answerable to Schaefer.

Public education, however, was not the chief concern of the Schaefer administration. Schaefer focused his energy, and the city's revenues, on downtown redevelopment.[39] Indeed, during the Schaefer years, spending on the schools and other city agencies contracted in order to help finance downtown redevelopment.[40] Superintendents Crew and Pinderhughes respected Schaefer's budget priorities. "School expenditures, which required the approval of city hall, were subjected to careful scrutiny by administrators who reported directly to the mayor's chief aide."[41] In an interview, Pinderhughes candidly admitted that she "never submitted a budget request to the board without first consulting Schaefer."[42]

Inadequate spending on the city's public schools had a significant effect on the quality of instruction.[43] As a result of low spending levels, the schools operated with a shortage of books and low staffing levels in libraries and counseling offices. Eliminated from the school budget were enrichment programs, such as art and music. In addition, low teacher pay hampered the city's efforts to recruit high quality teachers.[44] The influential *Baltimore 2000* report, issued shortly before Schaefer resigned to become governor, condemned the city's schools:

> In 1960, Baltimore's public schools, though overcrowded, were generally regarded as good. Some had quite distinguished records. By 1970 decline was well under way. The system is now widely condemned as ineffective,

undisciplined and dangerous. The fact remains that, on leaving the school system, very few Baltimore students have been pressed to the limit of their intellectual potential, many are unprepared for any but menial employment and some are unready for jobs of any kind.[45]

Critics and supporters agree that Mayor Schaefer's handling of school issues reflected his governing style: he preferred quick, decisive action aimed at visible problems and tended to eschew more complex policy issues. Moreover, as a city council member in the 1950s and 1960s, he had watched as previous mayors struggled with challenges (and the racial controversies) in the school system. In Mayor Schaefer's opinion, the school system was a political land mine, and heavy involvement in school affairs offered few rewards. Schaefer typically left school policy (other than the budget) to trusted associates on the school board and to African American administrators who owed their appointments to city hall.

Bonds of Personalism

In addition to establishing educational policy, the people at the top of the BCPS have authority over thousands of jobs. Wilbur Rich, in his study of school politics in Detroit, Gary, and Newark, has argued that "schools are one of the major linchpins of the urban economy."[46] With their huge budgets and the authority to enter contracts for the purchase of goods and services and to hire thousands of workers, big-city school systems are important to the local economy.

Despite declining revenues, the Baltimore school budget is still significant. In 1995, the BCPS' total budget was over $629 million. With the outmigration of manufacturing jobs and declining employment opportunities in wholesale and retail trade in the city center, the BCPS has emerged as a principal employer. Indeed, the public school system is the largest employer in Baltimore city (see Table 5.1). In 1995 the BCPS employed 11,414 workers. The largest private employers are the local electric and gas utility, Baltimore Gas and Electric Company, with 8,000 employees, and Johns Hopkins Hospital with 6,500 workers. As an employer, the BCPS is labor intensive, offering jobs across the entire spectrum of class and occupation.

There is also a racial dimension to the school system's employment base. African Americans now hold over 70 percent of the 11,000 jobs. Due largely to a diminished industrial base, continued racial discrimination in the private sector, and decades of political patronage, the public schools have historically provided an avenue through which African Americans could find employment, and a large sector of the African American community—particularly the middle class—continues to work in the public schools.[47]

By 1986, at the end of Schaefer's long tenure, Baltimore's top school administrators were a group of middle-class African Americans who had worked their way up the system's bureaucracy. Many of them—like then-superintendent Alice

Table 5.1. Baltimore's Largest Private-sector Employers, 1995

Firm	Nature of Business	No. of Employees
Baltimore Gas & Electric Company	Electric & gas utility	8,000
Johns Hopkins Hospital	Health care	6,500
Giant Food, Inc.	Retail food/pharmacy	6,139
Bell Atlantic	Telecommunications	6,083
AT&T	Telecommunications	4,000
Nations Bank Corp.	Banking	4,000
Sinai Hospital of Baltimore	Health care	3,001
USF&G Corp.	Insurance	2,287
First Maryland Bancorp	Commercial banking	2,075
Baltimore Sun Co.	Newspaper	1,818
Baltimore City Public Schools		11,414

Source: Greater Baltimore Committee, "Largest Private-sector Employers in Baltimore Area," Baltimore, 1995.

Pinderhughes—had gone through the turmoil of the 1970s when racial and class antagonisms ran high. They had survived the 1980s when the city's contribution to the education department grew smaller in real terms. They had listened in the 1970s and early 1980s as civic and business leaders began to criticize the schools as ineffective and dangerous. And many of them could recall when the *Baltimore Sun* had carried uplifting stories about the BCPS' accomplishments and how the newspaper's coverage had changed in the 1970s when it began to print news stories, and occasionally a series of feature articles, about the system's problems and failures.

A demographic snapshot of the top ten administrators in 1995 is revealing (see Table 5.2). Eighty percent of the top ten are African Americans; 60 percent are women. The top administrators have extensive experience in education. Significantly, seven of them have spent almost their entire career as educators in the BCPS. In other words, these are men and women who worked their way through the system, perhaps as teachers, then principals, and then central-staff administrators. These senior administrators have been together for most of their careers. In 1988 a close observer described the BCPS' administrators as a "tightly knit group of survivors" who controlled power in the school bureaucracy.[48]

A similar pattern is found among the entire professional staff—teachers, counselors, librarians, principals, and assistant principals. In 1993, 63 percent of the professional employees were African American.[49] Teachers in the BCPS are a closely knit group who have long years of experience in the city's public schools. Statewide, Baltimore City has one of the largest proportions of teachers with twenty-one years or more of experience; nearly 35 percent of the teachers in the BCPS have over twenty-one years. By way of comparison, the statewide average

Table 5.2. Demographics of Top Ten Administrators, Baltimore City Public Schools, 1995

Position	Race/Gender	Years in Education	Years in BCPS
Superintendent	B/M	31	4
Deputy superintendent	B/F	34	3
Chief of staff	B/F	30	25
Asst. area supt.	B/F	28	21
Asst. area supt.	B/F	28	28
Asst. area supt.	B/M	36	36
Asst. area supt.	W/M	20	20
Asst. area supt.	W/F	32	32
Asst. area supt.	B/F	27	27

Source: Department of Personnel, Baltimore City Public Schools, 1995.

is 28 percent. The BCPS also has the smallest percentage of teachers (22.5 percent) with less than ten years of experience.

With over one-third of the teachers having twenty-one years or more of experience in the BCPS, a large proportion of them—like their colleagues in the central administration—have been around since the tumultuous 1970s. They have not only worked together for decades, but they have also developed a personal affinity—a kind of personal bond. These "bonds of personalism" did not begin—nor do they end—at the central administration or at the school site.[50] The majority of the city's teachers and administrators share similar middle-class backgrounds. Many of Baltimore's black educators attended the same colleges and universities. Many of them (such as Alice Pinderhughes, for example) graduated from Coppin State College or Morgan State University, two historically black institutions located in Baltimore. Moreover, many of them are members of the same fraternities and sororities. Reportedly, when Alice Pinderhughes was superintendent, her sorority, Alpha Kappa Alpha, was well represented among the professional staff.[51] As one top administrator stated in a 1988 interview, "You've got to recognize a little bit of tradition in terms of blacks. Many of us went to black colleges and universities, and the social outlet there was the fraternities and sororities. That was the orientation for us."[52]

The bonds of personalism are further strengthened by the fact that many teachers and administrators attend the same middle-class black churches. Union Baptist Church and Bethel African Methodist Episcopal Church are two of Baltimore's most prominent African American churches whose congregants include principals, teachers, administrators, and other school system personnel. They are also two of the most influential churches in city politics.[53]

THE CHALLENGE OF SCHOOL REFORM IN BALTIMORE

What does this context mean for educational reform in Baltimore in the 1990s? The political events and shared experiences of the 1960s, 1970s, and 1980s have left important legacies that influence how Baltimore leaders perceive and respond to educational problems today. I illustrate this by examining Baltimore's three-year experience with a private firm hired to manage nine of the city's schools.

Mayor Schmoke and the Challenge of School Reform

Kurt L. Schmoke's 1987 election consolidated school reform on the local agenda. From the beginning of his administration, it was clear that Schmoke intended to play a more active role in school affairs than Mayor Schaefer had. Schmoke's vision for the schools included site-based management and the involvement of outside interests in educational policymaking.[54]

In 1989, after rejecting the initial choice of the school board's majority for superintendent, Schmoke asked the board to appoint Richard Hunter to succeed the retiring Alice Pinderhughes. Hunter came to Baltimore from North Carolina (the first superintendent recruited from outside Baltimore since Roland Patterson). Hunter, however, turned out not to be a strong supporter of site-based management. He and Mayor Schmoke clashed repeatedly. In December 1990, citing Hunter's lukewarm support for site-based decision making, Schmoke asked the school board not to renew his contract.

In August 1991 the board named Walter G. Amprey to replace Hunter. Amprey is a Baltimore native, a graduate of the city's schools and Morgan State University who started his career as an educator in the BCPS. In 1973 he moved to neighboring Baltimore County and eventually became a well-regarded associate superintendent. While working in the Baltimore County schools, Amprey maintained contact with school administrators, teachers, and black leaders in Baltimore City. In a sense, Amprey arrived in his new job as both an insider and an outsider.

By the time Superintendent Amprey took over, Mayor Schmoke had become frustrated by the slow pace of change in the schools. Well into the end of Schmoke's first term, the BCPS had reformed very little and Baltimore's students continued to perform poorly. A study of the management of the BCPS, released in 1992, found that many of the systems' school-based and central-office administrators were incompetent and that a "culture" existed in the school system that did not support "effective management."[55] Perhaps the best indication of Schmoke's frustration with the quality of the schools, according to local observers, was the mayor's decision in 1992 to transfer his sixth-grade daughter out of the BCPS and into a private school.[56]

Contracting Out as a School Reform Strategy

In 1992 Baltimore gained national attention when school officials, with Mayor Schmoke's support, hired a private firm, Educational Alternatives, Incorporated (EAI), to operate nine of its public schools (eight elementary schools and one middle school). Schmoke believed that EAI could show that public personnel, using private management techniques, could improve performance and the quality of education in the BCPS. He also saw EAI as a way around the teachers' union and the school bureaucracy, which were finding ways to "slow down" and "choke" efforts to decentralize the schools. Moreover, Schmoke viewed private management of the nine schools as consistent with his goal of giving schools more autonomy. Ultimately, Superintendent Amprey became an ardent supporter of EAI.

EAI is the brainchild of its chief executive officer, John Golle.[57] A prosperous business executive, Golle founded EAI in 1986 after more than twenty years as a salesman. Prior to the Baltimore contract, EAI ran two private schools in Minnesota and Arizona and one public school in Miami. EAI's trademark instructional model, known as the Tesseract method, relies heavily on computers, individualized educational plans for each student, and heavy parental involvement. The model also calls for a second adult in the each classroom to intensify teaching and to lower student-teacher ratios.

EAI officials promised to improve student performance and to make a profit, using no more money than the school system spent per pupil and keeping the existing teachers and staff. Under the terms of the contract, the school system retained authority over the assignment of all professional staff, although EAI could recommend assignments and transfers and set final staffing levels. EAI, however, could hire its own paraprofessionals—teachers' aides—and transfer those employed by the BCPS. The five-year contract could be terminated at any time with a ninety days' notice.

When the contract was announced, a number of Baltimore's civic and political leaders praised the decision. The editors of the *Sun* opined that Mayor Schmoke, the school board, and the city's new school superintendent "should be applauded for being willing to try this new approach."[58] Business leaders, who had long advocated implementing private management techniques in the operation of the schools, liked the idea of having a business firm operating public schools. Although soon to turn hostile, the BTU had been impressed by EAI's record in Miami. The BTU president appeared in public session before the school board to endorse the contract.[59]

EAI got off to a decent start in Baltimore. The schools underwent extensive renovations: the buildings were painted, new carpeting installed, broken windowpanes replaced, leaky faucets fixed, broken toilets repaired, and rubble-strewn schoolyards were cleaned and landscaped. Teachers and principals in the schools were pleased with the additional resources EAI provided: bright new tables and chairs in each classroom, a telephone on each teacher's desk, and a working copier in each school. Students and parents were excited about the new computers—four in each classroom and a new computer lab in each school. Initial reports showed that attendance increased.[60]

Things quickly turned sour, however, when one of the school system's most powerful constituents, the teachers union, withdrew its support. After EAI transferred ninety teachers' aides from the Tesseract schools and replaced them with less experienced, and less costly, recent college graduates, the BTU launched an aggressive campaign to kill the experiment. The practice of having neighborhood people work as teachers' aides was a holdover from the 1960s when Mayor D'Alesandro began using Title I monies to hire people from the surrounding communities to work in the classrooms. The BTU questioned the wisdom of replacing experienced teachers' aides—people who lived near the schools and were among the few who held jobs in those neighborhoods—in favor of college interns who were willing to work for less money and no health benefits. EAI officials argued that the interns, all of whom were college graduates, were better qualified than the BTU's teachers' aides.

The episode concerning the teachers' aides—combined with EAI's earlier decision to reassign union custodians from the nine schools and replace them with nonunion janitors—convinced union officers that EAI's strategy was to save money and make a profit by replacing relatively expensive union personnel with less costly nonunion personnel. It also heightened the BTU's concern about the long-term job security of its membership. In response, the BTU boycotted EAI's teacher-training sessions. Mayor Schmoke eventually had to step in to negotiate an agreement that left some aides in the nine schools (some EAI classrooms thus had three aides) and that found jobs elsewhere in the school system for the rest.

BUILD, which in 1983 helped mobilize community support for school reform and worked closely with Mayor Schmoke on several policy issues, took a strong stance against the EAI experiment. A BUILD leader told the mayor, "We will fight you on this because the whole thing is contrary to public education."[61] BUILD leaders asserted that EAI's major concern was not schooling but generating a profit. It should be emphasized that the teachers' union is a constituent member of BUILD. Irene Dandridge, the immediate past president of the BTU, noted in an interview that her union joined BUILD in the early 1980s because "we wanted to align ourselves with a group that had some power. It was that simple."[62] In addition, the Interdenominational Ministerial Alliance (IMA), an organization representing about 166 black ministers, joined with BUILD and BTU to stop EAI.

In 1993 I interviewed several African American ministers, many of them active in BUILD and the IMA, in an attempt to discern their concerns about Tesseract and the reasoning behind their opposition to EAI. The interviews revealed the perception that some educators could lose their jobs, which concerned many church leaders. As one BUILD leader pointed out,

The fact is that many of our major attractions—civic center, convention center, the Baltimore Arena, etc., operate with employees who are not city employees. Employees now are temporary or part-time, or employees of a contract company. It destroys some of the employment base of the city. Of course, because Tesseract is a move towards privatization of the school system, and as more schools are turned over to Tesseract, Tesseract then has the authority to hire and fire, to reallocate, to reassign employees at will, and that's very threatening to a person. That's their livelihood in the school system.[63]

Later, I tried to gauge the extent to which the concern about the job security of black educators might compete with the concern of improving education for the city's children. When I asked the same minister what BUILD's position would be if a reputable, independent evaluation found that EAI significantly improved student performance in the nine schools, he answered, "We'd still be leery of the privatization of a traditional government function."[64] Most of the African American ministers responded similarly. The unions had a powerful ally in their fight to end the EAI experiment: black church leaders.

Political opponents of Mayor Schmoke also joined the chorus of opposition. Mary Pat Clarke, then the president of the city council and later an unsuccessful challenger to Schmoke in the 1995 mayoral election, was a vocal opponent of EAI. As a member of the Board of Estimates, Clarke voted against the EAI contract. Other city council members also criticized the experiment. The city council eventually voted to urge Mayor Schmoke to delay any expansion of EAI before an independent evaluation of the experiment was completed.[65] A columnist for the *Sun* explained the opposition:

> The Baltimore Teachers Union has bitterly opposed Tesseract because the contract threatens union bargaining power and EAI cuts costs by hiring lower-paid but better-educated non-union teaching interns. The Interdenominational Ministerial Alliance and Baltimoreans United in Leadership Development (BUILD) oppose Tesseract because they fear they'll lose political influence over the schools. Administrators and bureaucrats oppose Tesseract because it will ultimately cost many of them their jobs. Some city politicians oppose the program because they pander to these constituencies.[66]

Lurking beneath the surface of the opposition to EAI was also a concern that the privatization meant a shift in racial control of the schools. Although Mayor Schmoke and Superintendent Amprey did not face the vocal opposition from African American residents that Washington, DC superintendent Franklin Smith faced when he sought to promote EAI management of fifteen Washington schools, racial concerns were not absent from the Baltimore case.[67] Given the history of racial politics in the city, especially in local school affairs, the fact that the head of EAI was a white businessman was not lost to many black educators and the larger African American community. Take, for instance, the comments of another African American minister:

> I'm against [EAI] because, first of all, it demoralizes and diminishes the talents and effectiveness of teachers that are already present in our school system. . . . Number two, it also says that persons are not quality-equipped to teach and I don't believe that. I don't see some midwestern white corporate firm coming in that knows nothing about our city leading us.[68]

Another black respondent, a former teacher and retired administrator in the BCPS, stated emphatically her opposition to EAI in racial terms:

> Walter [Amprey] likes Tesseract. I ain't gonna never want no white folks to come in and run my school system for me, but that's because he and I are different people. He feels good about it, and if he feels good about it, I have to feel good about it for him, not for me. It's helping him achieve his goals. It ain't helping me achieve my goal as a community leader. They ain't gonna put no Tesseract up here in my school, I can tell you that. The school in my community, while I'm president of that neighborhood association, no Tesseract is coming in there, because there's nobody white that can come in there and run my school system with a value system far removed from the people who they serve.[69]

Although the race issue never became a major part of the public debate, John Golle attempted to allay criticism that EAI, whose top executives were white, was profiting at the expense of the African American community. In 1995, as opposition to Tesseract intensified, EAI hired two African American executives from the Xerox Corporation and gave them visible roles in the Baltimore experiment. William Goins, a graduate of Morgan State, became the second-in-command at EAI. Ramon Harris, an African American, was hired to oversee the day-to-day operation of the Baltimore experiment.[70]

The End of EAI

EAI's demise became apparent in 1994. The first set of standardized test scores showed that the Tesseract experiment failed to improve student performance significantly in the two years since EAI had begun managing the schools.[71] Moreover, financial analysis showed that despite EAI's initial claims, the Tesseract schools were receiving more money per pupil than the other schools in the system.[72] The release of the test scores intensified critics' opposition and led the BTU to call for an immediate end to the contract. With an election year looming, Mayor Schmoke was forced to announce that EAI's fate depended primarily on student test scores and the results of an independent evaluation.

Ultimately the success or failure of Tesseract is going to be determined for most people by the academic performance of the children. . . . Our system has been judged for so long by how our kids do on these tests that we cannot ignore the fact that test scores are going to be a significant determinant in the success or failure.[73]

In August 1995 the first outside evaluation of the EAI experiment was completed. The report, conducted by the University of Maryland, Baltimore County, found that the Tesseract schools showed little difference from comparable city-run schools on test results, attendance, parental involvement, or even cleanliness.[74] Three years into the experiment, the evaluation found that student scores on the Comprehensive Test of Basic Skills were about the same as in 1992, the year of EAI's arrival, for the Tesseract schools, the control schools, and the city as a whole. Significantly, the evaluation found that Baltimore City was spending about 11 percent more (approximately $628) per student in the Tesseract schools than in comparison schools.

EAI's management of the Tesseract schools ended on March 4, 1996, a year and three months short of the original five-year contract. In announcing the end of the experiment, Mayor Schmoke and Superintendent Amprey pointed to the researchers' financial information. The report asserted that "the promise that EAI could improve instruction without spending more than Baltimore City was spending on schools has been discredited."[75] In actuality, the contract termination came after Mayor Schmoke and John Golle failed to come to an agreement on a renegotiated contract. Schmoke offered to continue the contract "at a rate 16 percent less than EAI was projected to receive under the average per-pupil cost formula."[76] Golle refused. Mayor Schmoke maintained that the city, facing a budget deficit, could not afford to keep EAI. Superintendent Amprey told reporters, "We have only so many dollars."[77]

Philip Abrams argues that events are "transformation device[s] between past and future" that are significant "markers of transition."[78] The course of events in Baltimore in the late 1960s and early 1970s marked a decisive conjunction of actions that helps shed some light on school affairs in the 1990s. First, as white students became a minority in the schools, white residents and civic leaders were more reluctant to identify with the BCPS. The BCPS began to attract criticism from individuals who charged that the schools were unsafe and ineffective. "The criticisms," as Edward Berkowitz has observed, "were not unrelated to the' fact that Baltimore was becoming a black city."[79] The teachers' strike, the controversy surrounding desegregation, and the botched attempt to fire the first African American superintendent exposed the racial tensions within the school system. The strike also established the teachers' union as a powerful player in city politics.

Mike Bowler has described this period as "the low-water mark" in the BCPS' history.[80] Finally, the appointment of Roland Patterson marked the transition from white to African American administrative leadership over the school system. The school system became the largest municipal institution under the direct administration of African Americans. The subsequent permanent superintendents have been African Americans. In short, the highly charged political atmosphere of the 1960s and early 1970s significantly altered political relationships around school affairs in Baltimore. These alignments foreshadowed relations for the next twenty to thirty years.

In a seminal article, Robert Salisbury has argued for a greater role for mayors in public education.[81] Salisbury believes that a mayor would "play a major role in giving over-all program and fiscal direction" to school affairs. The Baltimore experience suggests that it is not that simple, however. Under Mayor Schaefer, the BCPS increasingly was viewed as an institution ripe for political patronage. The true function of public education—mastery of sufficient knowledge and skills to assume the rights and responsibilities of citizenship—was lost during the Schaefer era. Even in the diplomatic language of the *Baltimore 2000* report, the recognition that Schaefer did little to help the schools is clear. Future mayors, the report suggested, should play a more substantial role. "The mayor appoints the school board and can set its course. No substantial renovation of the school system can be accomplished without his deep interest, steady pressure, and willingness to apply the political weight of his office to insure results."[82]

One cannot understand the politics of school reform in Baltimore without first understanding the important and sometimes defining role the school system plays in the city's economy. The school system is the largest employer in Baltimore, and a large sector of the black community is on its payroll. As Wilbur C. Rich puts it: "The school pie feeds many families, and slicing it is a major event within the local economy."[83]

Baltimore's experiment with EAI demonstrates how critical concerns about jobs and job security also play a major role in big-city school affairs. EAI's decision to transfer union-affiliated teachers' aides and custodians illustrates BCPS' significance to the local economy. The teachers' union's opposition to the experiment crystallized long before any evaluation of EAI's capacity to improve student performance was carried out. As the city's largest employer, the BCPS is a source of thousands of jobs. In Baltimore's declining economy, this is no small matter. In her comparative study of teachers' unions and contract provisions in six suburban, rural, and urban school districts, Susan Johnson found that union contract provisions tied to job security were enforced more stringently in urban districts where the local economy was in decline.[84] "The expansion or decline of enrollments and the local economy seemed to influence the progress of negotiations and the prominence of the contract. Where there were fewer students and fewer dollars to divide among all local employees, negotiations became more strained and contract provisions tied to job security were enforced more stringently district-wide."[85] Throughout her study, Johnson found that "Metropolis" (Philadelphia) always represented the "extreme," "unique," or "important exception" when it came to negotiating and enforcing contract provisions tied to job security. In big cities with declining economies, such as Baltimore, and where displaced school workers cannot easily take jobs outside of education, union leaders and their allies can be expected to oppose initiatives perceived to threaten job security.[86]

The institution of African American administrative control over the BCPS was firmly established during the Schaefer era. Over 80 percent of the students are African American, as are 70 percent of the school system's employees. The unspoken political reality is that politicians and civic leaders (blacks and whites) have come to view the education department as the black agency of municipal government. For the people who work in the schools, this is "their" system. Any criticism of the system, especially by individuals outside the schools, is looked upon with suspicion and has the effect of strengthening the "bonds of personalism" that exist among the thousands of administrators, teachers, and other system employees. As one top administrator said, "What bothers me is that there are a lot of people outside the schools who believe they can run the schools better than the professionals. We are always criticized for what we don't do. People ought to give us credit for having some ability and some skills."[87]

The political influence of black professional educators in Baltimore is further bolstered by the fact that many attended the same colleges and universities, are members of the same fraternities and sororities, and often are active members in major church congregations. Black teachers and administrators are prominent and active members of the black church, and they are supported by a powerful ally — African American churches and their ministers. The various economic, political, and social linkages among black professional educators mean that the school bureaucracy in Baltimore has an especially broad and powerful constituency upon which they can draw. Such a network magnifies their impact.

What lessons do we draw, then, about school reform from the Baltimore experience? First, the history of school affairs in Baltimore suggests that big-city school reform is context sensitive. One cannot simply craft a reform idea and initiate it in a community without considering its history and the relationship between major players and their motivations. Reform ideas must take into account the history and political context of a community.

Second, school reformers cannot ignore the fact that in many economically distressed cities the public school system is an important source of jobs. The Baltimore case suggests that for many teachers, administrators, and other school system employees, concerns about improving education for children may coexist and even compete with concerns about the viability of the school system as a source of wages, professional development, and economic advancement. In an atmosphere of corporate downsizing, mergers, and acquisitions, the thousands of positions in the school system are vital to Baltimore's economy. School employees' concerns about job security, as well as elected officials' desires to provide services and patronage to their constituents, put an extra burden on school reformers in Baltimore.

Third, the Baltimore case suggests that the widespread concern about jobs is not simply an expression of self-interest. Although self-interest is very important, it must be understood that what is happening is more than a small group of selfish elites trying to protect their privileged position. The economic role of the school system, and especially of black professional educators, is significant within the African American community. There is a general sense within Baltimore's black community that black professional educators have a direct positive social impact on the local community. Thus, for many black community leaders the public school system plays what Robert Merton has called a "latent function" as a black employment regime.[88] The unwillingness of black clergy to attack black professional educators reveals this understanding.

Public choice theorists, conservative analysts, and other observers have emphasized the role that the public school bureaucracy can play in blocking school reform.[89] The Baltimore case, however, shows that historical and contemporary forces make race an important part of this story that often goes untold. Because racism impeded their ability to penetrate stable and lucrative occupations in commercial and industrial organizations, African Americans have depended disproportionately on public-sector employment.[90] Today a large segment of Baltimore's black community, particularly the middle class, works in the public schools.[91] The role of public schools as large employers affects the politics of school reform in all large districts, but the fact that African Americans occupy important positions in the decision-making apparatus and in political life and that a majority of the administrators, teachers, other school-system employees, and students are African American gives school reform a particular racial dimension.

NOTES

1. Kurt L. Schmoke, "Inaugural Address" (Office of the Mayor, Baltimore) December 8, 1987, pp. 7–8.

2. Fellicia Hunter, "Mayor Says Schools' Woes Still 'Serious,' " *Sun,* October 20, 1996, p. B3.

3. Joseph L. Arnold, "Baltimore: Southern Culture and a Northern Economy," in *Snowbelt Cities: Metropolitan Politics in the Northeast and Midwest Since World War II,* ed. Richard M. Bernard (Bloomington: Indiana University Press, 1990), pp. 25–39.

4. Sherry H. Olson, *Baltimore: The Building of an American City* (Baltimore: Johns Hopkins University Press, 1980); George H. Callcott, *Maryland and America: 1940–1980* (Baltimore: Johns Hopkins University Press, 1985); Robert Brugger, *Maryland: A Middle Temperament* (Baltimore: Johns Hopkins University Press, 1988).

5. Ira Reid, *The Negro Community of Baltimore,* report of a study conducted for the Baltimore Urban League, 1935 (Baltimore).

6. Robert L. Crain, *The Politics of School Desegregation* (Chicago: National Opinion Research Center, 1968), pp. 75–84; Harry Bard, "Observations on Desegregation in Baltimore: Three Years Later," *Teachers College Record* 59, no. 5 (February 1958): 268–81; Eric M. David, "Blurring the Color Line: The Desegregation of the Baltimore Public Schools, 1954–1994," *Urban Review* 26, no. 4 (Summer 1994): 243–55.

7. Quoted in Reed Sarratt, *The Ordeal of Desegregation* (New York: Harper and Row, 1966), p. 79.

8. Ibid.

9. Ibid., pp. 110–11.

10. Sharon Perlman Krefetz, *Welfare Policy Making and City Politics* (New York: Praeger Publishers, 1976), pp. 31–32.

11. Ibid., p. 34. A split among the key factions of the Democratic party was an important factor that aided McKeldin's election.

12. Ibid., p. 35.

13. Peter Bachrach and Morton S. Baratz, *Power and Poverty: Theory and Practice* (New York: Oxford University Press, 1970), p. 81.

14. Mike Bowler, *Lessons of Change: Baltimore Schools in the Modern Era* (Baltimore: A report commissioned by the Fund for Educational Excellence, 1991), p. 11.

15. Ibid.

16. Ibid., p. 13.

17. Quoted in Mike Bowler, "Board Stands up to Be Counted," *Sun*, February 21, 1996, p. B2.

18. Bowler, *Lessons of Change*, p. 9.

19. William Ryan, *Blaming the Victim* (New York: Pantheon Books, 1971), pp. 55–59; Estelle Fuchs, "How Teachers Learn to Help Children Fail," *Transaction* 5 (September 1968): 45–49; and Robert Rosenthal and Lenore Jacobson, *Pygmalion in the Classroom* (New York: Holt, Rinehart and Winston, 1968).

20. Nora Frenkiel, "A Last Hurrah: Tommy D'Alesandro Found There Was Life After Big-City Politics," *Sun*, August 26, 1990, p. H1.

21. Quoted in Marion Orr, "Urban Regimes and Human Capital Policies: A Study of Baltimore," *Journal of Urban Affairs* 14, no. 2 (1992): 180–81.

22. Mike Bowler, "Patterson Is Hired by School Board," *Sun*, July 17, 1971, p. B18.

23. On Schaefer's election, see Marion Orr, "The Struggle for Black Empowerment in Baltimore: Electoral Control and Governing Coalitions," in *Racial Politics in American Cities,* ed. Rufus P. Browning, Dale Rogers Marshall, and David Tabb, 2d ed. (New York: Longman Press, 1997), pp. 201–19, and G. James Fleming, *Baltimore's Failure to Elect a Black Mayor in 1971* (Washington, DC: Joint Center for Political Studies, 1972).

24. Bowler, *Lessons of Change*, p. 14.

25. Ibid., p. 13.

26. Kenneth K. Wong, *City Choices: Housing and Education* (Albany: State University of New York Press, 1990), p. 87.

27. Patterson's tenure is discussed in Hugh J. Scott, *The Black Superintendent: Messiah or Scapegoat?* (Washington, DC: Howard University Press, 1980), pp. 102–18, and Barbara L. Jackson, *Balancing Act: The Political Role of the Urban School Superintendent* (Washington, DC: Joint Center for Political and Economic Studies, 1996).

28. Edward Berkowitz, "Baltimore's Public Schools in a Time of Transition," paper, George Washington University, November 15, 1996, p. 16.

29. Ibid., p. 18.

30. Richard Ben Cramer and Antero Pietila, "Board's Whites Try to Fire Patterson," *Sun,* August 9, 1974, p. C1.

31. Ibid.

32. Ibid.

33. Editorial, "Fresh Start for the School Board," *Sun,* January 4, 1975, p. A14.

34. Ibid.

35. In my interviews with key civic leaders, top educational administrators, business executives, and other school activists, some white leaders denied the existence of such an agreement. Many black educators and other black respondents acknowledged that such an agreement was made, however. Of course, this type of "distributional" arrangement is familiar to students of American urban politics. Steve Erie, in his study of the Irish political machines, discusses how machine bosses extended their longevity by distributing a variety of public-sector positions to their fellow Irishmen, who typically got police and fire jobs; teaching positions went to the Jews, and the Italians received jobs in sanitation. See Erie's *Rainbow's End: Irish-Americans and the Dilemmas of Urban Machine Politics, 1840–1985* (Berkeley: University of California Press, 1988), and Dianne M. Pinderhughes, *Race and Ethnicity in Chicago Politics* (Urbana: University of Illinois Press, 1987).

36. Wong, *City Choices,* p. 119.

37. Bowler, *Lessons of Change,* p. 18.

38. Wong, *City Choices,* p. 115.

39. Marc Levine, "Downtown Redevelopment as an Urban Growth Strategy: A Critical Appraisal of the Baltimore Renaissance," *Journal of Urban Affairs* 9 (fall 1987): 103–23.

40. Barbara Vobejda and Gwen Ifill, "Education Issue May Spell Trouble for Schaefer," *Washington Post,* July 28, 1986, p. C1.

41. Wong, *City Choices,* pp. 113–14.

42. Veronica D. DiConti, *Interest Groups and Education Reform* (Lanham, MD: University Press of America, 1996), p. 115.

43. Mayor Schaefer and his supporters were quick to point out that the state government failed adequately to support the city's schools that enrolled the highest proportion of disadvantaged students of Maryland's twenty-four school districts. In 1979 the city sued the state in an effort to revamp Maryland's local school-aid formulas and to increase funding for Baltimore. The city lost the suit, but the legislature subsequently adopted a new funding formula that brought more state funds to the city's schools. On the disparities in state funding for Maryland school districts, see Robert E. Slavin, "Funding Inequities Among Maryland School Districts: What Do They Mean in Practice?" paper, Center for Research on Effective Schooling for Disadvantaged Students, 1991, and the Abell Foundation, "A Growing Inequality: A Report on the Financial Condition of the Baltimore City Public Schools." (Baltimore: Abell Foundation, 1989).

44. Slavin, "Funding Inequities Among Maryland School Districts," pp. 11–18.

45. Peter Szanton, *Baltimore 2000: A Choice of Futures,* report to the Morris Goldseker Foundation, 1986, p. 10.

46. Wilbur C. Rich, *Black Mayors and School Politics: The Failure of Reform in Detroit, Gary, Newark* (New York: Garland Press, 1996).

47. Employment discrimination in Baltimore's private-sector economy is documented in Joint Center for Political and Economic Studies, *Moving Up with Baltimore: Creating Career Ladders for Blacks in the Private Sector* (Washington, DC: Author, 1991); Dewayne

Wickham, *Destiny 2000: The State of Black Baltimore,* report from the Baltimore Urban League, 1987; and United States Commission on Civil Rights, *Greater Baltimore Commitment: A Study of Urban Minority Economic Development* (Washington, DC: GPO, 1983).

48. Will Englund, "Tightly Knit Group of Survivors Controls Power," *Sun,* May 3, 1988, p. 1A.

49. Interestingly, no other department of city government is as thoroughly managed by African Americans. Excluding the education department, African Americans constitute only 50 percent of the municipal workforce. In 1994, 36 percent of the administrative and 37 percent of the professional positions in the Baltimore city government were held by African Americans. There remains a number of city departments that have yet to be headed by an African American. For data on the racial composition of Baltimore's municipal workforce, see Marion Orr, "The Struggle for Black Empowerment," pp. 211–13.

50. I borrowed the term "bonds of personalism" from Alan Rosenthal, *Pedagogues and Power: Teacher Groups in School Politics* (Syracuse, NY: Syracuse University Press, 1969).

51. Englund, "Tightly Knit Group of Survivors Controls Power."

52. Ibid.

53. The pastor of Bethel AME, Dr. Frank M. Reid, is Kurt Schmoke's stepbrother. The Reverend Vernon Dobson, pastor of Union Baptist Church, was active in the civil rights movement in Baltimore and a founding member of BUILD. See Harold McDougall, *Black Baltimore: A Theory of Community* (Philadelphia: Temple University Press, 1993), pp. 123–26, and Eugenia Collier, "House Built on Rock: Union Baptist Church," *Negro History Bulletin* 47, no. 4, (October–December 1984); 3–7.

54. See Marion Orr, "Urban Politics and School Reform: The Case of Baltimore," *Urban Affairs Review* 31 (January 1996); 314–45.

55. Associated Black Charities, *A Report on the Management of the Baltimore City Public Schools,* Baltimore, 1992, pp. 1–5.

56. Michael A. Fletcher, "Mayor May Transfer Daughter," *Sun,* March 28, 1992, p. B1.

57. For a thorough discussion of EAI, its corporate structure and investors and for background on John Golle, see Craig E. Richards, Rima Shore, and Max B. Sawicky, *Risky Business: Private Management of Public Schools* (Washington, DC: Economic Policy Institute, 1996).

58. Editorial, "Schools in Another Dimension," *Sun,* June 11, 1992, p. A12.

59. Galerah Asayesh, "Baltimore Board Weighs Private School Operation," *Sun,* May 17, 1991, p. B1.

60. Mark Bomster, "Nine Schools Start to Mend," *Sun,* November 15, 1992, p. B1.

61. Mark Bomster, "Schmoke Facing Challenge Tonight on School Reform," *Sun,* July 20, 1992, p. B1.

62. Quoted in DiConti, *Interest Groups and Education Reform,* p. 143.

63. Interview with author, September 29, 1993.

64. Ibid.

65. Gary Gately, "Council Members Call for a Delay on EAI Expansion," *Sun,* May 26, 1994, p. A1.

66. Tim Baker, "Reinventing Schools," *Sun,* January 3, 1994, p. A13.

67. Sara Horowitz, "A Public Defeat on Privatization," *Washington Post,* March 3, 1994, p. B1, and Charles Mahtesian, "The Precarious Politics of Privatizing Schools," *Governing* 12 (June 1994): 46–51.

68. Interview with author, September 29, 1993.

69. Interview with author, September 30, 1993.

70. Mike Bowler, "EAI Taps Xerox Executive to Take Over in Baltimore," *Sun,* May 6, 1995, p. Bl.

71. Gary Gately and JoAnna Daemmrich, "EAI Fails to Improve Elementary School Scores," *Sun,* June 17, 1994, p. Al.

72. For a detailed analysis of spending in the Tesseract schools, see Roberts, Shore, and Sawicky, *Risky Business,* pp. 79–124.

73. Gary Gately and JoAnn Daemmrich, "Mayor Links Future of EAI to Test Scores," *Sun,* October 21, 1994, p. Bl.

74. Lois C. Williams and Lawrence E. Leak, *The UMBC Evaluation of the Tesseract Program in Baltimore City* (Baltimore: Center for Educational Research, University of Maryland, Baltimore County, 1995).

75. Ibid., p. 115.

76. Lois C. Williams and Lawrence E. Leak, "School Privatization's First Big Test: EAI in Baltimore," *Educational Leadership* 24, no. 2 (October 1996): 57.

77. Jean Thompson, "City School Board Ends Effort to Privatize," *Sun,* December 1, 1995, p. Al.

78. Philip Abrams, *Historical Sociology* (Ithaca, NY: Cornell University Press, 1982), p. 195.

79. Berkowitz, "Baltimore Public Schools in a Time of Transition," p. 8.

80. Bowler, *Lessons of Change,* p. 14.

81. Robert Salisbury, "Schools and Politics in the Big City," *Harvard Educational Review* 37 (summer 1967): 409.

82. Szanton, *Baltimore 2000,* p. 41.

83. Rich, *Black Mayors and School Politics,* p. 5.

84. Susan Moore Johnson, *Teacher Unions in Schools* (Philadelphia: Temple University Press, 1984).

85. Ibid., p. 168.

86. Caroline Hendrie, "Politics of Jobs in City Schools Hinder Reform," *Education Week,* March 26, 1997, pp. 3–7.

87. Will Englund, "Huge Bureaucracy Drifts Without a Plan," *Sun,* May 1, 1988, p. 1A.

88. Robert K. Merton, *Social Theory and Social Structure* (New York: Free Press, 1967), p. 72.

89. John E. Chubb and Terry M. Moe, *Politics, Markets, and America's Schools* (Washington, DC: Brookings Institution, 1990), and Myron Lieberman, *Beyond Public Education* (New York: Praeger Press, 1986).

90. Martin Carnoy, *Faded Dreams: The Politics and Economics of Race in America* (New York: Cambridge University Press, 1994), pp. 161–63.

91. Between 1915 and 1960, the most numerous among black professionals were teachers. Black ministers were next. See Bart Landry, *The New Black Middle Class* (Berkeley: University of California Press, 1987), p. 51.

6

Grassroots Action in East Brooklyn: A Community Organization Takes Up School Reform

Timothy Ross

Calls for increased parental involvement, more community outreach, and improving the school-community connection are long-standing. Yet despite the reformist zeal for community participation, successful examples of it in inner-city neighborhoods tend to stand out because of their infrequent occurrence. Many observers see low levels of participation as a product of fragmented family structures and a lack of organization in low-income and minority communities. A closer look, however, suggests that deeply entrenched political obstacles often work against community participation. Contrary to the rhetoric of school administrators, teachers' unions, and other educational staff, urban school systems often discourage community and parental involvement in school operations.

The efforts of a community organization, East Brooklyn Congregations (EBC), to reform education in a section of Brooklyn, New York, will be explored.[1] The EBC experience shows that organizing around education can lead to some impressive achievements. The group implemented a plan establishing two new, small public high schools that have EBC members as principals and that incorporate a strong community involvement component. Still, EBC struggles with problems beyond the school level relating to teacher recruitment, the poor preparation of incoming students, building space, and union contracts. On the primary grade level, the group's efforts have faced stiff resistance. Despite a structure of governance intended to promote community participation, EBC has had little success in advancing less ambitious initiatives. Some background information will place the study in context.

EAST BROOKLYN AND EBC

East Brooklyn, which consists of the neighborhoods of Brownsville, Bushwick, and East New York, has been home to a high-poverty, predominantly minority population for over thirty-five years. Controversy concerning the school system's treatment of East Brooklyn minority children began in the 1950s, as thousands of southern blacks and Puerto Ricans migrated to the area. Conflict peaked with the Ocean Hill–Brownsville "school wars" in the late 1960s, which shut down the entire New York City school system for weeks at a time.[2] East Brooklyn schools continued to be a center of conflict, often of a racial nature, throughout the 1970s.[3]

EBC formed in 1978 when a group of seven local ministers hired the Industrial Areas Foundation (IAF), a group of professional organizers with over sixty affiliates nationwide.[4] EBC now consists of approximately fifty churches and controls a budget in excess of $200,000. Best known for building over 3,000 single-family, owner-occupied "Nehemiah" houses for low-to-moderate-income residents, the group also opened two neighborhood health care clinics, registered tens of thousands of voters, promotes community policing plans, works with the police to shut down drug-dealing locations, and deals with other neighborhood concerns such as poor-quality food in neighborhood markets, street lighting, road repairs, and illegal trash dumping. EBC also has a history of efforts to reform education.

NEW YORK CITY'S SCHOOL GOVERNANCE SYSTEM

Following the Ocean Hill–Brownsville controversy in 1969, the state legislature passed decentralization legislation that largely determined the institutional structures that govern the New York City school system today. The decentralization law left responsibility for the high schools with the board of education (the central board); the elementary and junior high schools (the primary schools) fell under the auspices of thirty-two newly created community school boards (CSBs). The mayor appoints the board, while the CSBs are elected. Though some minor reform efforts succeeded, the governance structure remained largely unchanged until 1997 when the state legislature moved to strengthen the power of the chancellor.

CSB elections take place in springtime every three years, and the electorate consists of all registered voters in each district. The CSBs appoint and remove the superintendent and other administrators, though the boards may delegate some of these powers to the superintendent. The central board oversees the CSBs and provides various services to the local districts but cannot remove CSB members or overrule CSB decisions in most situations. Though the CSBs may hire and fire paraprofessionals and other nonteaching personnel, employment decisions regarding teachers must conform to the union contract. State law mandates that every school set up a parent advisory committee.

The decentralization law created the dynamics that EBC faces in its efforts to reform education in East Brooklyn. Because of the split in governance between the high schools and primary grades, EBC follows a two-pronged approach. Though this discussion treats EBC's efforts at the high school and primary levels separately, the group often deals with both levels at the same time while organizing around other issues not related to education.

EBC EFFORTS TO TRANSFORM HIGH SCHOOL EDUCATION

Nehemiah II

In 1986 EBC organized 120 members to conduct twenty-minute meetings with local juniors and seniors. The members split into seven teams, one for each area high school. In the meetings, students identified a number of problems: few children received information about college entrance exams, financial aid, or college applications. Many students felt that the school staff had little faith in their abilities and that limited job opportunities awaited them, regardless of their school performance.

EBC announced a program, dubbed Nehemiah II, to motivate students by offering jobs or scholarships to students who graduated on time and missed no more than five days of school a year. EBC contacted banks, large corporations, and government agencies to arrange placements for students recommended by the group. For a student to receive a scholarship, a college must first accept the student; to receive a job, employers requested that students pass an eighth-grade-level math test. EBC hoped to find jobs for 1,000 students over a five-year period.

EBC asserts that area high schools responded to the initiative by attempting to channel successful students into the program. This practice, called "creaming," reduced the chance that students would fail tests or perform poorly on the job. To EBC, the schools appeared more interested in avoiding public relations problems than in creating incentives for students. The group selected a more random sample of students: EBC hoped the program might spark average pupils to try harder instead of rewarding only the academically talented.

When EBC took the first group of seventy-five graduates to Manufacturers Hanover Trust (MHT) for the math test, seventy-three failed. EBC told MHT that they had no obligation to hire any of the seventy-three students. After MHT indicated that they wanted to hire the students anyway, the vast majority failed MHT's two-week training course, prompting MHT to end the program. EBC informed MHT that once they hired the students, the bank took on a fiduciary responsibility to train them. MHT extended the training program another four weeks. EBC organizer Elda Peralta reports, "The kids turned out to be excellent workers." Some of the students worked at the jobs five years later, unusual for bank tellers, who have a high turnover rate.

EBC finished Nehemiah II in 1991 after placing 600 students in full- and part-time jobs (out of 1,000 job slots) and awarding 200 scholarships.[5] The group reached two conclusions from the experience. First, the school system failed to educate students properly, including those who attended classes on a regular basis and received good grades. Second, the schools proved impervious to the standard pressure techniques EBC employs. "The school system is encased in their own hopelessness," comments former lead organizer Dave Nelson.

EBC also furthered its understanding of the political strength of various elements of the education system. In addition to the protection provided by union contracts, teachers and principals benefit politically from their financial strength — EBC believes the banks refused to criticize the schools too severely because of large deposits held by the United Federation of Teachers (UFT) and other union employee pension funds. Public employee unions in New York City make campaign contributions, lobby the legislature, constitute a large voting bloc, and may supply large numbers of educated campaign workers. Ultimately, EBC concluded that Nehemiah II did not adequately address the deficiencies in the school system or improve the educational experience of East Brooklyn's children. EBC ended its association with the program, though it continues to function under other auspices.

EBC High Schools for Public Service, Part 1: Crisis Drives Policy

East Brooklyn contains several high schools, but two large schools in particular worried EBC: Thomas Jefferson and Bushwick High Schools. Both contain thousands of students housed in antiquated buildings. Bushwick's register of students put the school at 180 percent of capacity in 1990, and students scored an average of 285 on the math SAT. Thomas Jefferson suffered from overcrowding, poor educational performance, and a disturbing level of violence: in 1992 school security reported that over fifty assaults, robberies, drug and weapons possessions, and murders occurred in the school. Half of Thomas Jefferson's students dropped out without graduating, and only three students graduated with a Regents' diploma in 1991.[6]

In early 1991, EBC met with the Center for Educational Innovation (CEI), a wing of the Manhattan Institute think tank. At first, EBC wanted to take over Bushwick and Thomas Jefferson, but CEI argued persuasively that such a strategy would generate stiff political opposition and that EBC probably could not run the schools any better. The problem with the schools, in CEI's account, lay in their long-established culture of failure. CEI and EBC agreed that starting two new, small high schools with a school culture based on EBC's ideals of performance, accountability, responsibility, and public service had a better chance for success. According to CEI's Ray Domanico, "This was a radical idea at the time. No one was discussing this type of thing publicly."

When EBC leaders first broached the new schools idea with Chancellor

Joseph Fernandez, they received a polite reception but no firm commitments. EBC then recruited the chancellor of the City University of New York, Ann Reynolds, to support the idea. At the same time, assembly member Roger Green advanced an initiative for a "Ujamma" school to teach an Afrocentric curriculum in an all-black male high school. Green secured the endorsement of the president of Medger Evers College, where EBC hoped to form an enrichment academy for ninth-graders who would otherwise attend high school at Bushwick or Thomas Jefferson. Chancellor Fernandez suggested the two work together.

EBC rejected the offer. The group had no interest in the all-black-male concept or a purely Afrocentric curriculum. Instead, EBC sought to create a high school based on an academic, college-prep curriculum. Politically, working with Green and Ujamma put EBC in a compromised position. In the face of weak public support for the Ujamma school, opposition appeared likely. If controversy flared, EBC either would have to support an unpopular and divisive concept or reject Ujamma, which enjoyed support in parts of the black community. If the central board scuttled Ujamma, it could use a rejection by EBC as political cover against charges of racism or insensitivity. CEI believed that the central board consciously sought to use EBC to blunt the criticisms of black radicals. EBC continued to negotiate, but the new schools idea languished.

On February 26, 1992, a day scheduled for a visit and speech by Mayor David Dinkins, two students died of gunshot wounds inflicted inside Thomas Jefferson High School. Dinkins arrived shortly after the shootings to find the school in chaos and mourning. The assembled media shifted its attention from the mayor and onto the shootings, which garnered considerable coverage for several days. In a classic example of crisis driving policy, the *New York Times* reported that the central board was studying a proposal for two new EBC schools—one in East New York, the other in Bushwick—four days after the shootings.[7] Four months later, the schools received official approval.[8] In negotiations with EBC, Chancellor Fernandez reserved the right to withdraw his support unless the schools opened by September 1993.

With the help of CEI's Lew Smith, EBC leaders wrote a concept paper that included a mission statement; twenty-eight goals the schools should accomplish; plans for administration and management, instruction, curriculum, and staff development; and a weekly schedule for incoming ninth-graders. The paper proposed a governing board consisting of four EBC members and four members selected by the board of education, empowered to play an ongoing role in selecting principals and staff and to set guidelines for the schools' operation. EBC sought to augment classroom education through public-service placements with local service providers. On July 8, 1992, EBC held a meeting, which over 2,000 people attended and at which Chancellor Fernandez and board of education president Carl McCall agreed to the proposals in the concept paper.[9]

EBC High Schools for Public Service, Part 2: Navigating the System

EBC then faced the need to make a host of decisions regarding siting, supplies, and most important, choosing project directors for each of the schools.[10] The group sought to play a prominent part in this process. The central board of education, however, did not have standard operating procedures (SOPs) that allowed community groups to play such a role. Indeed, following the organizational imperative to avoid uncertainty and to maintain tight control of operations, SOPs of the board resisted attempts by community groups to influence policy. The head of High School Division and a former member of EBC's high school governing board, John Ferrandino, explains that Chancellors Fernandez and Ramone Cortines pushed hard for the involvement of community organizations and that the idea "was a major change from accepted practice."

Meetings of the governing board revealed the difficulties inherent in the process. At the initial meetings in late October 1992, the central board members raised a number of objections to the EBC concept paper. Ferrandino pointed out that the group could not violate the union contracts and had to meet various legal requirements. Central board members also objected to the term "governing board" because it might provoke the UFT by stirring memories of the Ocean Hill–Brownsville controversy. Though EBC found the meetings productive, the group felt that the insistence on political, bureaucratic and legal "necessities" foreshadowed future obstacles.

In March 1992 Fernandez threatened to abandon the idea unless EBC found sites for the schools within three weeks. EBC's Peralta scoured the area for days before finding two locations that looked acceptable. In East New York, Peralta discovered an unused warehouse whose owner—a Latino immigrant who had built a successful moving company—expressed enthusiasm at the prospect of renovating the building for use by local children. Problems with the Bushwick site appeared immediately when the owner, who lived in California, designated his real estate broker as his negotiator. By December 1, 1992, the lease on the East New York site, though not signed, appeared secure. The Bushwick owner, however, continued to negotiate.

The schools still needed to be designed and the buildings renovated, in addition to a long list of other tasks. EBC reports that they encountered a series of SOPs and a level of bureaucratic incompetence that nearly destroyed the project. Despite repeated requests, the central board failed to fax EBC the standard design plan for schools holding 600 students. The central board leasing office sent the wrong lease forms to the East New York owner. When the owner mailed back the wrong forms, the leasing office took two weeks to send out the standard set of forms—without the changes to which the owner and the central board had previously agreed. Each error delayed renovations for weeks, causing the work to start three months late on June 1, 1993. During this period, negotiations for the Bushwick site broke down. The schools would have to open in the same building in East New York, which now faced extreme time pressure because of the delay.[11]

EBC also needed to recruit students for the schools. New York City operates a limited choice system at the high school level: students rank their choices and are assigned to public high schools by the central board. Guidance counselors in the junior high schools did not publicize the new schools until late in the year, forcing EBC to spend precious time on advertising. Once the recruitment efforts yielded an acceptable number of students, both the project directors and the central board refused to give EBC the names of the students, citing confidentiality requirements. EBC could not contact parents to explain why the schools did not yet have buildings, which caused acute problems in Bushwick when inquisitive parents saw no renovations taking place at the school's address. To make matters worse, while EBC struggled to attract students, the central board's Office of Automated Admission Services sent out notices to some parents saying that EBC schools were full.

Nothing caused as much consternation to EBC, however, as the first two project directors. The governing board selected two candidates for each school and forwarded the names to the chancellor. In each case, the chancellor selected the candidate favored by the four representatives of the central board, not by EBC. Bureaucratic politics flared immediately. Despite EBC's request that the project directors work at EBC headquarters in Brownsville, the directors chose to work out of the central board's office in downtown Brooklyn. A battle for control of the schools quickly developed, with EBC on one side and the project directors and the head of Brooklyn High Schools, Joyce Coppin, on the other. Coppin and the project directors appeared tied to SOPs, routines, and programs used by the High School Division for opening new schools.[12] EBC wanted involvement precisely because it feared the development of standard high schools that had failed in the past.

EBC's demand for participation not only threatened the legitimacy of the High School Division by questioning its expertise, but it also held the potential of prompting similar demands from other community groups. As one study notes, "The New York City school system is a *machine bureaucracy* in the classic Weberian sense. It is under strong pressure . . . to deliver services in a way that is uniform across the city, that shows no 'favoritism' to particular groups."[13] If the school system allowed collaboration with EBC, it would have to work with other community groups who wanted to set up schools. Not only did the central board not have SOPs for collaborative schools, but EBC was encroaching on Coppin's turf.

Within a couple of months, the relationship between EBC and the project directors soured. EBC felt the directors made unilateral decisions, and the directors resented EBC's demands for involvement. Consultant Lew Smith describes his efforts to facilitate a meeting between the two: "It was one of the most frustrating professional experiences I have ever had. EBC did not want business as usual, and the directors did not respond. Now granted, they were in a tough position. At some level they felt they owed their jobs to Joyce Coppin. This put them right in the middle between Coppin and EBC." During the last week of the Fernandez administration, EBC prevailed upon the chancellor to shift administration of the schools to the more flexible Office of Alternative Schools (OAS). Aware of EBC's intense dissatisfaction, the project directors resigned. OAS acceded to EBC's request that Genivive "Ginger" Wright, an EBC activist with twenty-five years of classroom experience, be appointed project director for both schools.

With just over two months before opening day, the schools had a new project director with no administrative experience, no building, and few teachers hired. Wright, Peralta, and others made strenuous efforts to prepare the schools for opening day. Even with their exertions, the school managed to open on time only because an asbestos scare delayed the opening of all city schools by eleven days.[14]

EBC High Schools for Public Service, Part 3: Implementation

EBC held an energetic celebration attended by Chancellor Cortines at the schools' opening in September 1993. Indeed, the opening represented a triumph in terms of process. No other community group in East Brooklyn ever exercised such control over the selection of administrators or the direction of local high schools. No other school contained independent parent organizers with offices in the school. And never before had an East Brooklyn community organization had its own name on a public high school. EBC's thousands of person-hours devoted to creating the schools had finally paid off.

EBC quickly found out that creating and running a school constitute two separate tasks. Although a full evaluation of the schools is premature, patterns are emerging that are cause for both concern and optimism.

On the positive side, the atmosphere at EBC schools is palpably different from that at the large, traditional schools.[15] The institution of advisories—small groups of students who meet with an adviser for twenty-five minutes twice a week—allows students to make attachments not generally possible at larger high schools. Guidance counselor Melanie Kellogg comments, "The groups provide an intimacy developing situation. At big high schools, there are no personalized relationships, or at least they are much less likely to occur. . . . [At EBC schools] there are three or four stopgaps before a student gets into trouble. Before they see me, an adviser or a principal or a teacher who knows the student all have a chance to take care of things." Students often lead discussions, which may include topics concerning school, family, or friends.

Students often receive public recognition for their work at awards assemblies, an infrequent honor reserved for only the best students at most large schools. Twice a year the schools hold seminars directed by volunteers recruited by EBC and the schools. The seminars address a broad range of topics: for example, how to find work in the entertainment industry, AIDS, the realities of raising a child, and how to interact with the police. Students take frequent trips to museums, the theater, and other cultural events. The school building also contains a day care center so that student mothers may continue their education.

Parental outreach efforts are extensive and institutionalized. A parent or parent representative must meet with a school staff member each time the schools distribute report cards. The school notifies parents of such events and will not release a report card until the meeting takes place. The schools invite parents to awards assemblies; and in the Bushwick school, teachers must call every parent at least once a month. One adviser comments, "Students do not fall through the cracks the way they do at larger schools. If a student starts acting out, we try to find out what the problem is and deal with it. We don't want parents coming in and saying 'why wasn't I told?' "

The public-service placements have produced some success stories. Community service students work at their placements twice a week. Day care centers, public schools, and law offices employ the students for tasks ranging from photocopying to conducting interviews to writing reports. Eneida Lopez, the coordinator of the placements for the Bushwick school, describes one student who became a math tutor at an elementary school, despite mediocre math grades. Lopez explains that the student developed a renewed commitment to learning: "He came in and said to me, 'I have to learn math, because that little boy is counting on me to teach him.' "

Despite these accomplishments, the schools continue to encounter difficulties, many tightly tied to the politics of education in New York. Four problems stand out: student attendance, building space, the union contract, and the level of talent in the teaching pool.

First-year attendance figures placed the East New York school in the bottom quartile of all schools, and the Bushwick school below the average.[16] Explanations for the low attendance figures vary. Though one interviewee suggested that the attendance-taking practices of new teachers caused errors in the statistics, other factors appear to have contributed to the problem. Because the schools opened under enormous time pressure, the library, the computer lab, the gymnasium, and the cafeteria were not yet finished. Students complained of eating bag lunches day after day instead of hot food. The computer teacher taught without computers or a chalkboard the first semester. Physical education classes needed to improvise. With the two schools packed into one building, demands for the limited amount of space created tension.

These might be considered short-term problems easily alleviated by the opening of a separate building for the Bushwick school. As of January 1997, however, renovations on the Bushwick building had not begun. After pulling out of negotiations with the first Bushwick site, the central board signed a lease on another building in fall 1995, to be opened in fall 1996. EBC members periodically visited the site but saw no signs of construction. At the central board's monthly meetings, EBC and the owner exchanged claims and counterclaims concerning progress on the project. By May 1996 the central board acknowledged, albeit unofficially, that no renovations were taking place. Though EBC urged it to take action, the central board said that it planned to wait until the contract expired and then sue the owner.

In summer 1996, two buyers, who both owned construction companies, made offers to buy the site and assume the liens on the property taken out by the current owner. The central board said it would approve the deal but insisted that penalties for not completing the renovations by August 1996, written into the original lease, be left in place. Realizing that turning a shell of a building into a school that could pass inspection would take far longer than the two months remaining before the penalty date, both prospective buyers withdrew their offers. EBC asserts that the central board voiced fears that amending the lease might cause the press to claim that the new buyer received a "sweetheart" deal, a charge the board was especially sensitive to, considering the recent scandals in the leasing office.[17] Despite repeated protests, the central board has taken no action, and EBC's schools remain crowded into one building.

Other problems also explain the low attendance figures. The schools attempt to create a rigorous learning environment by assigning homework every night and enforcing dress codes. Many students who attended area elementary and intermediate schools are not used to this level of responsibility. Though some respond positively to the heightened expectations, others evade the increased responsibility by skipping school. The move to the Alternative Schools Division, which usually serves students not performing or behaving well in traditional schools, may have resulted in the recruitment of a disproportionately troubled student body. One person connected with the schools described the students, inaccurately, as "kids who couldn't make it in the regular schools." If some school staff members see the schools as an alternative for troubled children, it is possible that junior high guidance counselors advising prospective students share that view.

Attempts at innovation have met frequent resistance from the teachers' union. Although the UFT offers rhetorical support for various educational reforms, the core interests of the organization lie elsewhere. Like most unions, the UFT's primary concerns relate to job conditions, pay scales, and protecting members from the arbitrary actions of administrators. At times, this stance results in a slavish conformity to the union contract. Educational reforms often call for teachers to play different roles or assume new tasks. The top echelons of the UFT, generally regarded as more liberal than the rank and file, usually praise reforms. At the school level, however, union representatives routinely respond to innovations by characterizing changes as violations of the union contract and filing grievances that prevent reforms.

The ideological differences between the leadership and the rank and file are not the only explanation for this divergence. Politically, projecting an image of cooperation and caring usually serves the UFT better than one of confrontation. By offering support to reform ideas, top UFT leaders garner positive media coverage and help the union avoid charges of intransigence. At the same time, school-level challenges prevent changes that teachers dislike, usually without generating negative publicity.

Union chapter leaders at EBC's schools, for example, objected to the advisories on the grounds that they constituted unpaid time. In one of the schools, this objection resulted in reducing each class period by two minutes—a loss of fifty minutes of instruction a week. Though this solution removed the issue of unpaid time, the proposal circumvented the union contract and thus required approval of 75 percent of the school's teachers. One of the schools agreed, but the other did not, necessitating further negotiations.

In another case, when the East New York principal decided to shorten the lunch period by ten minutes, the union demanded that the time be made up elsewhere, which forced a cut of forty minutes from the Wednesday afternoon staff development sessions. The sessions allow teachers to meet and plan activities—another unique feature of the school. Some teachers protested unannounced parental visits organized by EBC, contending that the union contract specifies that only professionals may evaluate teacher performance. Though many problems have been solved without filing grievances, the schools are not immune to the familiar tension between administrators and the union.

Nowhere have these problems flared with greater intensity than over questions concerning hiring and firing. The initial project directors hired very few staff before resigning. When Ginger Wright took over as project director only two months before the start of school, she needed to hire teachers very quickly. During the first year, EBC received a number of complaints concerning the East New York school's science teacher, who also happened to be the UFT chapter representative. EBC and Wright suggested that the science teacher transfer to another school. She refused. When the school raised the matter with the UFT, on one account, "The UFT said, 'She has twenty-five years of experience. She stays.' " Despite EBC's aggressive posture and continued evidence of the teacher's poor performance on EBC's account, the teacher remained. Only the threat of legal action by EBC and a systemwide buyout offer persuaded the science teacher to retire.

In early 1997 both principals, with EBC's support, were taking steps to remove poorly performing teachers. The union contract, however, strictly governs the removal process. Administrators must extensively document poor performance, provide written suggestions for improvements, attend several classes taught by the teacher, and make attempts to improve the teacher's skills. Administrators must follow this process, regardless of evidence of incompetence. In practice, removing a teacher takes an enormous amount of time, and minor deviations from the process elaborated in the union contract are grounds for filing a grievance.

These problems point to larger, systemic problems. First, it appears difficult to recruit teachers to East Brooklyn. EBC's schools contain many excellent and committed teachers, but East Brooklyn's tough reputation appears to impede recruitment. Combined with a systemwide budget process that often forces last-minute hiring, EBC schools must resort to the "hiring hall" system on occasion. The hiring hall generally, though not always, contains two types of teachers: castoffs from other schools or newcomers. Indeed, EBC's schools admit to having largely inexperienced staffs. This situation allows greater flexibility in creating a school culture, perhaps, but the cost may be high. The greatest improvement in teacher ability occurs in the first five to seven years, but it is unclear whether EBC schools can attract or retain experienced teachers.[18] Nor have EBC's schools avoided high teacher turnover, a problem endemic to city school systems generally.

EBC'S EFFORTS TO TRANSFORM PRIMARY SCHOOL EDUCATION

EBC created the new high schools only by overcoming substantial and deeply entrenched resistance to community involvement. A large portion of this resistance occurred because of the unwillingness of school bureaucrats to deviate from established routines. In contrast, locally elected officials were the leading source of opposition to EBC's efforts on the primary grade level. Though EBC managed to garner a few small successes, narrow organizational interests and political concerns have frustrated the group's efforts at virtually every step. As intransigent as the board of education might be, the community school boards (CSBs) in East Brooklyn have proven decidedly less amenable to change.

When the 1969 decentralization law established CSBs, the possibility of educational improvement induced a number of highly qualified candidates to run for office. This soon changed: "Starting with the 1973 elections, however, there was a noticeable shift from parent-oriented and professionally oriented community school board members to those supported by the teachers' union, political clubs, parochial school groups, and antipoverty agencies. Each had their own particular interest."[19] With budgets in the tens of millions of dollars, CSBs frequently become centers of corruption and patronage. From 1978 to 1995, members of CSBs in at least eighteen of the thirty-two districts were suspended, involved in scandals, and/or indicted.[20] At one point in the 1980s, separate criminal investigations targeted ten boards simultaneously.[21] In 1996, the *New York Times* identified ten districts as having "histories of corruption."[22] The bulk of these cases, and the worst instances of abuse, occurred in districts serving poor minority students. Numerous reports and audits called for reform, but no major changes occurred for twenty-seven years.

Because CSB elections take place in the spring, turnout is extraordinarily low—usually below 10 percent citywide and below 5 percent in many districts. The use of a confusing weighted voting scheme and the prohibition of party labels gives well-organized special interests an advantage. According to one observer, "What has emerged in some districts has been [CSB] control by local 'power brokers' who represent organizational interests that do not include parents and are not oriented toward educational considerations."[23] UFT loyalists frequently win election to the boards, and before recent changes in state law, 94 percent of CSB members received aid or endorsements from the UFT.[24]

EBC's first attempt to impact primary education occurred in early 1984 with its "East New York Children" campaign. EBC ran a slate of candidates against entrenched board members, winning four of nine seats. The failure of the group to win a majority, which Peralta attributes to racial bloc-voting that divided support for EBC's multiracial slate, left the winning members vulnerable. Former EBC lead organizer Dave Nelson describes the result: "Two were corrupted and lost, two retained their values."[25]

1989–1994: Building the Bushwick Parents Organization

EBC next made primary education an issue in 1989, when the group formed a member organization, the Bushwick Parents Organization (BPO). BPO, under the direction of Sister Kathy Maire, focused its efforts on District 32. Maire's one-on-one interviews with 600 residents revealed considerable anger concerning the primary-grade educational system. Students complained of a shortage of books, fermented juice from the cafeteria, rotten meat, cockroaches in school food, and toilets that did not work.

Maire started holding monthly meetings, teaching parents to analyze the distribution of power in the school system. The analysis tracked the flow of money in particular—who pays into the system and where the money goes. Maire's analysis suggested that assembly member Vito Lopez controls District 32, largely due to his political organization in senior citizens' homes and a patronage base in the schools (the assembly is the lower house of the state legislature). Tito Velez, a Lopez ally, has chaired the CSB for more than twenty years. With the budget for the district totaling over $72 million, abundant opportunities exist for patronage and corruption. A grand jury report in 1991 concluded, "In the case of District 32, public money has been expended as a consequence of non-professional hiring, which reflects the use of public jobs as a reward for private political activity."[26] One superintendent testified that political pressure caused him to hire over 100 people.[27] A CSB member elected in the wake of the scandals commented, "People who knew nothing about education, who could barely read and write, got jobs. People even paid for jobs."[28]

The first action BPO took, scheduling a meeting with the principal of a local junior high school, indicated that the school system did not welcome the group's attempts to encourage parental involvement. When the parents came for the meeting, the principal did not show up—her secretary informed the group that her boss could not talk to the parents because of her busy schedule. BPO assigned a parent to write a letter demanding an apology and another meeting. A student hand-delivered the letter. When two weeks passed with no response, the group wrote another hand-delivered letter. After two more weeks, BPO informed the principal that twenty-five parents planned to march to the school to demand an answer to why they could not get a meeting.[29]

Within an hour, the superintendent phoned Maire, threatening to call the police if the parents showed up at the school. During a tense meeting, Maire informed the group that parents had a legal right to enter the school. Many in the group, which contained a large number of immigrants, had memories of the way police treated protesters in their home countries. Moreover, relations between the New York Police Department and many minority communities suffer from frequent tensions. When BPO arrived at the school, they were met by a group of police officers, the principal, and the superintendent. The parent leader of BPO asked why the principal refused to meet with them. The principal insisted she never received their letters. After BPO and the principal scheduled a meeting, the parents started to leave. According to Maire, the superintendent responded by yelling that the parents had no right to leave yet because he was going to tell them what they could and could not do in his district.

Why would a community school board superintendent call out the police on a local parent group, especially when the law mandates CSBs to solicit parental input? By circumventing the traditional form of parental involvement—the parent groups set up by the principals of each school—BPO challenged the competency and legitimacy of the district's officials. David Rogers and Norman H. Chung's examination of ten CSBs supports this explanation: "One of the disappointments of decentralization has been the limited participation of parents in school affairs. . . . Principals set up parent advisory councils, for example, to absorb parent leaders and then use them as informants on actions and intentions of those still outside."[30] The CSB saw BPO as a potential political rival and sought to undermine their support by denying the group any substantial victories.

The pattern of nonresponsiveness continued. On open-school night, BPO members walked through the district's schools, noting maintenance and equipment problems. They found broken windows, exposed wires, broken drinking fountains, and unclean bathrooms as well as roaches and dirt in the cafeteria. Parents at Intermediate School (IS) 291 found an open sewer line in a boys' bathroom, with no partitions surrounding it—a situation the custodial staff admitted had existed for months.

The principal of IS 291 blamed the situation on the maintenance contracts with the central board of education, which specify that a school cannot replace a toilet, only repair it. The principal claimed the school filed a PO-18 form requesting a new toilet, but the central board's backlog of PO-18s numbers over 40,000. BPO soon discovered the school never filed a PO-18 when the school secretary, also the spouse of the custodian, went on vacation: her absence allowed other people to look at the repair files. A BPO parent then pointed out the difficulty in imagining a student carrying a toilet out the front door. The school finally "discovered" a toilet in the basement of the building. Weeks dragged on as BPO fought for partitions around the toilet. Despite an appeal to the central board, the partitions were not installed until the parents threatened to erect them. This possibility prompted the custodial union to step in and finish the job. From discovery to completion, the toilet fiasco took over a year.

By 1994, BPO's efforts led to improvements in some of the worst conditions in district schools. Their actions, however, failed to affect the basic power structures that undergird the primary school system. The impact on the classroom in particular seemed negligible. While BPO received signed commitments from 400 parents to monitor homework, read to their children every day, and set aside a well-lit study place in their homes, the schools rejected BPO's suggestion to set aside twenty minutes each day for students to read.[31] BPO decided they needed allies if they wanted to take on bigger issues.

1994–1995: Banging Heads

In early 1994, BPO started to work with the Public Education Association (PEA), the oldest and most respected educational reform organization in the city. The entry of the PEA into District 32 raised the stakes of the conflict considerably. The PEA lent legitimacy to BPO's efforts and possessed the capacity to focus widespread attention on the district.

The PEA's initial activities with BPO involved parent training sessions concerning the governance and budget process of the school system and the legal rights of parents.[32] In October 1994 the executive director of the PEA, Ray Domanico (formerly of CEI), wrote the CSB indicating the PEA's intention to produce a parents' guide to District 32's intermediate schools.[33] At a November 17 CSB meeting, the board voted unanimously to "irrevocably [end] four years of a cordial, professional relationship" with BPO.[34] Despite criticism from newspapers and the PEA, the CSB refused to change its decision. In a letter to Domanico, board chair Velez claimed that BPO worked "to undermine our parent associations, underrate our staff and slam the district administration." The Council of Supervisors and Administrators (CSA) of District 32 applauded the CSB's "decision to sever any and all relationships" with BPO. In March 1995 Velez publicly accused Sister Maire of promising BPO parents "apartments, houses, whatever," in return for their support.[35]

The PEA issued a report on the intermediate schools in April 1995.[36] The report gives passing grades to only two of the district's six intermediate schools and advises parents of children in two schools to "seek alternative school placements for their children."[37] One of the passing schools, IS 383, is a magnet school that requires high test scores for admission. Seventy percent of IS 383's students come from outside the district.[38] The PEA report documents a variety of below-average test scores; outside of the magnet school, no school reported more than 33 percent of their students scoring at or above the national average in either math or reading. Only 16 percent of IS 111's students met that standard in math.

The CSB sharply criticized the PEA report. Chair Velez sent home a one-page "Chairman's report" with every district student on May 18: "[The PEA report] is a *cesspool of lies* and no *value* to *Parents*. Mr. Ray Domanico, Executive Director has brought discredit to P.E.A. Sister Kathy Maire and Father Powis, of Saint Barbara's Church have so influenced the Bushwick parents Association that they are unwilling to acknowledge their own children's academic achievements." Shortly thereafter, CSB officials denied BPO parents entrance to a school on the grounds that a principal must be present during a parental visit and that principals were attending a district meeting. When a BPO parent tried to make an appointment with a principal shortly after the incident, the principal informed her that she would have to wait until September.[39]

The PEA attempted to draw the attention of Chancellor Cortines, but he resisted. When the chancellor finally responded on June 7, he urged the PEA, BPO, and the CSB to "work together," despite the CSB's decision to "unrecognize" BPO at a March 1995 meeting. Cortines had his own organizational and personal concerns: the CSB is the legally recognized community representative. Siding against the local board would create considerable political furor. Furthermore, responding to Mayor Rudolph Giuliani's persistent criticism occupied a great deal of Cortines's time and eventually led to his resignation.

The Last Resort: The BPO Lawsuit

After six years of frustration, BPO filed a lawsuit in 1995 charging the state commissioner of education with failing to monitor New York City's bilingual education program. Typically, community organizations avoid legal strategies because they drain resources, often take years, and do not develop leadership. Legal victories may require extensive follow-through, and tangible benefits may never appear. "Trust me. It was not something we wanted to do," remarked Maire.

A brief tour through the bilingual system contributes to an understanding of the political concerns that drive the CSB. Students enter bilingual programs when they score below the 40th percentile on a test called the Language Assessment Battery (LAB). In practice, many districts test all Hispanic-surnamed students, regardless of the language spoken at home. In grading the test, comparisons between a student's English and Spanish language abilities are often overlooked, despite a mandate to monitor them. Thus, a student might score in the 20th percentile in Spanish and the 35th percentile in English and still be placed in a bilingual program. District 32 schools have placed students who functioned in English-language Head Start programs into bilingual education because of their test results.[40] In some cases, schools placed U.S.-born Hispanic-surnamed students with English-speaking parents into bilingual classes, even though they did not understand Spanish. To leave the bilingual program, a student must pass a test at the end of the school year. When little or inappropriate education takes place, a continuing stream of students enters bilingual education, and very few leave it. In District 32, only 2.8 percent of the students test out of bilingual programs each year.[41] In the worst school, IS 111, only 0.6 percent test out.

The original legislation called for students to spend a maximum of three years in bilingual education. A citywide Latino interest group, ASPIRA, challenged that rule on the grounds that some children might not be ready for monolingual (English) classes after three years. In a consent decree, a court allowed exceptions to the three-year rule in special circumstances, though no child may spend more than six years in bilingual education.

Exemptions to the three-year rule are now routine, which forms the basis of the BPO lawsuit. Board of education data show that 90 percent of junior high school students and roughly 50 percent of kindergartners who enroll in bilingual education stay in the program longer than three years.[42] BPO argues that the state's Department of Education bears the responsibility for monitoring the use of exemptions and that a substantial number of students stay in bilingual education beyond the legal time limit. The issue is not a small one: the number of students enrolled in bilingual programs increased by 65 percent in New York City in the last seven years, and over $10 billion is spent on bilingual education nationwide.[43] The rising number of Latinos migrating to New York City accounts, no doubt, for some of the increase. The 65 percent figure, however, far outstrips the 26.8 percent increase in New York's Latino population registered by the U.S. Census from 1980 to 1990.[44] Children of other ethnic groups also enroll in bilingual education, but Hispanics account for the majority.

Schools have an incentive to place and maintain students in bilingual education because of the additional funding they receive for these programs. As Maire explains, "Routine exemptions allow the City of New York and especially District 32 to build up politically useful programs because of the money coming into bilingual programs." A severe shortage of qualified bilingual teachers exacerbates the problem by giving the schools more latitude in hiring, which makes patronage appointments easier to justify.[45]

Some observers might argue that the extra money does not hurt education in District 32. BPO's parents, however, claim that bilingual programs stifle their children's educational progress and prevent them from developing language skills appropriate for employment and college. Some parents report that after six years in bilingual education, their children cannot read in either English or Spanish. Maire points to the poor placement record of bilingual students: "The elementary schools repeatedly claim success, but almost none of the bilingual students get into the [junior high] magnet school." The district administration benefits from the extra dollars, creating an incentive to perpetuate failure, or at least not to attack poor performance aggressively. As to funding, Maire asserts, "The schools are not short of money, they are short of education."

Parents who try to remove their children from bilingual education claim that administrators accuse them of not having pride in their heritage. When parents persist, BPO claims, school officials whisper warnings that the school cannot protect their children from attacks by black students. School officials may also prevent mainstreaming by refusing to give parents the proper forms to fill out.

Change or Business as Usual?

Courts twice rejected BPO's lawsuit, and the case is on appeal. The pressure created by the suit, however, led to an agreement in which the central board agreed to stop automatic testing of students with Hispanic surnames. Chancellor Rudolph Crew also announced an investigation into the bilingual program. Maire called the agreement "a paper victory." Reports from BPO's parents indicate that school practices have not changed.

On December 17, 1996, the state legislature "enacted the most significant overhaul of New York City's schools in a generation."[46] The new law strips most of the hiring power from the CSBs and gives the chancellor veto power over the selection of district superintendents. Days before the state legislature passed the new law, CSB 32 voted for a three-year renewal of their superintendent's contract, though it did not expire until June, and the mandatory performance review never took place. BPO received assurances from Crew and board of education president William Thompson that the contract would be ruled invalid, but Maire indicates that the group is taking no chances: "We will be having 200 parents writing letters. . . . We fax the Board of Education four times a day."

COMMUNITY PARTICIPATION AND SCHOOL REFORM

What does the EBC experience tell us about community participation in school reform efforts? A number of caveats must precede any answer. New York City's size, governance structure, and history of corruption suggest caution in making generalizations to other cities. Further, EBC's strategy, which includes the use of confrontational tactics, is only one of many approaches to community participation. Other forms, such as the School Development Program developed by James Comer, explicitly reject confrontation in favor of consensus decision making.[47] Although it is important to recognize these circumstances, the difficulties the group encounters are familiar. Turf wars, resistance to change by public employee unions, cumbersome bureaucracy, and political considerations trumping policy outcomes are typical forms of resistance to citizen participation in many policy areas. Moreover, tensions between schools in low-income, minority neighborhoods and the communities they serve are common in many other cities.

One lesson suggested by the EBC experience is that community participation in urban school reform is not a simple matter of exhorting parents and community leaders to become more involved in education. Multiple barriers to participation operate on many levels. Appeals from high-profile sources such as mayors or chancellors may sound hollow to communities with a long history of negative experiences with local school officials. Efforts to involve communities in school improvement efforts often have to overcome a high level of cynicism and suspicion.

The EBC experience also suggests that resistance to community participation is deeply ingrained. Crises may briefly lower the usual hurdles to involvement, but ongoing participation requires some form of organization with access to resources. These resources include money, organizational skills, and expertise in educational issues. Few community organizations are able to generate such resources entirely on their own. Indeed, EBC's ability to recruit allies such as CEI and PEA played a key role in the successes they achieved, not only by providing expertise, but also by expanding the group's access to political and financial resources. Without such resources and allies, isolated efforts by community groups are unlikely to have the staying power needed to promote reforms successfully or to see that they are properly implemented.

Moreover, the EBC experience shows the importance of governance structures in shaping participation. Consider the demands that EBC and BPO made at each level. On the high school level, the two new schools required a recurring commitment of millions of dollars and the institution of new procedures not welcomed by the central board staff. On the district level, such a proposal would constitute a major investment. The central board's $8 billion budget, however, made the financial commitment relatively insignificant. Because the mayor, the chancellor, and the board attract frequent media attention, positive coverage partially offset the costs in accepting EBC's proposal. Though it took a crisis to persuade the board to approve the proposal, EBC succeeded in having the plan accepted, though not yet fully implemented.

In contrast, BPO put forth far less taxing proposals. For example, the group asked the schools to make a number of minor repairs. Routine procedures exist to process such requests and require no ongoing effort on the part of either the CSB or school personnel. Funding for repairs is included in school budgets. Nonetheless, the CSB vigorously resisted BPO's demands. Given the extent of the CSB's patronage operation, as indicated by the 1991 grand jury report, the political threat posed by BPO easily outstrips possible gains from responding to the group's requests. Individual CSBs rarely attract media attention, and ignoring a community group usually does not lure a media acclimated to frequent reports of CSB corruption. Even the indictment of District 32's superintendent failed to create a crisis large enough to blunt the CSB's opposition to BPO's proposals. District 32's CSB, moreover, is not known as especially unresponsive and does not have as extensive a record of corruption as many other local boards.

The EBC experience shows the potential difficulties encountered when low-income inner-city neighborhoods seek to have meaningful input on educational issues. Though this account contains many discouraging aspects, that should not overshadow the fact that EBC and BPO put forth proposals that the school system enacted. Moreover, it seems reasonable to conclude that these changes would not have occurred without EBC's and BPO's activities. Just as the EBC experience demonstrates the difficulties associated with community participation, it also suggests that participation is possible and desired in inner-city communities.

NOTES

1. This chapter draws on a larger study of East Brooklyn Congregations (EBC) involving over forty interviews. See Timothy Ross, "The Impact of Community Organizing on East Brooklyn, 1978–1995" (Ph.D. diss., 1997).

2. See Diane Ravitch, *The Great School Wars* (New York: Basic Books, 1973).

3. Jonathan Reider, *Canarsie* (Cambridge: Harvard University Press, 1985).

4. For discussions of the modern IAF, see Jim Rooney, *Organizing the South Bronx* (Albany: State University of New York Press, 1995), and Mary Beth Rogers, *Cold Anger: A Story of Faith and Power Politics* (Denton: University of North Texas Press, 1990).

5. Amey Stone, *Hold Fast to Your Dreams,* EBC paper, p. 3.

6. Ibid., pp. i–ii.

7. Joseph Berger, "Officials Study New School Near Site of Students' Deaths," *New York Times,* March 1, 1992, p. A1.

8. Lynnell Hancock, "Two Alternative Schools for Brooklyn," *Daily News,* July 6, 1992.

9. Stone, *Hold Fast to Your Dreams,* p. 6.

10. Until a high school holds four grades, the principal is referred to as a project director.

11. In 1996 scandals forced the resignation of the director of the leasing program. See Sarah Kershaw, "Mix-up on Leases Costs NYC Schools $30 Million," *New York Times,* April 26, 1996, B1, B5.

12. Stone, *Hold Fast to Your Dreams.*

13. David Rogers and Norman H. Chung, *110 Livingston Street Revisited* (New York: New York University Press, 1983), p. 10 (italics in original).

14. Edna Negron, "Place of Hope: Born of Failure, New High Schools Filled with Promise," *New York Newsday,* September 2, 1993, p. 15.

15. This conclusion is based on interviews, visits to the schools, and my experience as a public high school teacher in New York City.

16. Public Education Association (PEA), *1995–1996 New York City Public High Schools at a Glance; A Consumer's Guide* (New York: PEA, 1995).

17. Kershaw, "Mix-up on Leases."

18. Mibrey W. McLaughlin and David D. Marsh, "Staff Development and School Change," in *Schools as Collaborative Cultures,* ed. Ann Lieberman (New York: Falmer Press, 1990), pp. 213–32.

19. Rogers and Chung, *110 Livingston Street Revisited,* p. 216.

20. This statistic comes from my examination of the *New York Times Index.*

21. Samuel G. Freedman, *Small Victories: The Real World of a Teacher, Her Students, and Their High School* (New York: Harper and Row, 1990), p. 110.

22. Matthew Purdy and Maria Newman, 1996, "Students Lag in Districts Where Patronage Thrives," *New York Times,* May 13, 1996, pp. A1, B4.

23. Rogers and Chung, *110 Livingston Street Revisited,* p. 217.

24. Freedman, *Small Victories,* p. 219.

25. Stone, *Hold Fast to Your Dreams,* p. 3.

26. Andrew Yarrow, "Brooklyn Grand Jury Finds School Patronage Pervasive, *New York Times,* February 5, 1991, p. B4.

27. "Brooklyn School Chief Barred by Fernandez," *New York Times,* June 12, 1991, p. B3.

28. Yarrow, "Brooklyn Grand Jury."

29. Edna Negron, "Parents Band to Better Their Schools," *New York Newsday,* December 18, 1990.

30. Rogers and Chung, *110 Livingston Street Revisited,* p. 221.

31. Stone, *Hold Fast to Your Dreams,* p. 4.

32. PEA, *Speaking Truth to Power: A Case Study of Parent Involvement in Bushwick, Brooklyn* (New York: PEA, 1995).

33. Letter from Domanico to Felix Vasquez, October 12, 1994. Domanico supplied copies of letters between the PEA, the chancellor, the CSA, and the CSB.

34. Chris Mitchell, "Parents' Group Feels Orphaned," *Daily News,* December 8, 1994.

35. Jim Dwyer, "Bilingual Blues," *New York Newsday,* March 29, 1995, p. A3.

36. PEA, *A Consumer's Guide to Middle Schools in District 32, Brooklyn* (New York: PEA, 1995). See also Annette Fuentes, "Parents' IS Guide Has Staffs Fuming," *Daily News,* May 10, 1995.

37. PEA, *Consumer's Guide,* p. 11.

38. PEA, *Speaking Truth to Power.*

39. Emphasis and capitalization in original of Velez's report; letter from Domanico to Cortines, May 25, 1995.

40. Dwyer, "Bilingual Blues."

41. PEA, *Consumer's Guide.*

42. See "Review and Outlook; Bust the Bilingual Establishment," *Wall Street Journal,* November 24, 1995, p. A8, and Susan Headden, "Tongue-tied in the Schools," *U.S. News and World Report,* September 25, 1995, pp. 44–46.

43. Headden, "Tongue-tied in Schools."

44. Department of City Planning, *Demographic Profile; A Portrait of New York City's Community Districts from the 1980 and 1990 Censuses of Population and Housing* (New York: New York City Department of City Planning, 1992).

45. Headden, "Tongue-tied in the Schools," p. 46.

46. James Dao, "Albany in Schools Accord to Give Chancellor Power and Weaken Local Boards," *NYT,* December 18, 1996, p. A1.

47. See James Comer, *School Power* (New York: Free Press, 1980).

7

Strategy and Tactics in Subsystem Protection: The Politics of Education Reform in Montgomery County, Maryland

Cheryl L. Jones and Connie Hill

Educational politics in Montgomery County emerges from a background different from the context of many other U.S. school systems. Instead of struggling with an overburdened system composed of children living in poverty, Montgomery County has operated a strong system with ample resources. Many residents have long considered the public school system to be the most attractive quality of the county.

Montgomery County borders the District of Columbia. With a growth rate of 30 percent since 1980, the county is currently the largest in Maryland with a population more than 790,000.[1] Furthermore, the population is affluent and well educated. The county's median family income of $61,988 ranks fifth in the United States.[2] Over 49 percent of adults in the county have at least a bachelor's degree and over 73 percent have had some college education.

Given the environment from which it emerges, it is not surprising that the Montgomery County Public Schools (MCPS) system has had a long tradition of academic excellence. Yet our examination found a school system with many of the same concerns facing older urban school systems: (1) an increasingly minority and poor student population with critical educational needs; (2) a teaching staff seen by some observers as inadequately trained to teach a diverse student population in the 1990s; (3) less than adequate parental involvement, especially among poor and minority parents; (4) less than adequate infrastructure, i.e., overcrowded or deteriorated buildings; and (5) tight funding, especially in a period of increased demand.

To be sure, the magnitude of the difficulties faced by Montgomery County is not nearly as great as those found in many inner cities. Yet these problems are significant and left unaddressed may grow to the crisis stage. Already, changes in the educational environment have prompted some observers to call for reform. The current educational context and challenges raise several questions. Can the traditional political arrangements in the county be adapted to meet the needs of a changing population? Will these arrangements hinder or foster coalition building between traditional education actors and new county residents? How will MCPS react to a changed political environment? In this chapter we seek to determine what kind of political leverage is exerted in a "good government" county when no crisis exists to prompt change.

THE POLITICS OF EDUCATIONAL REFORM

The American policymaking system is not one highly cohesive system but a set of policy subsystems organized around particular policies and programs. Each subsystem contains actors with strong interests in the particular policy area and a desire to control policymaking in the subsystem. In controlling the policymaking process, actors establish what Frank Baumgartner and Bryan Jones call a "policy monopoly," with a definable structure and a "supporting idea."[3]

Having a definable institutional structure responsible for policymaking allows the actors in the monopoly to establish formal and informal rules that discourage access to the policymaking process by those outside the monopoly. Restricting access limits possible challenges to the monopoly. The existence of a powerful supporting idea helps shape the prevalent understanding of the policy area and serves to legitimize the policy monopoly.[4] As such, this supporting idea buttresses the policy monopoly and is key to its continuance. Accordingly, the first step in mounting a successful challenge to the monopoly is attacking the ideas that undergird it. But this process is not spontaneous. It requires a conscious effort to do what is not normally done and often meets with strong resistance from the policy monopoly.

In the educational subsystem, school systems often act as policy monopolies.[5] The Montgomery County Public Schools system is no exception to the rule. The idea supporting MCPS is that it is a school system whose activities have produced a tradition of academic success, and continuing that success requires only minor adjustments that educational professionals are in the best position to make.

Because many county residents are well-educated professionals—often issue specialists—they expect a highly professional government, are not intimidated by credentials, and desire active involvement in government affairs. The public's desire for active involvement, however, is in competition with the system's desire for autonomy. The monopoly has accommodated the public's desire by using citizens' commissions and advisory boards. That these boards serve only an advisory role sometimes causes frustration among issue-oriented parents. Nonetheless, this strategy has allowed school officials to channel the public's involvement into an advisory role while positioning itself as the final decision maker. Holding in check the tension between citizen involvement and professional autonomy is key to the monopoly's continued existence.

The citizen-based procedures used by the school system were developed for a homogeneous, middle-class population. Today, the school system faces new challenges as the county's demographics change. An influx of minority, low-income, and immigrant families has produced pockets of poverty within this primarily middle-class community. At issue are how these new residents relate to the school system and how well the traditional citizen-involvement structures in the county serve new residents in bringing about change. Meanwhile, there is growing dissatisfaction with these structures from traditional county residents.

Increasingly, many see the school system as excessively bureaucratic and slow to respond to rapid increases in enrollment. In 1995 MCPS enrolled over 120,000 students, an increase of 20 percent since 1990.[6] Along with a general rise in enrollment has come the demand for more or expanded programs or both for the increasing number of students with special needs. The combination of growth and diversity has created conflicts about attendance boundaries, placement of magnet schools, and location of new facilities. As a result of these conflicts and the school system's inability to deal quickly with these issues, there have been many calls for decentralization of the system and a shifting of power from the central administration to individual schools. As one parent described MCPS, "It's a mainframe school system in a PC world."

Along with calls for openness, concerns have risen about the school system's tightening resources in a period of heightened needs. The county's economic downturn began in 1990 and ended in 1993, running longer and deeper than the national recession. Though the budget remains near $1 billion, cuts have been made at all levels of administration and staffing. This atmosphere of scarcity has put a strain on traditional coalitions, threatening to break them into smaller, individual interest groups. The resulting fragmentation may work against reform by making it difficult to build new coalitions as groups resort to competition in order to pursue their own particular needs.

SYSTEM CHALLENGE AND RESPONSE

Individuals wanting to challenge MCPS and effect systemic educational reform must begin by challenging MCPS' supporting idea. This will be no easy task, as the system has been effective in its use of parent-satisfaction surveys and national rankings as evidence of the good job the schools are doing. Montgomery County has enjoyed a positive reputation for its attention to education, and the people controlling the education subsystem have benefited from this reputation. There are, however, cracks in the armor. In December 1996 the state of Maryland released progress data on its school performance-testing program,[7] which show that MCPS students are not improving at a rate consistent with the county's position in the state. The state's goal is to have 70 percent of all students pass the tests by the year 2000. Currently 50.8 percent of MCPS students pass the test, ranking

Montgomery County fifth out of twenty-four districts in the state. Even more telling, the county's rate of improvement from 1993 to 1996 was 4.4 percent, the second lowest in the state. The figures hardly reflect the facts that Montgomery County parents have the highest level of education in the state and that the county had the highest per pupil expenditures in the state.[8]

Moreover, a state report on academic achievement showed that in 1994, 44 percent of the MCPS students attending the county's community college required remedial math assistance and 22 percent required remedial reading help.[9] The school system points out that these students were not the system's best and that many had not been in the system for a long time. Although this may be true, these students were not dropouts but graduates who were supposed to be ready for higher education or entry into the workforce. These results, coupled with the fact that the academic achievement levels of African American and Hispanic students continue to lag behind those of whites and Asian Americans, point to significant shortcomings. How MCPS and the other political actors in the county respond to these and other challenges will determine whether the county will maintain its coveted reputation.

We shall explore three issues (the school budget, diversity, and calls for decentralization) that present challenges to the policy monopoly. Though not the only issues confronting the monopoly, these illustrate the tactics and strategies used by the people who would test the monopoly and by MCPS itself as it tries to safeguard its position. The illustrations also provide insight into whether the county's problems can be addressed early and effectively, and what tools or resources are needed to do so.[10]

The School Budget

The County's Fiscal Squeeze. A tightening budget has changed the way the county thinks about education in the 1990s. County budgets are tight and are forecast to remain so. This situation is a far cry from the economic growth of the 1980s when there was ample money for government services, chief among them being education. With abundant resources, it was easy to aggregate and maintain an education coalition.

One reason for the stability of the education coalition was the school board's ability to provide generous salary and benefit packages for its employees, who are among the highest paid in the state.[11] Generous compensation satisfied a key constituency: the unions. Moreover, the board was able to provide these benefits without major opposition from other constituencies in the community. Until the recession, community support for teachers' raises was strong, with particular support from the Montgomery County Council of Parent Teacher Associations (MCCPTA).[12] In return, the teachers' union, Montgomery County Education Association (MCEA), was supportive of the PTA's initiatives, and the two formed a powerful coalition.

Along with the ability to keep employees satisfied, ample resources allowed the school administration to restrain the voices of people discontented with the school system's performance. Whenever parents and concerned community activists challenged the system's performance, the administration could address the concerns by offering a new program or by expanding an existing one. Economic prosperity also made it unlikely that those interested in other, noneducation issues would challenge the amount of county funds directed toward public education. Thus, the county's abundant resources served to avert any sustained confrontation while reinforcing the position of the actors controlling the education arena. With these resources reduced, MCPS finds itself subjected to increased scrutiny and criticism. Moreover, this new fiscal conservatism has led to increased competition among the groups asking for new initiatives.

An example of this increased competition is seen in the Union–PTA coalition's split during the 1991 budget cuts.[13] When staff raises were pitted against class size, the MCCPTA fought to maintain the latter while the MCEA held to the former. Prohibited from striking, teachers vowed to "work to rule." Some members even suggested that teachers refuse to write letters of recommendations for seniors unless they or their parents wrote letters in support of the union.[14] By pushing for the raise under these conditions, the union was seen as placing its own interest above those of the students. The MCEA lost this struggle and much of its credibility with Montgomery County parents.

The county's fiscal problems have been further complicated by a taxpayer revolt. County government agencies now find themselves under spending affordability guidelines imposed on them through referendum.[15] This tax revolt affects all areas of the budget, but MCPS is nearly 50 percent of the county budget, making it a major target. Since only one-quarter of the households in the county have children in the public school system, education spending has little built-in protection against a taxpayer revolt. The last three elections have seen referendums on tax limits placed on the ballot. Although none has passed, each has drawn significant support.

The Budget Process. At the center of education politics in Montgomery County is the school budget. Though MCPS' budget is actually two separate budgets, an operating budget and a capital budget, the former is the one most likely to generate controversy. From start to finish, MCPS' operating budget process covers nearly nine months, almost the entire school year. Not surprisingly, the budget process is where those controlling MCPS have tried hardest to protect themselves.

One self-protection strategy frequently used by MCPS is the controlling of information pertaining to itself. This strategy requires that MCPS limit the flow of information, particularly if it is negative. An example of how information, or lack of it, has a significant impact is in the area of contract negotiations with school system employees.

Separate negotiations are conducted between the school board's negotiator and representatives from the county's three employee unions—MCEA, the Montgomery County Council of Supporting Services Employees, and the Montgomery County Association of Administrative and Supervisory Personnel. Generally, negotiations are held away from public view, with the unions and the school administration agreeing not to comment on specific points until an agreement is reached. This secrecy makes it nearly impossible for other parties to monitor the proceedings or influence the process or its outcomes. This arrangement is particularly significant, considering that employee salaries and benefits account for nearly 90 percent of the entire operating budget.[16]

Of further significance, contract negotiations are rarely completed before the superintendent must submit his budget. It is not unusual for negotiations to be unfinished by the time the board must submit its budget. Thus without exact numbers, budget estimates must be used without any guarantee that they are accurate. This process can have catastrophic effects on the ability of the board to keep the budget under the spending limits set by the county council. For example, during the 1996 fiscal year budget process, the board negotiated a 2.7 percent cost of living raise for teachers.[17] However, the county council's approved budget contained only enough money to fund a 2 percent increase. The board was forced to choose between rolling back the negotiated raise or cutting spending from other areas of the budget. Going against the council's recommendation, the board gave priority to honoring the negotiated contract and chose to reduce spending by increasing class size, thus putting the demands of its employees above the demands of parents.

The length and secretive nature of the contract negotiations devalues the public process by giving a tremendous advantage to particular members of the education subsystem, namely the people negotiating contracts. Further, because of the negotiating process, most of the budget is removed from public control. The public is left to debate over the 10 percent not negotiated by collective bargaining. Community activists argue that opening up the negotiating process would give the public more influence and would require both sides in the process to act more responsibly.

This struggle over access and information extends past contract negotiations to other budgetary issues and ultimately to larger concerns about accountability. To whom is MCPS accountable? County residents would most likely argue that as a public institution, MCPS should be accountable to them. But in order to hold the school system accountable, citizens must have access to information. Accordingly, there has been a call for MCPS to release more quality information about its activities, particularly budget activities.[18]

A frequent criticism of the school system is that it puts money into projects without determining whether the projects are effective, the costs justifiable, or both. With more information, citizens could begin to gauge the impact of programs for themselves. Accordingly, the MCCPTA and minority activists have lobbied to get more detailed data on all schools and school clusters in order to determine exactly where and how the school system's resources are being spent. The central administration has tried to resist these efforts, and the school board has not been eager to force it to provide the information. However, continued demands for information and dissatisfaction with the budget process have moved the school system to provide more data than it has in the past.

At the recommendation of several groups, MCPS added cost data to its annual school profile report in 1994 and expanded that data in 1995. Although some people saw this change as an attempt by MCPS to move in the right direction, others complained the information was no more useful than before because the document failed to give per pupil cost figures for each school and included "allocated" cost figures, not "actual" amounts.[19]

MCPS also produced a new document, the *Citizens' Accountability Report.* According to the superintendent, "The report is designed to demonstrate the progress that Montgomery County citizens can expect when they invest tax dollars in public education."[20] The production of this document suggests that MCPS does sense the growing dissatisfaction with the budget process. Yet the document does not provide new information; instead, it is a summary of several other documents already published—documents that activists have criticized as incomplete.

Although MCPS can keep tight control over the information it releases, the system cannot carefully control information coming from others. Thus the media are a potentially powerful threat to those controlling the subsystem. Whether the media are actually a threat, however, depends on the types of issues that draw their attention.

An informal survey of *Washington Post* articles from January 1993 to December 1995 shows the dominance of the school system's budget as a topic.[21] Of the education articles surveyed, 31 percent focused on either the budget process specifically or other budgetary concerns. Surveying the *Montgomery Journal,* a local newspaper serving the county, produced similar results: 20 percent of the articles focused on the budget process. When compared to the amount of coverage given to topics such as academic achievement (3 percent for the *Post,* and 5 percent for the *Journal*) and curricula and education programs (8 percent and 9 percent), the magnitude of the coverage devoted to the budget becomes clear.

What is the impact of such intense budget coverage? During this period of austerity, the coverage tends to make the budget process more contentious by focusing much of the public's attention on it, intensifying the already heightened competition and increasing the probability of fragmentation. This fragmentation strains existing coalitions and makes it difficult for new ones to form. For example, during the fiscal year 1996 budget process, the MCCPTA's leadership was quoted as supporting the county executive's desire to reign in MCPS' budget.[22] This position drew the ire of the school board and the school system.[23] As a result, PTA members say they had a difficult time getting support for their efforts.

Letting the budget consume so much time and resources makes reform more difficult by requiring all actors to spend most of their time on the budget. Because the process is so demanding, it saps the energy needed for other efforts, including mobilization. The lack of adequate budget information has not been a serious problem in the past because the county's prosperity seemed boundless, and most actors appeared to get what they wanted. There was little effort to reform a school system that was seen as one of the best. Today, fiscal shortages and a time of increased needs have resulted in a transformation of the political environment. More people are fighting over slices of the pie. Those previously uninterested in education are now joining the fray, and the process is highly acrimonious. These dynamics put education supporters in a difficult position. They need to be critical of the system if they are going to effect change, but that criticism might serve as ammunition for taxpayer groups hostile to education spending in general. Thus, these supporters must walk a delicate line.

Such intense focus on the budget almost entirely precludes attention to topics such as academic achievement, curricula, system accountability, or other issues that might serve to question the supporting idea. Only 6 percent of the *Post*'s articles and 5 percent of the *Journal*'s articles dealt with reform issues, loosely defined. The failure of the media to focus more attention on broader issues diminishes the likelihood of systemic reform. This failure, coupled with the difficulty in obtaining information from MCPS, works against efforts to implement current reform proposals. Further, the fragmentation caused by budgetary constraints, and exacerbated by media coverage, makes the possibility of substantive reform remote.

An Increasingly Diverse Population

The issues surrounding diversity show how MCPS as an institution resists or fails to change, sometimes unwittingly. These issues also bring into question the validity of the supporting idea by lending credence to the opinions of individuals who suggest that MCPS' success is due more to the quality of its students than the quality of its services. Though Montgomery County continues to be a majority white school system, it is increasingly much less so, moving from 78.3 percent white in 1980 to 55.8 percent white in 1995.[24] MCPS is also becoming more international, having students who represent more than 138 countries and 122 languages.[25] With these new students come new or different needs or both.

Integration. In 1972 an adjacent school system underwent court-ordered busing to desegregate its schools. The actors inside the education subsystem, sensing a clear and powerful outside threat, chose to be proactive rather than wait to respond to court challenges and face a similar fate. In 1977 MCPS developed a voluntary desegregation plan using magnet schools.

Montgomery County's magnet schools have a reputation for academic excellence, but the real success of any magnet program lies in its ability to ensure integration. Montgomery County's magnets were supposed to increase the number of white children attending schools with a high-minority enrollment and to reduce the possibility of massive white flight from the most urban part of the county.

The magnet schools have been criticized as ineffective tools for desegregation. A 1994 study of the MCPS magnet program found a low number of transfer requests, suggesting that the lure of magnets is not sufficient to encourage families to leave their neighborhood schools.[26] This finding is not surprising, given the level of quality in the MCPS school system overall. For many parents, a magnet's increased quality does not offset the cost of sending their children to a school outside their neighborhood. The study also found that if all requested transfers were granted, magnets would actually increase segregation.

The county's magnets frequently fail to integrate classrooms in the schools where they are located. Although the magnet programs are located in high minority schools, students in the magnet tend to be separated from those outside the program, producing a school within a school. It would appear that the magnets' strength lies in their ability to keep white students in the school system instead of in increasing opportunities for minority students. These findings were echoed by another study that reported that the outcome of the county's desegregation practices has been "slipping segregation."[27]

Moreover, this study found that there was an increased concentration of poverty in some schools for the 1988–1993 period. The number of schools qualifying as high poverty schools climbed from six in 1988 to nineteen in 1993.[28] More significantly, the study revealed that during this period the percentage of Asian students attending high poverty schools rose from 6 percent to 17 percent. The percentage of students attending high poverty schools increased from 11 percent to 25 percent for African Americans, and from 14 percent to 40 percent for Latinos. Since the overall poverty rate rose only 4 percent for the entire school system, these findings are particularly striking.

Further, the report highlighted a problem referred to by several respondents —that the increase in diversity—racial, economic, or otherwise—is not evenly dispersed throughout the county. It tends to be concentrated significantly within a limited number of school clusters. Undoubtedly, as the superintendent argued, much of this disparity is due to residential patterns over which the school system has no control.[29] However, MCPS, while recognizing this pattern, has done little to counter its effects and to address the issues typically associated with having large concentrations of poor and minority students.[30]

MCPS and the school board could have dealt with the concentration of poverty and the more general problem of increased enrollment by redrawing school boundaries. Yet the system chose not to propose new boundaries, realizing that such a proposal would most likely spark a firestorm of protest in the potentially affected communities. The topic of school boundaries is one of very few issues that seem capable of mobilizing public sentiment against the school system. Because the issue is so explosive, and because the system wants to avoid any issue that might threaten its position, a discussion of whether boundary shifts would counter the effects of racial and economic concentration has never taken place. Instead, the system continues to rely on magnets even as they appear to be declining in effectiveness.

Academic Achievement. Minority and poor students often have significant difficulties in schools, performance gaps appearing between blacks and whites, rich and poor.[31] These gaps are particularly large in urban schools. Studies also suggest that poor and minority children are more frequently subject to disciplinary actions and overrepresented in special education classes.[32] Although the circumstances in Montgomery County are somewhat different from other urban school systems, MCPS is not immune to these problems.

The *Gordon Report,* a 1990 study commissioned by MCPS to assess minority achievement, points out that the circumstances for ethnic minorities in Montgomery County, Maryland, differ in three ways from minorities in many other areas of the United States.[33] First, in line with the educational level of the parents, the overall quality of the public school system is relatively high. Second, minority achievement is relatively high in Montgomery County compared to ethnic minorities in other school systems, despite the gap in achievement between ethnic minorities and white students. The third difference is the high number of ethnic minorities from the middle-class range.

While praising previous efforts by the school system, the *Gordon Report* points out that minority students still tend to be overrepresented in special education classes and underrepresented in gifted and talented programs. The report also emphasizes that minority groups saw the school system as insensitive to minority students' needs and saw teachers and school staff as having lower expectations for minority students and making less effort in teaching them. Overall, the report finds that though many minority students possess the same readiness to learn as the traditional white MCPS student, others, particularly those of new immigrant or low-income families, present a different challenge for the public schools.

MCPS responded to the *Gordon Report* by adopting a new education policy in 1992 called Success for Every Student (SES), the overarching policy to guide the school system in setting priorities. MCPS describes it as "a plan to improve the achievement of low to average achieving students with special and critical emphasis on the needs of low to average achieving African-American, American Indian, Asian-American and Hispanic students."[34]

SES focuses on the universal goal of raising everybody's level of academic achievement in an attempt to affect the achievement of specific minority groups. But why did the school system concentrate on universal goals instead of on a more targeted plan? According to community activists, the plan's universal goals are designed to appease white middle-class families. Over the past several years, there has been a growing backlash against programs targeted for specific populations. There is wide sentiment that the school system has forgotten about the "average" student—the child in the middle without any special needs. This attitude most likely stems from concerns over the tightening resources available for education and about MCPS' ability to maintain its tradition of excellence as it adapts to a diversified student population.

MCPS saw SES as a plan that would allow it to address minority achievement without provoking opposition from the larger population. Instead, SES has opened the system to criticism that the goals are far too general without specific strategies for improving performance goals for minority students. The board's own Advisory Committee for Minority Student Education has been critical of the plan:

> Our analysis of Success for Every Student proved to be a formidable undertaking. The main reason for this was a lack of data and information, or superficial or inadequate responses. Too often it appeared that implementation efforts were planning exercises that led to another plan! The Advisory Committee's conclusion is that if Success for Every Student is to succeed, more monitoring is essential at the implementation level. There seems to be great potential in the overall plan, but it requires more accountability for implementation efforts and results.[35]

Although the committee applauded the goals of SES, it notes that there had been no substantial progress made on outcomes or the mechanisms to reach these outcomes. It adds that the plan failed to provide disciplinary procedures for those staff members and schools not making adequate progress toward the goals.

SES, and ultimately MCPS, receives even harsher criticism from the Citizens' Minority Relations Monitoring Committee (CMRMC), a self-appointed monitoring group. The CMRMC releases an annual report concentrated largely on how well the school system has done in educating African Americans. Their 1994–1995 study agrees with previous findings that African Americans are overrepresented in special education classes and underrepresented in gifted programs.[36] The CMRMC also expresses concern about the low test scores and high percentage of suspensions and expulsions among African American students. Its report goes further than other reports, asserting that minority achievement today is no better than when it released its 1983–1984 report. Although the CMRMC report received some media attention, its call to action seems to have gone largely unheard by the school system, whose only response was for the superintendent to say that he would like to discuss the matter with the group.[37]

Despite reports criticizing MCPS' response to minority and low-income students, there have been some successes at the school level. One innovative effort by the county is *Linkages to Learning*. The program provides social services within schools for children and their families. This comprehensive service model follows national trends of linking social services to families within a school setting and is seen as a shift in how schools operate.[38] Currently, the program is operating in five facilities, with plans to expand to three more.

The system has other programs to address the needs of low-income students.

By contributing sixty-seven cents per federal dollar (forty-seven cents more than required), the county is able to run a Head Start program for all federally eligible children and some "near poor" students. Further, the county has a Head Start Transition program designed to sustain the gains made in Head Start. And although fiscal concerns have forced the county to eliminate most of its all-day kindergarten classes, all-day kindergarten is provided in those schools that are deemed to have the most vulnerable children.

A recent report showed that some Montgomery County schools in high-poverty, high-minority neighborhoods performed well on state reading tests.[39] This success is credited to the creative efforts and innovative programs of the school-level staff. These pockets of achievement serve as evidence that the obstacles to improved academic achievement can be overcome—if school systems are dedicated to doing so. Of course this raises the question, why are not all the Montgomery County schools performing well, as the system's reputation would suggest? Some schools are performing adequately, but others clearly are not.

In spite of their frustration with the inadequacy of school system policies, the efforts of the CMRMC and others have failed to mobilize parents against the system. One problem in doing so may be that academic achievement issues do not receive much media attention. But even internal criticisms have failed to change the current policies.

In the Montgomery County education subsystem, minority groups and low-income residents have typically had little institutional access. This may be due to several factors. First, minority and low-income parents are underrepresented in the MCCPTA, the primary parents' advocacy group. Second, many of the organized minority groups in the county have interests other than education. Multiple agendas weaken the potential for gaining access since institutional challenges almost always require sustained, consistent focus.

Third, the perceived quality of the school system and the relatively high achievement of minority students, especially compared to neighboring jurisdictions, have tended to mute criticisms. As one respondent suggested, things have not changed because many minority parents believe they have found "the promised land" in Montgomery County. That is, minority parents see the situation in Montgomery County as much better than neighboring jurisdictions, most notably Washington, DC. Consequently, they are unwilling to complain and challenge the monopoly.

Fourth, MCPS has made some limited responses but has used the budget squeeze to justify the minimal nature of these responses. And by putting minority members on its advisory boards and committees, the system can claim it has given minorities access. But doing so also allows the administration to absorb the criticism without forfeiting control of the arena. All of these factors have prevented the kind of crisis that would mobilize groups to demand new policies.

Special Education. Authority over any one policy area is frequently shared by several different groups of policymakers. The existence of these multiple "policy venues" or areas of control can assist individuals who wish to access or alter the policy subsystem since each venue offers a different entry point.[40] The case of special education provides an example of how a change in policy venue can have a profound impact on the subsystem. It also offers an example of how the people outside the subsystem can gain access and have significant influence over a subsystem.

Parents, unhappy with the special education department's handling of their children's education, felt frustrated by the department's response, or lack of response, to their concerns. They began looking for alternative ways to bring pressure upon the special education department to get the action they wanted. They found their alternative entry point in the federal courts.[41]

Parents petitioned the courts to force the county to provide their children with the kind of quality education required by law. Because of administrative inefficiency or mismanagement, the special education department repeatedly missed state and federal deadlines for filing paperwork and conducting evaluations. Missing the deadlines automatically caused the system to lose cases it would ordinarily win and also caused it to incur significant costs. The procedural problems became so bad that school officials, convinced they would lose, began settling cases before they even went to trial. By turning to the courts, special education parents were able to gain access to the subsystem and to get what they wanted for their children.

The general public was largely unaware of these problems until a leaked administration report revealed that MCPS was losing more than $4 million a year in legal fees and private-school placements because of the inept management of special education cases and inattentiveness to parents' concerns.[42] Such unnecessary expenses in a time when money was already tight provoked an immediate negative response from the community. The school system had to act or risk being acted upon. In summer 1995 the superintendent announced a thorough overhaul of the special education department, including reassigning staff, reorganizing the department, and computerizing cases and deadlines.[43]

On the surface it would appear that the system acted swiftly and effectively to the betterment of special education quality and service; a closer inspection shows this not to be the case. The computer system designed to alleviate problems only created more as employees found it time-consuming and difficult to access. It was abandoned less than six months after it became operational, and missed deadlines again became a problem. Legal fees continued to run over budget in 1995 and 1996. While the system argues that the legal fees are now under control, those with intimate knowledge of the system counter that costs are still larger than necessary. The difference is that the costs are now spread across departments, hiding their full impact.

The efforts of a few parents and the media changed the character of special education discussion in the county, at least temporarily. By gaining access through an alternative policy venue, parents were able to achieve improvements that MCPS had refused to give them. By shifting the special education focus from the quality of programs and practices to the quality of the department itself, the media exposed the department's weaknesses and made it vulnerable to attack. The system was forced to act. Ironically, the situation could have been avoided, or at least considerably reduced, had the system heeded earlier warnings. Previous reports had identified the inefficiencies that led to the inflated legal costs, but these reports were ignored.[44] Some observers would say that MCPS paid a price for this. After the initial firestorm, however, the issue has largely faded from public consciousness, allowing MCPS to appear responsive and responsible while continuing to maintain control.

Site-Based Management

For many years school systems have tried to keep parents and the larger community at arm's length.[45] Site-based management (SBM) has the potential to bring parents and other community members into greater contact with policy and to increase the accountability of the school system to parents and the community. SBM, in Montgomery County, has become an important test of MCPS' willingness to open up the school system.

As the educational environment changes, a growing concern in the community has been whether established mechanisms provide adequate access for new residents as well as for long-term residents. A response to this concern was the school system's appointment of a Long Range Planning Task Force to develop a long-term vision for MCPS. The task force's primary recommendation called for an SBM plan to be implemented by MCPS. The plan would require shifting power from the central office to individual schools and providing student, resource, and financial information for each school.

The task force's recommendation came almost ten years after a similar recommendation by the 1985 Commission on Excellence in Teaching. As part of a series of recommendations, the commission advocated SBM as a means of encouraging effective education.[46] It described MCPS as a system that is "becoming increasingly bureaucratic, inflexible, and top-down in its management style. Problems are identified, strategies are developed, and resources deployed mostly at the Board and central office level, then presented to the schools for implementation."[47] The commission saw SBM as a vehicle for correcting these problems.

Despite the support of the task force and other groups, SBM is largely untried in Montgomery County. There are many supporters of SBM in principle, but countywide implementation has faltered. Following the initial recommendations, MCPS installed a "flexibility" pilot program in nine schools in 1990. This pilot differed from other SBM plans in that it focused on shared decision making, allowing the central administration to retain primary control of school management and budgeting. In an internal evaluation of the pilot, most of the participants strongly supported the shared decision-making approach.[48] However, survey participants cited as obstacles the lack of central- and area-office administrative support, the absence of board policy on shared decision making, and an insufficient amount of training, time, and money.[49] No new schools have volunteered for the program since its inception, and some of the original participants have since abandoned the project.

SBM in Montgomery County was destined to failure because it was not the school system's basic reform strategy.[50] Instead, it was just another policy in a sea of policies. The evaluation team has noted that "neither the Superintendent of Schools nor the Board of Education initially made any commitment to extend the pilot beyond a trial period or to institutionalize it if successful."[51] Official policy calls for voluntary participation in SBM, but the board spends no effort promoting it. The abandonment of SBM shows the strength of the institutional status quo in Montgomery County. Since a pilot plan was already under way, policymakers were able to circumvent attempts to define and sell SBM.

Given the strength of some local PTAs and the political astuteness of many people in the county, it may be that parents have created their own informal style of site-based decision making. These parents may decide what their local school needs and then try to get these needs placed on the county agenda or fill them themselves. Local PTAs often raise extra money for their schools or provide services that might not otherwise be supplied.[52] The question is whether all local school PTAs will be in a position to aid their schools. Will those less affluent, less politically sophisticated, and less knowledgeable about the system gain access? It remains to be seen. Informal SBM may enlarge inequities between schools. Yet if properly implemented, formal SBM could eliminate or at least minimize some of the disparities that currently exist.

The success of local-level PTAs does not transfer to the county level. Indeed, such success may hinder the ability of the organization to gain power on a county wide basis. Some activists see a divide and conquer strategy; they argue that those local PTAs that play along with MCPS are rewarded with resources. Some respondents identified a "PTA style" of interaction with the central administration that is highly conciliatory in nature and designed not to rock the boat. The central administration, it is feared, marginalizes those groups who take a more confrontational approach. By adopting a nonconfrontational style, local PTAs reinforce the power of the monopoly.

Reform requires a change in thinking about the place of education in the community and the role of the community in education. Once this vision is developed, sustained cooperation between the various political actors in the community is needed to support a reform movement long enough for it to produce a successful challenge to the policy monopoly and the idea supporting it.

What, then, are the prospects for educational change in Montgomery County? Despite significant pockets of criticism, there is no general plan to overhaul the school system. Site-based management, which is typically seen as the blueprint for comprehensive, systemic reform, has been neutralized by the school system.

Still, community activists continue to call for more openness and accountability. They complain that there is too much bureaucracy and that the budget cannot be traced back to schools and programs. But the competitive atmosphere created by scarcity means these complaints are not unified. Scarce resources force issues of equity between white and minority parents, between middle-class and poor parents, and between parents of high-achieving (gifted) students and average students. Funding battles between the MCCPTA and the MCEA make a broad-based reform coalition difficult to achieve. Moreover, because of the county's changed fiscal condition, individuals calling for change must temper their criticism of the school system in order to protect the county education budget from other activists wishing to fund their own policy arena or to lower taxes.

In Montgomery County, the level of discontent with the school system has not reached critical mass. Although there is frustration, there has been no sustained challenge to the policy monopoly held by the school administration. PTA members have become fragmented in their vision, focusing on their own cluster or breaking into interest groups around specific programs. The people without children in the system are unlikely to be a part of challenging the institution since their perceptions are colored by memories of their own past experiences. Those memories are of a school system that was an innovator and that served them well. They seem largely unaware of the changes that have taken place.

With a past reputation of academic excellence, achieved in serving a homogeneous, educated middle class, MCPS is able to fend off the idea that major change is needed. Piecemeal adaptations suffice. MCPS' supporting idea is still fully entrenched within much of the public psyche. At the same time, traditional community support mechanisms, particularly task forces, give the appearance of citizen input while ignoring any substantive criticisms. The advisory nature of these citizen committees, combined with an entrenched supporting idea, provides substantial protection for the school system's policy monopoly. Accordingly, the school system is able to maintain its control on the subsystem by deflecting and absorbing challenges.

At this stage, political support for the school system has only loosened, not fully destabilized. A broad challenge coalition is not yet in place, and opposition is too fragmented to be effective in more than a piecemeal manner. Mindful of past school system accomplishments, key parts of the county's civic leadership feel no sense of urgency about reform. Ad hoc responses and small-scale initiatives hold a broad-based challenge at bay and leave control of the education subsystem in the hands of MCPS.

NOTES

1. Maryland National Capital Park and Planning Commission, *1994 Planning Area Profiles: Demographic Data by Area and Structure Type* (Silver Spring, MD: Montgomery County Planning Department, November 1995), p. 6.

2. Bureau of the Census, *City and County Data Book 1994* (Washington, DC: Department of Commerce, 1994).

3. Frank R. Baumgartner and Bryan D. Jones, *Agendas and Instability in American Politics* (Chicago: University of Chicago Press, 1993).

4. Baumgartner and Jones, *Agendas and Instability in American Politics,* p. 7.

5. Charles E. Bidwell, "Toward Improved Knowledge and Policy on Urban Education," in *The Politics of Urban Education in the United States: The 1991 Yearbook of the Education Association,* eds. James G. Cibulka, Rodney J. Reed, and Kenneth K. Wong (Washington, DC: Falmer Press, 1991), pp. 193–99.

6. Montgomery County Public Schools, *The Citizens Budget FY 1997* (Rockville, MD; December 1995).

7. Dan Beyers, "Four Largest Md. School Districts Show Little Progress on Scores," *Washington Post,* December 12, 1996, p. G1.

8. In 1996 MCPS' per pupil expenditures were $7,697, $900 more than the next highest district. Maryland State Department of Education, *The Fact Book 1995–96: A Statistical Handbook* (Baltimore, 1996).

9. Stephanie Barrett, "Older Students Lack Remedial Skills," *Montgomery Journal,* January 22, 1997, p. A1.

10. In order to understand the educational politics in Montgomery County, sixty-eight interviews using a structured interview schedule were conducted beginning in 1993. These interviews included elected officials, media representatives, civic leaders, the business community, activists, and education specialists. We have drawn heavily on the responses from these interviews as well as on newspaper articles and primary data to describe education in Montgomery County.

11. Maryland State Department of Education, *The Fact Book 1995–96.*

12. Amy Goldstein, "Montgomery Poll Backs Teacher Raises," *Washington Post,* March 20, 1990, p. A12.

13. "The Teachers Don't Get It," *Washington Post,* November 16, 1991, p. A26.

14. "Teachers' Union Talks Go to Mediation," *Silver Spring Gazette,* February 21, 1996, p. A27.

15. The spending affordability guidelines are the result of a 1990 charter amendment designed to limit increases in property taxes. The amendment limits property tax rate adjustment to the rate of increase in the consumer price index unless seven county council members agree to a higher increase. Every October the council must estimate the amount of local revenues available in the upcoming year and set estimated budget limits (called spending affordability guidelines) for all county departments and agencies.

16. Montgomery County Public Schools, *The Citizens Budget FY 1998* (Rockville, MD: December 1996).

17. Dan Beyers, "Montgomery Board Increases Class Size to Balance Budget," *Washington Post,* June 14, 1995, p. B1.

18. Dan Beyers, "Cutting up the Pie in Education," *Washington Post,* January 12, 1995, p. MD1.

19. Judith Sloan Deutsch, "Revised Spending Breakdown Still Comes up Short, Critics Say," *Silver Spring Gazette,* February 7, 1996, p. A30.

20. Montgomery County Public Schools, *Citizens' Accountability Report* (Rockville, MD: 1995), p. 3.

21. In addition to articles in the paper's front and metro sections, articles also appear in a weekly section ("The Montgomery Weekly") that focuses on the county and is dis-

tributed in papers sold in the county. The articles surveyed do not include sports reports, editorials, columns, or letters to the editor.

22. Dan Beyers, "PTA Praises Cutbacks," *Washington Post,* March 30, 1995, p. MD1.

23. Dan Beyers and Michael Abramowitz, "School Board Takes the Fight to the PTA," *Washington Post,* June 29, 1995, p. MD1.

24. The percentage of students who are minorities increased 35.8 percent between 1970 and 1995. In 1970, there were 125,344 students, and 91.6 percent of them were white. In 1995 the student population was 120,788, of which 55.8 percent were white, 19.4 percent were African American, 12.0 percent were Hispanic, and 12.5 percent Asian American. See Department of Facilities Planning and Capital Programming, *Requested FY 1997 Capital Budget and the FY 1997 to FY 2002 Capital Improvements Program* (Rockville, MD: Montgomery County Public Schools, 1995).

25. Montgomery County Public Schools, *Our Commitment to Quality: A Guide for the 1996–97 School Year* (Rockville, MD: 1996), p. 8.

26. Jeffrey R. Henig, *Rethinking School Choice: Limits of the Market Metaphor* (Princeton: Princeton University Press, 1994).

27. Susan E. Eaton, "Slipping Towards Segregation: Local Control and Eroding Desegregation in Montgomery County, Maryland," paper prepared for the Harvard Project on School Desegregation, August 1994.

28. A high-poverty school is defined as one in which 40 percent of the student population were eligible for free or reduced-price lunch.

29. Judith Sloan Deutsch, "Vance Blasts Harvard Desegregation Study," *Silver Spring Gazette,* July 13, 1994, p. 1.

30. Robert E. England, Kenneth J. Meier, and Luis Ricardo Fraga, "Barriers to Educational Opportunity: Educational Practices and Minority Students," *Urban Affairs Quarterly* 23 (June 1988): 635–46.

31. Gary Natriello, Edward L. McDill, and Aaron M. Pallas, *Schooling Disadvantaged Children: Racing Against Catastrophe* (New York: Teachers College Press, 1990). Kenneth K. Wong and Margaret C. Wang, eds., *Rethinking Policy for At-Risk Students* (Berkeley, CA: McCutchan, 1994).

32. James Gordon Ward and Patricia Anthony, eds., *Who Pays for Student Diversity? Population Changes and Educational Policy* (Newbury Park, CA: Corwin, 1992).

33. Edmund W. Gordon and John M. Musser, *A Study of Minority Student Achievement in Montgomery County Public Schools* (Pomona, NY: Gordon and Gordon Associates in Human Development, November 16, 1990).

34. Montgomery County Public Schools, *Success for Every Student Plan* (Rockville, MD: January 6, 1992), p. 3.

35. Advisory Committee for Minority Student Education, *1994 Annual Report* (Rockville, MD: Montgomery County Board of Education, July 25, 1994).

36. Citizens' Minority Relations Monitoring Committee, "African American Community Response to the Montgomery County Public Schools' Annual Report on Systemwide Outcome Measures (1994)" (February 14, 1995).

37. Andrew D. Beadle, "Black Leaders Say Schools Fail," *Montgomery Journal,* February 15, 1995, p. A1.

38. James G. Cibulka, "Urban Education as a Field of Study: Problems of Knowledge and Power," in Cibulka, Reed, and Wong, eds., *The Politics of Urban Education in the United States,* pp. 27–43.

39. Maryland Education Coalition and MD Kids Count Partnership, "Living in Poverty: Must Students Pay the Price?" issue brief (Source Publishing: September 1995).

40. Baumgartner and Jones, *Agendas and Instability in American Politics,* p. 38.

41. Dan Beyers, "Montgomery's Special Ed Called Inefficient, Costly," *Washington Post,* January 27, 1995, p. A1.

42. Ibid.

43. Dan Beyers, "Montgomery Special Education Still Struggling with Legal Costs, Red Tape," *Washington Post,* January 31, 1996, p. B6.

44. Jan E. Bowman and Joy A. Frechtling, *Study of the Special Education Initial Referral and Placement Process in MCPS Elementary Schools* (Rockville, MD: Montgomery County Public Schools, Department of Educational Accountability, September 1991). Department of Educational Accountability, *A Study of the MCPS Learning Disabilities Initiative* (Rockville, MD: Montgomery County Public Schools, 1991).

45. Bidwell, "Toward Improved Knowledge and Policy on Urban Education."

46. Commission on Excellence in Teaching, *Attracting, Keeping and Enabling Excellent Teachers,* report prepared for the Montgomery County Board of Education, Rockville, MD, 1987.

47. Ibid., p. 43.

48. Antoinette B. Brown, *The Flexibility Pilot: Two Years of Shared Decision Making in Selected Montgomery County Public Schools* (Rockville, MD: Montgomery County Public Schools, Department of Educational Accountability, January 1992), p. 19.

49. Ibid., p. 20.

50. Paul T. Hill and Josephine Bonan, *Decentralization and Accountability in Public Education* (Santa Monica, CA: Rand, 1991).

51. Brown, *Flexibility Pilot,* p. E-1.

52. Andrew D. Beadle, "Schools Relying on PTAs," *Montgomery Journal,* March 24, 1995, p. A1.

PART III
Business Involvement and the Struggle for Reform

Educational improvement has become a nearly universal concern in urban school districts, and a major proponent of reform is corporate business. But what is the impact of business involvement? Part 3 examines experiences in three large urban districts. Dorothy Shipps shows that business involvement in the Chicago school system has an extended history that runs much deeper than is generally recognized. In particular, the recent move to elevate managerial control in Chicago springs from a long-running series of business initiatives, some of which have not been highly visible. In Charlotte-Mecklenburg, business participation has been highly public, and business leaders were integrally involved in backing desegregation through a controversial plan of busing. Houston provides a third case of extensive business influence, and in this instance school-business partnerships are the principal vehicle for business involvement in the education process.

Each of these cases is rich in significant detail, but they also pose some broad questions about business influence on the direction of school reform. Business seems little inclined to pursue issues of pedagogical reform. "Businesslike" management rather than classroom techniques draws the reform spotlight that business shines. Houston provides an interesting variation. In that city, from a growing concern with crime and youth gangs, business has focused on school-linked services and community improvements to provide a more promising context for the education process. Unresolved, however, is the issue of how to balance voluntary effort with regularized public support. Houston's history of elite-level voluntarism, Thomas Longoria suggests, may be a means whereby public expenditures are kept at a minimum. Moreover, Houston's style of business participation draws considerable suspicion from community groups, and it has contributed to tensions between the Latino and African American communities. Despite—and to some extent because of—business partnerships, civic capacity on behalf of educational reform in Houston is incomplete and halting.

Charlotte has a more developed form of civic capacity than most cities, which was key in that district's success with busing. However, as Stephen Smith shows, demographic change has weakened that city's once formidable biracial coalition. The consolidated character of the Charlotte-Mecklenburg district gives it an outer ring of suburbs and a set of business interests distinct from the old-line establishments based in the central business district. Population growth has brought increased political fluidity to the city, and, as Smith points out, Charlotte's established business leaders have proved somewhat clumsy in the game of electoral politics. Yet Charlotte business has a long record of involvement in education. In addition to being a major partner in the school-desegregation coalition, business has funded educational initiatives and was a key supporter of innovator John Murphy as school superintendent. Still, as Smith notes, though business support seems necessary to sustain an activist agenda, business involvement is not sufficient—particularly to bring into being a genuine performance regime.

These three cases show that business involvement is no cure-all for school problems. Business has enormous resources and considerable influence, but its understanding of the issues tends to be narrow. Moreover, the part that business can play is limited. It is more comfortable on management ground than on the pedagogical terrain, and it is often more at ease behind the scenes than it is engaged in the process of community mobilization.

It is well to remember that the level of business involvement varies from city to city. San Francisco, as we saw in chapter 4, has little business participation in education. In other cities, Atlanta for example, business involvement may fluctuate over time. But does this matter? There is no simple formula for explaining the difference that business participation makes. The considerable weight that it can carry behind the scenes may work counter to broad popular participation. Yet business is also a force for accountability, a force that can help break through school insularity. Though business involvement often rests on too narrow a body of concerns to carry the burden alone, school accountability may, then, be weaker without business participation than with it. In any event, there is no indication that an absence of business involvement has a liberating effect on educators, who often show little inclination to pursue a wide-ranging agenda of schooling. Thus, although business involvement is insufficient by itself to work wonders in educational improvement, there is also little evidence that its absence unleashes the creativity of education professionals. The participation of noneducators appears to be crucial.

8

Corporate Influence on Chicago School Reform

Dorothy Shipps

In June 1995 the state legislature of Illinois enacted a reform law for the Chicago Public Schools that gave sweeping new powers to a school district management team whose titles read more like those of a Fortune Five Hundred Corporation than an urban public school system.[1] Replacing the general superintendent is a chief executive officer, chief financial officer, chief operations officer, chief purchasing officer, and a chief education officer. This team, directly appointed by the mayor of Chicago, works with a new, five-member board of trustees, also mayoral appointees. Together they have authority to determine which schools require intervention; to dismiss, lay off, or reassign any and all personnel in them; and to dissolve elected Local School Councils. They are also empowered to cut costs, privatize work usually performed by employees, and abrogate many collective bargaining agreements.[2]

Seven years earlier, another school reform law had legitimated a governing strategy that appeared quite different. The Chicago School Reform Act of 1988 has been referred to as an experiment in social activism. Historians and policy analysts agreed that it was an example of radical decentralization in school governance.[3] It appeared to take community control further than any previous experiment by making parents and community members the statutory majority on each of about 550 Local School Councils (LSCs), giving them powers to hire and fire the school principal, determine the school's educational priorities, and approve the spending of state Chapter 1 funds eventually amounting to about $500,000 per elementary school and $850,000 per high school.

Striking differences in the allocation and use of power seem to distinguish these two laws, and most commentators emphasize the differences. In this chapter I clarify how Chicago's 1995 school law is linked to the 1988 law through the corporate business community's involvement in both.

Recent reform laws can be traced to a resurgence of corporate activism that began shortly after the death of Mayor Richard J. Daley, when local bankers and other corporate business association leaders restructured financial control of the system. This led them to an intensive, unilateral effort to rationalize and decentralize central office operations between 1980 and 1984. Discomfited by central office resistance, in 1987 they invited other civic and community groups to form a cross-sector coalition to restructure the school governance system. The unlikely coalition ultimately wrote, lobbied for, and helped implement and interpret the 1988 law. Leaders and staff of these same business associations eventually developed a critique of the 1988 law, which in turn informed their participation in drafting new legislation in 1995. When reform is described with this history in mind, it reflects the refinement of long-standing corporate concerns rather than a pendular reaction from one reform strategy to the next.

In this chapter I discuss the governance consequences of corporate business involvement; others have documented the educational consequences of these reforms.[4] The new governing system forged in these two laws strengthens corporate links to systemwide bureaucrats and political agents while it simultaneously limits parents' influence to individual schools. Chicago school reform of the last fifteen years is misconstrued without an understanding of how corporate business has influenced school politics to create these new alignments.

A frequently recounted popular mobilization prior to the 1988 law differentiates Chicago's experience from the politics of reform in many other urban school systems. Yet the view of the two reforms that emerges when the corporate role is understood focuses less on the growth of parent power and democratic revitalization than on the replacement of professional control with business management. Chicago's community advocates made common cause with organized business, powerful allies who helped them achieve substantial benefits. Their constituency, parents and community groups, became school-level policymakers. But the price was high. The reform of 1988 empowered parents and community members as the dominant voice on each school's LSC but simultaneously weakened their influence as citizens with interests in the system of schools serving all of Chicago's children. That voice was left to corporate business, formally guiding systemwide policy through its influence on an oversight authority and using its informal political resources to shape the system. By 1995 corporate influence was institutionalized through a strong district CEO with a financial background—but no education credentials—and a corporate-style board. This management team is accountable only to the mayor, who is actively pursuing an economic development agenda.

Explaining how this situation came about shows how the reform of urban school governance is shaped by history-dependent institutions of city government. It also demonstrates how corporate interests in public education are shaped by business association rules and roles. Though it has been frequently noted that corporate influence is often manifest through school board membership, adopt-a-school, and other special programs, these forms of influence are increasingly overshadowed by the systemwide governance reforms of organized corporate groups. The Chicago case demonstrates that this seemingly new form of corporate influence in education has a long and vibrant history.

It presents an opportunity to examine how local corporate involvement occurs. What resources did business bring to school policy formation? How have Chicago's history and political institutions encouraged and constrained corporate activism? How has corporate mobilization influenced the recent course of system change? As it turns out, institutional strengths—the extraordinary organizational resources of Chicago's business groups, its long legacy of intervention in the governance and organization of the city's schools, and the mayor's reliance on corporate support—help to explain the role of corporate business in Chicago.

Chicago's corporate leaders also have a long history of collaboration with the local Democratic machine, in addition to enjoying the support of Republican politicians statewide. The mayor of Chicago has long had a strong influence on school policy (he or she has always appointed the school board, for instance), and organized business has been a crucial part of the mayor's governing coalition. The recent role of business in city politics has been shaped by nearly fifty years of highly centralized government. These structural and institutional factors have reinforced the public policy advantages that Chicago's corporate business associations share with all others, making the Chicago story a cautionary tale.

My analysis aims at understanding how organized business used its power to affect the school system between 1979 and 1995 and the extent to which the city's school reform laws reflect the interests and activities of business association representatives. I begin by describing the organizational strengths of Chicago's corporate business associations and the legacy of school activism inherited by current members. Next, their solution for the troubles of the school system is described as it evolved, during a transition from Chicago's fabled machine governance to black-led populism and back to control of the school system by city hall. Last, some concerns about the impact of this kind of corporate involvement on democratic governance in Chicago's public schools are explored.[5]

CORPORATE ACTORS IN CHICAGO SCHOOL POLITICS

Chicago's recent reforms are simultaneously a response to chronic concerns about poor performance and the most recent manifestation of a long struggle for control of the city's public schools. The basic facts include decades of declining enrollments accompanied by rising proportions of poor, bilingual, and handicapped students and a crumbling stock of buildings with the attendant increases in the costs of education. In the 1970s and 1980s widespread dissatisfaction with Chicago schools was solidified by a financial crisis, encouraged by educators who appeared indifferent to calls for change, and spurred by documentation of poor academic performance, high dropout rates, violations of state regulations, and a decline in low-skill manufacturing jobs in the city. The struggle over who will control and reshape the city's schools has engaged many organizations over the last century, and business associations have been among them as soon as they were formed.

The Early Years

The core business interests in the coalitions that negotiated the 1988 and 1995 school reform laws are a group of four related associations. Each of the three younger associations was founded and is largely funded by the elite, Commercial Club of Chicago, organized in 1877. By the early 1990s it had grown to include 275 leaders of the city's top industrial, commercial, and financial institutions as well as the heads of the city's main philanthropic and civic institutions. The mayor of Chicago and the governor of Illinois have been ex-officio members of the Commercial Club for about twenty years.

Almost as soon as it was founded, the club became an important venue through which its members pooled their resources to develop and influence legislation on the organization and control of the nascent public school system. By its fifth year, it had opened one of the city's first vocational education schools; within a decade it was cosponsoring legislation to centralize, bureaucratize, and hierarchically manage all the public schools; and by the middle of the depression it controlled the budget and financing of the school system. In these early years, its role in school policymaking was hotly contested by teachers' unions as well as by other professional and civic groups.[6]

By the depression, the cumulative effects of mayoral corruption and unpaid taxes had plunged the school system into bankruptcy. As conditions worsened, the club formed a large group of business leaders to demand cutbacks in every aspect of schooling, from kindergarten to vocational schools. When this group disbanded in 1937, Chicago's political culture had changed. By that time, Democratic machine mayors were already providing the centralized power and social stability necessary for corporate influence to flourish. The club's influence on school policy moved from center stage to behind-the-scenes. Club members acknowledged that their advantage in the new political context depended upon two key elements: the threat of a fiscal crisis severe enough to put their "private" money in charge of the school's finances and a mayor who had "complete political power to see that his orders were carried out."[7]

Close relationships forged with the emerging Democratic machine, along with its own earlier activism, were to form the basis of the club's interest in the schools. It became a key member of the governing coalition supporting the Democratic machine. Club leaders had direct access to the mayor, who was sympathetic to their requests. In turn, the club provided technical expertise, private support, and independent resources for city projects—including school projects—that the mayor sought. The club's public voice returned only after the death of the last machine mayor, Richard J. Daley, in 1976. In the intervening years, corporate business encouraged mayoral control of the school system and kept a low profile.

The Next Generation

The three younger members of the Commercial Club family, Chicago United, the Civic Committee of the Commercial Club, and Leadership for Quality Education (LQE), were founded by club leaders well after the depression-era public activism had become history. Yet each inherited the club's legacy of concern about the control, financing, and organization of the public schools.

Chicago United grew out of a group formed by three Commercial Club leaders. In early 1969 they determined that race riots and racial discord over segregated housing and schools demanded they learn to talk to black Chicago. The civil rights movement had begun to challenge Daley's regime, and the Commercial Club responded, albeit secretly at first. Club leaders gathered about ten other sympathetic members and found an equal number of their counterparts among the local African American leadership to begin a private dialogue, meeting regularly for early breakfasts in one or another of the hotels of the city. The group addressed the volatile racial issues that the mayor publicly eschewed.

In 1972 they incorporated as Chicago United and developed the structure retained through the early 1990s. Half of the approximately sixty members had to be leaders of Chicago's minority communities, preferably business leaders. Chicago United itself, as well as each of its six Task Forces, was to be co-chaired by one African American member and one white member (later, Hispanics were added). Early on, its African American members insisted that unequal schooling was a root cause of the glaring economic, political, and social inequality in the city, and education became a key topic of discussion and planning. The Chicago United Education Task Force that led the business side of the 1988 school reform coalition had its beginnings in these racially charged times. Their projects included career education for students and management training for principals; later, they focused on decentralization and the job-preparedness of graduates.

Following the death of Mayor Daley in 1976, the school policy arena shifted from the mayor's office to Springfield. Private, personal access to the mayor no longer ensured policy influence; more public means were once again required. Daley's successors, Michael Bilandik (1976–1979) and Jane Byrne (1979–1983) were unable to recentralize power and sought advice from Chicago United and a few of the club's officers.

At the same time, a national recession hit the Chicago school system hard, providing a new opportunity for the bankers of the Commercial Club to control school finances. It also provided an impetus for creating the Civic Committee of the Commercial Club, which was intended to be the club's first public policy arm since the 1930s. It was formed wholly from the membership of the club, and nomination was intended as a special honor. The Civic Committee concentrated and centralized the club's resources and voice. The group's avowed concern was the decline of jobs in metropolitan Chicago, but members quickly related jobs to workplace skills and made the link to public schooling. By the time the 1988 reform law was being hammered out in mass meetings of a reform summit, the Civic Committee was heavily involved in guiding the school reform plans of Chicago United, and both were attributing local economic prospects to the human capital produced by schools.

The populist African American mayor, Harold Washington (1983–1987), sought advice from both the Civic Committee and Chicago United. He faced the aftermath of recession without the power of a machine or the club's electoral backing and wanted corporate business in his governing coalition. One of his outreach efforts was to seek a business–school district partnership to stem the flow of unemployable high school dropouts. The partnership never materialized, but the initiative eventually led to the 1988 reform law.

In spring 1989, about two months after the 1988 reform act was signed, the Civic Committee and Chicago United created Leadership for Quality Education to help implement the new law. Mayor Washington had died in office. His successor, Eugene Sawyer (1987–1988), was uninterested in school reform, as was Richard M. Daley (1988–present) initially. But negotiations that had enabled the 1988 law had developed their own momentum. As Mayor Daley came to realize, systemwide school reform remained on the public and corporate agendas. Gradually, he too embraced reform.

LQE became the voice of corporate business in public schooling, inheriting the status from Chicago United. It was largely responsible for supporting the community organizing effort that made the first LSC elections a success. LQE also provided professional staff to the interim board of education during the transition period after enactment, commissioned surveys of school council members, and underwrote a number of reform advocacy groups, eventually developing its own agenda of charter and small school advocacy.

By creating three subsidiary associations to address different aspects of social policy, Commercial Club leaders were responding to successive changes in the local political culture. First was the threat to the Democratic machine posed by civil rights struggles in the 1960s. It spurred the creation of Chicago United. The collapse of the machine left Daley's successors unable to cope with the recession of the late 1970s, engendering the Civic Committee to focus corporate clout on economic revitalization. Next came Harold Washington's inclusionary regime. It highlighted Chicago United's role as a bridge between the corporate and black communities and generated corporate interest in forming a coalition with community groups on school issues. Ultimately, it helped produce LQE, with its mixed board of corporate and community leaders.

Common Organizing Principles

The relationship linking these four organizations goes beyond their being founded by the same patriarch association. There is also a high proportion of membership overlap among the white members of the four groups. The groups share induction processes and membership rules that bind them to a common vision of civic life in Chicago, operating procedures that stress members' discipline and control, and decision-making patterns that encourage cohesion. Common organizing principles help to clarify how these groups achieved the capacity for policy negotiation. Structural commonalities underscore the strong historical ties among them, provide a framework within which the motives of individual members are actualized, and make more comprehensible the thesis that they have a collective and cumulative role in Chicago school reform.

Principals Only and the Requirement of Civic Service

Members of these associations are a highly selective group of corporate businessmen and a few nonbusiness civic leaders. A new member may be nominated only if he or she is both the principal (CEO, president, director) of his or her organization and has a resumé of civic service in Chicago. Insisting that each member have authority to deliberate and act on behalf of his or her firm facilitates their collective ability to create binding decisions. The requirement of civic service ensures that members of the four associations have similar experiences with Chicago's elected policymakers and appointed bureaucrats; they learn to speak about local policy problems in a shared language. The public service rule has also meant that each succeeding generation of members builds on the local policy network established by its predecessors.

Member Control

Another important property of these organizations is that they are run by members. CEOs, presidents, and directors do most of the work and sit on the committees. Corporate members deliberate on and decide all internal organizational matters as well as determine the public policy stands each association will take. New members often begin their tenure with an assignment to work on a citywide task force or to co-chair a committee with more experienced members. Committee assignments serve as a kind of policy apprenticeship for members; they learn about the salient issues in a policy arena, come to know key governmental policymakers, and learn how to interact with them on behalf of the corporate community.

Member control has also worked to centralize authority in each of the associations. Lead officers in each association and executive committee members act as the primary decision makers, and small staffs reinforce their authority. Stability and clout remain linked to the active involvement of principal members, even though the small staffs of Chicago United, the Civic Committee, and LQE are highly respected for their expertise. Larger staffs would dilute the association's central political resources: direct access to the wealth of big business through CEO–initiated dues and donations and their active engagement in the policymaking for the city.

Consensus Decision Making and Public Unanimity

These associations also operate under the principle of consensus decision making. Votes are rare, usually called only when it is known beforehand that they will be unanimous. The often spirited debate that precedes decision making is safeguarded by confidentiality. Conflict takes place within the associations. Publicly, members usually speak with one voice. For instance, widely differing opinions among members meant that no consensus could be formed to support vouchers during Chicago United's internal debates over school reform in the mid-1980s. Hence, no public position was taken on the issue. Consensus decision making creates the useful appearance that members have similar opinions, despite sometimes sharp disagreements, and facilitates disciplined, concerted action.

These membership criteria, structures, and decision-making processes foster uncommon cohesiveness. They encourage members to become actively engaged in local policymaking, despite their personal histories of activism, mitigating the long-recognized tendency of multinational corporate leaders to be focused on national and international concerns to the exclusion of local interests.[8]

The reemergence of business as a school policy actor was possible because Chicago business had uncommon institutional strengths. It had a legacy of school policy innovation and advocacy dating from the turn of the century. It had internal organizational structures and processes that facilitated cohesion and the ability to act in concert. Its own staff helped to define issues and alternative solutions and was supported by powerful corporate members. By creating subsidiary organizations that formed different coalitions around social policy issues—Chicago United with Chicago's African American leadership, LQE with community-based school reform advocacy groups—corporate business was able to mobilize other constituencies (and antagonisms) that might have remained dormant. The rules of membership, induction, and apprenticeship within these related associations prepared corporate business to take on the role of school policy kingmaker with what otherwise might seem to have been astonishing speed. But this capacity to act is inseparable from a history that led to one of the most radical cases of urban school governance reform in fifty years.

BUSINESS AND CHICAGO SCHOOL REFORM, 1979–1995

What began as a corporate bailout in 1979 was to become a wholesale appropriation of modern management rhetoric and governance forms by the Chicago school system. In the years leading up to 1995, corporate leaders took command by detailing administrative changes they sought from the central office, selecting school board members, and overseeing the system's finances and systemwide reorganization while drafting and promoting successive pieces of legislation.

A Financial Crisis Highlights Business Resources

Just as control over school finances had been the last of the club's public efforts to reorganize schooling in the early years of the twentieth century, so a second financial crisis fifty years later became its rationale for a new wave of public activism. The financial crisis of 1979 also set the stage for the reform of 1988. Club leaders had restructured their own businesses in response to changing markets. Insolvency, they reasoned, was strong evidence that the centralized and bureaucratic school system their predecessors had helped create also needed restructuring.

The crisis of 1979 was actually a delayed reaction to long-festering problems. Mayor Richard J. Daley had managed to keep the schools open throughout the 1970s by settling frequent teachers' strikes with promises of money the system did not have, convincing legislators to make minor changes in state aid, and asking club bankers to ignore the unusual accounting and financial procedures used to keep the district's bond ratings high. One result was that Mayor Byrne faced employee strikes and the financial collapse of the $1.2 billion school system. But she washed her hands of an impending $85 million shortfall in operating-fund debt payments. Club members, concerned about the negotiability of debt notes, went to the governor. Over a New Year's weekend meeting they assembled a bailout plan. It gave an emergency loan to the school system, forced the entire board of education to resign (the superintendent and his business manager had already resigned), and launched a legislative investigation. They also created a five-person Chicago School Finance Authority (SFA), giving it the statutory power to oversee school finances and approve all major budgetary decisions.

The first SFA members were businessmen and attorneys, appointed for fixed terms by the mayor and the governor. They were accountable to no single group or officeholder since the SFA reported only once yearly to the governor and the legislature, the mayor and the city council. The SFA's legitimacy was based on the putative financial and management expertise of corporate business. As in the depression, the governor and the legislature had legitimized a corporate role in school governance through creation of a financial oversight group. The SFA was scheduled to wither away after six years of balanced budgets. Balanced budgets never materialized. Instead the SFA was to be strengthened in 1988. Thus, within three years of Richard J. Daley's death, the state was sharing its financial oversight with corporate business, ensuring that the city's business associations would influence any further school reform efforts.

The club's influence was not limited to financial matters. Despite protests from African American groups, Mayor Byrne also asked Chicago United to select the new school board. Once appointed, this racially mixed board chose the district's first African American superintendent, outsider Ruth Love, passing over the African American inside candidate, Manfred Byrd.

Building on a new administration and fiscal control, Chicago United and the Commercial Club then partnered in a widely publicized attempt to restructure the central office. They garnered eighty-two loaned executives to conduct a fourteen-week analysis of the management of the school system. According to one of the signatories to the ensuing report, it was a "management audit . . . so (Love) would know what she was getting into." Administrative decentralization—devolving authority from the general superintendent to district superintendents, but not to principals—was primary among the 253 recommendations in the Special Education Task Force report. One task force staff member remarked that businessmen did not recommend devolving authority to schools:

> Our view in 1980 and '81 was that the Chicago school principals were not ready to take on the actual formal responsibility of being in charge of their schools because they were in a bureaucratic system in which they were rewarded for not taking responsibility on. . . . We didn't think that the principals had the tools to do the job. It would take some time to first decentralize the district superintendents, who would then train the principals so that they could then be in a position that if they were given the authority, they could have a chance to succeed.

Two years later, Chicago United was still dedicating significant resources to implementing its recommendations, even funding an Office of Systemwide Reorganization, but with only superficial success. The man Ruth Love selected to run the OSR was her rival for the superintendency, Manfred Byrd. He was eventually blamed for the lack of change in the central administration. According to one co-chair of the Chicago United Education Task Force, Byrd had frequently "stonewalled" them, although Byrd described his own job as "being put in charge of looking out the window."[9] Club members were later to describe Byrd's recalcitrance as an example of the general principle that change could not be initiated from within an organization.

Despite members' concerns, Byrd was appointed superintendent in 1983. Mayor Harold Washington had been under some pressure from his African American supporters to replace the unpopular Love. African American community activists had many reasons for their discontent: the combination of a financial "overseer" and a school board selected by businessmen, central office downsizing that accompanied financial oversight and threatened newly won African American jobs, Byrd's having been passed over for an outsider, and Mayor Byrne's replacement of two African American board members with white women. Their dissatisfaction contributed to a grassroots electoral campaign that eventually elected Harold Washington as Chicago's first African American mayor.[10]

Mayor Washington reached out to the Civic Committee, asking them to study the city's finances. White club members who claimed to be surprised by his election seized the opportunity to build a closer relationship. As they had done for the Special Education Task Force, the committee put together a group of financial and management experts from among their membership and dubbed it the Financial Research and Advisory Committee (FRAC). FRAC was charged with conducting a city audit and then serving as the mayor's financial advisor.

Meanwhile, Chicago United kept trying to decentralize and rationalize the system. Every two years between 1981 and 1987, it sponsored another report on the public schools. Its 1987 report was an explicit "reassessment" of its 1981 conclusions, this time recommending decentralization of authority down to school principals. The reassessment made a strong impact on members because it judged the 1981 effort a failure, laying blame on the central administration and characterizing it as having "swelled to an intolerable degree." In one particularly telling passage, readers were asked to compare the twenty-three administrators for the Catholic Archdiocese schools with the 2,950 administrators assigned to Pershing Road. This "waste and inefficiency" not only caused financial problems, but it also made clear lines of accountability difficult to find.[11] Five years later, several businessmen recalled that comparison when they described why a decentralized management structure with clear lines of central authority was more urgently needed than pedagogical reform.

Business was not alone in this assessment. Community advocates had begun to complain about the administration of the public schools by the early 1980s. Despite some shared terminology, advocates' analyses of the problem were quite different from businessmen's. Community advocates began by documenting high dropout rates and poor performance among high school graduates and faulty implementation of previously mandated remedies. Most went on to argue, in terms similar to business, that the problem with school performance lay in a bloated, entrenched central bureaucracy. Central office employees were judged indifferent to the needs of Chicago's students and unable to fix the system. Yet, by their reckoning, the system needed more, rather than fewer, decision makers. Activists sought an infusion of grassroots democracy powered by parents, who could be trusted to hold the interests of students above others. Their version of decentralization had intellectual roots in the community control movements of the 1960s. A few observers also recognized elements of the "effective schools" literature in these calls to strengthen school autonomy and discretionary resources.[12] For both reasons, activists were passionate about the potential of neighborhoods and parents to improve schools.

Mayoral Initiative Encourages an Unlikely Coalition

Mayor Washington responded to combined business and community dissatisfaction in 1986 by asking members of the Civic Committee to help him put together a summit to address the poor skills of many high school graduates. Having just formed a temporary alliance with seven other Chicago business groups, the Civic Committee asked that new alliance to respond. The Chicago Partnership designated Chicago United to represent its 4,000 affiliated businesses on school issues. Thus began a further centralization of the already highly cohesive corporate business voice on public schooling.

Mayor Washington sought a Chicago version of the Boston Compact,[13] which he dubbed the Learn-Earn Connection. In addition to staff from the mayor's office and some civic leaders, the forty-person summit included Superintendent Manfred Byrd, the teachers' union, and Chicago United's business representatives. Little came of the Learn-Earn idea. As one corporate executive put it: "We would propose a deal and (Manfred Byrd) would say 'No.' See, we were trying to get him to accept higher standards of performance. He would give us 400 reasons why performance couldn't be improved and why he couldn't be held to a higher standard. It was ridiculous."

Another Commercial Club executive saw a "latent problem": the union's hitherto unopposed salary and benefit demands were draining school resources, and bargaining with a weak administration was no contest for them. The problem erupted in fall 1987, only a few months after Chicago United had given up on the Learn-Earn Summit and released the reassessment report. The Chicago Teachers Union held a month-long strike—the ninth and longest since collective bargaining had been granted—enraging parents and providing the catalyst for a coalition between community groups and Chicago United that was forged in the ensuing year. Once again, the mayor responded. At a public meeting on October 11, 1987, he reinvigorated the summit by adding fifty-four parents and community advocates known collectively as the Parent Community Council (PCC). Mayor Washington gave the summit a new charge: to reform the entire public school system and to bring him a consensus plan by the end of the year.

Neither the PCC nor corporate executives were prepared for face-to-face negotiations with the other. But an unlikely coalition eventually coalesced around a common enemy: the central administration of the public schools. One club leader was clear about the binding force:

> In the summit when we all got thrown together to go over to city hall chambers, you sit around and here's [an African American community organizer] and [a white community advocate] and the Chairman of AMOCO and the Chairman of First Chicago [First National Bank] and me. And we're all lookin' at each other . . . and I'm sure they said [to themselves] "What are these rich guys from Winnetka doing here?" Well, it turned out that we found

out who the enemy was: the administration. So the coalition of rich folks and poor folks came together.

"No one trusts the administration," added an African American member of Chicago United, "because the administration does not respond to anyone from the outside."[14]

By the middle of spring 1988, Chicago United leaders had already decided that nothing they could support was likely to come from the summit process. Harold Washington died shortly after reviving the summit, and his immediate successor was uninterested. Nor was Superintendent Byrd or the board in support of the decentralization plans being floated. Moreover, three summit subgroups (two advocacy groups and the PCC) were preparing legislation for state enactment. Further reform was to be negotiated in Springfield. Chicago United's response was to form a business/community advocacy coalition. The Alliance for Better Chicago Schools (ABCs Coalition) met in its offices for the purpose of drafting a consensus bill for the 1988 legislative session.

Corporate Chicago Seeks Greater Central Oversight

At a strategy meeting of the Chicago Partnership it was agreed that corporate Chicago could not support any legislation in which implementation was left to system educators. An executive remembered someone saying, " 'You know we need something simple. Let's establish in the hierarchy, above the board, an entity like the Finance Authority. But to really insist that the board do things to reform itself. Because it can't do it on its own.' We all agreed that no one from within a bureaucracy had been able to reform it."

A new reform oversight authority became the one nonnegotiable demand of corporate business, even though it could be expected to engender as much African American opposition as the SFA. When Chicago United representatives announced the demand to the full summit, "all hell broke loose." African Americans in the district had never been reconciled to the SFA's control over the district budget. Now they were being asked to accept a management "overseer" who could determine how they responded to impending decentralization legislation. The African American leader of the PCC feared that "a powerful oversight panel to enforce reform was an attempt to rob blacks of power they have achieved in city government and on the school board." After all, he reasoned, "This system was messed up by them for a long period of time."[15]

As it turned out, none of the bills submitted in spring 1988 received sufficient votes to pass. During the last days of the 1988 session, the ABCs Coalition became the core group that redrafted a successful reform bill. Besides Chicago United, ABCs Coalition included the most well-organized of the reform advocacy groups. One of them, Designs for Change (DFC), was widely credited by businessmen as being the architect of the law's powerful school site councils. One club leader explained, "[Their] idea of decentralization [was] micro-management. Don Moore [DFC's leader] sold us on it in exchange for him accepting some kind of power in some place that would force it to happen." Working in coalition to write and then pass a reform law had forced both community activists and club leaders to compromise, although their fundamental differences resurfaced later. To corporate executives, the delineation of powers, obligations, election procedures, and training for 550 school councils risked overspecifying local school governance. Their objective in decentralization was quite different: a lean, systemwide management structure to hold principals accountable for the performance of teachers and students while also ensuring that principals had the authority to implement change.

Bound by the legislative constraint that no new money would be appropriated for reform, the management and governance changes negotiated between Chicago United, DFC, and other advocates became the core of the new legislation. A second constraint, that any bill must meet with the approval of the legislative Black Caucus, at first put roadblocks in the way of the oversight group demanded by Chicago United. But a compromise was worked out; the existing SFA would be given the new reform oversight authority and no additional body would be created.

Corporate leaders and their community allies had a new school law in December 1988, and they were determined that it should be implemented. The SFA notwithstanding, LQE was also created for just that purpose. For six years LQE remained a strong advocate for the 1988 reform. But in 1993 club members decided that LQE's support for community organizing and voter turnout campaigns was not producing better schools. Their initial skepticism about political decentralization as a reform strategy resurfaced. The outside agitator role might suit community groups but was ill-suited to corporate leadership. It was exacerbating a rift between them and the central administration. Club leaders were increasingly convinced that central office accountability was a necessary component of their vision of decentralization and a requirement for any substantive results. As the fundamental divisions between their vision of administrative decentralization and the political version held by community activists reemerged, activists felt betrayed. They protested the pull-back loudly but succeeded only in becoming less central actors in future reform efforts.

Corporate Oversight Sustains Their Reform Agenda

The scope of formal authority given to the SFA and the LSCs differed radically and highlights how community advocates' 1988 focus on school-level governance missed much of the reform picture. Elected LSCs were given school-level decision-making authority in a few crucial areas. But their decisions were to remain bound by the resources in schools and neighborhoods and those they were able to attract from a cottage industry of foundation-supported advisers. They were simultaneously constrained by central office administrators who were fomally accountable to businessmen on the SFA and to the mayor. On the other hand, the SFA was charged with fiscal, personnel, and administrative oversight for the district as a whole. It too had constraints, including mixed political authority and insufficient control over top administrators. But the limitations on the SFA's effectiveness were quickly noticed by corporate executives and were eliminated as soon as an opportunity arose.

In addition to overseeing a balanced budget and reallocating funds to schools, the SFA was authorized by the 1988 act to approve the board's reform implementation plan or to reject it and mandate its own. Until 1993 the SFA rejected every plan the board presented without mandating another. In 1992 its second chairman determined that the district had no intention of presenting a plan that met SFA requirements. The 1993–1995 decentralization implementation plan was commissioned by the SFA directly and adopted by them over the board's objections. It was a detailed document that described a strategy for turning the central district into a service center, in competition with private service providers. Yet the plan remained unimplemented; central-office restructuring along business lines was once again stonewalled.

Meanwhile, chronic fiscal problems continued. Richard M. Daley, the next elected mayor after Harold Washington, refocused city hall on downtown development and away from neighborhood concerns, favoring advice from a handful of corporate and civic elites. Once elected, he asked FRAC to perform an audit on the school system. Even so, corporate suggestions for cost-cutting and efficiency were only marginally better accepted by the system's career educators than the 1981 audit had been. Despite its formal, mayoral-sanctioned authority, corporate business remained unable to direct a decentralized management in the central office.

There were other signs of weakness in the corporate strategy of control by central office oversight. In 1991 the Civic Committee president signaled the group's worries about the limited expertise and resources of the SFA. "Originally established to oversee the financial operations of the public school system, the SFA in a last-minute legislative maneuver in 1988, was handed an ill-defined oversight authority for reform. Under the current legislation, the SFA is badly handicapped and lacks staff to fulfill its dual responsibilities: it should have additional cooperative assistance from the private reform infrastructure."[16]

The SFA's "ill-defined" reform oversight authority and its lack of resources turned out to be only two of many flaws club members would find in the 1988 law over the next six years. The SFA's financial oversight remained hamstrung by federal and state budgetary categories. Shortfalls that continued to plague the system were exacerbated by a generous three-year teachers' contract negotiated by a transitional, interim board. The interim board had also chosen Superintendent Ted Kimbrough to succeed the ousted Manfred Byrd. Despite their participation in his selection, club leaders quickly dubbed him "a centrist" and "a mistake," blaming him for a lack of leadership just as they had once blamed Byrd.

Corporate leaders had a litany of other concerns. The new law had created a community-based school board nominating commission. In their view, it unacceptably diffused the mayor's authority, and public vetting of school board candidates virtually eliminated club members' interest in serving. Subdistrict councils —also created in the 1988 reform—had virtually no function as they saw it, except to further embed district decision making in community politics. Principals still lacked sufficient authority to discipline building staff, and the pool of experienced principals was rapidly diminishing. LQE's president argued that too much attention had been paid to school councils and not enough to specifying the authority at the center. "It's the councils that are specifically empowered, and everything else is left to the central administration. More mischief, more damage, has been done to school reform in Chicago because of that than any other single thing."

Nor were there enough signs of educational success in the first five years to mollify corporate concerns. Although community advocates saw hope in even small improvements, corporate leaders sought more immediate results. Thanks to Chicago's relative abundance of foundations, reform effects were well documented. Surveys of teachers suggested that many remained unaware of how little had actually improved and revealed their mistrust of parents and community members. Meanwhile test scores, attendance patterns, and graduation rates were mixed, with no clear evidence of gains. One widely read report found that among elementary schools only one-third could be called improving. Unwilling to accept such results, and concerned about the structural problems they saw in central office leadership and decision making, club leaders drew the conclusion that more drastic change was needed.[17]

Events gave them the opportunity. A Republican landslide in 1994 unseated the Democrats, who had dominated the Illinois House of Representatives for decades, removing much of the teachers' union's state influence and decreasing that of the Black Caucus. Both the new Republican chair of the House Education Committee and the Republican governor held invitation-only meetings to gather ideas for a new Chicago reform law.

Large portions of the new law were strongly influenced by business groups. Advice from FRAC became part of the law as did recommendations from several business associations and the SFA. This time, the Commercial Club was joined by statewide business organizations more accustomed to working with downstate Republicans. The new business coalition included the Illinois Manufacturers Association, the Illinois Business Roundtable, the Illinois State Chamber of Commerce, and the Illinois Retail Merchants Association as well as the Chicago Civic Federation and the Chicagoland Chamber of Commerce. The group was dubbed the Illinois Business Education Coalition (IBEC). Though some community groups submitted legislative recommendations, they were not actively engaged in developing the 1995 law. The window of opportunity for their influence had closed.

The new, broader business coalition was unable to come to full agreement around common legislative wording. Club members' long history with school reform in Chicago gave them a different perspective from the statewide associations. The club supported increased funding for the Chicago schools, but statewide associations were skeptical about providing new money. All could agree on stricter accountability of principals to the district and on central office leadership modeled after an up-to-date corporation, as well as on reinstating unfettered mayoral discretion in the selection of the school board. Republican legislators were unwilling to increase school funding for Democratic Chicago but did agree to give a new business management team unprecedented fiscal flexibility that had been recommended by FRAC and the SFA. The law also gave Mayor Daley unprecedented power to select the management team for the system, a move that both challenged him and lowered the political liability of business should this new reform fail.

A New School Regime

Two months after his reelection in March 1995 with strong corporate support, Daley inherited the powers of the new school law. He had played little part in drafting it, campaigning instead on a different version of school accountability that included a smaller school board, principal performance contracts, peer review of teachers, and parent "partnership" contracts. But as soon as he was handed the new powers, Daley chose a trusted former chief of staff and his own budget director to be the president of the board and the CEO, signaling that he alone would hold the school system management team personally accountable. By virtue of the fact that he fully embraced the powers he was given in the 1995 law, he was soon being described as the nation's "education mayor" and became a national symbol of mayoral initiative in public schooling. Daley justified his new involvement in economic development terms: good schools would attract middle-class taxpayers (and corporate businesses) back to the city. "I believe that nothing is more important to the future of our cities than the quality of our public schools. . . . To keep and attract middle class families to our cities, it is essential for mayors to assume leadership and responsibility for this critical issue."[18]

The 1995 school law resolved most of the concerns Civic Committee leaders had identified. School board membership was once again attractive to corporate executives. Central office leaders were loyal to the mayor and had business and financial resumés. As a result of their unsatisfactory experience with Superintendents Byrd and Kimbrough, corporate executives abandoned the strategy of holding superintendents accountable for the schools. They preferred to deal directly with the mayor, as they had for decades with his father. They had sought for him the direct chain of command they enjoyed in their firms. The SFA's reform and budgetary oversight was temporarily suspended in favor of unfettered management by mayoral appointees as sympathetic to corporate concerns as was a mayor bent on economic development.

Moreover, twenty-five separate state funding streams that had hampered the

SFA's discretion were combined into two block grants, seven separate school property tax levies were consolidated, and the requirement of a balanced budget was suspended to encourage an orderly transition in the absence of increased funding. Principals gained almost complete authority over building staff. Budgetary and personnel powers given to LSCs in 1988 were constrained by the strengthened authority of the new CEO, while all restrictions on outsourcing and privatization were eliminated. For good measure, executives helped to ensure that the teachers' union would be weakened; strikes were outlawed for eighteen months following enactment, and all but bread-and-butter concerns were eliminated from the school code.

SOME CONCERNS ABOUT DEMOCRATIC SCHOOL GOVERNANCE IN CHICAGO

The formidable influence wielded by corporate business does not make elite capture of the Chicago Public Schools reform process a foregone conclusion. But it does challenge some common wisdom about the 1988 act and raises questions about the claims of democratic governance made about Chicago school reform.

The century-long saga of Chicago school reform is characterized by an enduring tension between populist democratic governance and professional management. The 1988 and 1995 reforms represent its most recent manifestations. It first took shape in the Progressive Era, when teachers' unions were attempting to advance working-class solidarity and teachers' governing councils while the city's businessmen linked arms with new administrators and academics to support the bureaucratization, centralization, and standardization of schooling. Responding to the next fifty years of machine politics, both business associations and unions consolidated, stabilized, and secured their place as unchallenged representatives of their members' interests. These political and organizational adaptations changed the goals of the two groups as well. Faced with the challenge of securing tenure and favorable working conditions for their members, teachers' unions lost interest in democratizing school governance. Beginning with the community control experiments of the 1960s, the union ceded its status as agent of popular democracy to Chicago's community organizations. For their part, the city's business associations became increasingly influenced by a new wave of "scientific management" that stressed accountability, enhanced by new technology and performance contracting. Adopting corporate practices of the late twentieth century to public schooling, they advocated administrative decentralization: the devolution of authority but with centrally controlled accountability.

In a desperate search to improve the depressing state of Chicago's public schools, community groups and business associations formed a temporary alliance in 1988, agreeing to compromise or to ignore their differences. But those differences remained, resurfacing in 1995. Enshrined into law, they will have on-going political consequences.

Taken together, the 1988 and 1995 reforms have created a new set of rules governing the public schools and new divisions of labor. Where there were once board members directing the schools, now there are business managers on the one hand and parents and neighbors on the other. The mayor's board once selected a professional superintendent, to whom school-level professional administrators were accountable through a complex and fragmented bureaucracy. Now the CEO and his management team hold direct political appointments made by the mayor, and principals are the political appointees of elected parents and neighbors. Schools are increasingly vulnerable to the competing demands of parents and managers, unbuffered by a bureaucracy; and systemwide leaders are explicit political agents rather than professional educators. A school system originally designed to encourage professional and hierarchical accountability has been redesigned to emphasize competing forms of political accountability. In Chicago's centralized political culture and highly segregated neighborhoods, this approach is not a recipe for participatory democracy in the schools.

The democratic aspects of Chicago's reform rest on a peculiarly local vision of representation and voice. The LSCs offer thousands of parents and community members access to a legitimate platform on which to speak their minds about their child's or a neighbor's school. But the same reform that created the LSCs also diminishes their voices as citizens who wish to say something about the pattern of resource inequities across schools. Nor do LSC members address the needs of all children: common standards for teaching and learning, basic guarantees of school adequacy and appropriate citywide assessment systems, or the policies that govern system-level accountability and small, dispersed student populations. Focusing on the role of parent (or neighbor) rather than on the role of citizen as the common criterion for voice in school governance presupposes what the correct stance toward schooling should be among the residents of the city. It suggests that a parent's role in schooling is best kept parochial, focused on gains that might benefit that parent's own children.

Many of the hoped-for benefits of enhanced democracy are actually hampered by this narrowly geographic view of community, especially in a city with housing patterns as segregated as Chicago's. The combination encourages and justifies inequities and divisions among schools. If an LSC functions well in representing the interests of a neighborhood and its parents, it is necessarily in competition with other LSCs for scarce resources (e.g., good teachers and principals, private funding, and other external support and expertise). Resources and attributes of schools and their surrounding neighborhoods are highlighted. Councils with sophisticated, politically well-connected, or relatively advantaged parents and community members do better at such competition. Councils in poor neighborhoods—primarily black and Hispanic neighborhoods in Chicago—are at a disadvantage. If their LSCs do not function well, the political premise of reform suggests they will be denounced as inept or corrupt and further isolated from the resources most needed to turn their schools around.

In contrast, corporate business is given a systemwide voice—perhaps even a veto—regardless of whether LSCs work or not. Together, the formal and informal sources of corporate influence allow it to take advantage of political openings to negotiate the terms of debate within which individual schools must survive. The committed corporate executives interviewed for this study relied on a model of reform that suited their managerial expertise. In so doing they helped to define the relationship between schools and public officials, limit the amount of local (and state) tax dollars that are spent on education, and specify the objectives and measures of good schooling. Each of these systemwide decisions has far-reaching equity implications across schools, and each constrains the decision latitude of LSCs. The SFA was established by corporate business to veto budgets and contracts, set district priorities and long-term goals, and unilaterally determine whether the district's plans for restructuring were adequate. Following the same model of corporate decision making, the new management structure has been given enhanced powers to privatize public school functions, abrogate prior law and precedent in collective bargaining, determine which schools and employees are failing, and even disband LSCs and reconstitute schools.

Equity concerns are not only the result of limited popular participation in decision making; corporate management influence at the central office also has produced some rapid shifts in employment with racial implications. SFA mandates had begun downsizing central office staff in 1980, at the same time that a Chicago consent decree was encouraging the hiring of African Americans and other minorities. By 1987 the total number of central office jobs had been cut by about one-third, decreasing the employment opportunities available to minorities even though African Americans still made up a plurality of teachers, principals, and administrators (49, 34, and 48 percent). Downsizing had cut the number of whites in district jobs by half and African Americans by almost 30 percent, while the initially small numbers of Hispanics increased by nearly 40 percent. After the 1988 reform, central office cutbacks continued: another 40 percent of jobs were lost over the next six years. By 1994 whites held only one-quarter and African Americans 40 percent of the positions they had held in 1987; Hispanic central office employees held on to half of their jobs. Since 1995 privatization and outsourcing have further decreased central office employment opportunities. The central office of the Chicago Public Schools did not become the large and secure source of middle-class jobs for African Americans as some had hoped when Ruth Love was selected as the first African American superintendent. Instead, African American employment in the central office has fallen but has made up a rising proportion (50 percent) of remaining jobs.

Principals' jobs have also been racially reshuffled by the governance changes. African American principals have secured a 54 percent increase since the 1988 law made these positions political appointments. Hispanic job opportunities in the schools continue to increase, reflecting the growing Hispanic population in the city: Hispanic principals increased 152 percent (from seventeen to forty-three) after the first round of LSC selections and have maintained a similar growth pattern since. Symbolically, it is significant that the current management team is once again headed by a white male, after a decade of African American superintendents. These employment changes have marked a realignment of leadership in the system in which whites once again are at the top; African American and Hispanics make up the middle and bottom ranks of an insecure (and shrinking) job hierarchy.

Corporate influence has not turned Chicago's schools into models of high performance or democratic governance, but it has helped to legitimate a more prominent corporate role in school system policymaking. Chicago's corporate businesses have provided a template of solutions for the system's manifest problems, drawn from contexts unrelated to schooling that executives know well: modern corporate management and restructuring. The 1995 law itself was an attempt to reorganize the school system on the model of a corporation in the hopes that restructuring would then follow patterns more familiar to business.

Club members (now the mayor and the CEO) hoped to direct a governance change that built on the best of what they knew about managing large organizations. Yet for all their genuine concern and prior efforts to work in coalition with "poor folks" and community activists, they are most comfortable thinking in terms of hierarchy, management, and structure, not in terms of participation, pedagogy, and the supports needed for learning. Few Chicagoans would argue that repeated financial crises and central office stubbornness have not been crucial problems underlying incapacity in Chicago's school system. Improvement in these areas can provide the stability on which educational improvements might be built. At the same time, management expertise and structural inclination can make all problems appear to be amenable to management solutions and structural reform. Yet the basic dropout, achievement. and instructional deficits in Chicago's schools are educational problems, whose solution requires the combined knowledge and experience of educators and citizens as well. Thus far, they have been given only limited roles.

The political processes by which corporate executives in Chicago have learned to deliberate about public policy issues—in small groups of like-minded and powerful executives whose relationships are based both on mutual reliance and common experience—exacerbate the difficulties of creating democratic participation and broad-based support for school change. The executives' insularity and cohesiveness greatly enhance their political influence but also limit their exposure to people who have different experience and expertise about school problems. Their essentially private conclaves were briefly expanded in 1988 when corporate executives joined in coalition with community activists; the mayoral summit of 1988 was a remarkable achievement for its inclusiveness. But it was a fleeting venture. Today as managerial understandings of performance dominate school reform, corporate cohesiveness and insularity threaten to limit the achievements of reform to those fiscal and management indicators that business-men and politicians can agree on.

Chicago demonstrates that with a combination of corporate political re-sources and big ideas, urban school systems can be radically changed, altering the basic relationships between communities and public schooling. Although the Chicago case may establish the current limits of school governance change, orga-nized business in other cities is also advancing governance reform. Two funda-mental questions that remain for Chicago are object lessons for everyone engaged in this process: Can we find a way to keep the public schools "public," even as corporate groups set the agenda? Can corporate influence be reconciled with pro-fessional expertise and democratic decision making?

NOTES

The research reported in this chapter was assisted in part by a grant from the Spencer Foundation. The data presented, the statements made, and the views expressed are solely the responsibility of the author.

1. For detail on corporate influence on Chicago school reform, see an earlier, much expanded version of this chapter, "Invisible Hand: Big Business and Chicago School Re-form," *Teachers College Record* 99, no. 1 (1997): 73–116.

2. Public Law 85-15.

3. Michael Katz, "Chicago School Reform as History," *Teachers College Record* 94, no. 1 (1992): 56–72; G. Alfred Hess Jr., "Race and the Liberal Perspective in Chicago School Reform," in *The New Politics of Race and Gender: The Yearbook of the Politics of Education Association,* ed. Catherine Marshall (Washington, DC: Falmer, 1993), pp. 87–96; Anthony S. Bryk and Sharon G. Rollow, "The Chicago Experiment: Enhanced Demo-cratic Participation as a Lever for School Improvement," *Issues in Restructuring Schools* 3 (fall 1992): 3–7.

4. See, for instance, Anthony S. Bryk, John Easton, David Kerbow, Sharon Rollow, and Penny Sebring, *A View from the Elementary Schools: The State of Reform in Chicago* (Chicago: Consortium on Chicago School Research, 1993).

5. Primary data used for this analysis were lengthy, semistructured interviews and documents collected between 1991 and 1997 for an extended case study of business in-volvement in Chicago school reform. Fifty-six prominent executives, business association staff and consultants, and community and school leaders were key informants. Except where noted, all quotations are from these interviews. A subsequent round of eighty-three interviews in 1997 provided secondary data.

6. Julia Wrigley, *Class, Politics and Public Schools: Chicago 1900–1950* (New Bruns-wick, NJ: Rutgers University Press, 1982).

7. Stephan D. London, "Business and the Chicago Public Schools, 1980–1966" (Ph.D. diss., University of Chicago, 1968), pp. 115–16.

8. Carol Ray and Roslyn Mickelson, "Corporate Leaders, Resistant Youth and School

Reform in Sunbelt City: The Political Economy of Education," *Social Problems* 37, no. 2 (1990): 178–90.

9. Jean Franczyk, "School Reform Pressure Continues: Competing Plans Vie for Support," *Chicago Reporter* 17, no. 1 (January 1988): 1.

10. See, for instance, Jeffery Mirel, "School Reform, Chicago Style: Educational Innovation in a Changing Urban Context, 1976–1991," *Urban Education* 28, no. 2 (1993): 116–49.

11. Chicago United, "Reassessment of the Report of the Special Task Force on Education, Chicago," Chicago United Incorporated, July 1987, p. 9.

12. G. Alfred Hess Jr., *School Restructuring, Chicago Style* (Newbury Park, CA: Corwin, 1991).

13. Eleanor Farrar and Anthony Cipollone, "After the Signing: The Boston Compact 1982–1985," in *American Business and the Public School: Case Studies of Corporate Involvement in Public Education,* ed. Marsha Levine and Roberta Trachtman (New York: Teachers College Press, 1990), pp. 69–119.

14. Franczyk, "School Reform," p. 1.

15. Linda Lenz, "School Summit Wants Outsiders Kept Out," *Chicago Sun-Times,* April 29, 1988, p. 1.

16. Larry Howe, "Reviving the Zeal for School Reform," *Chicago Enterprise,* December 1991, p. 4.

17. John Q. Easton, Anthony S. Bryk, Mary E. Driscoll, John G. Kotsakis, Penny A. Sebring, and Arie J. van der Ploeg, *Charting Reform: The Teacher's Turn* (Chicago: Consortium on Chicago School Research, 1991); Albert L. Bennett, Anthony S. Bryk, John Q. Easton, David Kerbow, Stuart Luppescu, and Penny Sebring, *Charting Reform: The Principal's Perspective* (Chicago: Consortium on Chicago School Research, 1992); Bryk et al., "A View from the Elementary Schools," and "Catalyst," *Voices of Chicago School Reform* 1, no. 1, to 4, no. 4 (February 1990–December 1994).

18. United States Conference of Mayors, "Best Practices in City Governments," vol. 3, "Focus on the Mayor's Role in Education" (Washington, DC: U.S. Conference of Mayors, 1996).

9

School Politics in Houston: The Impact of Business Involvement

Thomas Longoria Jr.

Houston, Texas, provides an informative case history of business involvement in the politics of education.[1] During the 1990s, realizing that the Houston school system was lacking in much-needed public support, the city's business community moved in to fill the void. In this chapter I rely on newspaper articles, school district documents, and a series of nonattributed interviews conducted in 1994 to examine some of the consequences of that move.

A city's business sector is a significant part of its tax base and a major provider of jobs. In many cities, Houston being a leading example, business leaders are key players in the voluntary sector as well. They have a unique ability to legitimate policy initiatives and to bring about community change. But what are the consequences of the business sector's playing an active role in the politics of education? After all, business executives operate largely outside the public spotlight. Their main concerns are company profits and market share, not building popular coalitions.

Two events in Houston demonstrate and illuminate the business sector's active role in that city's educational politics. One is the hiring of a new school superintendent, Rod Paige, an African American and the first minority person to head the Houston school system. The other event is the launching of an organized series of school-business partnerships. But first, some background.

PROFILE OF HOUSTON AND THE HOUSTON INDEPENDENT SCHOOL DISTRICT

With 1.6 million residents in 1990, Houston is the fourth largest city in the United States. Houston has experienced rapid population growth as well as demographic

184

changes that influence local politics and policymaking. In 1980 Houston's population was 54 percent white, 28 percent African American, and 18 percent Latino. By 1990 Houston was 39 percent white, 29 percent African American, 29 percent Latino, and 4 percent "other." As a result of an aggressive annexation strategy, Houston's population accounts for over half of the population of its metropolitan statistical area (MSA). Unlike many other major cities, where population declined between 1980 and 1990, Houston's population increased by 2 percent, and the city showed strong growth in private-sector jobs.

Houston is a mayor-council city that elects city council members through a mixed district and an at-large election system. In 1979 a series of municipal annexations that diluted minority voting strength led to litigation under the Voting Rights Act of 1965 and a change from a pure at-large system. Though the city is still primarily guided by a professional bureaucracy, civil service, and nonpartisan elections, the adoption of the mixed (district/at-large) election system and the growth of minority communities have increased the importance of local government in recent years. Prior to this reemergence of city government, the local business community's influence on city politics and policy went relatively unchecked.[2]

The Houston Independent School District (HISD) is the one of the nation's largest, with 198,209 students in 1992. However, HISD constitutes only 35.7 percent of the Harris County student population. As an independent school district, HISD does not have a formal relationship with the city of Houston, Harris County, or the surrounding school districts. There are twenty-two independent school districts in Harris County, and many of the suburban districts had growth rates exceeding 100 percent between 1980 and 1988. These suburban districts "lock in" HISD, which does not have the powers of annexation available to local governments. As a result, poor minority students are increasingly concentrated in HISD. Integration efforts emphasize magnet schools designed to attract white suburban students to HISD.

The property tax rate per 100 valuation in HISD was $1.38 in 1994, the second lowest among Harris County school districts and well below the metro average of $1.50. Local property taxes provided 70 percent of HISD revenues in 1992. Given the reliance on local property taxes to fund schools in Texas, there are substantial inequities in the resources available to urban school districts. Furthermore, funding-equity issues have gone unresolved since the late 1960s, despite the fact that the school funding system has been declared unconstitutional on several occasions.

Although there has been significant growth in the number of students attending HISD schools (from 189,467 in 1982 to 198,209 in 1992), the changing demographic patterns are a more important indicator of the challenges facing HISD. In 1982 African American students were the largest group at 44.1 percent, followed by Hispanics (32.4 percent), Anglos (20.3), and Asians and others (.03

Table 9.1. Racial Breakdown of City Population, Student Population, and Teachers, 1992

	City Population	School Bd. Composition	Student Population	Teachers
White	39%	44%	13%	45%
Black	29%	33%	36%	42%
Latino	29%	22%	48%	12%
Other	4%	0%	3%	1%

percent). By 1992 Hispanics surpassed African Americans as the largest group (48.1 percent versus 36.2 percent), followed by Anglos (12.9 percent), and Asians and others (2.9 percent).

As in most major U.S. cities, there are racial and social cleavages in Houston. Tensions among African Americans, Latinos, and Anglos are based on issues such as electoral representation, employment equity, government contracts, and other distributive issues. Latinos are underrepresented on the school board and in the teaching staff compared to Anglos and African Americans (for racial breakdowns of the city population, school board members, student population, and teachers, see Table 9.1). As a result, many Latinos feel locked out of nonbilingual education, HISD administration, and teaching positions.

One Latino community leader argued that the reason for the isolation between Anglos and Latinos compared to that between Anglos and African Americans is that "Anglos and the blacks are more similar culturally."[3] Some community activists regard the relative isolation of the Latino community as a remnant of the coalitions built during the civil rights movement.[4] When a white corporate executive was asked how various groups worked together, he noted, "I don't know how well they work together, if at all. Blacks have had a longer history of working with the system and have had some success, as opposed to the Hispanic groups in town. That has generated some resentment."[5]

THE ROLE OF THE BUSINESS SECTOR IN HOUSTON POLITICS

Houston's leadership has been focused on diversifying its oil-based economy, especially after the bust in oil prices in the 1980s, and on making public investments to produce growth.[6] In general, Houston's political and social character reflects and perpetuates the boomtown ethos fostered by the rapid development of the city. Nonetheless, it also has a strong tradition of philanthropy.

Another characteristic of Houston politics and culture is the emphasis on political entrepreneurship. Actors in Houston gravitate to ideas that seem "doable." Community leaders with a coherent plan are able to generate support from local elites, who are always looking for a way to make a contribution to the city. When community leaders were asked in personal interviews how plans were effected in Houston, two consistent responses emerged: (1) things get done in Houston through the "power of a good idea" that will generate sufficient attention and support from community leaders, and (2) things are done informally with little coordination either by government or civic organizations. Many linkages are ad hoc. As one respondent explained, groups "work together when there is a common policy. They come together for causes like that, but it's very sporadic, very short-term, and then they go back to their own group."[7]

Overall, citizen participation in local politics and policy is minimal, especially when it comes to education. There is only one consistently active parents' group in the city, and it is focused on tax issues. This lack of community involvement has an impact on the success of education reforms. For example, one of the proposed reforms was decentralization by means of site-based management. But for site-based management to work, principals and staff need to work with and involve parents and other community representatives. As a result, implementation of this reform initiative proved uneven: many schools lacked a tradition of parental participation, and school leadership was inexperienced in promoting it. Lack of parental participation is a problem currently being addressed by some school-business partnerships and nonprofit organizations.[8]

THE BUSINESS SECTOR'S INVOLVEMENT IN PUBLIC EDUCATION REFORM

Although some business leaders became active in Houston education politics and policy after the Nation-at-Risk report and the heightened attention to the education "crisis" of the early 1980s, broader and more sustained involvement occurred after the HISD administration proposed a large local property tax increase in 1993. The school district justified the request on the basis of the need to improve test scores and to lower the dropout rate. The proposed property tax increase was opposed by elected city officials, business leaders, and residents. Business leaders wanted results first in order to justify the expenditure of more resources by the public schools.

Open conflict between HISD and the business community broke out over a number of issues. Business representatives did not trust the accuracy of budget figures and academic performance measures and, as a result, criticized the district as inefficient and unbusinesslike. The implication was that if the school district could not balance the school budget, how could it educate children? Then-Superintendent Frank Petroziuelo's confrontational manner further strained the relationship between the school district and the business community at a time when, as one school board member noted, the "business community is always sort of yapping at our heels."[9] The conflict was addressed, in the minds of some members of the school board, by replacing Petroziuelo with popular school board member Rod Paige. While Paige was school board president, according to a school board colleague, he had the reputation of being close to the business community. Again, according to a board colleague, Paige gave business leaders carte blanche to identify areas of HISD's budget that should be cut or increased.

The appointment of Paige as superintendent in 1994 was symbolic of the new relationship between the school district and the business community. Previous superintendents had been education administration professionals and outsiders. Moreover, Paige was the first African American (and first minority) superintendent.

Once appointed, Paige quickly formed a joint business–school district commission to study ways to make the school district more efficient and effective. He also developed and publicized a list of goals and priorities and articulated a mission statement for HISD. These actions reflected the business community's expectations of changing the public schools by strategic planning and goal setting. The commission eventually developed recommendations on how to restructure HISD into smaller administrative units. Although much of the reform and reorganization had begun under previous superintendents, the efforts acquired greater legitimacy under Paige because he was trusted by business-community leaders.

The opening up of the school district to external involvement was also perceived as necessary by dissatisfied community leaders. The president of a community-based organization active in the schools noted, "Up until maybe the 70s, schools didn't want to collaborate; they [HISD] said 'look we can do it, we don't need you, don't come or come and don't stay too long, and now I think they have just opened their doors and said 'help, we can't do this by ourselves.' "[10]

After Paige's appointment, HISD administrative and elected officials consulted the business community on management issues, strategic planning, accounting practices, and outcomes measurement. The decision to reach out to business was motivated by a desire to improve HISD's legitimacy in the minds of the business community, taxpayers, and the media. For example, a senior HISD administrator noted, "You just can't ask the business community and taxpayers for money and not show results, which is why all the accountability measures have now been implemented to hold people accountable."[11]

Gaining legitimacy was a major reason HISD began cooperating with the business community. According to a school board member, "We have asked business community groups to help us for two reasons: They have expertise, and we don't have clout." The board member continued, "We are part of the 'bad guys,' so we need some independents to come in and not only help us develop ideas, but also bless the ideas we have, so the public will treat us good."[12]

Educating the business community about how difficult it is to improve HISD without additional support and resources is another reason for the new era of openness and cooperation. For example, according to one school board member, "They [business groups] came in and said 'well it is too big a job and we can't do it. It is too complicated; we can't figure out what you got. What you really need is a complete redo of your budget process and how you [HISD] handle various reports'; then we said 'Great, why don't you do that?' "[13]

Incentives for the business community are less obvious, but corporate executives involved with the school district frequently expressed a sense of civic responsibility and investment in the future. They also cited the need for improving the quality of the workforce and reducing the crime rate. For example, in discussing his involvement with HISD, one sponsor of a partnership program noted, "I think we run the risk of ending up like a third-world country in the not too distant future if we don't do something better than what we're doing now." This same business executive noted the emergence of gated communities to reduce crime and argued that improving schools was a better strategy because "you just can't build the fences high enough."[14]

The business community's growing interest in improving urban education is the positive face of the public-private interaction noted in the urban political economy literature. The school district has become more businesslike to appease taxpayers and businesses and has agreed to work toward the common goal of improving the workforce. The consequences of business-sector involvement are less positive, however, when the only goal is controlling school expenditures.

SCHOOL-BUSINESS PARTNERSHIPS AS A RESPONSE

The business community is composed of individual business leaders and several business organizations that emphasize education reform as a major portion of their activities. In their view, the school district faced two major problems: (1) additional spending would not improve student achievement because of an insulated and unbusinesslike school bureaucracy, and (2) the isolation of schools from the community limited the ability of the schools to address social problems that are root causes of low achievement. Many members of the business community believe that education and its reform cannot occur in isolation. Schools need to address health care, counseling, and job-skills training in addition to improving school administration, curriculum, and teaching. Corporate "adopt-a-school" programs are designed to address both social and education issues.[15]

Houston's premiere business organization, the Greater Houston Partnership (GHP), has been active in the area of education reform and social policy for at least a decade. The Greater Houston Coalition for Education Excellence (GHCEE), a business-sponsored education-reform advocacy group, has its origins within the GHP but is now an independent organization that supplements and reinforces the GHP's efforts.

The GHP has developed a number of programs and committees dedicated to enhancing the quality of public education. Their Houston Business Promise program was designed to support the school system and families through business-sponsored programs that help children receive a quality education. The GHP asks companies to sign the Houston Business Promise compact, which has eight points, including encouraging "meaningful" partnerships with schools. These partnerships encourage and foster employee participation in volunteer efforts, contribute materials, encourage students to achieve by providing scholarships, increase student awareness of career options, and prepare students for the workforce. Although the Houston Business Promise is not binding or specific in its expectations, it has shaped ad hoc business involvement into a more coherent effort and has become a priority for business leaders. Despite the strong support of the business community, however, the vast majority of partnerships fall short of school compacts, which guarantee a job interview or scholarship on graduation. A small number of partnership programs do include a postschool transition to work or college.

The goals of another business-sponsored organization—the Greater Houston Coalition for Educational Excellence (GHCEE)—are explicitly focused on providing an environment that improves the lives and education of children and youth. The GHCEE was created to "bring together all the stakeholders in education in Houston—educators, businesses, religious leaders, parents, and community members—to work toward specific goals in improving Houston's educational system." Lawrence Payne, director of the GHCEE, notes in the organization's brochure that "teachers, parents, businesses, the community at large—we all need an educational system that develops competent adults who are skilled and productive members of the community. And no one group can achieve that goal alone. We are interdependent." Another group working along similar lines is the Texas Business and Education Coalition, one of the first statewide networks of local business-education partnerships.

By 1993 there were approximately thirty community-business-education coalitions in Houston, most dominated by business-sponsored advocacy groups since there are no "independent" parent and community groups with equal levels of organization and resources involved in public-private partnerships. Largely as a result of business-sector advocacy, there were 2,322 individual school-business partnerships in 1994.[16] Though many of these partnerships were narrow in scope (i.e., providing a mentor for individual students, donating equipment, funding rewards for perfect attendance), more comprehensive efforts are now under way. For example, in describing the partnerships at her school, a middle-school principal listed several nonprofits and businesses and indicated that the focus of their efforts is a Saturday workshop series that addresses the "whole child." Persuading individual business and nonprofit-sector partners to work together on a project organized by the principal was difficult, she acknowledged, but about twenty organizations and businesses participate on a regular basis.[17]

James Ketelsen is widely acknowledged as the person who began to change the relationship between the business community and the school system in the early 1980s. Ketelsen was chief executive officer of Tenneco, a major energy company, and is respected by elected officials, the media, and others as one of the most powerful individuals in Houston. He is also an active leader of the GHP and now independently finances his own education-reform advocacy organization. Ketelsen's involvement sends a signal to other business community actors that education reform is an important focus of philanthropic and voluntary attention.

Ketelsen's involvement is important as an inspiration to others, but he has also brought new thinking into the relationship between schools and businesses. He argues that the pattern of individual linkages among businesses, corporations, and schools will never have a major impact on students. The problem, in his view, is that students progress through high school "feeder patterns" that at times provide comprehensive support for at-risk students and at other times do not. Ketelsen believes that school-business partnerships need to address these feeder patterns in a coordinated and comprehensive way.

As a result, a diverse set of local actors have developed partnerships with Jefferson Davis High School and the schools that feed into it. Representatives from all sectors of the community are represented in partnerships that provide tutors, motivational speakers, rewards for academic achievement, and after-school programs. Ketelsen, still in partnership with Tenneco after his retirement, helped organize much of this feeder-pattern activity. Support programs delivered by nonprofit organizations—for example, Success-by-Six and Communities in Schools—are also placed in key feeder-pattern schools to support parents and help them encourage their children's education.

The Metropolitan Organization (TMO) project demonstrates the broad scope of the Jefferson Davis program:

> TMO walks the blocks at the beginning of school. Knocks on the doors of all 9th graders and tells the parents about the Jeff Davis scholarship program in English and Spanish. And tells them to come see the school. Parents sign a contract saying they are going to do their best to provide a homestead in which that child can study and graduate. The program is the glue on the campus that links each child with the remedial courses they need, summer jobs they need, the cross intervention they need, the social services they need, to make it all work so that child is connected with the Tenneco scholarship program.[18]

Tenneco has given a $1,000 scholarship to every student who attends a summer institute, keeps a good grade-point average, and graduates. As a result, according to advocates of the partnership program, the number of graduates who go to college from Jeff Davis has increased from five students to over one hundred.

Other reform-minded elites are trying to establish additional feeder-pattern projects. Thus, this approach to developing and coordinating programs is being supported in Houston by a broad range of actors, including Mayor Bob Lanier and community-based organizations. Education and social programs are seen as human investment policies and are linked to gang prevention and crime reduction as well as to the need to provide an environment supportive of economic development. That the public and private sectors have worked together to develop specific strategies for feeder-pattern programs suggests that a significant level of civic capacity exists in Houston, although the low level of parental involvement remains a weakness.[19]

Using partnerships to address external social and economic factors that limit academic achievement works because partnerships do not call for heavy involvement in affairs that are deemed "school matters." This approach also works to HISD's advantage, since supporting such programs protects the district's autonomy: a focus on social and economic conditions has diverted the civic energy of businesses from such issues as privatization, school choice, and vouchers.

CONSEQUENCES OF THE BUSINESS SECTOR'S PARTICIPATION

In Houston, the consequences of the business sector's involvement in education include real changes in academic achievement as well as some unintended results. One outcome is that the larger community has not always been appreciative of the expanded role of business in education. When asked to comment on the ties between the school district and the business community, the president of a parents' advocacy organization said, "One of those knee jerk conservative organizations [GHP] said 'bloated bureaucracy' and if you really want this tax increase you must streamline your bureaucracy."[20] She added that this relationship between the school district and the business sector had existed for a number of years, and, as a result, programs to improve the quality of teaching have suffered from budget cuts.[21] In response to such sentiments, however, HISD can point to some measurable academic improvements.

Improved Test Scores

In 1992, with the advice and guidance of consultants supported by the business community, HISD adopted a new accountability system that ranks schools based on the percentage of students passing the Texas Assessment of Academic Skills. Although thirty-one schools were "low performing" (0 to 34.9 percent passing) in 1992, there were no low-performing schools in 1996. The number of "exemplary" schools (90 to 100 percent passing) increased from ten in 1992 to forty-three in 1995. Fifty-seven percent of HISD schools were rated either "exemplary" or "recognized" (75 to 100 percent passing). In 1996 HISD students scored from ten to ninety-four points higher than other urban school districts on the Scholastic Aptitude Test. Fifty-three percent of HISD seniors took the SAT, and the average score was 832. The scores of HISD students were higher than, for example, students from Dallas (45 percent took the test, 767 average score), Los Angeles (50 percent took the test, 797 average score), and Baltimore (51 percent took the test, 738 average score).

Superintendent Paige is attempting to capitalize on the good news with a public relations campaign to help further the connection between the public and the schools and to improve communications with "everyone who has a stake in Houston's schools."[22] Project Reconnect outlines Paige's effort to overcome the public's image of the public schools by developing a strategy that fights the tendency of the media and other critics to "define public education by its weaknesses rather than its strengths."[23] Business and community efforts and parental involvement are more likely to succeed, given the improvements in student achievement.

Despite the real improvement in student performance, however, many business and community members believe that even if the feeder-pattern program is successful in the short run, there will be little possibility of sustained effort because of the costs involved. A former elected official sees the involvement of the voluntary and philanthropic sectors moving through a typical pattern in which volunteers and foundations try to "make a go of it" themselves but eventually ask the city to expand a small-scale program that, though successful, is expensive and difficult to replicate.[24]

The transition from short-term charity to long-term policy is a concern for business community leaders who support education reform. In the view of one business leader, the issue is one of greater maturity in policy so that more focused "adopt-a-school" efforts are substituted for efforts to "take care of [improving student achievement] in one swoop." He also said that more effective partnerships between schools and businesses will occur when "we get a policy and procedure and money to get it done, and institutionalize."[25]

Improvements in academic achievement certainly indicate the long-term potential of Houston's partnership programs. And the fact that business leaders engage in self-evaluation, consider results, and take steps to ensure broader community participation also suggests that the connections between businesses and the school district are not solely about agenda and issue control. If such were the case, information and evaluation would most likely be unacknowledged or hidden. Instead, Houston's school district and business leaders are working together to improve education for reasons of mutual interest.[26]

Unintended Consequences

The appointment of Superintendent Rod Paige also came about as a result of new cooperative linkages between the school district and the business sector. But the process by which Paige was appointed had a number of unintended political costs. His appointment was made without an extensive national or internal search. This decision angered some school administrators, who saw politics taking precedence over qualifications, training, and administrative experience. Suspicions of an inside political deal were further aroused because the selection process was not open: deliberations by white and black school board members were carried out in an informal meeting prior to the formal meeting of the full school board, which included two Latinos. No matter how potentially important for enhanced governance and reform, the closed process angered a significant number of people involved in education politics and policymaking. The fact that Paige was not a certified superintendent (a waiver from the Texas Education Agency was obtained after a series of highly publicized actions by Gov. Ann Richards) contributed to the view that the school board was blindly responding to the business community, despite potentially negative consequences.

One of the results of this process was strained race relations. The Latino community, including Latinos employed as senior administrators, protested Paige's appointment. The two Latino school board members had not been informed of the meeting where the informal agreement to nominate and appoint Paige was allegedly made. As a result, a lawsuit was filed by a newly formed Hispanic education advocacy group claiming a violation of the Open Meetings Act and the Fourteenth Amendment. The plaintiffs were unsuccessful, but the lawsuit illustrated the Latino community's feelings of exclusion. The marginalization of that group's elected officials, school teachers and administrators, activists, and parents is especially serious, given that the school population is now approaching a Latino majority.

One of the reasons for Paige's appointment was to further the goal of improving schools through partnerships with the business sector. Paige may be, as one business executive put it, a known "homegrown entity" and the first minority superintendent who "understands the issues of the people and who knows the business community."[27] Yet even Paige's supporters thought that the selection process, although justified, was seriously flawed.[28] Business practice often entails closed negotiations, but within the public arena, the expectation is openness and inclusion. The selection process violated this expectation, leading to heightened tensions and the politicization of education policymaking in Houston.

The Pattern of Weak Parental Involvement

Besides contributing to the isolation of the Latino community, the involvement of Houston business groups may limit community participation in general.[29] In a city with low levels of citizen participation, the involvement of the business community may further marginalize parents and citizens. The motives of the business sector are questioned by some community activists. For example, both Latino and black grassroots activists were highly critical of the decision-making process that led to Paige's appointment and blame the emerging alliance between the school board and business interests. Thus, though Paige's appointment was a way to foster goodwill between the school district and the business community, it was also viewed as an instance in which the school district and the business sector acted in bad faith with other groups, especially Latinos.

The perception of Latino exclusion was reinforced at a news conference where, according to one observer, newly appointed Superintendent Paige was surrounded by African American administrators; that no Latino administrator was on the stage sent a signal of exclusion. Two years later, Paige's contract was extended on a 7 to 0 vote, the two Latino members of the school board abstaining.[30] And a major reorganization of the upper hierarchy of HISD bureaucracy in 1995, according to a Latino administrator, left only one Latino with direct access to the superintendent. Moreover, the sense of exclusion extended beyond administrative appointments. One Latino activist described HISD policy and school politics as a "political economy" designed to channel construction contracts into the traditional business sector. His point was that Latinos were largely without access to the school system's distributive benefits.

The cynicism that emerges from a politicization of education policy extends to members of the school board as well. For example, one community activist charges that school board members respond to parental demands to create magnet schools not to improve urban education but to build a base of support before running for higher office.[31] Helping parents gain access to magnet schools for their children is seen as a way of building a list of supporters.

Community wariness about the political consequences of business involvement is also part of the picture. Given the importance of political protest as a resource for neighborhood and minority groups, some actors may resist inclusion in partnerships, especially if such arrangements are accompanied by the image of a businesslike organization. Business executives indeed are often interested in depoliticizing interactions. Attaining "buy in" from parents and community-based organizations is an expressed goal of business leaders active in education matters, and they encourage potential protest groups to see the advantage of linkages between the business sector and the public schools. For example, the Metropolitan Organization, a Saul Alinsky–style group, now has close ties with the business community. But instead of organizing poor communities for public protests in the traditional Alinsky model, TMO participates in partnerships with other community-based organizations and business-sponsored partnerships to empower parents and improve schools. According to a business leader,

> TMO is really focusing on youth, and that's their very positive view. They weren't that way when they started. They turned, over a fifteen-year period, into a very effective organization. They started out as something of a community organization, with a "got to rattle the cages in order to get anything done" attitude and they've turned that around and are much more effective now. They first came in for business support years ago and I said "gee, with the tone of programs you've got I can't in good conscience support you," and we had a long discussion on the subject. Today, if I were running a company and they came in for money, I could in good conscience give them what they ask for.[32]

TMO's headquarters is located in a mixed Latino and Anglo working-class neighborhood, and its president is Latino. However, TMO is no longer viewed by some activists as a grassroots group. At the same time, TMO is widely respected by local elected officials and the business community. The depoliticization of TMO, and the message this shift sends to other community groups, is one reason the chances of mass protest are limited in Houston.

Moreover, some community activists are concerned that the issue of financial support for the schools has been inadequately addressed. They see the feeder-pattern approach as simplistic and as a distraction from more meaningful, systemic reforms.[33] In short, there is a wide range of reactions to business involvement in school politics, and some of the community-based actors are quite hostile.

It is easy to dismiss cynical and seemingly unnuanced characterizations of school politics. School construction, payroll, and operating costs are a small, but significant, part of Houston's economy. Yet the school district is one of the few opportunities for minorities seeking stable professional employment and a chance to move into the middle class. For minority small businesses, even a modest contract from HISD can be the foundation of a successful enterprise. As a result, some Latino leaders are more concerned with getting their share of HISD jobs and contracts rather than with systemic reform. When asked if the school district was focused on systemic reform, an Anglo school board member joked that a Latino school board member did not even know what systemic reform means.[34] Some African Americans see calls of mismanagement as a threat to their leadership of the school district, a tendency that concerns one African American activist who claims that, for some HISD administrators, protecting jobs is more important than educating children.[35]

In two respects, education reform efforts in Houston have been modest: there have been no major increases in spending, and there have been no ambitious, systemic reforms. Neither magnet schools nor school-business partnerships are considered especially innovative by education experts. However, the encouraging aspect is that influential Houstonians are focused on the external problems of poverty, neighborhoods, and parenting in addition to taxes, spending, and bureaucratic insulation. Time will determine whether comprehensive support programs will be placed in all the schools that need them. Test scores must continue to improve to convince other actors waiting on the sidelines to join in Houston's educational reform efforts.

Cooperative public-private partnerships have the potential to transform public education. Elites in Houston recognize that partnership efforts must be comprehensive and coordinated to address the range of problems facing children and youth. There is an effort both to rationalize and focus the programs as well as to foster more community involvement. These concerns seem to emanate from a few actors in the business sector, however, and not from teachers, administrators, and parents, many of whom express concerns regarding the distribution and content of school-business partnerships.

A related concern is the extent to which business-school partnerships, motivated by philanthropic impulses as well as by concerns regarding the quality of the workforce, will be institutionalized and sufficiently long-term to have a continuing impact on student academic performance. The interest, energy, and effort that create and maintain individual school-business partnerships, though important, may not translate into comprehensive reform.[36] Cooperative partnerships have considerable symbolic value and support, but they also have a privileged position in policy debates and may keep other options—such as higher property taxes to invest in schools or statewide funding equalization—off the agenda. Grassroots groups and community-based organizations that could be working for the restructuring of school finance and higher school taxes now function within the parameters set by the business-partnership ideology.

Currently, Houston's school-business partnerships, which are elite-driven and entrepreneurial, do not result in a comprehensive education reform program. Community-level actors and parents do not play a prominent role in the formation and development of cooperative public-private partnerships. This circumstance leads many community actors to be cynical about the motivations of elite actors. The linkage among citizen demands, responsive policymaking by elected officials, and implementation by education bureaucrats has little influence on the formation and content of cooperative public-private partnerships.

All parties concerned with education in Houston need to monitor and assess the business sector's potential for bypassing democratic policymaking and accountability. The motivations of the business community and the outcomes and unintended consequences of its involvement must be part of a critical inquiry. It is true that business interests have been a catalyst for education reform and that the public interest has been served by an infusion of new ideas. Nevertheless, it may also be the case that business involvement, Houston style, tends to preclude some ways of rethinking and reforming public education.

NOTES

1. Business involvement in public education has been examined in M. Levine and R. Trachtman, *American Business and the Public Schools: Case Studies of Corporate Involvement in Public Education* (New York: Teachers College Press, 1988); M. Levine, "Approaches to Private Sector Involvement in Public Education," in *The Private Sector in the Public School: Can It Improve Education?* ed. M. Levine (Washington, DC: American Enterprise Institution, 1985), pp. 3–10; and J. Shive and J. H. Rogus, "The School-Business Partnership: A Concept Revitalized," *Clearing House* 52 (1979): 286–90.

2. R. D. Thomas and R. W. Murray, *Progrowth Politics: Change and Governance in Houston* (Berkeley, CA: IGS Press, 1991).

3. Community activist 1, interview by author, July 1994. (Community activists include members of community advocacy groups.)

4. Ibid.

5. General influential 1, interview with author, April 1994. (General influentials include elected officials and business executives.)

6. Thomas and Murray, *Progrowth Politics,* pp. 64–65.

7. Program specialist 2, interview with author, June 1994. (Program specialists include school administrators, teachers, and social service providers.)

8. General influential 2, interview with author, June 1994.

9. General influential 4, interview with author, June 1994.

10. Program specialist 4, interview with author, July 1994.

11. Ibid.

12. General influential 4, interview with author, June 1994.

13. Ibid.

14. General influential 1, interview with author, June 1994.

15. Levine, "Approaches to Private Sector Involvement in Public Education."

16. Houston Independent School District, *Community Partnerships Catalog,* 1995.

17. Program specialist 5, interview with author, July 1994.

18. Program specialist 3, interview with author, June 1994.

19. See C. N. Stone, M. Orr, and D. Imbroscio, "The Reshaping of Urban Leadership in U.S. Cities: A Regime Analysis," in *Urban Life in Transition,* ed. M. Gottdiener and C. G. Pickvance (Newbury Park, CA: Sage, 1991), pp. 222–39, for a discussion of civic capacity.

20. Community advocate 2, interview with author, June 1994.

21. Ibid.

22. Rod Paige, "Project Reconnect: Re-Enfranchising the Community in Support of Public Education," HISD: www.houston.isd.telnet.edu/~reconn/recon.htm, 1996.

23. Ibid.

24. General influential 5, interview with author, April 1994.

25. General influential 3, interview with author, July 1994.

26. See R. P. Stoker, "Baltimore: The Self-Evaluating City?" in *The Politics of Urban Development,* ed. C. N. Stone and H. T. Sanders (Lawrence: University Press of Kansas), pp. 244–66, for a discussion of self-evaluation of informal partnership structures.

27. General influential 3, interview with author, July 1994.

28. Ibid.

29. Although public-private partnerships for education and partnerships for economic development are different, the issue of controlling citizen involvement is significant in the former. See L. Jezierski, "Neighborhoods and Public-Private Partnerships in Pittsburgh," *Urban Affairs Quarterly* 26 (1990): 217–49, for a discussion of these issues.

30. Melanie Markley, "HISD Extends Paige's Contract Two Years," *Houston Chronicle,* March 20, 1997, p. 1A.

31. Community advocate 4, interview with author, July 1994.

32. General influential 2, interview with author, June 1994.

33. Community advocate 2, interview with author, June 1994.

34. General influential 4, interview with author, June 1994.

35. Community advocate 5, interview with author, July 1994.

36. M. Gittell, "School Reform in New York and Chicago," *Urban Affairs Quarterly* 30 (1994): 136–51.

10

Education and Regime Change in Charlotte

Stephen Samuel Smith

To students of urban education, the Charlotte-Mecklenburg School District (CMS) has long been known as the one that gave rise to *Swann,* the 1971 Supreme Court decision allowing intradistrict busing for desegregation. In the wake of that decision, CMS developed a busing plan that was generally considered among the nation's most successful. In the early 1990s, however, CMS attracted attention for a quite different reason: an ambitious program of educational change initiated by its high-profile superintendent, John Murphy, soon after he took office in July 1991. Both the superintendent and CMS' reforms drew lavish praise from some of the nation's most prominent proponents of educational change,[1] even though— and in some cases, because—a key aspect of the reform program was the implementation of a system of magnet schools to replace much of the district's nationally touted mandatory busing plan.

In addition to the magnet schools, Murphy's program included a new system of goals and accountability, bonuses for teachers and schools who attained specified goals, international baccalaureate programs, many other changes in curriculum, and tougher discipline standards. Murphy also effected a large turnover in CMS personnel; approximately 50 percent of the district's schools had new principals within two years of his arrival. Taken together, these efforts constitute a sweeping program of educational change, which immediately gives rise to a question: What political conditions allowed these many reforms to be introduced so relatively quickly and, compared with many other districts, so easily?

To that question, a second can be added: What political conditions might be necessary to *sustain* these many reforms?[2] The latter question assumes special importance in light of the political tumult that engulfed CMS in 1995. In May of that year, voters rejected a large school bond package, the first defeat of a comprehensive school bond package since the 1960s. A smaller bond package passed in November, but that same election day saw Susan Burgess reelected to the school board by a margin large enough to make her the new board's chair. Relations between Burgess and Murphy had been strained, and his supporters in the business elite had tried to thwart her reelection bid. Burgess's ascension to the chair of the newly elected board prompted Murphy's resignation, effective the day before the board was installed.

Murphy's resignation should not be taken as an indication that CMS is undoing many of the changes that he introduced. Both the new school board and the superintendent it hired expressed a desire to continue along many of the lines that Murphy had laid out. Nonetheless, his resignation, along with that of his top aides, left a gaping administrative hole. Filling that hole would be difficult no matter how great a commitment there might be to staying whatever course he had charted. Furthermore, the contrast between the acclaim given Murphy's program outside Charlotte and the political setbacks he suffered within the district demands explanation.

To address these two questions about the initiation and continuation of school reform, I draw upon Clarence N. Stone's application of regime theory to the politics of education. Noting "that it takes broad mobilization of civic capacity to bring about a thorough-going effort at educational improvement," Stone argues reform will take place "not by coalition *pressure on* the school system, but by a realignment of the relationships between the school system and various sectors of the community." Although they enjoy a degree of autonomy, "even the internal operations of schools as organizations are affected by relationships to the community."[3] The realignment of such relationships is especially important for the development of performance regimes (see chapter 1), the goal of which is to improve academic outcomes (however defined) for economically disadvantaged students, a large percentage of whom are members of minority racial and ethnic groups in most urban areas. In that respect, a performance regime in education can be viewed as an example of what Stone in earlier work called a lower-class opportunity expansion regime. Such a regime differs markedly from one whose main concern is promoting development because the tasks of governance are so demanding. Economic development can proceed largely through the coordination of institutional elites (often through the use of selective material incentives), but opportunity expansion requires the regulation, perhaps coercion, of these institutional elites. Such regulation is "most sustainable when backed by a popular constituency."[4] In addition to providing the political clout necessary to sustain the regulation of institutional elites, mass mobilization is also necessary to ensure the effective functioning of the educational, health, housing, and employment programs designed to serve the poor. But such mobilization is not easily effected, in part because the long history of most of these programs' failing to meet the needs of the urban poor has contributed to cynicism and withdrawal.

In exploring the possibility of CMS' developing a performance regime, it is especially important to discuss the extent to which the school system has realigned its relationship with two sectors of the community. The first is the business elite, which has played a crucial role in educational politics. The second sector is the black community because in Charlotte-Mecklenburg, as elsewhere, education is intimately involved with matters of race. Also key to understanding changes in educational policy are discussions of the relationships between CMS and whites and between the school district and the organizations that represent its employees.

BACKGROUND

As befits the district whose experience gave rise to *Swann,* CMS consciously aspires to be the "premier urban, integrated public school system in the nation."[5] That such an aspiration is within the realm of possibility indicates a major difference between CMS and many other urban districts: a majority of CMS' students are white. In the 1997–1998 school year, approximately 51 percent of CMS' 96,000 students were white, 41 percent were African American, and the remaining 8 percent were Asian, Hispanic, or Native American. Since 1960 the district has, as the name suggests, been a consolidated one, covering all of Mecklenburg County, 78 percent of whose population lives in the city of Charlotte.

Consolidation contributed to the success of the busing plan. Even more important to its success was the courage and determination of the African American community. The business elite, on the other hand, provided scant support for the federal district court's initial desegregation order. Only after the Supreme Court affirmed the lower court's order did business leaders come largely together to marshal broad community support for the busing plan. Also playing a major role was a twenty-five-member Citizens Advisory Group. Composed of both busing proponents and opponents, this group helped craft many aspects of the busing plan that was eventually adopted. Furthermore, the group's political as well as demographic diversity facilitated broader community acceptance of the busing plan.

Once busing was successfully implemented, the business elite touted the city's desegregation accomplishments and, in the battle to attract new investment, benefited from Charlotte's reputation for progressive race relations and its image as "The City that Made it Work."[6] Moreover, business support for school desegregation was intimately linked to the nature of Charlotte's regime from approximately 1963 to 1987. Key to this regime was a progrowth electoral coalition between the business elite and the leadership of the black community that dominated much of local government and enabled the Democratic candidate to win all but one of the mayoral elections during this period. The election of Harvey Gantt, Charlotte's first black mayor, in 1983 and 1985 exemplified the electoral clout of this coalition.

The busing plan and Charlotte-Mecklenburg's concomitant reputation for progressive race relations greatly facilitated dramatic economic growth. By the mid-1990s, the city had landed both a National Basketball Association and a National Football League franchise and was among the nation's three largest banking centers. This financial eminence stems from the fact that Charlotte houses the corporate headquarters of NationsBank and First Union, which in the mid-1990s were the nation's fourth and sixth largest banking companies.

Charlotte's growth had broad political consequences. A combination of in-migration, the city's ambitious annexation plan, which gave many newcomers a vote in city elections, and poor campaign tactics led to Harvey Gantt's upset defeat by Republican Sue Myrick in the 1987 mayoral election. Since then, no Democrat has been elected mayor, strong evidence that the coalition between the business elite and the leadership of the black community presently lacks the electoral clout it once had. As a result, the local regime is clearly in flux. As journalists Neal Peirce and Curtis Johnson note, "The leadership clique, led by the bank CEOs and other corporate chieftains, has not disappeared. But it is less cohesive, and rebellions against it more serious."[7]

Linked to these broad political changes were those in education. The area's economic growth in the 1970s and 1980s occasioned the relocation to Charlotte of both businesses and individuals from all over the country. Unlike more established Charlotteans, these newcomers had not lived through the tumultuous days of desegregation and took little pride in the city's accomplishments in this area. Moreover, many of the white newcomers, especially mid-level managers, had come from suburban school districts in other parts of the country where their children had attended predominantly white school systems. Once in Charlotte, these executives had little use for a desegregation plan that often involved busing their children into heavily black, inner-city neighborhoods. These newcomers' demands for change were initially resisted by the area's established business leaders. But the newcomers' concerns acquired additional force because they dovetailed with broader political currents in the late-1980s: diminishing federal support for mandatory desegregation plans, the advantages of choice as a school improvement strategy, and increasing concern about academic performance.

Echoing national concerns prompted by *A Nation at Risk,* many middle-class white newcomers to Charlotte-Mecklenburg viewed curriculum and instruction as inferior to what it had been "back home." Furthermore, even among longtime black Charlotteans there was growing concern that the district's desegregation achievements had not produced a concomitant increase in black educational achievement. Added to such concerns were those of Charlotte's established business elite. Although leading corporate executives had previously seen Charlotte's reputation as "The City that Made it Work" as helping attract investment, by the late-1980s the business elite saw perceptions of poor academic performance as jeopardizing growth. As a result, prominent executives undertook a wide range of measures to change education policy. One especially important step came in the 1988 school board election when they successfully supported a dramatic change in the composition of the board. One of the newly elected board members, a close associate of NationsBank's CEO Hugh McColl, was key in effecting the 1990 resignation of the incumbent superintendent, whose ability to function as a "change agent" was very much in doubt.[8] This same executive also chaired the search that led to the hiring of John Murphy.

Murphy's ability to function as a change agent had already attracted national attention exemplified by a front page *Wall Street Journal* article, "Forceful Educator Gets Teachers and Children to Be More Productive." The article noted that in his previous superintendency Murphy had emphasized magnet schools, enrichment programs, tests, accountability, and a self-described management philosophy of "applied anxiety" that had led to the demotion of principals, the transferring of teachers, and the freezing of salaries "when he didn't see results."[9] Critics charged that the magnets were creaming resources, teachers were teaching to the test, and that this majority black district should soon have a black superintendent. Intensifying such criticism was Murphy's demand for additional compensation.

REALIGNING RELATIONSHIPS

The Business Elite

Of the various relationships whose realignment accompanied the onset of school reform, the clearest changes involved CMS and Charlotte-Mecklenburg's business elite. One of the main aspects of this realignment was that the differences that had previously characterized relationships between CMS and the business elite, or among different components of the latter, decreased significantly in the whirlwind of change that characterized the first two years of Murphy's tenure. Both the substantive and symbolic aspects of the reform agenda contributed to the lessening of these differences. Of the substantive aspects, two are especially important: the magnets and the system of goals and accountability.

Adopting the Magnet Plan.   The magnet plan reflected a broad political realignment. The busing plan was a defining characteristic of the pre-1987 coalition between the business elite and black political leaders that had dominated local politics, but the magnet plan reflected a more fluid political situation in which there was less political cohesion among African Americans and in which established business leaders had to take greater account of other actors, many of them new to Charlotte and many of them physically located on the county's periphery. In this fluid situation, one of the magnet plan's advantages was that it seemed to be a way to have the cake and eat it, too: to placate those opposed to "forced" busing, to hitch CMS' wagon to the rising star of school choice, and to maintain a desegregated school system along with the presumably progressive race relations associated with such a system.

Murphy's system of accountability and financial bonuses for the achievement of benchmark academic goals also earned high marks among Charlotte's business elite because of its apparent similarities to corporate management strategies. And

Murphy received generally high marks from the business elite for his willingness to effect large-scale personnel turnover in a system that many business leaders apparently believed had too many timeservers.

To these substantive changes, Murphy added crucial symbolic touches, the most important of which were the World Class Schools Panels, which met during his first year in Charlotte. Financed by corporate donations, these panels brought to Charlotte some of the country's most prominent proponents of educational reform for three meetings about the direction of educational change in CMS. However, some participants were unfamiliar with the agenda, and others lacked knowledge about what was actually taking place in Charlotte. Furthermore, the discussion was often extremely general. Thus, the World Class Schools Panels were symbolic politics, and very effective symbolic politics insofar as they further enabled CMS to realign its relationship with the business elite.[10]

The consequences of this realignment became apparent shortly after Murphy's arrival when the CEO of the area's largest utility led a drive to create the Charlotte-Mecklenburg Education Foundation (CMEF). In addition to funds for educational innovation, support from the business elite took the form of partnerships, task forces, and lobbying. For example, in 1993, when the school board met in private to consider a raise for Murphy, who had threatened to leave Charlotte, First Union CEO Ed Crutchfield "wanted to speak to the elected officials on Murphy's behalf" and waited in a nearby office during the board's deliberations.[11] Even after the unexpected defeat of the school bonds in 1995, Crutchfield called Murphy "the best guy in the country."[12]

Another of downtown's influential businessmen, the publisher of the city's daily newspaper, the *Charlotte Observer,* also strongly supported Murphy. In a column that preceded the November 1995 school board election, the publisher called Murphy "a shadow candidate," cited CMS' many reforms and national recognition, and concluded, "If America is clamoring for what Charlotte has, shouldn't we be careful to cherish, celebrate, and retain it?"[13] In the late-1980s the paper had called for major changes in local education policy, but its strong support for Murphy in the 1990s was additional evidence of the extent to which the superintendent's program had realigned CMS' relationship with the business elite.

The 1995 School Board Election. Additional evidence of Murphy's support among the business elite comes from the 1995 school board election. Until 1995, board members were elected at large, but in 1995 CMS switched to a system of representation in which six of the nine members would be elected from districts. Because a plurality would determine the winners in the districts, both the superintendent and business elite were worried that members of the new school board would be concerned mainly with "single issues" such as sex education. The perceived electoral threat both to school reform and Murphy's superintendency led the CMEF to switch its focus from educational innovation to school governance and to launch an educational campaign about the requisites for effective service on the board of education. In addition, many CMEF leaders together with the chamber of commerce initiated the Charlotte-Mecklenburg Alliance for Public Schools. A political action committee (PAC), the purpose of which was to support candidates who would continue education reform, the alliance counted among its leaders and supporters a virtual who's who of corporate Charlotte. As a result, it was able to raise and contribute more money to school board candidates than any PAC in CMS history.

Although the alliance's formation had been prompted largely by concerns about the six district races, its activity in the three at-large races proved the most controversial. It endorsed all incumbents seeking reelection except Susan Burgess, who had first been elected in 1990 with support from the business elite. Although she had generally supported Murphy's policy innovations, relations between the two of them were tense. Part of the explanation for the tension was that she had refused to rubber-stamp even those reforms with which she agreed and part was that she and Murphy had differed over several issues involving equity and personnel matters. Some of their disagreements had been public, and the superintendent's dislike of her was well known. For a variety of reasons, five members of the board—including most of Murphy's strongest supporters—decided not to seek reelection. Their decisions not to run raised the distinct possibility that Burgess might lead the at-large field, become the new board's chair, and thus prompt Murphy to resign. In the ensuing controversy over its endorsements, alliance leaders confined the public defense of their activities to statements such as "we endorsed those we thought would best continue the reforms."[14]

Burgess, however, skillfully exploited the alliance's nonendorsement. She portrayed herself as a candidate who was independent of special interests and who supported educational change but who was willing to stand up to a superintendent whose applied-anxiety management style, volatile personality, and frequent demands for additional compensation infuriated many voters. She received over 25 percent more votes than her nearest rival and laid successful claim to the chair of the newly elected board. Among her strong supporters on the new board were representatives from two swing districts whose candidacy the alliance had also failed to support.

The outcome of the election and Murphy's subsequent resignation are evidence that, as Peirce and Johnson note, rebellions against what they call "the leadership clique, led by the bank CEOs and other corporate chieftains" are more serious than in the past. These journalists' observations can be phrased more precisely, however, with the help of regime theory. As Stone says in his discussion of Atlanta, "There is not much of an activist agenda that can be accomplished" without the cooperation of the business elite.[15] Like most activist public officials, John Murphy realized this need and successfully realigned CMS' relationship with a willing business elite. But although business elite support was *necessary* for the initiation of an activist education agenda, it was not *sufficient* to sustain it. Moreover, the business elite rarely distinguished between those aspects of

the agenda that might benefit all children and those that might benefit particular groups. To be sure, corporate involvement in education was based largely on
the belief that "good schools" are intimately linked to economic growth. But
would "bad schools" mean that Charlotte businesses would not get adequately
trained entry-level workers? Or would "bad schools" mean that the children of
middle-level managers and professionals would not be adequately prepared for
college and the restructured economy? The business elite typically did not distinguish between those two questions even though policies designed to address the
first might be quite different from those aimed at dealing with the second. But in
Charlotte-Mecklenburg's black community there was intense debate about who
was benefiting from Murphy's program.

Educational Change and Blacks

Although Murphy generally received credit for acknowledging CMS' past weaknesses in educating black students, especially poor ones, and for stressing that "all
children can learn," there was considerable debate in the African American community about whether policy jibed with rhetoric. The onset of school reform —
especially the magnet component of it — sharpened certain divisions among black
leaders as well as between many of them and CMS. Some of Charlotte's most
prominent blacks supported the magnet plan. Among them was a bishop of the
AME Zion Church who chaired the school board as well as a woman whose
pioneering attempt to desegregate a Charlotte high school in the 1950s had trig-
gered the events leading to *Swann*. On the other hand, the most vocal objections
to implementing the magnet plan came from African Americans who feared that
it would facilitate resegregation. At the standing-room-only public meeting at
which the school board finally voted to adopt the magnet plan, whites applauded
enthusiastically but blacks remained silent. Though unable to stop the magnets
or postpone their implementation, black opponents together with white allies did
manage to secure several modifications of the original plan. Furthermore, the
school board appointed a twenty-five-person citizens' committee (C25) to monitor the effect of the magnets on desegregation and resource allocation.

The debate over the magnet plan foreshadowed much of the future relationship between Charlotte's black community and Murphy's program. Among
some African Americans there was persistent opposition to aspects of his reform
agenda, especially its perceived threat to desegregation, equitable resource allocation, and the employment of various black teachers and administrators. Thus
black dissatisfaction was undoubtedly part of the complicated causal web that
contributed to Murphy's departure. But African American opposition to the general thrust of Murphy's program was basically unsuccessful. A precondition of
any effective opposition, presumably, would have been substantial cohesion and
political mobilization among blacks, given the fact that they constituted only 27
percent of Charlotte-Mecklenburg's population and 40 percent of CMS' student

body. But, in fact, substantial differences among the city's black leadership persisted, as events surrounding the dismissal of the C25 and voting on school bond referenda indicate.

The Dismissal of the Committee of 25. Although a large majority of the committee's membership was white, the C25's mission involved equity issues traditionally more salient to blacks than to whites, and its first chair was an African American business executive well known for his civil rights activity. In July 1994 the committee prepared reports calling attention to the disparity in resources between the magnets and other schools and claiming that the district's new pupil assignment plan was leading toward a multitiered system, with many schools likely to remain or become racially isolated. The reports provoked considerable controversy. The chair of the school board refused to accept the reports for several months until CMS staff had a chance to prepare a rebuttal. Two weeks after accepting both the C25 reports and the staff rebuttals, the school board voted 4 to 3 to dismiss the C25. In the view of the board's chair, the committee was abusing its charge by trying to direct school board policy. In the view of another board member who had voted against the dismissal motion, the board was killing the messenger who had brought the bad news.[16]

A month after its dismissal, many C25 members joined with the Black Political Caucus to discuss the committee's findings and to develop plans for following through on them. However, virtually nothing came of this meeting. The watchdog committee had been put to sleep for barking, and there was insufficient political will and/or resources among its members and supporters—black and white—to sustain an organized attempt to address the issues to which its reports had called attention. Part of the difficulty in pursuing these issues lay in the fact that several influential members of the black community argued that the C25's reports grossly exaggerated the trend toward resegregation. They also said that Murphy's program provided schools in black neighborhoods with hitherto unavailable resources, gains that, in their view, easily compensated for whatever resegregation might be occurring.

School Bond Referenda. Black support for bond packages traditionally has been high and was key to the alliance between the business elite and the black community that had dominated local politics from 1963 to 1987. Even after the demise of that regime, there was strong support among black voters for all bond packages. Of the thirty-seven Mecklenburg County bond referenda held from 1985 to 1995, there was only one in which there was less support among black voters than white voters.[17] That issue was a 1993 school bond package that graphically indicated the divisions within the black community about Murphy's program.

The 1993 package provided, among other things, for the building of seven new schools, many of which would presumably be located in outlying, overwhelmingly white areas. Such locations tend to "complicate integration," as the

Observer noted. To integrate many of these new schools, the story continued, "many black students will travel farther than whites. School board members last year promised to build all new schools in integrated areas. But later, they exempted the two southeast elementaries from the promise."[18]

Partially because of concerns about resegregation and partially because relatively little money was allocated to repair older schools in predominantly black neighborhoods, Arthur Griffin, one of the school board's two black members, broke ranks with the board and vigorously campaigned against the bond package, as did the Black Political Caucus. However, the bonds were supported with equal vigor by the African American chair of the school board, AME Zion bishop George Battle, and by an influential black county commissioner. These differences among black political leaders were reflected in the vote. Only about 50 percent of black voters supported the bonds. This figure was much lower than in previous referenda, but it was enough to secure the bonds' passage, given support for the package by approximately 53 percent of white voters.[19]

The 1995 School Bond Package. The May 1995 package would have provided for the construction of nine new schools, most of which would have also been built in heavily white areas. However, almost all of the black community's prominent political leaders and organizations — including Arthur Griffin and the Black Political Caucus — endorsed the May 1995 bonds largely because this package provided for more renovations and repairs in schools in black neighborhoods than the 1993 package had. Such endorsements notwithstanding, undercurrents of opposition remained. The caucus had been divided over the issue, and some members campaigned against the bonds. Although the package received a majority of black votes, the margin was considerably less than in the years prior to 1992. Furthermore, the margin of victory in black precincts was insufficient to compensate for the bonds' lack of support among whites. The bonds failed by a narrow margin, the first defeat of a comprehensive school bond package since the mid-1960s.

The May package was then trimmed, and a smaller package placed on the November 1995 ballot. The cuts largely satisfied conservative whites who had spearheaded opposition to the May package. After considerable debate, the Black Political Caucus also endorsed the package, as did Arthur Griffin. It passed overwhelmingly, receiving 72 percent of the total vote.

That large margin among both blacks and whites notwithstanding, an analysis of trends in Mecklenburg County bond voting called attention to a drop in black support for school bonds after 1992, the year in which the magnet plan was implemented. That drop was greater than the decline in white support for school bonds as well as greater than the decline in black support for nonschool bonds.[20] In the absence of survey data, it is impossible to ascertain fully the causes of this drop in black support for school bonds. Yet the history of events surrounding the post-1992 referenda suggests that concerns about resegregation and resource allocation are an important part of the explanation. Consequently, the history of school reform in Charlotte-Mecklenburg calls attention to this policy dilemma: In substituting magnets for many aspects of the mandatory busing plan, Murphy sought, among other things, to decrease white opposition to desegregation and thus to allow CMS to proceed with other aspects of educational change. But while laying a political foundation among whites for such change, the magnet plan and other aspects of Murphy's program may have jeopardized CMS' ability to meet its growing financial needs by alienating that segment of the electorate—blacks— historically most likely to support school bonds. From that perspective, Murphy's program of educational change may have realigned part of the relationship be-tween CMS and the black community, but it did so in a counterproductive manner.

Educational Change and Whites

The extent to which Murphy's program realigned relationships among whites, or between them and CMS, is difficult to ascertain. Much of the difficulty lies in the fact that no set of issues has defined white involvement in education the way that concerns with desegregation and equity have historically characterized black involvement or the way that concerns with attracting new investment have historically characterized business involvement. To be sure, white families, like everyone else, are concerned with a "good education," but that term admits of so many differing interpretations that it cannot easily be linked with specific policy positions.

Perhaps the best short summary that can be offered about the extent to which Murphy's program realigned relationships between whites and the school system is that his agenda failed to overcome some of the centrifugal tendencies inherent in the many political, economic, and social changes that have affected Charlotte-Mecklenburg in the past ten years. Of these changes, three interrelated ones are especially relevant to the politics of education: the increased clout of the county's rapidly growing outlying areas, the increase in the number of Republicans, and the increased influence of fiscal and social conservatives in local affairs.

The growing importance of the county's outlying areas was manifest in the events that led to six members of the school board being elected from districts. Although both Murphy and the business elite feared the switch would jeopardize his program, district representation came about through complicated political ma-neuvers in which political leaders from an outlying white area played pivotal roles in explicit efforts to give their constituents greater voice on the school board.

The increased influence of conservatives and Republicans was also evident in the May 1995 school bond referendum. In that campaign, white, conservative Christian, Republican county commissioner Tom Bush led public opposition to passage of the school bonds. Aiding Bush was a predominantly white citizens' group that had challenged local fiscal policies for a decade. In the absence of survey data, there is scant hope of assessing the extent to which fiscal concerns (as opposed to, say, dislike of Murphy) were responsible for the rejection of the bonds by a majority of white voters. But it is clear that these fiscal concerns mobilized conservative activists to get out the No vote.[21]

The defeat of the bond package prompted Murphy to lash out at certain political officials for misleading the public and to decry Charlotte's lack of world-class leadership.[22] These public outbursts did little to dispel his image as a volatile, irascible superintendent. His obvious anger, resentment, and frustration also symbolized CMS' inability adequately to realign its relationship with a significant section of Charlotte's white population.

Educational Change and Employee Organizations

Organizations of school system employees can have a large effect on educational policy. In CMS, however, employee organizations played a relatively small role. They were especially ineffective in addressing the large-scale turnover in personnel that took place during the Murphy years. There are two reasons for this small influence. The first is a weakness rooted in North Carolina law prohibiting local government agencies from engaging in collective bargaining. The second involves the way in which Murphy dealt with the leaders of the two largest teachers' organizations.

In his previous superintendency, Murphy had thrown the president of the largest teachers' union out of his office and did not speak to her for two years, but in Charlotte-Mecklenburg, events never approached the confrontational stage.[23] Early in his administration, Murphy appointed the president of one of the organizations to a full-time position at CMS' downtown headquarters. The president of the other, larger, and more influential organization, Vilma Leake, retained her teaching position but was appointed to several advisory positions and given special access both to Murphy and his aides. In minimizing whatever opposition Leake might have had to CMS' many changes, including the large turnover in personnel, Murphy was helped by her close relationship with George Battle, the AME Zion bishop who was one of Murphy's strongest supporters on the school board. Leake's late husband had also been a bishop of that church, and the ties between Battle and Leake extended to politics as well. When Leake ran (unsuccessfully) for school board in 1995, Bishop Battle's wife chaired Leake's campaign. Early in Murphy's administration, Leake had criticized some aspects of his program, but she was generally supportive of it. When Murphy indicated in 1994 that he might leave CMS, Leake said, "He has the children's interest at heart. . . . And I would hope he would not leave. He needs to stay here and finish the job he started."[24] When he eventually resigned she was "heartbroken."[25] In sum, to the extent there was any significant realignment between CMS and these organizations, it was achieved by Murphy's securing their leaders' support.

DISCUSSION

This account of the extent to which relationships have been realigned in CMS calls attention to three themes: politics matter, sustaining educational change is different from initiating it, and CMS' school reform efforts have important implications for the rest of the country.

Politics Matter

Although the notion that politics matter is one of this volume's guiding principles, it bears emphasis here because the politics that have mattered most in CMS' recent history is the most basic nuts-and-bolts ability to win a majority of votes in an election or a referendum. The May 1995 bond referendum and the November school board election make clear that political skill can play an important role in affecting the fate of educational change.

In the May 1995 referendum, the corporate executives who headed the Bond Task Force followed the advice of consultants who thought that a low-profile campaign and concomitant low turnout would facilitate passage of the package. Thus, despite access to the considerable financial resources of the business elite, the task force made relatively little effort to mobilize broad support for the package. This strategy proved disastrous. While bond proponents were counting on a low turnout, conservative activists waged a carefully targeted door-to-door and telephone campaign to get bond opponents to the polls. There is no way to determine whether their self-described "stealth" campaign made the difference in the 51 to 49 percent defeat of the bonds. But it is evident that the Bond Task Force had little idea of what was taking place among the electorate.[26]

In the November 1995 school board elections, the Alliance for Public Schools —an organization, like the Bond Task Force, with deep roots in the business elite—made similar miscalculations. Although the alliance was able to raise a considerable amount of money, its attempts at influencing the election were largely unsuccessful. In addition to dealing with Burgess's candidacy in an inept and self-defeating manner, the alliance was ineffective in the districts. In one swing district in which there were eight candidates, the alliance was unable to use its considerable resources to persuade any candidate to drop out. As a result, the candidate endorsed by the alliance split the vote with two candidates with similar platforms, thus allowing the field's most liberal candidate to eke out a victory with only 23 percent of the vote. This person became one of Susan Burgess's strong supporters on the newly elected board. Just the opposite happened in another district. Here there were only two candidates, neither of whom had a background that indicated she would, if elected, unqualifiedly support Murphy's program. One was a conservative Christian with a strong base among religious fundamentalists; the other was a liberal League of Women Voters activist who had worked closely with the C25. The alliance endorsed the conservative Christian as the lesser, from its standpoint, of two evils, especially because it figured, correctly as things turned out, that she would win handily. But the alliance's inability to recruit a more suitable candidate in this affluent, heavily white district is another indication of its failure to act in a politically effective manner.

These political shortcomings during the Murphy years become especially apparent when compared with the much greater savvy that became evident in the years following his resignation. Especially important was the way that CMS, under the guidance of Murphy's successor, Eric Smith, began mending relations with other political leaders, including Tom Bush. In 1997, as in May 1995, Commissioner Bush opposed a bond package. However, in 1997, unlike in 1995, he agreed not to campaign publicly against the package even though it was 33 percent larger. In Bush's view, if you wanted anything from John Murphy, "You had to kiss his ring . . . [but] Eric Smith has that unique capacity of making people feel very important." Furthermore, Bush noted, he and Smith "came to the conclusion that the best way for the school board to deal with Tom Bush is to do it privately through Eric Smith."[27]

Moreover, the tax watchdog group that had also fought the 1995 bonds supported the 1997 package, citing differences between Murphy's and Smith's leadership as one reason for the endorsement.[28] Finally, the 1997 bond campaign was the first in which bond proponents saw fit to open a satellite campaign headquarters in an African American neighborhood. Facing only scattered opposition, the referendum received 73 percent of the vote.

The Difference Between Initiating Change and Sustaining It

The electoral events of 1995 call attention to a second theme in CMS' recent history: the conditions necessary to sustain school reform may be very different from those necessary to initiate it. Within a year of Murphy's taking office in 1991, educational policy changed dramatically. The relatively low level of opposition reflected the mandate for change that existed within the district at the time. In hiring Murphy, the school board was looking for the kind of "change agent" the previous superintendent had not been. Within the school system, the weakness of employee organizations created fewer obstacles than can be found in some other districts. Demographic changes, political developments, and economic growth combined to make the environment within which CMS operated a fluid one. To these circumstances can be added the resources of a business elite quite willing to support a superintendent whose national prominence would allow Charlotte to continue to attract new business investment.

Taken together, those conditions were sufficient to allow the *introduction* of major policy innovations. However, the defeat of the May 1995 school bonds and the resignation of John Murphy suggest that these conditions may not be sufficient to *sustain* large-scale educational change. In seeking the additional conditions that may be necessary to sustain this change, it is useful to draw on earlier comments about the governance tasks associated with different kinds of regimes. In development regimes primarily concerned with promoting growth, coordination among a relatively small set of institutional elites can suffice to fulfill regime goals. With a few notable exceptions—e.g., Commissioner Bush's opposition to the May 1995 bond package—the Murphy administration was relatively successful, especially during its early years, in enlisting elite support for its sweeping agenda.

But educational change, especially the creation of a performance regime, requires a civic capacity that is quantitatively greater than and qualitatively different from what is typically required for altering land-use patterns. Because altering land-use patterns is often controversial, "development activities are often insulated from popular control." Furthermore, the goals of development regimes "impose no motivational demands on the mass public and are advanced easiest when the public is passive."[29] By contrast, building a performance regime in education is more akin to building an opportunity expansion regime: it requires mass mobilization and widespread participation in activities ranging from support for bond referenda to family involvement in many school-centered activities. The governance tasks associated with developing a performance regime in education are thus immense, and the Murphy administration fell considerably short of satisfying them. The shortcoming in relations with the African American community was especially important, given the large number of blacks among CMS' economically disadvantaged student population. African American critics were unable to prevent or slow the adoption of key aspects of Murphy's program. Yet black opposition was sufficiently broad and deep to preclude the Murphy administration's developing the mass involvement and support upon which any hopes of creating a performance regime ultimately hinged.

Given the many generic difficulties of establishing an opportunity expansion regime, it remains problematic whether any school district will succeed in fulfilling the governance tasks that a performance regime in education would demand. Still, post-Murphy events exemplify some likely first steps in tackling several of these tasks and the ongoing difficulties of fulfilling them.

Among the first issues facing the Smith administration were changes in pupil assignment necessitated by the opening of two new high schools. CMS developed three proposals for the new assignments and solicited public comment. The result was arguably the most contentious round of pupil assignment meetings since the early 1970s. Particularly vociferous in their opposition to the proposals were white families in three outlying areas whose children were not assigned to the high schools closest to their homes. Although CMS developed a fourth proposal that satisfied many residents in these areas, there remained sufficient public anger to trigger the formation, with considerable media attention, of Citizens for a Neighborhood School System (CFANSS), which promised to fight for neighborhood schools by lobbying in the state capital and by defeating any candidate for school board who did not support neighborhood schools.

In response to these events, CMS created a task force to develop recommendations about pupil assignment and facilities planning. Each of the school board's nine members appointed three people to this task force, and the superintendent appointed six.[30] Members included leaders of CFANSS, leaders of the NAACP's and the Black Political Caucus's Education Committees, several prominent corporate executives, and a wide range of citizens and education activists.

Although issues facing the task force were similar to those with which the C25 had dealt, the two groups differed in several crucial respects. The C25 was appointed to monitor the operation of the magnet plan, which had already been developed by CMS, but the task force was much more proactive insofar as its charge was to develop recommendations to guide future CMS decision making. Because the C25's role was that of watchdog, it was easy for the relationship between it and CMS to become adversarial. But because the task force's role was proactive, it was relatively easy for relations between it and CMS to remain extremely cordial, especially because the superintendent and board hoped agreement within the task force would prevent future pupil assignment donnybrooks.

In August 1997 the task force released a unanimous report. Among other recommendations it emphasized the need to bring older schools up to acceptable standards by devoting unprecedentedly large percentages of funds to renovations, repairs, and maintenance; drew on the court orders of the 1970s to recommend that the percentage of black students in all schools be within plus or minus 15 percent of the systemwide average; and acknowledged CFANSS concerns by recommending that CMS generally limit mandatory bus rides to thirty to thirty-five minutes. To facilitate implementation of these substantive recommendations, the report also called for the creation of zone-based citizens' advisory planning councils.[31]

As these recommendations indicate, the task force dealt only peripherally with the complex curricular and instructional issues associated with improving educational outcomes. Rather, the group saw itself as helping remove whatever school-planning and pupil assignment barriers might interfere with the pursuit of educational achievement. However, insofar as pupil assignment and related issues often consume disproportionate amounts of attention and resources, any diminution of these barriers would most likely contribute to the development of a performance regime in Charlotte-Mecklenburg.

The task force's ability to issue a unanimous report suggests progress toward that goal, but the district's commitment to desegregation remained controversial. Shortly after the report's release, a CFANSS member, who had not been on the task force, filed suit in federal court challenging CMS' use of racial guidelines in assigning students to magnet schools. Viewing that lawsuit as a threat to all CMS desegregation goals, the law firm that had represented the plaintiffs in *Swann* filed a motion in October 1997 seeking to reactivate that case. Moreover, in the November 1997 school board elections, a neighborhood schools activist won the seat held by the liberal desegregation proponent whose 1995 victory had been facilitated by the eight-candidate field. That electoral outcome together with other changes in membership intensified divisions on the board over many issues, including pupil assignment.

Although these electoral outcomes and legal developments may render moot much of what the task force sought to accomplish, it would be premature to overlook the possible implications of its work. Just as the Citizens Advisory Group helped reconcile competing viewpoints in the divisive desegregation battles of the 1970s, the task force's efforts can be understood as an attempt to draw on similar traditions of civic involvement and consensus building. That chairs of organizations with as differing perspectives as CFANSS and the NAACP's Education Committee could agree to a report addressing a range of equity and pupil assignment issues was a first step in drawing on that tradition.

A second step involved extending the consensus on the task force to the larger community, and the Smith administration moved quickly in that direction. Approximately one month after the task force presented its report, CMS created five zone-based community advisory councils ranging in size from twenty-nine to forty-six members, appointed by the school board and principals of schools located in each zone. The advisory councils were charged with first learning the contents of the task force's report and then developing specific proposals for CMS planners that would enable the report's substantive recommendations to be implemented. To develop these proposals, in November 1997 council members scheduled focus groups at all schools in their zones to solicit citizen input about, among other issues, the changes in pupil assignment that would be necessitated by the opening of six new schools in the next two years. Such widespread, institutionalized, proactive involvement of hundreds of citizens in desegregation, equity, and planning issues is unprecedented in CMS history. This involvement may be interpreted as an attempt to enlarge civic capacity if only because the Smith administration clearly hoped that the community advisory councils would succeed in transferring the task force's consensus to wider sections of the community. However, at this early date (December 1997), it is unclear to what extent this transfer will take place and to what extent the advisory councils will have merely provided forums in which opposing groups organized their forces and marshaled support for future political and legal battles over pupil assignment. This uncertainty is additional evidence of CMS' ongoing difficulty in overcoming barriers to the development of a performance regime and of sustaining educational change.

Civic Capacity and Educational Change in Charlotte-Mecklenburg

The implications of events in CMS are enormous, as some remarks by Eric Smith indicate. While talking to a group of parents and teachers several months after becoming superintendent, Smith explained why the job was such an attractive one by suggesting that the audience scan, as he had done, a list of the twenty-five school districts in the United States which are larger than CMS. All but a few, he noted, faced much greater obstacles to achieving significant educational change than Charlotte-Mecklenburg does.[32]

Precise comparisons among districts are difficult, but Smith was almost certainly right in noting that CMS faces relatively low obstacles. Because of Murphy's electoral setbacks in 1995 and continuing controversy over desegregation, in much of this chapter I have focused on the difficulties that CMS faced in realigning various relationships. These difficulties go a long way toward explaining why sustaining educational change in CMS has been more problematic than initiating it.

Such difficulties should not, however, obscure the fact that CMS has important things going for it that are absent in many other large urban districts. Perhaps most important, the district is a consolidated one. Just as consolidation greatly facilitated desegregation in the 1970s, it now allows the district to minimize many of the political, fiscal, and social problems that are intensified, if not created, by the fragmented character of most contemporary metropolitan areas. Second, compared to many other urban districts, CMS is located in a metropolitan area that, economically speaking, is much healthier. Third, the weakness of employee organizations frees CMS' administration from constraints that in some districts have retarded educational change. Further, the business elite's long-standing involvement in education could also augur well for the future of educational change in CMS, though the assumption that the interests of local business leaders and schoolchildren are largely identical deserves much closer scrutiny than it typically receives in Charlotte-Mecklenburg. Finally, the district has a long tradition—exemplified by the Citizens Advisory Group in the 1970s and the task force in 1997—of community involvement and building consensus in matters dealing with public education. That much of this tradition draws on a concern for educational equity and racial justice provides relatively favorable grounds for addressing the issues of race and social class that polarize so much of urban politics.

Accompanying these many advantages are some disadvantages that further highlight the difficulties of CMS' developing a performance regime. Because it is consolidated, the district may have access to more resources than many urban districts, but it also has more claimants upon these resources. The typical political advantage of these other claimants, especially middle-class whites, is compounded in Charlotte-Mecklenburg by the various weaknesses of organizations whose primary constituency is the poor, the working class, or African Americans. Labor unions are very weak, and few community-based organizations are much stronger. Although more African Americans than ever before walk the corridors of government and corporate power in Charlotte-Mecklenburg, the same demographic changes that have given rise to a black middle and upper-middle class have also geographically dispersed the black population and rendered it less cohesive politically.

In some cities, community-based organizations have helped mobilize broad public support for educational programs aimed at increasing the academic performance of economically disadvantaged students. An especially carefully studied example is the activity in Baltimore of BUILD, an affiliate of the Industrial Areas Foundation.[33] However, attempts to organize a similar affiliate in Charlotte have been slow in getting off the ground and, as of late 1997, had done relatively little to change local politics.

As a result of the general weakness of organizations representing the poor, the working class, and African Americans, numerous actors ranging from Arthur Griffin to John Murphy may succeed in putting the question of the academic performance of economically disadvantaged children on the policy agenda. Yet whatever mass involvement and participation occurs in education has been mobilized at least as much from the top down as from the bottom up, as the origins of the zone-based community advisory councils indicate. Whether such top-down mobilization is sufficient to sustain an opportunity expansion regime in any policy arena is problematic.

Consequently, conditions in CMS would seem to favor the development, up to a point, of both civic capacity and a performance regime. But unless the local political landscape changes significantly, CMS may also serve to indicate the difficulties of creating a performance regime in the absence of organizations with wide and deep roots among the economically disadvantaged. These two considerations make the course and consequence of educational change in Charlotte-Mecklenburg extremely worth watching.[34]

NOTES

The research reported in this chapter was supported by grants from the Winthrop University Research Council and is part of the author's continuing study of education policy in Charlotte-Mecklenburg, another published report of which is "Hugh Governs? Regime and Education Policy in Charlotte, North Carolina," *Journal of Urban Affairs* 19, no. 3 (1997): 247–74.

1. See, for example, Louis V. Gerstner with Roger Semerad, Denis P. Doyle, and William Johnston, *Reinventing Education* (New York: Dutton, 1994).

2. An obvious third question is how these many reforms affected both opportunities to learn and educational outcomes. Although that question is a crucial one, its systematic discussion is well beyond the scope of this chapter, the focus of which is on the political aspects of school reform. For an analysis of educational outcomes during the Murphy years, see Stephen Samuel Smith and Roslyn Arlin Mickelson, "Symbol and Substance in School Reform: The Case of Charlotte, North Carolina," paper presented at the 1997 annual meeting of the Southern Political Science Association, Norfolk, VA.

3. Clarence N. Stone, "The Politics of Urban School Reform: Civic Capacity, Social Capital, and the Intergroup Context," paper presented at the 1996 annual meeting of the American Political Science Association, San Francisco.

4. Clarence N. Stone, "Urban Regimes and the Capacity to Govern: A Political Economy Approach," *Journal of Urban Affairs* 15, no. 1 (1993): 1–28.

5. These words are part of CMS' vision and mission statement.

6. Davidson M. Douglas, *Reading, Writing, and Race: The Desegregation of the Charlotte Public Schools* (Chapel Hill: University of North Carolina Press, 1995), p. 251.

7. Neal Peirce and Curtis Johnston, *The Peirce Report: Shaping a Shared Future* (Charlotte, NC: *Charlotte Observer,* 1995), p. 1.

8. Joseph Martin, interview with author, Charlotte, NC, September 15, 1994.

9. Gary Putka, "Forceful Educator Gets Teachers and Children to Be More Productive, *Wall Street Journal,* June 5, 1991, pp. A1, A7.

10. Roslyn A. Mickelson, Carol Ray, and Stephen Samuel Smith, "The Growth Machine and the Politics of Urban Educational Reform: The Case of Charlotte, North Carolina," in *Education in Urban Areas: Cross-National Comparisons,* ed. Nelly P. Stromquist (Westport, CN: Praeger, 1994), pp. 169–95.

11. Kevin O'Brien, "Eye on Access: Districting for School Board on Ballot," *Charlotte Observer,* October 5, 1993, pp. 1A, 4A.

12. Liz Chandler, "School Bonds' Loss Ignites Debate," *Charlotte Observer,* June 1, 1995, pp. 1A, 6A.

13. Rolfe Neill, "Vote 'Yes' on Murphy," *Charlotte Observer,* November 5, 1995, p. 3C.

14. Tucker Mitchell, "Burgess Says New Group's Endorsements 'Smell,' " *Charlotte Leader,* September 22, 1995, p. 1.

15. Clarence N. Stone, *Regime Politics: Governing Atlanta, 1946–1988* (Lawrence: University Press of Kansas, 1989), p. 197.

16. Del Stover, "Board-appointed Advisory Bodies Don't Always Have the Right Answers," *School Board News,* October 11, 1994, p. 5.

17. Stephen Samuel Smith, "Black Political Marginalization? Regime Change and School Reform in Charlotte, NC," paper presented at the 1995 annual meeting of the American Political Science Association, Chicago.

18. Kevin O'Brien, "Sites for Two New Schools Complicate Integration," *Charlotte Observer,* October 15, 1993, p. 20A.

19. Smith, "Black Political Marginalization?"

20. Ibid.

21. Jim Morrill and David Mildenberg, "Low-key Campaign 'Caught Off-guard,' " *Charlotte Observer,* June 1, 1995, p. 6A.

22. Chandler, "School Bonds' Loss Ignites Debate."

23. Putka, "Forceful Educator."

24. Neil Mara, "Murphy's Possible Departure Rouses a Split Community," *Charlotte Observer,* April 21, 1994, p. 1A.

25. Vilma Leake, interview with author, Charlotte, NC, July 17, 1997.

26. Morrill and Mildenberg, "Low-key Campaign."

27. John Deem, "Superintendent of Sales," *Leader,* August 1, 1997, p. 14.

28. Debbie Cenziper, "Tax Watchdog Group Endorses School Bonds," *Charlotte Observer,* August 16, 1997, p. 4C.

29. Stone, "Urban Regimes," pp. 18–19.

30. The author was appointed to the task force by Susan Burgess and helped draft early versions of some sections of its report.

31. Future School Planning Task Force, *A Vision to Overcome Barriers to Educational*

Excellence Related to Future School Planning and Student Assignment (Charlotte, NC: Charlotte-Mecklenburg Schools, 1997).

32. Eric Smith, speech at parents' meeting at East Mecklenburg High School, October 21, 1996.

33. Marion Orr, "Urban Regimes and Human Capital Policies: A Study of Baltimore," *Journal of Urban Affairs* 14, no. 2 (1992): 173–87.

34. For additional discussion of the socioeconomic and cultural context within which the political developments discussed here took place, see Roslyn Arlin Mickelson and Carol Axtell Ray, "Fear of Falling from Grace: The Middle Class, Downward Mobility, and School Desegregation," *Research in Sociology of Education and Socialization* 10 (1994): 201–32.

PART IV
The Elusive Search for Civic Capacity

We move now from individual cases to more general patterns. In chapter 11, Kathryn Doherty considers an extensive body of research on attitudes toward public education in the United States. She finds that the citizenry continues to give public education a positive rating but nevertheless perceives it to be plagued by problems much more serious than those in private schools. Big-city districts are seen as especially problem-laden and ripe for fundamental change. Educators would be well advised to pay close attention to these findings. Part of the conventional wisdom within schools has been that external players are always critical and that they push ill-conceived reforms soon to be replaced by other hastily conceived reforms, but none of it amounts to anything greatly consequential. In this view, educators can outwait critics and reformers, and life will go on much as it has in the past.

Doherty's analysis suggests that this "life goes on" view is naive and specifically that it misses a significant decline in the standing of public education. The very legitimacy of the public system is at issue, particularly in the case of low-performing urban districts. Piecemeal reform is no longer the only alternative under consideration. Public discourse now gives major attention to a fundamental reordering of how education is provided, and the edge that private schools enjoy in the eyes of the citizenry poses a threat to public education that practitioners in the present system would be foolish to ignore.

If discontent with public education runs so deep, one might expect that support for reform would be easy to organize. Not so, Doherty's analysis shows. Various stakeholders have differing understandings of the nature of the problem and therefore of how to solve it. There is no hidden hand of politics that moves to solve policy problems. Instead, those individuals with the immediate responsibility of meeting a functional need often are inattentive to growing signs of dissatisfaction, and they tend to protect those practices that are familiar. Especially is that the case when familiar practices also bestow significant benefits.

Far-reaching change comes only when a wider body of actors mobilizes and is able to create a new set of institutional practices. Thus the overall pattern of change may best be described as "punctuated equilibrium"—a period of stasis followed by a disruptive mobilization and the creation of new arrangements.[1] Public education shows every sign of heading toward such a period of fundamental reordering. For teachers, administrators, and their unions, the question increasingly becomes one of whether or not they want to play a part in the process of reordering or if they want to defend established practices at the risk of being left out of the construction of new arrangements.

Change follows no single path. As Doherty's analysis shows, understandings of the education problem vary. Hence it may matter enormously who is part of the coalition that puts together a redesigned system of education. Because everyone's understanding is partial, the narrower the redesign coalition the more limited the understanding that is likely to guide a new set of arrangements. Conversely, the more inclusive a reform coalition, the broader the set of considerations taken into account. There is more to the story than simple perception and information, however. In all areas of policy, and especially in education, the nature and the extent of the effort made depend on more than who participates in policy deliberation. They also depend on who contributes what—on the resources brought to bear. To see policy in this light is to think about policy change in a new way. Change comes about not so much by putting pressure on a given body of decision makers as by rearranging relationships, by changing who is involved and on what basis.

This line of thinking stimulated the concept of civic capacity. For education, the questions are who is involved in the governing coalition and what does each contribute? If civic capacity is to be developed, more than talk must take place. The ideal is that, as varied stakeholders engage one another around a common problem, each is drawn into a broader understanding of the problem and a commitment to be responsive to needs defined in community terms. Doherty's findings indicate no natural tendency toward a broad and shared conception of the education issue. In chapter 12 Clarence Stone shows how rare it is to develop a high degree of civic capacity and how difficult it is to maintain it. Powerful forces work against a mutual understanding and stand as a barrier to broad and sustained cooperation.

Is there an alternative, then, to building civic capacity? Can a hegemonic actor—state or federal courts, for example—compensate for the strong centrifugal forces in an urban community? The case of Charlotte-Mecklenburg has demonstrated that a court decision could precipitate coalition building. San Francisco also shows that court action can provide a means for bringing key actors together, but that city's case also reveals that a partial mobilization of concerned stakeholders can lead to conflict, as excluded groups organize to challenge decisions of which they are not a part.

In the eleven-city study reported by Stone, only Pittsburgh approximated an inclusive coalition, and a court desegregation order was the precipitator of the city's education coalition. Boston's more tenuous education coalition came during the aftermath of that city's desegregation crisis. In Los Angeles, the precipitating crisis was demographic change brought about by a huge in-migration of Latinos. In Baltimore, there is widespread support for school reform, but it has taken state intervention to prevent the effort from completely unraveling. Thus, though external intervention is contested, it may yield results nonetheless.

Despite desegregation and other crises, some cities have not built broad and lasting education coalitions. Again, no invisible hand produces a result simply because it is needed. Civic capacity is a politically constructed response, and urban conditions themselves are far from conducive to the needed coalition building. Someone has to see the need and have the ability to create conditions that bring people together around civic concerns.

Many cities have formed public-private coalitions for economic development and the restructuring of urban land use. But one of the points Stone makes is that civic mobilization in one policy area does not automatically extend to another. Spillover is possible, but essentially the wheel of civic capacity has to be invented, problem area by problem area. Thus Stone's overview of the eleven-city study is a reminder that civic cooperation is itself a challenge, and it may have to be met before the further challenge of educational improvement can be undertaken. Changing relationships so that they address *community* problem-solving is no easy matter.

NOTE

1. Frank R. Baumgartner and Bryan D. Jones, *Agendas and Instability in American Politics* (University of Chicago Press, 1993).

11

Changing Urban Education: Defining the Issues

Kathryn M. Doherty

Why are schools so hard to change even when the demand for reform is high and claims of crisis in education are frequent? The contributors to this volume demonstrate that although much leverage can be brought to bear on school systems and educators by a variety of stakeholders—from courts and the state to business, parents, and community—there is no simple formula for successful education reform. The cases highlight the ways that efforts at reform are shaped by the particular circumstances of local environments. In this chapter I take another approach, examining the broad context of education politics and looking at the ways education stakeholders, in the aggregate, frame the question of educational reform.

The views communicated through survey research reveal patterns that are important to our understanding of current school reform efforts. First, opinion data show that reform is being pursued in an atmosphere where the very legitimacy of public education is at risk. Though support for the system remains fairly wide, it does not run very deep. Furthermore, the data illustrate no natural tendency toward a broad and shared conception of reform among important stakeholders; rather, various actors tend to have only partial understandings of the problems facing public education.

As a consequence, educational reform efforts are proceeding on tenuous ground. Since support for public schools is shallow, reforms that fail become further evidence of the inadequacy of the system. The effect of diminished confidence in public schools can be defensiveness among education professionals. A defensive education system potentially reinforces a narrow sense of obligation from stakeholders outside the system. And since the numerous actors who have a role to play in educational reform have incomplete understandings of the issues at hand, efforts tend to become fragmented. They are further splintered by racial and class tensions. One feature of the education landscape, then, is a dearth of actors for whom the collective interests of all children are a central mission.

Trends in survey data indicate that the call for accountability is wide. But how can performance be improved? And who should be accountable for improving public schools? In answer to those questions, blame and finger-pointing are prevalent, and there seems to be little common understanding of how schools might change to meet higher expectations and demands.

THE LEGITIMACY OF PUBLIC EDUCATION

In view of the frequently alarming rhetoric about the condition of public education, recent studies at first glance suggest a good deal of confidence in public schools. As one survey indicates, 42 percent of the American public express a great deal or quite a lot of confidence in public education. And, although this figure may seem low, when put in the context of the more general decline of American trust in public institutions and professionals, schools do not fare badly. In the same survey, only 15 percent of Americans expressed the same level of confidence in Congress, and just 19 percent were confident in the federal government. Public education fared better than both state and local government as well, which were rated with confidence by only 20 and 23 percent of the public.[1]

Indeed, when asked to rate their own local public schools, Americans appear even more supportive of public education, and they have been over time. In a twenty-five-year compilation of data from Gallup/Phi Delta Kappa, local public schools were given grades of A or B by 40 percent of the public and failing grades by no more than 7 percent of those surveyed. These ratings are consistent over the entire period of the survey—there has been no significant change, according to this data, since 1969 when the survey instrument was first used. Overall, the average grade assigned to local public schools by Americans has been a C+. Although this rating does leave much room for improvement, it is not nearly the failing scenario one would expect, given the tone of much discourse on the condition of public education. Similarly striking, over half of the public, and 71 percent of parents with children currently in school, give their community schools an "excellent" or "good" rating.[2]

Without denying the fact that serious problems face American schools, the case for a wholesale crisis in education may be tenuous.[3] Survey research does not yet show widespread evidence of public abandonment of the system. And empirical data also question the crisis claim. As Jeffrey Henig explains:

> The declaration of an education crisis rests on a partial and one-sided reading of the available data. Just as powerful are figures that tell a somewhat different story: one of progress in expanding educational achievement, lowering drop-out rates, improving performance as measured by some tests of reason-

ing and substantive knowledge, narrowing educational differences between whites and racial minorities, and maintaining a stable base of public support and appreciation.[4]

Although there have been areas where students have shown declines in scores on achievement tests, when one takes into account the higher expectations and larger breadth of education Americans now demand of schools, the extent of the commitment to giving all children the opportunity to learn in this country, the rise in public school enrollments, and the questionableness of recent test data interpretations, some of the attacks on public education may not be warranted.

Shallow Support for Public Education

Yet this is not to say that all is well. There may be more confidence in schools than one might expect, but support for public education is quite shallow. Although not in the case of their own children and schools, the public does seem to regard schools in general as in trouble. The grade assigned to public schools nationally is less impressive than the grades assigned to local schools. In 1997, 46 percent of Americans give their schools a grade of A or B, but only about half that number were willing to give public schools in general the same grades. The public is also increasingly supportive of the idea of allowing choice among public and private schools at government expense.[5] Further, 47 percent of Americans surveyed no longer believe that a high school diploma ensures that students have learned the basics; 63 percent of employers believe the same. Leaders are even more skeptical; 65 percent do not think a high school diploma is a sign of student competence. In one survey, even one-third of teachers and administrators admitted that a high school diploma does not necessarily signify that basic competencies have been mastered by students.[6]

One might further gauge the depth of American confidence in public schools by comparisons that have been made between public and private education. At first they would seem to suggest that the fever pitch of much rhetoric is exaggerated. A cursory look at the data indicates that confidence in private education does not exceed public education by large margins. When asked to compare them, the public is fairly evenly split. Thirty-nine percent say private schools in their community provide a better education and 33 percent think that local public schools are superior. Forty-five percent of Americans reported "quite a lot" or "a great deal" of confidence in private schools in 1994—only three percentage points higher than confidence in public schools.[7]

But there is less than straightforward optimism about how public schools measure up to private schools. Upon deeper probing, and as questions become more precise, support for public education does seem to erode, and the data offer some revealing insights about where people see weaknesses in the public schools. Such studies indicate that people believe private schools surpass pub-

Table 11.1. Percentage of Parents Identifying Issues as Problems

	Private School	Public School
Child safety in school	3%	30%
Child safety out of school	14%	45%
Gang violence	4%	48%
Drugs	6%	39%
Poor achievement	9%	49%
High dropout rate	2%	35%
Education of non-English speaking	8%	24%
Education of low-income students	16%	36%
Resources	34%	37%
Parental say in schools	32%	53%
Lack of parental involvement	41%	60%

Source: Dan A. Lewis and Kathryn Nakagawa, *Race and Educational Reform in the American Metropolis* (Albany: State University of New York Press, 1995).

lic schools on a number of criteria. In one survey, public and private (including Catholic/Christian) schools were compared on thirteen dimensions, including teaching techniques, instilling work habits, preferable class size, and discipline. On eleven of the thirteen dimensions, private schools were deemed to be more successful than public schools.[8] Another survey demonstrates similar findings (see Table 11.1). As these data illustrate, even though many Americans remain somewhat loyal to public education, they are clearly unhappy with the ways public schools handle a number of their important responsibilities.

Comparisons of teachers' attitudes in public and private schools reveal differences as well. According to a U.S. Department of Education survey, private school teachers are more likely than public school teachers to feel that they work in a supportive environment, that teachers play an important role in decision making at their schools, and that they receive a great deal of support from parents.[9]

The Crisis in Urban Education

Although the call of crisis may not be warranted for many American public schools, the one area where a sense of urgency is profound is in the case of urban and inner-city schools and in the opinions of minority parents. Current statistics show that the forty-seven school districts serving the nation's largest cities educate a student population that represents a full 40 percent of the country's low-income pupils and almost 75 percent of the nation's minority students.[10] In these schools, financial and social problems are acute. Surveys of urban and minority parents reveal them to be far more troubled than white suburban parents about the conditions of their local schools. Eighty percent of black parents think that

Table 11.2. Percentage of Teachers Rating Aspects of Their School as "Excellent" or "Good."

	City	Suburb
Quality of teachers	92%	98%
Curriculum	77%	86%
Academic standards	74%	90%
Parental and community support	37%	75%
School funding	43%	56%

Source: Louis Harris and Associates, *Metropolitan Life Survey of the American Teacher 1984–1995* (New York: Met Life, 1995), p. 22.

drugs are a serious problem in schools, compared to 58 percent of white parents. Seventy percent of black parents believe academic standards in their schools are too low, compared with less than half of white parents. Black parents are also likely to report that urban schools are underfunded and that the best teachers avoid inner-city schools.[11] In a Washington, DC, survey, 65 percent of city residents rated the quality of public schools as "not so good" or "poor"; only 22 percent of suburban residents surveyed rated their schools as low.[12]

A 1997 survey reveals that 69 percent of the public believes that problems facing urban students are more serious than those facing other students.[13] One of the most striking pieces of data is the discrepancy between urban and suburban teachers in their ratings of parental and community support for their schools. Urban teachers suffer far more than their suburban counterparts from a sense of isolation and poor relationships with the communities they serve. Responses by urban and suburban teachers on several criteria for judging their schools are revealing (see Table 11.2).

In American cities, concern about education invokes the crisis label from leaders as well. Research from the Civic Capacity and Urban Education Project found that 61 percent of community advocates and urban leaders identified education as a major problem facing their cities.[14] In an annual survey of municipal officials, education and youth crime have been identified as the two most important conditions to be addressed in the nation's cities. Almost 30 percent of U.S. city officials surveyed think that the quality of education in their cities had worsened since 1995. And education is high on municipal officials' top-ten list of "most deteriorated" urban conditions in the past five years.[15]

DEFINING THE EDUCATION PROBLEM

Whatever disparities there are in perceptions about the condition of public schools, across the board current demand for education reform is strong, and defense of the status quo has become increasingly difficult to maintain. But does the

Table 11.3. Percentage Saying "Not Enough" Investment in Education

	Public	Students	Parents	Employers
Preschool education	61%	69%	56%	73%
K-12	71%	81%	77%	78%

Source: Committee for Economic Development, *An Assessment of American Education: The Views of Employers, Higher Educators, the Public, Recent Students and Their Parents* (New York: Harris Education Research Center, 1991).

education system need to be tinkered with? A major overhaul? Curriculum reform? More money? Improvement in school-community relations? An incremental or systemic approach? Though poll results consistently show a need for improved education, the question of how to achieve reform elicits mixed responses.

For a long time, the inadequacy of school funding was the focus of concern for improving education. When asked whether we spend enough on education, stakeholders believe that we are not doing enough (see Table 11.3). In 1997, half the public saw lack of funding as a serious problem for education, but the position that stresses the link between money and educational improvement is becoming less viable.[16] Despite their concerns about funding, Americans also feel that more expenditures on education would be analogous to throwing money down the drain. Community leaders (63 percent) tend to think that schools use lack of funding as an excuse for their poor performance.[17] Although 64 percent of educators in one Connecticut survey believe that more money would help make schools better, the same proportion of public officials hold that unless schools are fundamentally overhauled, more money will be wasted. Other sources show the public evenly split about the effect more money would have on improving local schools.[18] And when it comes to spending money on teachers, although 44 percent of educators believe that better teachers' salaries have substantially improved education, 65 percent of the public and 70 percent of public leaders say that salary increases have done very little to improve education.[19]

Many people who reject the claim that schools need more money point to the growth of large public school bureaucracies as the largest obstacle to high quality education. Bureaucracy is a serious concern not only for the general public but is also the number one focus of business complaints about schools. Once seen as a great improvement in education, the development of a professionalized educational cadre is now considered the enemy of school reform. Sixty-six percent of business executives and 60 percent of teachers cite bureaucracy as an obstacle to improved public education. Recent investigations into big-city school districts have uncovered systems dominated by cronyism, waste, and the protection of administrative jobs at the expense of classrooms and students.[20] For many parents, bureaucracy stands as an inflexible and impersonal structure, wasting taxpayer money and set on making communication between school and community difficult. For teachers, bureaucracy limits classroom freedom, constrains time, and stands in opposition to innovation and change. Only education administrators themselves disagree—with just 20 percent reporting excessive administration as a problem for education.[21]

With bureaucracy as a target, public support for structural education reforms such as school privatization, charter schools, and vouchers has grown in strength in the last decade—although support remains more cautious and less ideological than is often presented in public discourse, perhaps partly because of uncertainty about how such a system would work. Support for parental choice, when set in the vaguest of terms, is strong, holding at 69 percent in 1995. The annual Gallup/Phi Delta Kappa polls indicate that 54 percent of the public now support charter schools, a figure that has not grown dramatically but has been steady in recent years. Polls do show increasing support for voucher systems. In the past four years, support for parental choice that includes sending children to private schools at public expense has risen from 24 to 44 percent.[22]

Many of these types of market reforms are aimed at increasing the accountability of schools and at breaking the stranglehold of centralized school bureaucracy. But other critics focus on the quality of teachers as the central problem of education, supporting reforms aimed at raising the accountability of education providers. Although 70 percent of teachers claim that outside critics underestimate the good things going on in schools, 40 percent of influential urban actors point to the quality of schools, including poor teachers, as a major problem for education in their cities.[23] Thirty-three percent of Americans believe that teachers are worse now than when they themselves were in school.[24]

The view is popular, then, that if classrooms are run properly, student achievement will improve. Thus, for example, the public strongly supports merit pay as a way to provide incentives for improved teaching accountability. The public also strongly favors strengthening the ability of school systems to remove poor teachers. Even though teachers have resisted such policies through their representative unions, 89 percent of them also say they support making it easier to remove incompetent teachers.[25]

Curricular reform is another classroom-level focus for critics of the educational system. No group in any surveys examined here believes that American students currently have too much academic pressure. Most think that curriculum falls short of student needs. The public is supportive of higher academic standards for students and believes teachers should be more willing to fail high school students who do not learn. In one survey, 89 percent of parents support high school graduation exams. When asked about the consequences of tough standards—more dropouts for example—the public, at least rhetorically, seems prepared to accept such risks.[26] Despite the political fight waged over Pres. Bill Clinton's Goals 2000 legislation, the concept elicits overwhelming support in surveys of public opinion. Sixty-two percent of educators and 82 percent of business executives call for common national standards.[27] An overwhelming 82 percent of Americans are convinced that "the nation needs common national standards of performance that all schools should be expected to live up to."[28] Noteworthy is the case of inner-city respondents. Though much of the protest over the standards movement has emphasized a potential bias against disadvantaged students, inner-city residents are equal to affluent communities in their belief that their children should be expected to achieve the same high standards as other public school students in the nation.[29]

The bulk of educational reform efforts are directed at increasing school and teacher accountability, but educators are not the sole source of concern. Thirty-eight percent of influential actors in eleven cities named social issues as a major problem for education in their cities.[30] And both parents and teachers agree that a student from a stable, supportive family in a poor school is better off than a student from a troubled family who attends a good school.[31]

By this account, teachers do not believe that they can bear the brunt of blame for mediocre student performance. Educators observe that "schools are trying to meet all the needs of children, social as well as educational, and we aren't equipped for that. We're not properly prepared to deal with . . . the many, many problems they bring to school."[32] When asked why students with high grades do well, two-thirds of teachers say it is because parents support education.[33] Sixty-six percent of teachers blame the failure of students in school on the family and the home life of children.[34] Academic achievement, they recognize, depends on "social supports" for education that come from the community. Thus, much of what hurts student performance begins at home and is beyond the control of schools and classroom teachers.[35]

As some observers suggest, the problem facing education today may not be fundamentally about the need for school reform but about the lack of commitment from parents, adults, and society in general toward school and learning. One of the most profound changes in American schools may be the growing proportion of students who are disengaged and have "checked out."[36] A recent extensive study finds that students today do not seem to take learning seriously. Over one-third say that they get through the day at school by "goofing off with their friends," and almost 40 percent say that they neither try very hard nor pay much attention when in class. American students also spend precious little of their time studying or doing homework, and peer culture downplays academic success.[37] Indeed, more than half of the students surveyed in the study said that they could bring home grades of C or worse and not upset their parents. One-third reported that their parents had no idea what they were doing in school, and one-sixth said their parents didn't care.[38] Another study reports that 51 percent of students say their parent or the adult in their home never or only once in a while checks to see if they have done homework.[39]

As one teacher put it, "Without parental support, it makes it very hard to educate their kids—you have no feedback; you have no support. . . . They just

Table 11.4. Percentage Agreeing Parents and Members of Community Need More Say in Public Schools

	Teachers	Principals	Business	Public
Allocation of school funds	26%	14%	56%	59%
Curriculum	17%	27%	48%	53%
Selection and hiring administration	28%	15%	48%	46%
Salaries	17%	10%	40%	39%
Books and materials	16%	10%	19%	43%
Selection and hiring teachers	12%	8%	27%	41%
Books in school libraries	13%	10%	13%	38%

Source: Stanley Elam, *The Gallup/Phi Delta Kappa Polls of Attitudes Toward the Public Schools 1969–1988* (Bloomington, IN: Phi Delta Kappa, 1989).

want a finished product. They want to drop him off in kindergarten and pick him up in senior year."[40] Parents agree in principle that lack of parental responsibility is a grave problem for today's students; almost nine in ten see deficient parenting as a major obstacle to student performance. But even though 56 percent of teachers think students face most of their stress from their home lives instead of in school or with friends, only 22 percent of parents agree.[41]

The importance of active parent participation in education does not let schools off the hook. In a national PTA survey 25 percent of parents say they do not get involved more in their children's education because they feel intimidated in the school environment.[42] One parent describes attending conferences with teachers: "You know, it's just like going to the doctor's. And it makes you feel a little inferior to them."[43] Rhetoric about deficient parental involvement aside, when asked about increasing the power of parents in schools, teachers often seem less than enthusiastic. Educators are very supportive of parental activity at home and of their volunteering as chaperons at school activities, but they often seem to prefer that parents accept a position of "distant assistants" and help teachers only when invited to do so.[44] Professional educators and administrators express much lower levels of interest in community participation in other areas of public school life. In one survey, only 18 percent thought it would be "very valuable" to have parents on a school curriculum committee, and only 26 percent thought it would be valuable to have parents on a school management team (see Table 11.4).[45]

Although parents are ultimately responsible for becoming involved in their children's education, a recent study suggests that school and teacher practices may be the single most important factor in determining parental involvement— more important than student and family background, income, or parents' education levels. These findings have important implications for those individuals who believe that changing the school-community relationship is central to education reform.[46]

SOURCES OF DIVISION AMONG STAKEHOLDERS

What do these various understandings of the education problem tell us about the likely shape of change? In describing the sources of the problems of education—from poor teachers and curriculum to school bureaucracy, social and economic inequality, poor parenting, or pervasive social problems—differences in framing issues emerge among education stakeholders. And although the contributors to this volume stress that there is no one leverage point for changing schools, the data examined here reveal that many stakeholders do emphasize single causes for the education "problem." Whether blame lies with teachers, parents, administrators, or somewhere else, the search for a silver bullet is prevalent.

It is no surprise then that the reform landscape reveals thousands of programs aimed at everything from changing curriculum, enhancing professional development, and altering patterns of school governance and parental involvement to raising teacher and school accountability for enforcing higher academic standards. But it is likely that all of these factors are part of the public education problem. No one actor's views of the situation seem to capture the full picture. In fact, it is more accurately the case that stakeholders have only partial understandings of the issues, based on their relationships with the public education system or within it. If this is true, it is not enough to illustrate differences of opinion to explain fragmented efforts at educational improvement. We also need to look at the underlying obstacles to more convergent understandings of the challenges of educational reform and the solutions that might improve conditions. Where are the fault lines?

The School-Business Relationship

Two-thirds of employers say high school graduates lack the skills to succeed as workers. Business support for education is considered instrumental in reform efforts, both in financial support for schools and the provision of jobs for graduates. But surveys that ask businesspeople about their perceptions of public education show consistently and conspicuously negative responses. Seventy-nine percent of business executives say the nation's public schools are seriously off on the wrong track, an opinion that only 32 percent of school superintendents share. Among businesspeople, opinion does not improve much when the question is asked about local schools: 56 percent of business executives say that even their own communities' schools are headed in the wrong direction. And although nine in ten teachers rate their schools highly, that number drops significantly for many political leaders, barely half of whom describe schools as "excellent" or "good."[46a]

Businesspeople are outsiders to the school system. Their work is managed by different principles and under different conditions from that of educators. The work process in education is not as tangible as production in other occupations.

Perhaps because of their own take on how to improve performance and their own reading of the ease with which schools ought to be able to operate, business-people are more optimistic than most groups about the possibility of change in the public school system.

Despite this optimism there are challenges to getting the business sector involved in education reform. Although businesses have shown themselves to have the potential to become highly mobilized around community problem-solving efforts—in development issues, for example—the process of improving schools is a more long-term effort that does not have immediate and tangible returns. As stakeholders in the education system, businesses have often seen their work with schools as charity, not as part of their own interests.[47] The perspective of business also leads to its focus on efficiency and managerial reforms as key in fixing schools.

Despite businesspeople's complaints about students' basic math, science, and writing skills and their deep dissatisfaction with schools, they may be doing little to encourage student achievement in these areas. First, businesses report relying much more on interviews than on student grades, rarely using transcripts in making hiring decisions. A survey conducted in 1991 by the Michigan Department of Education reported that the five most important attributes considered by employers are absence of substance abuse, honesty, ability to follow directions, respect, and punctuality. The five least important attributes were skills in math, social sciences, natural sciences, computer programming, and foreign languages.[48]

But business has been taken to task on its limited role in reform efforts. During a 1996 national education summit of educators, governors, and CEOs, companies were challenged. The corporate agenda focused on standards and technology, avoiding most of the controversial issues of school reform and their own responsibilities in the process, but the group did pledge to focus on grades in their hiring decisions as a way to encourage students to work harder. One educator present at the summit offered the important observation that "it would help us motivate kids if there was a connection between grades and job prospects."[49] Many people would like to see a stronger connection between businesses and schools on this level, with relationships not just on the basis of donating computers or money but in the form of opportunities for transitions out of school and into productive work. Even though there are a number of examples of business-school partnerships, there are few citywide initiatives that signify a large-scale commitment from businesses to the graduates of public schools.[50] Few observers believe that business is sufficiently involved in helping to produce the very workforce it demands for the future.

The School-Community Relationship

The nature of the tension between parents and teachers and their perceptions of educational problems are clearly illustrated when one compares the top problems cited by each group. A pattern of mutual blame surfaces. Parents point to the difficulties in getting good teachers, and teachers stress lack of parental support, lack of pupil interest, and lack of discipline among students.[51]

Although the relationship between parents and teachers is recognized as important to most education stakeholders, parents' regard for and faith in teachers is mixed. Over one-third of parents do not trust teachers to make decisions about how the public schools are run. Some observers see the public's call for the basics as a revolt against education professionals, a return to old-fashioned teaching techniques, and a rejection of methods that are seen to be new-fangled, self-esteem-centered approaches to education.[52] Thirty-seven percent of Americans currently believe that teachers are more interested in making students "feel good" than in making them learn. Despite this perception, a comparison of teachers' responses between 1964 and 1984 found that teachers in the 1980s were more likely than in earlier years to emphasize basic tools for acquiring and communicating knowledge and more likely to describe themselves as "no nonsense, get the learning of the subject matter done" educators.[53]

Part of the tension does seem to reflect a persistent pedagogical disjunction between parents and teachers. In a 1969 survey of parents and teachers, 62 percent of parents said they believed that discipline was more important than "self-inquiry"; only 27 percent of teachers agreed.[54] The public supports memorization and enforcing grammatical rules as tried-and-true techniques of learning, but teachers more often promote practices such as creative writing in their classrooms.[55] In contrast to general opinion, teachers believe that one of the keys to effective classrooms has been a willingness to throw out traditional practices.[56]

Education insiders see other aspects of their work quite differently from parents and community as well. Teachers often claim that parents and families make their jobs as educators more difficult. As one teacher commented, "The families in our school don't solve problems; they create them. . . . You can't believe what I have to do to find parents. If I actually do make contact, some say, 'Why are you calling me? You should know what to do. You are the teacher!' "[57]

Teachers do not feel respected and are often frustrated about their roles as professionals. Although job satisfaction has gone up in recent years, at the same time only one teacher in ten agrees strongly that they are respected as teachers in today's society.[58] One teacher described her experience with parents during a time of transition:

> I believe a piece of us felt that parents should have had more faith in our judgment of what we believed was educationally sound for their children. Thus we felt not only frustrated at being ineffective in communicating our message, but also angry and sad that our role as teachers seemed diminished.[59]

It is not surprising, given these tensions, that survey data reveal a great potential for burnout and defeat among teachers. When asked whether they can really make a difference in the lives of the children they work with, 83 percent agree strongly before their first year of teaching. After the first year, the figure drops to 68 percent.[60] The problem of teacher burnout is particularly severe in urban schools.

Overall, educators can feel threatened and sometimes demoralized by problems they cannot control. Where reforms are taking place, teachers often feel that there is too much change happening too fast.[61] They suffer from little interaction with each other and little support from the public and from parents. Even as parents and outsiders are focused on increasing teacher accountability, teachers already see themselves as inundated with demands such as paperwork and mandates that leave them overwhelmed.

The problem of poor parent-community-school relations is particularly acute in urban schools (see Table 11.2). Here, not only is there distance, but more often than not, hostility. In urban schools, parents often do not see professional educators as interested and willing to work together with them. In disadvantaged neighborhoods, school and community are often caught in a cycle of mutual frustration and recrimination, each seeking to blame the other for problems in the schools. Teachers blame parents for the deficiencies in children who do not come to school ready to learn. Community members blame educators for failing to instill discipline and to teach needed skills.

Discussion of parental involvement, and of community and business support for education, points to a need to think of education as a process broader than the confines of school buildings and textbooks. Majorities of teachers and parents, along with many businesspeople, recognize that a lack of community involvement is a significant contributing factor to the education problem.

Much current urban education reform seems to pay lip service to the idea of increased community participation in schools. And there are many honest efforts to involve the community, particularly parents, in the life of their children's schools. But a recent study by the U.S. Department of Education reveals that attempts to increase parental involvement were reported in only 18 percent of high-poverty school districts surveyed. A Rand evaluation of federal programs intended to support innovative practices in public schools found that although some practices, like local evaluation efforts, continued after the regulatory thumb of the federal government was lifted, parent involvement consistently came to a halt in almost all school districts when it was no longer mandated.[62]

City officials observe a dearth of collaborative effort on education issues. Only one-third of public officials believed business is involved or very involved in addressing the needs of children. City officials also cite as substantial problems a "lack of shared responsibility," lack of information, and poor communication among community sectors.[63] It is unclear if the issue is insufficient community involvement in schools or if community involvement is not considered a prime factor in determining educational success, but "either way, viewing the school as an institution isolated from community involvement seems to be pervasive."[64]

Of course, even when parents do participate in education, and the community gets involved in relationships with schools, positive outcomes are not guaranteed. Increased school-community interaction can bring conflicts to the surface. Moreover, such interaction is often unwelcome (see Table 11.4). As one teacher puts it, "Personal responsibility, good sense, respect for the process—when these elements are absent, even a very few individuals can disrupt the well being of many."[65] Dorothy Shipps suggests that community involvement in Chicago school governance, which focused on the public input of *parents* rather than on *citizens*—the latter might have had a more general interest in improving education for all children—may have furthered a narrow and parochial agenda.[66]

The potential for conflict does not necessarily serve as a good reason to avert the leverage that parents and community can bring to bear on schools. But making school-community interaction a positive experience takes effort. A number of programs have been developed with attention to improving the quality as well as the quantity of interaction among school and community actors, particularly in disadvantaged neighborhoods. The Comer School Development Plan, for example, is a program implemented in almost 600 schools and is focused on creating relationships of trust between parents and schools. Comer's approach, based on principles of respect, collaboration, and nonblame among education stakeholders, has been adopted as a model for many other school reform efforts that strive for positive relationships between school and community.[67]

The Internal Dynamics of Schools

Beyond external pressures on teachers, the complexity of the school environment itself is an often overlooked source of tension and strain. Daily incentives and constraints on teachers shape their views—habitual patterns, external demands, little internal control—conditions that are not immediately obvious to outsiders.[68] Some of the difficulties facing reform efforts are related to these circumstances, including repeated experience with failed reforms and frustration with what some teachers call "administrivia."[69]

Part of the problem is that the American school is characterized by an "egg crate" structure, built around traditions of mutual noninterference among educators and isolation of individual classrooms and teachers.[70] Education policy thus takes on a special character. With classroom interaction between students and individual teachers as central, the context of that interaction is extremely important.[71]

The egg crate structure of classrooms also contributes to a certain distance from and limits on policies or demands made on teachers and schools from the system level. This highlights a second important internal dynamic of school life—the tension between the professional autonomy of teachers and the bureaucratic controls of administrators. Given the size of education administration in this country, this tension may be even more pronounced. Studies show that the United States far outspends other industrialized nations on education administration. It devotes 24.6 percent of total education spending to nonteaching personnel, compared with 20.2 percent in Canada, 17.7 percent in the UK, and 15 percent in Japan.[72] In Baltimore, to cite one example, there is estimated to be an administrator for every eight teachers in the public school system.[73]

From the teachers' point of view, school administrators are often seen as a major problem for public education. In one survey, under 15 percent of teachers strongly agreed that they themselves participated in making important education decisions in their schools.[74] As one teacher puts it, "People aren't leaving education because of children but because of other adults: incompetent principals, supervisors, and board members."[75] By this account, much teacher burnout and low morale are related to lack of support and professional treatment by administrators. Teachers are often expected to "comply rather than invent," in order to mass-produce learning.[76] The system has been described as one of "dual captivity" for students and teachers. Even though classroom work is highly decentralized, school officials often try to micromanage, seeing teachers as agents charged with implementing detailed specifications developed by central administrators.[77] Furthermore, decisions over issues of school budgets, personnel, and professional development are generally highly centralized.

Under trying circumstances of working with both students and professional colleagues, the psychological benefits of teaching can lose ground to job security and material concerns. A Chicago survey reveals that commitment to and collective responsibility for schools by teachers dwindle under difficult conditions.[78] Inner-city schoolteachers often believe that reform efforts are futile.[79] The teachers on the front line become resistant to "reform du jour" cycles and grow "tired of constantly trying out the ideas in someone's master's or Ph.D. thesis."[80]

Although by this account it would seem that school reforms aimed at restructuring the organization of school hierarchy or instituting alternative schools would appeal to the public and to teachers, breaking both the bureaucratic dominance of the educational system and countering teacher resistance, there are mixed signals from the community and from educators on this front. When we look at opinions about what people see as the ideal public school, the mandate for change is unclear. Much of the American public is supportive of a traditional, hierarchical school structure. In one study of a New York City school, parents seem most supportive of an authoritative school principal.[81] And although teachers report that they resent administrative control, still they are in favor of maintaining the ability and the promise of being able to move up, and sometimes out of, the classroom. Thus, while education specialists, teachers, and citizens may complain about it, most professional educators and the general public seem to prefer the traditional structure to the many alternative-school concepts. The idea of the "real school" remains "a cultural value in and of itself, quite apart from how effective it proves in educating children."[82]

The School as Employment Regime

Recognizing the tensions between school and community and the internal strain of the school environment is important in discerning much of the context in which school reform must take place. Education is not simply about straightforward attention to the needs of children. We must understand that schools are also about jobs and benefits. Calls for major restructuring of the education system threaten the livelihood of many education stakeholders. Urban school systems, in particular, are often the largest employers in their cities.

On this front, teachers' unions have been cited by many frustrated education reformers and many people in the popular press as a major obstacle to school reform efforts. Eighty-six percent of business executives believe that unions are an important part of the problem. In fact, combining "strongly agree" and "somewhat agree" responses, even a small majority of teachers agree with the statement that education reforms are usually resisted by unions and administrators.[83] Still, teachers usually stand by unions. In a Public Agenda (1994) report on Connecticut schools, 59 percent of educators agree with the statement that teachers' unions are a positive force for education. In contrast, 71 percent of public officials believe that unions have been a negative force in education. And in a survey asking the public about their levels of trust in different groups to make decisions about their community's schools, teachers' union representatives were second only to elected officials as least trustworthy.[84]

When we look at particular employment issues, teacher defensiveness is apparent. In a time of teacher shortages in some urban school districts, 92 percent of teachers support incentives to help students choose careers in teaching, but at the same time 59 percent think it would have a negative effect to allow school districts to hire talented people not certified as teachers.[85] The protection of rewards in the form of administrative jobs also remains important to teachers. Sixty-six percent would leave unchanged or increase career-ladder opportunities. Ironically, teacher support for this career ladder is maintained, despite recognition that it has virtually no relationship to, or effect on, student learning.[86] Thus although school bureaucracy is seen as a problem by teachers, as well as the public, the bottom line is that the public school system is also a major source of jobs, particularly in the nation's largest cities.[87]

The Class and Racial Context of Public Education

The conditions of life for poor children and inner-city families are particularly grave. Large numbers of children in American cities live in a social environment of decay, overwhelmed by poverty, drugs, violence, and their consequences—family instability, teen pregnancy, school dropouts, malnutrition, abuse, and suicide. The geographic concentration and isolation of these conditions in inner cities only exacerbates such problems. The city of Baltimore, for example, con-

Table 11.5. Percentage of New Teachers Whose First Two Years Were "Very Satisfying"

	All/many low-income	Few/none low-income
Your students	70%	75%
Other teachers	56%	68%
Your principal	45%	61%
Administrators	32%	40%
Parents	18%	43%

Source: Harris, *Metropolitan Life Survey.*

tains only 31 percent of the metropolitan population yet an overwhelming 71 percent of the children who are poor. The city of Atlanta is home to 14 percent of the metropolitan area's total population but 40 percent of the poor children. Statistics from other American cities reflect similar patterns.

Thus, when it comes to solutions, urban stakeholders are more supportive of strict and pervasive reform efforts, yet at the same time, urban schools have more obstacles to overcome. Social supports are generally weaker in lower-income neighborhoods. School bureaucracy may be more deeply entrenched. Teachers are less satisfied with their working conditions.[88] And inner-city families often are isolated and may lack the skills or confidence to participate in their children's education. They are often intimidated by the school atmosphere and feel that professional educators look down on them. Urban education stakeholders are generally the least optimistic in their beliefs that things can change and in their expectations for school improvement and student achievement. The experience of teachers who work in disadvantaged communities is also worse (see Table 11.5).

Students are affected by these perceptions among the adult members of their communities. Low-income students are more likely to lack confidence that their teachers will like them, to have lower expectations of themselves, and to feel that they receive more than their share of punishment compared with high-income children.[89]

What James Comer has described as a "culture of failure" is a prominent feature of urban education.[90] Milbrey McLaughlin and Joan Talbert describe many teachers in this situation as "disengaged, furious, resigned and frustrated."[91] A number of studies indicate that minority parents believe that they, more than their white counterparts, are unwelcome at school. Minority parents also are more likely to describe their interactions with teachers and administrators as confrontational and stress a lack of respect or compassion from professional educators.[92]

There is a large racial divide in opinion on why and how inner-city schools are so often low performing. Findings from a survey of Connecticut residents reveal different understandings of the plight of inner-city schools. Across the board, less than half of whites agree with the majority of blacks' perceptions about the discrepancies in performance between urban and suburban public schools (see

Table 11.6. Opinions on Low Performance of Inner-city Schools, Percent Responding "Very Important"

	African Americans	Whites
Inner-city schools have much less money	69%	41%
Inner-city teachers have low expectations	59%	39%
Best teachers avoid inner-city schools	58%	42%
Racial discrimination	53%	26%

Source: John Immerwahr, *The Broken Contract* (New York: Public Agenda, 1994); see also John Immerwahr, *Committed to Change: Missouri Citizens and Public Education* (New York: Public Agenda, 1996).

Table 11.6). Indeed, these data reveal that white respondents downplay many of the factors that black respondents see as significant reasons for the low performance of inner-city schools.

Although almost all respondents are concerned about financing education, in surveys white respondents attribute less importance to funding disparities as a problem for education than do black respondents. Thus it is not surprising that white and suburban stakeholders are ambivalent about issues of funding equity and continually unwilling to redistribute education funds. Indeed, although the general public seems to pay lip service to providing equal education for all children, including inner-city youth and minority students, the depth of that concern is questionable. Less than one-third of public educators in Connecticut were willing to say that residents of their state were committed to providing quality education for poor and minority children on par with their own children. In the same study, only 28 percent of business executives regarded revenue disparities across school districts as a serious obstacle to educational achievement.[93]

In theory, people seem to be unsure about how more money would make a difference to schools. But in practice, the unwillingness of taxpayers to spend more on schools is a prominent feature of the political landscape. A Florida survey found that over 80 percent of voters believe overcrowded classrooms were a major problem facing their community, but less than half would support a bond issue to raise money for building schools.[94] A number of states have experienced "tax revolts," with referenda and initiatives aimed at radically limiting property taxes as a source of revenue that is available for education. And these revolts often have been unaccompanied by plans for revenue replacement.[95] Urban public officials also highlight the importance of taxpayer resistance to new spending as a major obstacle to addressing the problems of children and youth, 66 percent of city officials and 72 percent of leaders from large cities citing this as a barrier.[96]

Comparing responses by race reveals other differences in the views of white and minority parents. Despite greater obstacles, black parents, for example, are still more hopeful than whites and teachers in general that a good education or a good school can overcome other troubles. They also have a more radical notion of reform than most professional educators. Blacks are less skeptical of vouchers, privatization, and school choice schemes than whites and are more likely to support school uniforms, discipline enforcement, and national standards. And though blacks are even more likely than whites to think that Catholic schools succeed in giving children a solid education and are more critical of the condition of public education, nevertheless, black support for the potential of the public school system to educate children adequately is greater than it is among other groups.

My point has been to show the diversity of perceptions about the education "problem" in order to understand the context within which the politics of school reform must take place and change occur. One of the themes of this volume is that the direction education policy takes largely depends on the extent to which various sectors of the community can supply leverage and can be mobilized on behalf of a problem-solving effort. Therefore the way that problems are defined and issues framed, and the extent to which those perceptions are held in common by stakeholders, is an important element in the effort. The way issues are framed can define the scope of actors who see themselves as having a stake in the matter.[97] Ideas are also important for changing institutional arrangements. As Frank Baumgartner and Bryan Jones explain, education is an example of a policy subsystem that is characterized by a "strategic struggle over the definition of issues." Long periods of stability in a policy subsystem can be fundamentally altered by participation around a new definition of the situation.[98] And developing shared orientations and approaches to problem solving may be essential for school reform efforts. For example, studies have found that in successful comprehensive, citywide, business-school partnerships, participants were able to reframe the education problem and come to a shared understanding of its complexity. This process of "issue crystallization" was critical for collaboration to occur and be sustained.[99]

There are areas of convergence in public opinion on education issues. Across categories of groups there is a fairly stable understanding of what the public schools ought to accomplish and a belief that they have the capacity to achieve such goals.[100] But opinions diverge, and often very sharply, on what it would take to get schools to improve student performance along such criteria. These divisions among stakeholders stand out as potential roadblocks to generating agreement about shared social purpose, especially differences between education insiders and outsiders, teachers and parents, urban and suburban residents, and black and white families.

Even for dedicated teachers, schools are a source of career ambitions and income. Professional educators and administrators have much to lose in a major disruption of the current system. But they are also under increasing pressure to be more accountable for educational improvements that they cannot possibly produce alone. Defensive positions thus are common among professional educators and their union representatives. Parents have great interest in school reform, yet despite their opinions on tighter standards, many resist accepting the possibility of their own children failing. Parents are much more willing to blame schools or teachers rather than themselves or their own children's efforts for lack of educational achievement. Businesses have their own financial interests at stake in the results of American education. Yet despite complaints about the job preparedness of American students, there is little systematic effort by business to participate with schools to help achieve the quality of students necessary for the economy of the future. Although many businesses help provide equipment and technology to individual schools, very few offer apprenticeships or job partnerships to school districts.

The complexity of the factors that determine academic achievement and school reform success shows that increasing accountability for educational outcomes most likely rests on more than just teachers' shoulders. Change depends also on parents, business, and other community members and institutions. But the fact that many sectors of our society have a stake in educational practices and are dissatisfied with the current system does not easily lead to a shared understanding of and concerted effort at educational reform. Part of the task, then, is to find a means to change the way the issue of education reform is framed and to focus disparate interests so that some common solutions seem plausible and palatable and other positions less urgent.

Difficult questions arise, given the data presented here: If a concerted effort among actors is not the natural outflow of the recognition of a problem, where can a shared understanding and effort come from? How can competing interests be focused? How can a new configuration of interests be promoted? Education seems to be an area where focus on a common goal is possible by concentrating, not on the needs of business or the economy per se or on the protection of teachers in the system, but squarely on the needs of children. A shared definition of the issues surrounding education, and the establishment of common goals among reformers, may be at least more promising than efforts built only on a shared disdain for the current system.

Great obstacles still loom on the path to educational reform. The task is not simply one of changing opinions and reframing issues. The sentiments presented in this chapter are reflections of deeper issues of power and resources that cannot easily be resolved. The often overlooked challenge remains one of how to build new relationships among actors so that efforts for coalition building for educational reform can become sustainable over the long term. This is the task of building civic capacity.

NOTES

1. Independent Sector, *Giving and Volunteering in the United States: Findings from a National Survey* (Washington, DC: Independent Sector, 1994).

2. Stanley Elam, *How America Views Its Schools: The PDK/Gallup Polls, 1969–1994* (Bloomington, IN: Phi Delta Kappa Educational Foundation, 1995). Some cautions about the interpretation of opinion data are worth noting. For example, approximately 40 percent of respondents in any given year admit knowing "very little" about their local public schools. Yet despite this lack of knowledge, on average, no more than 18 percent of respondents in any of the Gallup polls declined giving a grade to their local schools. See also Kate Zernike, "Education Poll Finds Parents Satisfied," *Boston Globe,* December 3, 1996, p. A1. Massachusetts parents of public school students rate their schools very highly, but their perceptions may not match reality.

3. David Berliner and Bruce Biddle, *The Manufactured Crisis: Myths, Fraud and the Attack on America's Public Schools* (New York: Addison-Wesley, 1995).

4. Jeffrey R. Henig, *Rethinking School Choice: The Limits of the Market Metaphor* (Princeton: Princeton University Press, 1994), p. 32.

5. Forty-eight percent of Americans support allowing students and parents to choose a private school to attend at government expense. Lowell C. Rose, Alec M. Gallup, and Stanley Elam, *The 29th Annual Phi Delta Kappa/Gallup Poll* (Bloomington, IN: PDK Educational Foundation, 1997).

6. Louis Harris, *Metropolitan Life Survey of the American Teacher, 1984–1995* (New York: Met Life, 1995); Jean Johnson, *Assignment Incomplete* (New York: Public Agenda, 1995); Education Week, *Quality Counts 98* (Washington, DC, 1998) XVII: 17.

7. Independent Sector, *Giving and Volunteering in the United States.*

8. Johnson, *Assignment Incomplete;* see also Stanley Elam, "The 28th Annual Phi Delta Kappa Gallup Poll" (Phi Delta Kappa, 1996).

9. U.S. Department of Education, *School and Staffing Survey, 1993–1994* (Washington, DC: National Center for Education Statistics).

10. Council of Great City Schools, National Urban Education Goals: 1994–95, Indicators Report (Washington, DC: 1996).

11. Jean Johnson and John Immerwahr, *First Things First: What Americans Expect from the Public Schools* (New York: Public Agenda, 1994), and John Immerwahr, *Committed to Change: Missouri Citizens and Public Education* (New York: Public Agenda, 1996).

12. *Washington Post,* March 11, 1996, pp. A1, A8.

13. Time/CNN Cable News Network Poll (Feb. 1997).

14. Whitney Grace and Bryan Jones, "Convergent and Divergent Views of Educational Policy Among Urban Elites: A Preliminary Report," paper presented at the Annual Meeting of the American Political Science Association, San Francisco, September 1996.

15. National League of Cities, *The State of America's Cities* (Washington, DC: National League of Cities, 1996).

16. Time/CNN Cable News Network Poll; Charles Mahtesian, "The Quagmire of Education Finance" *Governing,* September 1993, pp. 43–46.

17. John Immerwahr, *The Broken Contract* (New York: Public Agenda, 1994), p. 12.

18. Immerwahr, *Broken Contract,* and Johnson, *Assignment Incomplete.*

19. Immerwahr, *Broken Contract,* p. 12.

20. See, for example, the series "D.C. Schools—Learning the Hard Way," *Washington Post,* February 16–21, 1997.

21. Steve Farkas, *Educational Reform: The Players and the Politics* (New York: Public Agenda, 1992).

22. Rose, Gallup, and Elam, *29th Annual Phi Delta Kappa/Gallup Poll,* 1997.

23. Grace and Jones, "Convergent and Divergent Views of Educational Policy."

24. Johnson and Immerwahr, *First Things First,* and Johnson, *Assignment Incomplete.*

25. Harris, *Metropolitan Life Survey.*

26. Rose, Gallup, and Elam, *29th Annual Phi Delta Kappa/Gallup Poll,* 1997; Mass Insight, *Education Reform—Year Three: The Public's View of Standards and Tests* (Cambridge, MA: Opinion Dynamics Corporation, 1996). See Zernike, "Education Poll Finds Parents Satisfied." Parents may have a "false expectation" about how many students will succeed if standards are raised and graduation exams are administered.

27. Farkas, *Educational Reform.*

28. Committee for Economic Development, *An Assessment of American Education: The View of Employers, Higher Education, the Public, Recent Students and Their Parents* (New York: Committee for Economic Development, 1992).

29. Johnson, *Assignment Incomplete.*

30. Grace and Jones, "Convergent and Divergent Views of Educational Policy.

31. Steve Farkas and Jean Johnson, *Given the Circumstances: Teachers Talk About Public Education Today* (New York: Public Agenda, 1996).

32. John Godar, *Teacher Talk* (Matcomb, IL: Glenbridge, 1990), p. 145.

33. Farkas and Johnson, *Given the Circumstances.*

34. Farkas, *Educational Reform* and Marilyn Cohn and Robert Kottkamp, *Teachers: The Missing Voice in Education* (Albany: State University of New York Press, 1993).

35. David Cohen, "What Is the System in Systemic Reform?" *Educational Researcher* 24, no. 9 (December 1995): 11. Although parents and the public in general seem willing to admit that many of the troubles faced by the schools stem from home life and social problems that are out of the direct control of teachers, they still blame teachers and schools. Only 42 percent of business executives agree with the statement that students come to school with so many problems that it is difficult for them to be good students.

36. Laurence Steinberg, *Beyond the Classroom: Why School Reform Has Failed and What Parents Need to Do* (New York: Simon and Schuster, 1996).

37. Ibid., p. 18. But see also Jean Johnson and Steve Farkas, *Getting By: What American Teenagers Really Think About Their Schools* (New York: Public Agenda, 1997).

38. Steinberg, *Beyond the Classroom.*

39. Penny Bender Sebring, Anthony S. Bryk, and John Q. Easton, *Charting Reform: Chicago Teachers Take Stock* (Chicago: Consortium on Chicago School Research, 1995).

40. Godar, *Teacher Talk,* p. 154.

41. Farkas and Johnson, *Given the Circumstances.*

42. National Parent Teacher Association, *First Annual National PTA Worldbook Survey of Elementary School Parents* (Chicago: National PTA, 1994).

43. Susan McAllister Swap, *Developing Home-School Partnerships: From Concepts to Practice* (New York: Teacher's College Press, 1993).

44. Dan C. Lortie, *Schoolteacher: A Sociological Study* (Chicago: University of Chicago Press, 1975).

45. Harris, *Metropolitan Life Survey.*

46. Joyce Epstein and Susan L. Dauber, "School Programs and Teacher Practices of Parent Involvement in Inner City Elementary and Middle Schools," *Elementary School Journal* 91, no. 3 (1991): 289–305.

46a. *The Public Agenda* (Winter 1998); Farkas, *Educational Reform;* Johnson, *Assignment Incomplete.*

47. Andrew Ashwell and Frank Caropreso, eds., *Business Leadership: The Third Wave of Education Reform,* Report no. 933 (New York: Conference Board, 1989).

48. Berliner and Biddle, *Manufactured Crisis.*

49. Jay Mathews, "Major Companies Vow to Focus on Grades in Hiring High School Graduates," *Washington Post,* March 27, 1996, p. A7.

50. See Ashwell and Caropreso, eds., *Business Leadership;* Leonard Lund, *Corporate Championing of Educational Coalitions,* Report no. 1033 (New York: Conference Board, 1993); and Sandra Waddock, "Lessons from the National Alliance of Business Compact Project: Business and Public Education Reform," *Human Relations* 46, no. 7 (1993): 849–77.

51. Elam, *Gallup/Phi Delta Kappa Polls,* 1989; Martin Haberman and William Rickards, "Urban Teachers Who Quit: Why They Leave and What They Do," *Urban Education* 25, no. 3 (October 1990): 297–303.

52. See, for example, a description of the elective curriculum of the 1970s in a high school in Gerald Grant, *The World We Created at Hamilton High* (Cambridge: Harvard University Press, 1988). Although these illustrations are twenty years old, there is still the perception today that schools have lowered their demands and expectations of students in response to pupil disengagement.

53. Cohn and Kottkamp, *Teachers.*

54. Louis Harris, "Poll: Collision Course in the High Schools," *Life,* May 16, 1969, pp. 22–39.

55. Immerwahr, *Broken Contract.*

56. Milbrey W. McLaughlin and Joan E. Talbert, "How the World of Students and Teachers Challenges Policy Coherence," in *Designing Coherent Education Policy,* ed. Susan Fuhrman (San Francisco: Jossey-Bass, 1993).

57. Cohn and Kottkamp, *Teachers,* p. 8.

58. Harris, *Metropolitan Life Survey,* 1995. But see OECD, *Education at a Glance* (Paris: Center for Educational Research and Innovation, 1995). In international comparisons with Western industrialized countries, teachers in the United States are rated as "very and fairly respected" by 68 percent of the public—higher than in any of the ten European countries surveyed.

59. Laraine K. Hong, *Surviving School Reform* (New York: Teachers College Press, 1996), p. 63.

60. Harris, *Metropolitan Life Survey,* 1991.

61. Hong, *Surviving School Reform.*

62. Milbrey W. McLaughlin, "The Rand Change Agent Study: Ten Years Later," in *Education Policy Implementation,* ed. Allan R. Odden (Albany: State University of New York Press, 1991), pp. 143–55.

63. National League of Cities, *State of America's Cities.*

64. Farkas, *Educational Reform.*

65. Hong, Surviving School Reform, p. 140.

66. Dorothy Shipps, "The Invisible Hand: Big Business and Chicago School Reform," Consortium on Chicago School Research, University of Chicago.

67. James P. Comer, *School Power* (New York: Free Press, 1980); James P. Comer, Norris Haynes, Edward T. Joyner, and Michael Ben-Avie, eds., *Rallying the Whole Village: The Comer Process of Reforming Education* (New York: Teachers College Press, 1996).

68. James Q. Wilson, *Bureaucracy* (New York: Basic Books, 1989).

69. Godar, *Teacher Talk,* p. 97.

70. Lortie, *Schoolteacher.* Less than one-half of teachers in a recent Chicago survey thought that teachers helped each other do their best (Sebring, Bryk, and Easton, *Charting Reform*).

71. Milbrey W. McLaughlin and David D. Marsh, "Staff Development and School Change," in *Schools as Collaborative Cultures,* ed. Ann Lieberman (New York: Falmer Press, 1990), and Edward Pauley, *The Classroom Crucible* (New York: Basic Books, 1991).

72. Gregory Fossedal, "Help for Schools? Try Deregulation," *Wall Street Journal,* March 27, 1996, p. A22. Yet some people dispute the growth of bureaucracy as a central problem for education. One study indicates that central-administration costs for education have been roughly stable since the end of World War II (see Eric A. Hanushek, *Making Schools Work* [Washington, DC: Brookings Institution, 1994]). An accounting of how the New York City school system spends its money estimated that no more than 4 percent of the overall budget goes to administration (see Jacques Steinberg, "School Budget Study Shows 43 Percent Is Spent in Classrooms," *New York Times,* November 21, 1996, p. B8).

73. Clarence Stone, "Urban Education Reform: On the Politics of Structural Change," paper presented at the Urban Issues Workshop of the Center for the Social Science and Barnard-Columbia Center for Urban Policy, November 1995.

74. U.S. Department of Education, *Schools and Staffing Survey, 1993–1994* (Washington, DC: NCES, 1996).

75. Godar, *Teacher Talk,* p. 199.

76. Susan Moore Johnson, *Teachers at Work: Achieving Success in Our Schools* (New York, Basic Books, 1990).

77. Lortie, *Schoolteacher.*

78. Sebring, Bryk, and Easton, *Charting Reform.*

79. Jean Anyon, "Race, Social Class, and Educational Reform in an Inner City School," *Teacher College Record* 97, no. 1 (fall 1995): 69.

80. Godar, *Teacher Talk.*

81. Mary Anne Raywid, "The Wadleigh Complex: A Dream That Soured," *Politics of Education Association Yearbook* (Washington, DC: Falmer Press, 1995), 101–14; see also Hong, *Surviving School Reform.*

82. Mary Haywood Metz, "Real School: A Universal Drama amid Disparate Experience," in *Politics of Education Association Yearbook,* ed. Douglas Mitchell and Margaret Goertz (Washington, DC: Falmer Press, 1990), p. 113.

83. Farkas, *Educational Reform.*

84. Immerwahr, *Broken Contract,* and Johnson, *Assignment Incomplete.*

85. Segun Eubanks, *The Urban Teacher Challenge* (Belmont, MA: Recruiting New Teachers, 1996); on teacher and union resistance to such policies, see Thomas Toch, "Why Teachers Don't Teach," *U.S. News and World Report,* February 26, 1996, pp. 62–71.

86. Mark A. Smylie and John C. Smart, "Teacher Support for Career Enhancement Initiatives: Program Characteristics and Effects on Work," *Educational Evaluation and Policy Analysis* 12, no. 2 (summer 1990): 139–55.

87. Marion Orr, "The Challenge of School Reform in Baltimore: Race, Jobs, and Politics," chap. 5 of this volume.

88. U.S. Department of Education, *Schools and Staffing Survey 1993–1994* (Washington, DC: National Center for Education Statistics, 1996). Teachers in schools with high percentages of children in poverty report higher levels of student misbehavior, dissatisfaction with salary levels, and dissatisfaction with the level of parental support.

89. Ellen A. Brantlinger, *The Politics of Social Class in Secondary School* (New York: Teachers College Press, 1993). Yet, in one survey, majorities of black and Hispanic Students say they routinely get away with being late and not doing their work—Steve Farkas, Jean Johnson, and others, *Getting By: What Teenagers Really Think About Their Schools* (New York: Public Agenda, 1997).

90. Comer, *School Power.*

91. McLaughlin and Talbert, "How the World of Students and Teachers Challenges Policy Coherence," in *Designing Coherent Education Policy,* ed. Susan Fuhrman (San Francisco: Jossey-Bass, 1993), pp. 220–49.

92. Raymond L. Calabrese, "The Public School: A Source of Alienation for Minority Parents," *Journal of Negro Education* 59, no. 2 (1990): 148–54.

93. Immerwahr, *Broken Contract.*

94. Lisa Arthur, "Build Schools—Just Don't Make Us Pay, Poll Says." *Miami Herald,* January 23, 1997, p. 1A.

95. Penelope Lemov, "Taxes: The Struggle for Balance," *Governing,* August 1996.

96. National League of Cities, *State of America's Cities.*

97. E. E. Schattschneider, *The Semi-Sovereign People* (New York: Holt, Rinehart and Winston, 1960).

98. Frank R. Baumgartner and Bryan D. Jones, *Agendas and Instability in American Politics* (Chicago: University of Chicago Press, 1993), p. 22. See also Deborah A. Stone, *Policy Paradox and Political Reason* (Glenview, IL: Scott, Foresman, 1988).

99. Waddock, "Lessons from the National Alliance of Business Compact Project, and *Business and Education Reform: The Fourth Wave* (New York: Conference Board, 1994).

100. Johnson and Immerwahr, *First Things First,* and Farkas, *Educational Reform.*

12

Civic Capacity and Urban School Reform

Clarence N. Stone

In this chapter I report on a study of urban education in eleven large and geographically diverse cities.[1] The study concerned efforts to change fundamentally not only the manner in which urban school systems are run internally but also the way schools and their communities are related. To direct attention to the extent to which the full scope of stakeholders, noneducators as well as professional educators, join in efforts to improve local schools, the eleven-city study used the concept of civic capacity.

Research for this project was driven by two questions: (1) Is there evidence that greater civic capacity leads to more extensive efforts to improve school performance? (2) And, if so, are there ways to facilitate the building of civic coalitions? Though these are fairly direct questions, neither, especially the second one, turns out to be easily answered.

SELECTED DEMOGRAPHIC CHARACTERISTICS

The cities studied were Atlanta, Baltimore, Boston, Denver, Detroit, Houston, Los Angeles, Pittsburgh, St. Louis, San Francisco, and Washington, DC. Three of the eleven were over 1 million in population in the 1990 census, and the three smallest were just under 400,000. Even with considerable range in size, all are among the nation's largest school systems, with enrollments varying from nearly two-thirds of 1 million in Los Angeles to in excess of 40,000 in Pittsburgh and St. Louis. These cities have large minority populations, and four of them have African American majorities. San Francisco has a sizable Asian American population, at 28.4 percent. Five of the cities have Latino populations greater than 10 percent, Los Angeles having the highest at nearly 40 percent.

To an even greater extent than the general population, the students in these

250

schools were of color and poor. None of the eleven systems had a majority of white students, and only Pittsburgh came close. Nine of the eleven had a majority of their students on federally assisted lunches; and in a tenth, Denver, virtually half of the students were under the program. For St. Louis, at the upper end of this measure of student poverty, the figure reached 85 percent.

Though there is significant variation among the eleven cities on various factors, as a group they do not seem to differ much from big-city systems generally. The proportion of minority teachers is lower than the proportion of students, but it is quite substantial. Six of the cities have "majority minority" teaching staffs, and the proportion reaches 83 percent in Atlanta. In addition, five of the superintendents are African American, and two are Latino.[2] None is Asian American.

The political ramifications of these figures are important. The socioeconomic profiles of urban school children are quite distinct from those of the voting-age population of their cities, and the differences between them and the adult populations of their metropolitan areas and states are even greater. Moreover, the school systems themselves face the harsh fact that, by background, a high proportion of their students is predicted to perform poorly by various measures of academic achievement.

AN APPROACH TO EDUCATION POLITICS

By focusing on civic capacity, the eleven-city study brings front and center the question of coalition building. Complex factors infuse this process. Although everyone thinks that schools should perform better and children deserve wider opportunities, as we have seen in chapter 11, people have varied ideas about the nature of the problem and how to respond to it. Moreover, rallying "the whole village" into an encompassing education coalition cuts against the convention of delegating to school officials the responsibility of educating children.

Important as these considerations are, they do not stand alone. As Marion Orr emphasized in chapter 5, race pervades education politics. Coalition building begins with that fact. Thus, I shall make further use of the Baltimore example to illustrate how any effort at coalition building in support of educational improvement cannot ignore the racial divide.

Of course, education politics is not simply about racial division and policy impasse. One of the puzzles is that there is much small-scale experimentation but little full-fledged reform. Why? Are there special difficulties in building coalitional support on behalf of systemwide change? That question encourages us to reexamine stakeholders from an intergroup perspective.

Table 12.1. Demographic Profiles of the Eleven Cities

	Population	White	African American	Hispanic	Asian American	Median Income	HS grad. or less	College
Atlanta	394,017	31%	66%	2%	1%	$25,145	70%	30%
Baltimore	736,014	39%	59%	1%	*	$28,217	67%	33%
Boston	574,283	59%	24%	11%	5%	$34,377	51%	49%
Denver	467,610	61%	12%	23%	2%	$32,038	44%	56%
Detroit	1,027,974	21%	75%	3%	1%	$22,566	66%	34%
Houston	1,630,553	41%	27%	28%	4%	$30,206	52%	49%
Los Angeles	3,485,398	37%	13%	40%	9%	$34,364	52%	48%
Pittsburgh	369,879	72%	26%	1%	2%	$27,484	62%	38%
San Francisco	723,959	47%	11%	14%	28%	$40,561	40%	60%
St. Louis	396,685	50%	47%	1%	1%	$24,274	64%	36%
Washington, DC	606,900	28%	63%	5%	2%	$36,256	48%	52%

Source: United States Bureau of Census, *1990 Census of Population and Housing.*

* Less than 1%

Table 12.2. Eleven-City School Profile

	Students	African American	Hispanic	Asian American	White	FARM[†]	Minority Teachers
Atlanta	58,744	91%	1%	1%	7%	71%	83%
Baltimore	110,662	82%	*	1%	17%	62%	65%
Boston	62,407	48%	23%	9%	20%	58%	37%
Denver	62,935	22%	41%	4%	32%	49%	23%
Detroit	175,036	88%	*	1%	8%	58%	65%
Houston	198,209	36%	48%	3%	13%	55%	55%
Los Angeles	653,619	15%	65%	7%	13%	65%	43%
Pittsburgh	41,160	53%	*	1%	45%	61%	20%
St. Louis	42,278	78%	*	1%	20%	85%	66%
San Francisco	64,986	19%	20%	47%	14%	31%	40%
Washington, DC	80,937	89%	6%	1%	4%	56%	78%
Council of Great City Schools Mean	113,002	42%	28%	6%	24%	59%	40%

Source: Council of the Great City Schools, *National Urban Education Goals: 1992–93 Indicators Report* (Washington, DC: Council of the Great City Schools, 1994).

* Less than 1%
† Eligible for the federally assisted school-lunch program

STAKEHOLDERS, CIVIC CAPACITY, AND EDUCATIONAL IMPROVEMENT

Political scientists and educationists alike see fundamental change as requiring a substantial widening of participation in schools and their politics.[3] The challenge, then, is to bring key actors into a different relationship. The language employed by reform advocates, particularly the term "stakeholder," signals just such an approach. It portrays major elements of the community, along with professional educators, as having a shared stake in educational improvement. However, at the same time that reformers argue the need for an external push, they also point out that sustained reform requires the involvement of education professionals.

The eleven-city project treats the *collective role* of stakeholders in terms of civic capacity, that is, the degree to which a cross-sector coalition comes together in support of a task of communitywide importance. So, although the task we are concerned with is educational improvement, civic capacity could apply to problemsolving in any of various areas.

Civic capacity is a concept that moves beyond what a single organization, like the school district, is able to do and brings to the forefront what multiple sectors can do when acting in concert. In the education arena, the capacity of any set of stakeholders is limited, and so long as various players think and act in terms of a narrow view of their duty, they miss the full scope of the problem they face and the response to which they could contribute. Though civic capacity can be thought of as a category of social capital, the term is not meant to imply that civic capacity in one area transfers easily into civic capacity in another area. Thus a city could mobilize civic capacity for urban redevelopment or for specific projects, such as building a new sports arena, but not in children-and-youth policy.

Since the literature on educational reform contains the proposition that reform is most likely when it is supported by a broad, cross-sector coalition, why use the term "civic capacity"? Why not simply rely on the term "stakeholder"? Mainly, civic capacity suggests a deeper involvement than stakeholder—to be a stakeholder implies only that various actors have a stake in (in this case) education, "capacity" suggests something more than that. It suggests that various sectors can contribute to educational improvement by their active involvement.

The term "civic capacity" is thus intended to accent the importance of a broad base of *active* involvement. This point is related to how regimes, in particular, opportunity-expanding regimes, operate. The ability of a regime to pursue an agenda depends on the resources that the members bring to the task of governance, and active involvement brings resources to bear. From this understanding of urban regimes, it follows that it takes broad mobilization of civic capacity to bring about a thoroughgoing effort at educational improvement. The means by which this happens, the analysis suggests, is not by coalition *pressure* on the school system, but by coalition contributions to critical policy tasks.

In education, the core elements in civic capacity are those who have the most to contribute to educational improvement. Teachers and school administrators clearly have a central part, and parents do as well—they contribute in various ways to the learning readiness of their children, give (within the limits of their resources and networks) important signals about the worth of schooling, and can reinforce numerous school-related attitudes and behaviors.

Business joins parents and educators as the third core group in civic capacity for educational improvement. A brief explanation is in order about the inclusion of business as a *core contributor.* After all, many institutions—churches, universities, and civic organizations—can contribute resources, provide tutors, and in various ways embrace educational aims. But business more than any other element represents the channel to the economic mainstream. For most middle-class families, the connection between school success and "real-life rewards in the form of good jobs and salaries" is taken for granted, but not so in the typical household served by urban school systems.[4] The business sector is in a special position to make that connection concrete and credible through, for example, various school-to-work programs.

Beyond a strengthened link between schooling and job opportunities, business can also promote the placement of educational improvement high on the community's action agenda. In American cities, business has a long history of being highly valued as "symbols of civic legitimacy."[5] Public officials and other community leaders, along with the news media, attach great importance to business involvement in an issue, and the greater the involvement, the more importance attached to it. A number of other elements in the community can play an auxiliary role in education, contributing resources and heightening the visibility of educational improvement as a citywide issue; but none can match the full potential of business involvement. Nor do any have the same close connection to the instructional process that parents and educators have.

CIVIC CAPACITY IN THE ELEVEN CITIES

As part of the eleven-city study of civic capacity, field researchers did in-depth case studies, following a common template. From these case studies, I made an assessment of the extent to which different groups are part of a community effort at educational improvement. This serves as a measure of civic capacity in education (see Table 12.3 for a summary of this information and a ranking of the cities).

General Observations

Some general observations are in order. Despite the institutional position of school boards as official policymakers, that potential was not realized. Occasionally a school board serves as the electoral front of a broad reform mobilization, but beyond that they rarely surface as a major force and thus are omitted from the table.

Table 12.3. Civic Capacity by City: Level of Involvement by Selected Actors in Educational Reform

	Business	Parent	Teachers	Sup't.	Other
Pittsburgh	Broad and institutionalized	Some, but not among the top actors	Included in reform coalition	Active promoter	Foundations, state govt., & CBOs
Boston	Broad and institutionalized	Varied, but not a cohesive force	Included in reform coalition	In trans'n to active promoter	Foundations, mayor, state goft., & CBOs
Los Angeles	Broad and institutionalized	Very little	Included in reform coalition	Active promoter	Foundations, advocacy groups
Baltimore	Somewhat broad and institutionalized	Very little	Very little	Highly selective promoter	Foundations, mayor, state govt., & CBOs
Houston	Rising and institutionalized	Very little	Very little to minor	New, but with ref'm support	Foundations, CBOs
Washington, DC	Institutionalized but guarded	Narrowly based	Resists reform	Lacks firm political base	U.S. Congress
Detroit	Institutionalized but contested	Mixed, but quite small	Resists reform	Reform supt. ousted	Foundations, state govt.
Atlanta	Small	Small	Very little	New appointee, following a nonleader	State govt., CBOs, J. Carter's Atl. Project
Denver	Small	Small	Quietly resists reform	Old no, new selective promoter	Foundations, nonprofits, state govt., fed. court
St. Louis	Small	Very little	Very little	Very little	Foundations, fed. court, mayor
San Francisco	Very little	Very little	Very little	Active promoter	Fed. court, advoc. grps.

The superintendent's office plays a less modest but still limited policy role. Though the superintendent is a key actor in several cities, the intense cross-pressures surrounding the office foster high turnover and often work against a central leadership role.[6] All things considered, superintendents are ultimately dependent on a supporting framework of some kind. To illustrate, in Detroit, when the reform movement suffered an electoral setback, the reform superintendent was ousted.[7] Thus superintendents show little ability to operate free of active community backing.

Teacher associations play perhaps the most varied role. In three cities, they are active members of the reform coalition, but in another three they are active forces of resistance. In the remaining five they are simply not major players.

The grassroots weakness of educational reform shows up in the anemic amount of parental involvement across the eleven cities. Along with the middle class becoming a diminished presence in big-city schools, parents have come to play a small part, despite a wide recognition of the importance of parental involvement and despite efforts to provide an institutional niche for parents in school-improvement processes. Lower-income parents, especially those with less education, face significant barriers, and, unless the schools themselves actively promote parental involvement, little is likely to take place.[8]

A number of other actors play varying parts in the eleven cities. The federal courts, state governments, foundations, and, in three cities, the mayors emerge as significant actors in educational reform. But none of these represents a grassroots constituency. In that category, community-based organizations (CBOs) and various racial and other advocacy groups play some part in about half the cities, but not in the remainder.

The role of business is also quite varied. In some cities, it plays a broad and institutionalized part, but in others, its place is extremely modest. It may include little more than organized support for an occasional reform-minded slate of school board contenders. In light of the big part that business has played in educational reform at the state and national level, this limited role at the city level calls for explanation. At higher levels of government, reform activism often consists mainly of an endorsement of broad and general principles. The policy aim is legislative enactment. At the local level, educational reform calls for concrete and particular steps. Costs become an immediate factor. Actual implementation is not only more contentious, but it is also a more drawn-out process and entails working with a specialized set of actors and procedures that are remote from the day-to-day activities of most business executives.

Educational reform is thus unfamiliar territory to many business executives, and as one St. Louis businessman explained, "It would take an incredible amount of time to deal with that bureaucracy." In today's competitive business world, he offered that "working in one election was enough of a commitment for me."[9] Contrary to what might have been expected, business involvement in other areas, such as redevelopment, or in specific projects, such as building a new sports stadium, does not necessarily lead to a role in education.

The Ranking

With business, educators, and parent groups significantly involved, Pittsburgh tops the list of eleven cities in civic capacity. Only in the relative disengagement of city hall is Pittsburgh less encompassing than the other cities on any count. Pittsburgh is typical of big-city school systems, specifically in having an independent school district with its own taxing power and therefore institutional independence from the general government of the city. Three of the eleven cities— Baltimore, Boston, and Washington, DC—depart from this prevailing pattern of independent school districts, and in Washington there is an elected school board, even though the general local government possesses financial control.[10]

Boston and Los Angeles, like Pittsburgh, have broad coalitions formed around school improvement, and these include both the business sector and teachers' unions. There are differences among the top three cities. Boston had to overcome years of bitter controversy over school desegregation, but the city's business-connected compact has served to bring various elements together. Pittsburgh's civic capacity was built cumulatively over a period of years, but the civic capacity of Los Angeles was mobilized from the top down in response to a perceived crisis, fed in part by rapid growth in immigrant student enrollment.[11] Only these three cities have both business and the teachers' union as members of the education coalition. In the three, the coalition is largely peak level, but Pittsburgh has a stronger community-based sector than the other two.

As an ideal, civic capacity entails not simply bringing a coalition together around the issue of educational improvement but beyond that engaging the members in activities and promoting discourse. In this way the limited concerns of particular groups—business leaders with economy and efficiency, parents with the opportunities available to their own children, educators with salary and professional prerogatives—might be expanded as they face a need to frame their concerns in communitywide terms and act on that basis. Only the top three cities come anywhere close to this ideal. Fourth-ranked Baltimore, for example, has a wide array of elements involved in education, but the discourse has been disjointed and activities disconnected except as forced by state intervention. Communitywide concerns have yielded at various points to more narrow considerations. No cohesive coalition has developed, and cooperation remains tenuous. The other cities have had even less cohesion, and Houston and Detroit have experienced high levels of community conflict.

Nevertheless, there is a range of experiences, with Pittsburgh, Los Angeles, and Boston grouped at the upper end of local civic capacity; Baltimore, Houston, Washington, and Detroit at an intermediate level; and Denver, Atlanta, St. Louis, and San Francisco at the lower end. Denver has been the target of extensive state intervention. San Francisco remains under a federal court order. Hence, for both, external intervention has substituted for local civic capacity in providing a major boost for school reform.

Significantly, though both Atlanta and Denver are noted for strong civic capacity in the area of economic development generally and downtown redevelopment specifically, both also have quite weak civic capacity in relation to educational improvement. Clearly civic capacity does not carry over automatically from one policy arena to another. A transfer that took place in Pittsburgh, for example, did not occur in Atlanta and Denver.

CIVIC CAPACITY AND EDUCATIONAL IMPROVEMENT

What about the impact on educational improvement of variations in civic capacity? Educational improvement is an open-ended term and can include quite diverse kinds of efforts, as, indeed, the recent school reform movement does. Yet many efforts share a rhetoric centering on the idea of fundamental reform.

After decades of seeing that various stand-alone initiatives had little or no impact, some reformers came in the 1980s to appreciate the systemic character of education reform.[12] In using the term "systemic," some advocates of current educational improvement would have the nation look beyond particular reforms *within* schools and pursue change in the way schools are related to the larger society and to the communities of which they are a part.[13]

Though these various proposals fit no neat formula, there are some common themes. One key theme, as emphasized earlier, is that all students can learn. The achievement of that goal, it is widely argued, is hampered by the shortcomings of bureaucracy and narrow professionalism. The prescription for a fundamental restructuring often includes administrative deregulation and radical decentralization (but with some form of accountability). A major concern is to shift from standardized classroom instruction to greater attention to the individual learning needs of students.

The full reform agenda calls for breaking down the isolation of education and educators from parents, business, and the community at large. Though there is little accord on the specifics of what new educational systems should be, there is wide agreement that the old model of professional autonomy needs to be replaced. As a consequence, today's educational scene teems with new ideas, pilot projects, demonstration programs, and experimental schools. Ironically, however, efforts at change rarely seem to be more than partial and fragmentary. Thus, despite talk about systemic reform, most efforts are still limited and fall toward the incremental side. Reform advocates are largely stymied by the challenge of how to "scale up" experiments and make them genuinely systemic.

Many efforts to stimulate reform rest on the belief that good practice need only be demonstrated. Once the demonstration occurs, it is assumed, others will rush to embrace the new practice. Thus proponents of reform are often inattentive to the political differences between a small- and a large-scale effort. It is one thing to get a few people to think anew about how education can be improved and quite another to bring about a general rethinking of education practice.

It is in this context that the eleven-city study was conducted and the propo-

Table 12.4. Educational-Improvement Effort

	Infrastructure of Support	Internal Moves	Comprehensive Effort
Pittsburgh	13.5	13.5	27.0
Boston	11.0	11.5	22.5
Los Angeles	11.0	12.5	23.5
Baltimore	9.0	9.0	18.0
Houston	8.5	7.5	16.0
Washington, DC	9.0	8.5	17.5
Detroit	9.5	6.0	15.5
Atlanta	8.0	5.0	13.0
Denver	7.0	10.0	17.0
St. Louis	8.0	6.5	14.5
San Francisco	8.5	7.5	16.0
Rank order correlation	.83	.71	.81

sition was offered that greater civic capacity would promote a greater effort at educational improvement. A set of indices was devised to gauge efforts at educational improvement (see Table 12.4). Four of the items fall under what has been called an "infrastructure of support,"[14] and they involve extra-school efforts to enhance the readiness of students to learn and to heighten their motivation to achieve academically through preschool, parent involvement, and school-to-work programs, plus the provision of school-linked services. The second set concerns efforts to alter internal school operations through site-based management, parent participation in school improvement teams and kindred bodies, the extent of the school system's reliance on research and evaluation for informing educational decisions, and the system's use of assessment measures to encourage active learning. Hence the index spans governance as well as other internal moves. Though the items are quite disparate, the third column totals them into a single figure as a rough measure of comprehensive effort.

The results indicate that greater civic capacity is associated with various efforts to improve education. That the measures are crude and that the fit is imperfect are also to be acknowledged. But Pittsburgh, with the highest ranking on civic capacity, also rates high on the various indicators of effort to promote educational improvement. Overall the rank-order correlations are quite respectable. Deviations from the general pattern are, however, worthy of note. Houston places in the top half mainly because of the city's business-led initiative to establish partnerships, but as shown in chapter 9, the school system has been caught in litigation and a significant conflict between the Latino and African American communities.

Denver and San Francisco also deviate from the general pattern, but in these cases their educational improvement scores are higher than anticipated on the basis of local civic capacity ranking. In both cities, important external forces are at work. In San Francisco, the significant factor is a consent decree under a deseg-regation order by the federal district court. Working with the school superinten-dent, the court's panel of experts has moved beyond numerical racial balance to the issue of school performance for minorities. A targeted set of schools has thus been reconstituted, and the authority of the federal court perhaps provides a sub-stitute for civic capacity in providing a context in which innovation can occur. In Denver, a teachers' strike enabled the governor to intervene and impose a contract settlement, which included an ambitious set of school reforms. So again, a power-ful external force was at work, providing an alternative to local civic capacity.

Exceptions notwithstanding, the connection between level of civic capacity and degree of effort at educational improvement seems quite solid. Differences among the eleven cities are, however, only part of the story. Though there are significant variations in the degree of reform across the eleven cities, none has put a fully comprehensive program into effect, and only Pittsburgh comes close. Thus, in many ways the most interesting finding is the abundance of small-scale and partial attempts to introduce change. Clearly, the old pattern of centrally run and professionally guided education lacks the legitimacy it once had. In its place the current pattern is one of piecemeal efforts. These exist in great abundance in most of the eleven cities, indicating a high level of policy ferment and a wide-spread search for a new systemic arrangement.

What, then, do these various findings suggest? Civic capacity is far short of full strength in almost all the cities. Particularly noteworthy is the feeble part played by local school boards. A few superintendents have had an impact, but without a base of support, their efforts at the systemwide level are enormously handicapped.

WHY IS CHANGE SO DIFFICULT?

The question posed by these findings is why substantial reform is so difficult. Support for the old order has eroded. Fresh ideas abound, and new participants are involved. The scene would seem to be set for a fundamental restructuring, but the old order displays persistence. Despite the intellectual ferment, *fresh and demonstrably workable ideas are not "scaled up."* Most efforts fall far short of sys-temwide institutionalization. Why? The answer comes in several parts. One is the bedrock strength of existing arrangements, and part of the answer may have to do with education itself, its nature as a policy task. Functional autonomy is not easily modified. Another part of the picture has to do with the group context of education politics, particularly in large cities. Race is an integral part of urban education. Let us look more closely at these factors, first through a general dis-cussion and then by an examination of the Baltimore experience.

Civic Capacity and Educational Improvement

The term "civic capacity" highlights the importance of a broad base of cross-sector participation. Though a policy aim like economic development can be pursued by a narrow, peak-level coalition, education is different. It involves a different kind of policy task, one in which the participation of professional educators and parents have essential roles to play. The business sector can be a significant contributor but has limited leverage in inducing educational change. Unlike the case of economic development, business withdrawal does not bring policy activity to a halt. If other stakeholders are reluctant partners in educational improvement, business backers of reform have few means to induce cooperation.

Moreover, business commitment to educational improvement can itself be sorely tested by the extent of effort required. Education professionals play the central operational role and have a long tradition of functional autonomy. Historically, business has been helpful in supporting bond issues or tax increases but has had little to do with operational details. Thus the business sector can establish a favorable climate for considering educational reform, but mere endorsement of the idea provides little leverage over complex practices, devised to ensure that day-to-day tasks are performed. At the operational level, change involves a substantial reorientation of the habits and understandings of a large body of educators—and the students and parents they interact with as well.

Further complicating the picture is the history of business involvement in education. In some cities, business leaders have been concerned primarily with efficiency and low taxes, not necessarily with educational improvement. Still, in a number of cities, they have played a significant role in promoting school desegregation, despite the high level of controversy surrounding the issue.[15] Indeed, business leaders have often been more supportive of desegregation than parents' groups have. Nevertheless, business has limited concern with the details of daily operation.

For African Americans, public education holds a special place. In many cities, historically the public schools provided the primary source of middle-class employment. Moreover, public education occupies a central place symbolically, as a policy area closely associated with the expansion of opportunity. Beyond that, education was a central arena in the struggle against racial subordination, and *Brown v. Board of Education* was the legal battering ram that first penetrated the walls of racial separation and exclusion in a predominantly white nation.

Different groups thus bring quite different concerns to the issue of educational improvement. Although the general aim is widely shared, a host of particulars imposes itself unless the general community stake in solid schooling can subdue more narrow interests. Parents and educators, for example, share the goals of good schooling for children, but educators also have a strong interest in professional prerogatives that make them wary of an active parental role. Moreover, educators typically see parents not in the role of general champions of improved education but as sources of particular demands.

As a concept, civic capacity calls for a perspective different from the conventional social science preoccupation with "who gets what, when, and how." Trained to look for the hidden particular interests behind a rhetoric of the public interest, acutely aware of the differences that drive identity politics, and heavily exposed to postmodernist skepticism about any shared truth, contemporary social science finds itself drawn to an understanding of public affairs as an arena of contending interests, none of which is normatively privileged. Thus does social science in the United States celebrate the adversarial character of American public life and largely ignore the politics of building support for community purposes.

Contrast with the privileging of adversarial politics the argument in Jeffrey Mirel's award-winning history of education politics in Detroit. Mirel treats Detroit schools as pulled between efforts, on the one side, to establish a vision of the common good, able to attract support from diverse groups and provide legitimacy for their support and, on the other side, the centrifugal forces of race and class. The virtual destruction of the idea of a common good in Detroit had no liberating effect but left the school system at the mercy of "self-seeking interest groups and blatant bigotry," in Mirel's words. With the breakdown of public support, "the system came apart politically, financially, and educationally." [16] Thus Mirel does not deny the reality of group conflict, but he does argue that, if unchecked, the political accentuation of differences can get in the way of a common effort. Implicit in Mirel's account is an understanding that a community has a capacity, albeit a highly fragile one, to pursue a widely beneficial program of education; but this pursuit can be realized only if there is a high level of concurrence across various sectors of community life about the nature of that program and a significant degree of loyalty to the effort to see it realized.

The Baltimore Experience

Baltimore offers an outwardly different scenario from Detroit. With a mayorally appointed school board, it has not had the kind of electoral conflict Detroit has experienced. The reform coalition has not sundered, as the one in Detroit did, but it also has not generated the level of cohesion needed to move on a systemwide effort. Like Detroit and many other cities, Baltimore has a profusion of small-scale experiments, several of them highly successful and widely praised. Yet, "scaling up" is not merely doing the same thing, only more of it. To move from small- to large-scale efforts is also a move from an *interpersonal* to an *intergroup* context and, in the citywide arena, intergroup competition stands as a formidable barrier to building and holding together civic capacity on behalf of educational improvement.

Baltimore ranked fourth among the eleven cities in civic capacity mobilized on behalf of educational improvement. Key stakeholders are only loosely aligned, though the idea of educational improvement remains high on the Baltimore agenda. The evolution of the city's school improvement effort shows both the potential and the fragility of a concerted effort. The initiating force behind educational improvement was Baltimoreans United in Leadership Development (BUILD), a community organization affiliated with the Industrial Areas Foundation. BUILD pushed for reform inside the school system, particularly site-based management, and also pressured the Greater Baltimore Committee, an organization of leading businesses, into supporting the Baltimore Commonwealth program with its dual school-to-work and school-to-college tracks. When Kurt Schmoke became mayor in 1987, he embraced the educational reform program of BUILD and brought the Commonwealth program into city government.[17]

Since the school system is a department of city government and the mayor appoints the school board, crucial pieces appeared to be in place for a concerted effort to transform education in Baltimore. In addition, the state of Maryland itself has adopted a broad educational reform program, supporting site-based management and the related structure of school-improvement teams, as well as a new statewide system of assessment. The state's Department of Education is also authorized to mandate the reconstitution of individual schools performing poorly. The state legislature has been on board for reform, and a key member of the House of Delegates, Howard "Pete" Rawlings, strongly supports school reform. Rawlings, an African American from Baltimore City, chairs the House Appropriations Committee and has the backing of other Baltimore legislators.

Other pieces have also fallen into place. The local Abell Foundation has supported a number of educational initiatives for basic change, and the school system had established several experimental programs, including two widely acclaimed initiatives in collaboration with faculty at Johns Hopkins University.[18]

When Schmoke's first appointee as school superintendent proved to be a reluctant backer of reform, the mayor replaced him. The issue of the level of state funding for the Baltimore school system has long been a source of tension, but with the election in 1994 of Parris Glendening as governor of Maryland, the city and Mayor Schmoke in particular had a close ally who also strongly backed educational improvement. With such an array of support, how could substantial reform miss?

The general consensus foundered on the particulars. An experiment with privatized management let the genie of employment anxiety out of the bottle and changed the political scene (see chapter 5). Even so, the issue of educational performance persisted. Two management studies made clear that the city's school system was deeply troubled.[19] Though some individual schools performed quite well and had high staff morale, the overall system was afflicted with a "culture of complacency" and low expectations. In a study sponsored by Associated Black Charities, consultants found the school system to be overly centralized but functionally fragmented, excessively concerned with monitoring and compliance procedures while too little focused on student achievement, and not cost-conscious despite budget stringencies.[20] Consultants found the flow of information to be strategically manipulated and employee attitudes to be a major barrier to system change.[21]

Staff competence came in for especially close scrutiny. The consultants reported that although the school system had a number of capable staff members, interviews suggested "that many school-based and central-office administrators are less competent."[22] The report noted further that many central-office staff are former teachers and principals "who lack the technical skills, training, and experience to perform in their current capacities"; that "burned-out teachers" and administrators with "a personnel problem" are placed in the central office; that some staff hired outside the system also "lack requisite skills, training, and experience."[23] Consultants found that union contracts contained "onerous" provisions, that sick leave was abused, and specifically that "procedures for termination are extremely cumbersome."[24]

The Baltimore school system operates in a context in which patronage politics has long been important.[25] Maintenance workers and other noneducational employees were outside the control of school-site administrators and are hired from lists provided by the city. Though in short supply, substitute teachers were required to be city residents.

The report made recommendations about streamlining various procedures, negotiating less confining provisions in the union contract, and putting in place processes for removing and replacing principals and other administrators "not performing effectively."[26] The report gave special emphasis to implementing the site-based management policy already officially adopted. Many of the recommendations were highly specific and detailed.

Three years later, a follow-up study sponsored by the state's Department of Education found that fundamentally little had changed. The system continued to be "top down," site-based management still lacked an effective implementation plan, and some central-office staff were reported to be resisting the policy. A "good-old-boy" network continued. Important contract provisions deemed onerous had not been renegotiated. And "ineffective principals and teachers" remained as a barrier to school improvement. Moreover, "no one could provide evidence that an 'ineffective principal' had been fired during the past ten years."[27] Yet the Department of Education has identified fifty of the city's schools as eligible for reconstitution because of poor performance.

In 1997, after a period of intense controversy, a consent decree brought a formal resolution by restructuring the school system's management under a Board of School Commissioners jointly appointed by the governor and mayor and allocating an additional $254 million of state money for the city's school system. The negotiation put the mayor in the difficult situation of being able to obtain new money for the system only by agreeing to a unique state role in managing it. These arrangements came under attack from BUILD and various city officials as a hostile takeover with strong racial overtones, and the mayor himself at one point accused the state of "a blatant power grab."[28] At another point, Mayor Schmoke referred to the state's insistence on management restructuring as "insulting and paternalistic."[29]

Concurrent with the effort to work out a settlement between the governor and the city, suburban officials objected to additional money going to the city, and they represent potential opposition in the future. A suburban newspaper, the *Montgomery Journal,* has kept up steady criticism of the arrangement, attacking the city schools as unreformable and touting the need to replace the current system with a voucher plan. The suburban position is that management improvement should come before additional funding, that poor management wastes resources. And a recent Governor's Commission on School Funding reported that "disparities in student achievement across Maryland, but particularly in Baltimore, far exceed disparities in spending."[30] In rejoinder the city points to the pernicious effects of concentrated poverty. The settlement for Baltimore thus has provided a jump-start for reform, but suburban opposition has a potential to overturn it, doing so in a manner that perpetuates the state's long-standing racial divide. The suburban voice in the debate so far has not acknowledged that concentrated poverty is a consideration.

Implications

What does the Baltimore experience tell us about civic capacity and the challenges it needs to address? First, it is clear that the Baltimore schools, like many other big-city systems, have been poorly managed. Hence the need for reform is acute. Second, several small-scale reform initiatives have been implemented and are regarded as highly successful; reform can occur. Third, a wide array of players—the mayor, the governor, the state board of education and state superintendent, BUILD, the Greater Baltimore Committee, the Abell Foundation, and Delegate Rawlings—has pushed actively for basic reform. Yet systemwide reform remains embattled. Why? Why didn't earlier initiatives become cumulative? Where, then, is the city's civic capacity, and why has it been so hard to mobilize on behalf of sustained educational improvement?

Once the general issue of improving education moved to the stage of concrete action, race became the overtowering factor. Still, the way in which race infused the situation is complex. BUILD, with its preponderantly African American base of support, was, after all, the initiator of the city's educational reform movement. Delegate Rawlings remains an outspoken critic of the administration of the city's school system. The Associated Black Charities sponsored the 1992 management study. And Mayor Schmoke has himself made several significant moves on behalf of reform. So there is no African American consensus that the schools are performing effectively; more the opposite is the case. Why, then, is it hard to mobilize and maintain support behind reform, especially given the fact that a number of promising innovations have taken hold in several places within the Baltimore school system? Several significant considerations come into play.

First, the school system represents a bundle of material benefits. Any move to restructure contains a potential threat to the existing racial distribution of those benefits; and the black middle class, which is a significant constituency of black churches and black elected officials, is anxious about possible job losses.

Second, conflict has centered on control over personnel and procurement decisions, not on philosophy of education. But jobs are only part of the picture. Given black political and administrative control of the city's school system, members of the African American community see restructuring as a threat to a long-in-coming, but still limited, power base. A major state role in school restructuring evokes special worries about diminished power.

Third, educational improvement does not present itself in a historical vacuum. It occupies a place in a process in which public authority was long used to perpetuate and even to aggravate black disadvantage. Neither state government nor white business leaders have a history of being dependable allies, and any action taken to restructure the city's schools cannot be easily taken as innocent of implications for competitive group advantage, especially given the generally adversarial character of American politics.

CIVIC CAPACITY, SOCIAL CAPITAL, AND THE SCALING-UP PROBLEM

The concept of social capital suggests that small-scale instances of cooperative action should nurture habits of reciprocity and trust.[31] As participants in community life learn these skills, they should be able to apply them to additional areas of activity, on a larger and larger scale. Thus the Baltimore educational riddle: Why do successful innovations and significant program initiatives not cumulate into a broadly supported move to reform a poorly performing school system? Numerous small-scale efforts bridge the city's racial divide and bring different sectors of community life together, but they do not build toward a city-level effort even though several key institutional actors back such a move.

The mayor, the state school board, the ministers of major black churches, the head of the Abell Foundation, the Greater Baltimore Committee, key legislators such as Delegate Rawlings, officers in the teachers' union, education specialists at Johns Hopkins and other universities, representatives of various parent groups, and numerous teachers and administrators have extensive experience working with one another in a variety of efforts. Collaboration on small-scale projects demonstrates the capacity of diverse actors to come together on behalf of a variety of educational improvements.

What, then, is the flaw in the social capital argument? We need to remember that social capital is a metaphor, suggesting something highly fluid, like financial capital. After all, money generated in one activity can be invested in another, and several small pools of money can be invested in one large activity. For financial capital, transferability is not a problem.

Social capital, however, seems not to be easily transferred. Aside from *skills* that might readily be applied to new situations, social capital (defined as an ability to gain social ends by cooperation, with minimal reliance on direct payments or coercion) also rests, in significant part, on a basis of *shared loyalty and duty*. Reciprocity and trust are thus circumscribed; they may apply within some circles but not in others.[32] The boundaries may be defined by interpersonal relations—*individuals* accustomed to transacting business with one another can develop habits of reciprocity and a high degree of interpersonal trust. Out of accumulated experience, they may develop feelings of obligation to one another. In some matters, they may even have a sense of common fate.

Yet take these same individuals and put them in an *intergroup* context, a context in which competitive *group* advantage is salient, and *interpersonal* trust and reciprocity may lose strength. Interpersonal social capital thus does not necessarily translate into intergroup social capital, that is to say, into civic capacity. In an intergroup context, the effort of any individual to extend trust and engage in reciprocal considerations is subject to challenge by others who assert *group loyalty* as the pivotal consideration. The intergroup context can thus override even well-established patterns of interpersonal trust and reciprocity. This is not to say that interpersonal social capital has no weight in an intergroup setting; it is only to say that it does not necessarily carry the day.

With the difference between interpersonal and intergroup social capital in mind, we can see why small-scale efforts at educational improvement do not readily cumulate into a large-scale mobilization for change. Because social capital has limited transferability, interpersonal acts alone cannot build civic capacity. If educational improvement is to enjoy a broad intergroup base of support, then steps are needed that will foster loyalty to the main task of educational improvement while diminishing distrust between groups and, in Baltimore, for example, demonstrating that educational improvement can be pursued without increasing the competitive disadvantage of the African American community for jobs and other distributive benefits.

Baltimore's experience thus indicates that, even with several major players committed to the need for fundamental reform, building a coalition devoted to improved school performance is a difficult task. State action, with the mayor's assent, has established a new management structure and brought new money to the city. However, follow-through remains uncertain at this writing. Several city players are concerned about the impact of reform on jobs, and some see the mandated change in management structure as racially driven. Suburban opposition to "special" money for city schools reinforces the racial divide and makes the building of civic capacity difficult. Yet the Baltimore picture is not discouraging on every count. State intervention and the resources it has brought have reactivated the reform effort. For example, the new school leadership in Baltimore has called for after-school programs citywide and sees this initiative as a road to greater involvement by what one former superintendent called "the little people."[33] A number of the city's superintendents have over the years maintained that school improvement in Baltimore will not move very far without extensive involvement of the community, and the new initiative holds some promise of increasing that involvement. The mandate and the money to carry it out provide significant leverage, and activity stimulated at the school level may have the bonus of minimizing intergroup tensions.

Overall, though experience across the eleven cities indicates that civic capacity is a useful facilitator of school-improvement efforts, the study provides no simple formula for building civic coalitions. The Baltimore experience shows that race is a major barrier, and Houston and San Francisco direct attention to the additional complication of frictions among minorities. The tempting solution is to bring elite-level stakeholders together and to promote interpersonal understanding and trust among them. The Baltimore case cautions against such an approach.[34] Difficult as it may be, civic capacity needs to be built at the intergroup level among the populace, not simply among elite players. Baltimore provides a test of whether or not that can happen.

Educational improvement looms as a major challenge facing many urban communities today. An eleven-city study offers evidence of enormous ferment—new ideas abound; a fresh set of actors has claimed the role of stakeholder; and pilot programs, experimental schools, and demonstration projects are a thriving industry. The future shape of urban education is far from clear, however, and the eleven-city study indicates that different communities are at different places in the change process. The operating assumption of the study was that change would be greatest in those communities with the strongest civic capacity. Generally the proposition holds, but important exceptions can be linked to the force of external intervention, particularly by the federal courts and state governments.

The education arena is analytically rich. On the one hand, educational improvement is universally applauded. And stakeholders in that process include not only professional educators and the parents of schoolchildren but business and other employers, politicians, nonprofits, advocacy groups, and a variety of community-based organizations. Further, as the African proverb counsels, "the whole village" needs to contribute. Counterposed to this inclusive social responsibility is the harsh reality of modern-day specialization and intergroup conflict, competition, and distrust. Significantly, a close examination of the Baltimore experience suggests that this conflict is often less about educational philosophy or differences in social values than it is about control of jobs, employment security, and career tracks. Taking this context into consideration, a major analytical challenge is how to account for these findings:

- Small-scale successes in collaboration do not necessarily cumulate into city-wide efforts, and, in fact, they rarely do.
- Civic capacity in one area—economic development, for example—does not necessarily transfer to another area, such as education.

These two findings point to some refinements in our understanding of social capital and its implications for civic capacity. Social capital seems not to be simply a set of skills or "habits of the heart" that can be readily transferred from one arena to another. In short, it seems issue- and group-bounded. This may be because some elements of social capital, namely trust and reciprocity, are linked to another element, that of duty or obligation. Trust and reciprocity operate most readily when there is a shared identity of some kind. This identity might be with a highly informal and even casual set of acquaintances or it might be with a widely recognized racial or religious grouping. It might be a neighborhood or a larger entity like the city. Often it is people who share in a task activity or are engaged in pursuit of a common goal.

Identity, however, can also be shaped in an oppositional manner, by who an adversary is. Thus it matters greatly whether the context of activity is interpersonal or intergroup. In an interpersonal setting, shared identity in task performance can be nurtured on its own terms. In an intergroup setting, shared identity in task performance has to contend with a past history, which may be conflict-ridden and rife with grounds for distrust.

This context brings us back to civic capacity, which entails an intergroup form of social capital. Civic capacity has strength to the extent that identity with, and therefore duty to, the larger community is strong enough to withstand competing claims. Building this capacity, then, is partly a matter of promoting communitywide identity. It is also partly a matter of allaying worries about *groups* that might seek a competitive advantage under the guise of a communitywide interest. Thus, though interpersonal bonds could be a starting point for building civic capacity, they are only a starting point.

Identity with the larger community and responsibility to it appear also to be influenced by areas of activity. Business executives may see themselves obligated to contribute to the economic health of the community, without necessarily feeling a companion obligation to contribute to its social health. This is why "problem definition" is potentially important and why institutionalization of commitment is as well.

The involvement of Pittsburgh's business sector in educational improvement is strong perhaps because, through the Allegheny Conference on Community Development, early on it institutionalized a social responsibility.[35] A comparable institutionalization did not occur in Atlanta, Denver, St. Louis, San Francisco, and many other cities in which business pursued downtown redevelopment without taking on a parallel responsibility for social reconstruction. Business leaders in different cities have seen their civic obligations in different ways and have therefore institutionalized these obligations in divergent ways.

Much remains to be learned about how responsibilities to the larger community are defined and institutionalized. Several cities outside our eleven — Chicago, Dallas, and New Orleans, for example — have called summit meetings to bring a wide cross-section of stakeholders together around the issue of educational improvement. But simply bringing representatives of various groups together to endorse a reform agenda falls short of being a strong instance of civic capacity. The test is a willingness to commit resources and to work actively to reduce intergroup frictions and mistrust. So far many may have been called, but few have chosen to make that kind of commitment.

The Baltimore case shows that verbal support for change is not enough. Even the formal adoption of reform measures can have little effect, especially when a substantial proportion of the school staff is dispirited. A currently touted reform strategy is to put forward a coherent set of directives around academic achievement for schools to follow. An assumption that underlies this strategy is that schools can be responsive, but only if the signals are clear. Baltimore points to a different scenario. The proximate barrier to action was not a set of contradictory directives. It was the unresponsiveness of school district employees. That unresponsiveness, the anxieties that feed it, and the capacity to deflect efforts to heighten accountability are best understood in community context. Perhaps, then, the best-advised strategy of reform is one that calls for change in the larger context in which schools are embedded. What may be most promising is not a continuation of the sponsorship of pilot projects, which are unlikely ever to be scaled up. Instead, it may be more productive to search for leverage points through which the school-community relationship can be altered.

NOTES

1. This chapter is a revised and abbreviated version of "The Politics of Urban School Reform: Civic Capacity, Social Capital, and the Intergroup Context," paper presented at the annual meeting of the American Political Science Association, San Francisco, August 29–September 1, 1996.

2. For 1993–1994, when field study for the project was conducted, the upper level of administration (the top ten positions in each city) was 56 percent African American, 29 percent white, 13 percent Latino, and 2 percent Asian American.

3. Frank Baumgartner and Bryan Jones, *Agendas and Instability in American Politics* (Chicago: University of Chicago Press, 1993), and John Goodlad, *A Place Called School* (New York: McGraw-Hill, 1984).

4. Jeannie Oakes, *Improving Inner-City Schools* (Santa Monica, CA: Rand, 1987), p. 27.

5. Peter Clark, "Civic Leadership," in *Democracy in Urban America,* ed. Oliver P. Williams and Charles Press (Chicago: Rand McNally, 1969).

6. Cf. Barbara L. Jackson and James G. Cibulka, "Leadership Turnover and Business Mobilization," in *The Politics of Education Association Yearbook 1991* (Washington, DC: Falmer Press, 1992), pp. 71–86.

7. Richard C. Hula, Richard W. Jelier, and Mark Schauer, "Making Educational Reform: Hard Times in Detroit 1988–1995," *Urban Education* 32 (May 1997): 202–32.

8. Joyce Epstein, "Parent Involvement: What Researchers Say to Administrators," *Education and Urban Society* 19, no. 2 (February): 119–36, and Nancy Chavkin, *Families and Schools in a Pluralistic Society* (Albany: State University of New York Press, 1993).

9. Lana Stein, "Education Reform and Civic Capacity," site report, St. Louis, Missouri (December 1, 1994).

10. Washington, DC, has a unique local government situation, with Congress granting only limited home rule. Even that limited amount is further restricted at this writing by a budget crisis and the creation of a Financial Control Board for the city. (This event came after the focal period for the eleven-city research.)

11. In Pittsburgh's case, the precipitating event was a desegregation controversy in the 1970s. (See Robin Jones, "Civic Capacity and Urban Education: Pittsburgh," site report [February 1995]).

12. Marshall Smith and Jennifer O'Day, "Systemic School Reform," in *Politics of Education Yearbook 1990,* pp. 233–67, and Susan Fuhrman, ed., *Designing Coherent Education Policy* (San Francisco: Jossey-Bass, 1993).

13. William Clune, "Systemic Educational Policy," in Fuhrman, ed., *Designing Coherent Education Policy,* and Goodlad, *A Place Called School.*

14. Dorothy Rich, "Building the Bridge to Reach Minority Parents," in *Families and Schools in a Pluralistic Society,* ed. Nancy F. Chavkin (Albany: State University of New York Press, 1993).

15. Robert Crain, *The Politics of School Desegregation* (Garden City, NY: Anchor Books, 1969), and Elizabeth Jacoway and David Colburn, eds. *Southern Businessmen and Desegregation* (Baton Rouge: Louisiana State University Press, 1982).

16. Jeffrey Mirel, *The Rise and Fall of an Urban School System* (Ann Arbor: University of Michigan Press, 1993), p. 369.

17. Marion Orr, "Urban Regimes and Human Capital Policies: A Study of Baltimore," *Journal of Urban Affairs* 14, no. 2 (1992): 173–87.

18. Epstein, "Parent Involvement," pp. 119–36; Joyce Epstein and Susan Dauber, "School Programs and Teacher Practices of Parent Involvement in Inner-City Elementary and Middle Schools," *Elementary School Journal* 91, no. 3 (1991): 289–305; and Robert Slavin et al., *Success for All* (Arlington, VA: Educational Research Service, 1992).

19. Associated Black Charities, *A Report of a Management Study of the Baltimore City Public Schools,* June 26, 1992; MGT of America, *A Report on Monitoring and Evaluating Implementation of Management Study Recommendations in Baltimore City Public Schools,* submitted to the Maryland State Department of Education (Tallahassee, FL: MGT of America, 1995). It should be noted, however, that criticisms of the school system in these reports were similar to those made by a management study *twenty years earlier,* covering the last years of white administrative control. See Christopher Lambert and Jennean Reynolds, *The State of Baltimore's Schools* (BALTIMORE: Advocates for Children and Youth, June 1997), 1:H-7. *Plus ca change, plus c'est la meme.*

20. As one component of the budget squeeze, special education consumed one-quarter of the system's instructional dollars (Associated Black Charities, *Report,* 1992, p. III-16).

21. Ibid., p. III-29 and p. I-5.

22. Ibid., p. III-23.

23. Ibid., p. III-23, p. III-24, and p. III-32.

24. Ibid., p. III-35; see also V-2.

25. Kenneth K. Wong, *City Choices* (Albany: State University of New York Press, 1990).

26. Associated Black Charities, *Report,* 1992, p. IV-13.

27. MGT of America, *Report,* 1995, p. VIII-21.

28. Charles Babington, "Clash over Schools in Baltimore," *Washington Post,* June 19, 1996.

29. Jean Thompson, "Schmoke Says School Aid Falls Short." *Baltimore Sun,* June 21, 1996.

30. Lambert and Reynolds, *State of Baltimore's Schools,* p. H-23.

31. Robert Putnam, *Making Democracy Work* (Princeton: Princeton University Press, 1993).

32. James Coleman labels this phenomenon "closure" (*Foundations of Social Theory* [Cambridge: Harvard University Press, 1990], pp. 318–20).

33. Lambert and Reynolds, *State of Baltimore's Schools,* p. H-17.

34. See also Julie White and Gary Wehlage, "Community Collaboration," *Educational Evaluation and Policy Analysis* 17 (spring 1995); 23–39.

35. Barbara Ferman, *Challenging the Growth Machine* (Lawrence: University Press of Kansas, 1996), and Jones, "Civic Capacity and Urban Education: Pittsburgh."

PART V
Conclusion

In an overview chapter, Michael Danielson and Jennifer Hochschild give an assessment of the "lessons, cautions, and prospects" that can be gleaned from the studies that make up this volume. They highlight the enormous complexity and variability of education politics at the local level yet point out that a defining feature is the continuing reluctance of both educators and noneducators to acknowledge openly the profoundly political character of public education.

Though duly skeptical that broad coalitions of education reform can be mobilized and sustained, Danielson and Hochschild nonetheless conclude that without such a coalition or some form of central direction (or possibly both), piecemeal incrementalism appears the most likely prospect for urban education. They caution, however, that incrementalism is unlikely to move us very far in the direction of robust opportunities for those children on the lower rungs of America's system of stratification. Thus despite sustained talk about an education crisis and the need for fundamental reform, there remains a gap "between what we are likely to do and what we need to do for our children's sake."

Overall the contributors to this volume give us a variety of perspectives on the politics of urban education. Nonetheless, missing is any indication that big-picture considerations—whether of the need for workforce preparation in a global economy or of educational equity for all children—are an organizing force with any vigor. The nation's anemic understanding of politics, as pursuit of private advantage in the public sector, thus continues to handicap us in our activities as citizens responsible for a system of education. Our inability to see, deliberate, and act as a civic body does not prevent change, but it does ensure that we have limited capacity to shape our collective fate. Piecemeal responses cumulate but without restoring confidence in the current system of education, especially its ability to serve those students who are in greatest need.

Danielson and Hochschild are aptly cautious about the future and see that any current characterization of schools could become outdated. Indeed, it is extremely difficult to see emerging trends as they first appear, especially in an environment as turbulent as the one surrounding today's schools. It is possible, then, to harbor less pessimism than Danielson and Hochschild do about the prospects for positive change. Reform nearly always takes longer than anyone expects. The process is messier and more diffuse than most people are comfortable with, and the path prescribed by reformers is rarely, if ever, followed very closely. But that does not mean that change is stymied.

It should be remembered that the now-faltering system of education run by autonomous and nonpartisan professionals came into being in a drawn-out process, spread unevenly over time and place. It is just possible that the piecemeal changes now cumulating may add up to a more profound alteration than we can grasp at this stage. Though systemic reform is an elusive goal, going back to the old ways seems unlikely. Change appears inevitable. Indeed it may be that experiences as diverse as reconstituted schools in San Francisco and EBC-designed schools in Brooklyn foretell a changed relationship between educators and community. Early signposts of change are not always clearly marked.

13

Changing Urban Education: Lessons, Cautions, Prospects

Michael N. Danielson and Jennifer Hochschild

Political scientists are often accused of emphasizing complexity, of focusing on the trees at the expense of mapping the forest.[1] With regard to the politics of education, however, the contributors to this volume demonstrate that knowing about variations among trees is essential to understanding the forest. Public education in the United States is a mammoth, decentralized, and diffused enterprise, and it is particularly complex in urban areas of the kind examined in this book. Context is critical to almost everything that matters in education. Whether and how cities are connected to suburbs, the degree of racial segregation in housing, the role of voters in making education policy, the funding formulas for state aid to school districts, and the enthusiasms of superintendents and corporate leaders — these and other idiosyncratic and varying factors determine the educational practices of school districts.

Within each particular context, educational policy, as Clarence Stone emphasizes, is shaped by interactions among an array of institutions and individuals, including boards of education, school superintendents, teachers and their labor unions, corporate leaders, parents and other constituents, local politicians, state and federal governments, and state and federal courts — although seldom by students. No element in this mix is a fixed quantity or has a precise relationship to the other factors. In the preceding chapters it is suggested that some interactions fit a common pattern across school districts; school boards have relatively minor policy roles everywhere, as do parents and community organizations. But other interactions follow no common pattern; the roles of superintendents, teachers' unions, legislative bodies, corporations, mayors, federal courts, and state education officials range from featured player to bit part in different places and at different times in the same place.

Given both the degree of complexity and the differences across districts in how that complexity plays out, what can we conclude about educational policy overall? Our task in this concluding chapter is to discern and map the forest while being simultaneously mindful of the variations among the trees.

A DISTINCTIVE POLICY SYSTEM

We begin by distinguishing schooling from other policy arenas in terms of those characteristics that shape its politics and prospects for reform. Our starting point is the recognition that, unlike most other local functions, public education is rarely an integral part of the general governmental structure. Schools either have their own governance structure and financing, or, as is the case with most of the urban systems examined in this volume, are connected to the local government through distinctive arrangements for the selection of school board members and for financing.

Partly due to these unusual structural arrangements, the education establishment typically has enjoyed more autonomy than have other governmental functions. Schools are most insulated from the usual government controls over policy, personnel, and financing when they are organized as independent districts with their own electoral and tax base. But school systems have considerable freedom of action even when school boards are appointed and financing is controlled by local elected officials. Most citizens consider politics to be incompatible with education. After all, schooling has great symbolic value, immense importance to society, and deep involvement in the sensitive tasks of transmitting ideas and values. Education is universally required, and almost nine-tenths of children satisfy that requirement in public schools. Schools are expected to educate children, train workers, foster democracy, and build a civic society. Thus the belief that schools and politics should not mix has throughout the twentieth century served to insulate schools from politicians even beyond the separation implied by the formal arrangements.

Educators and their supporters have capitalized on these beliefs and structures to insist that schools be the province of specially trained teachers and administrators, thereby producing relatively closed systems in which professional educators control most aspects of school policy. Within this professionalized world, school superintendents and other central administrative officials have consolidated power at the top, particularly in large urban districts. Ironically, school boards, which are formally authorized to set policy and to be the instrument for holding the professionals accountable to the citizenry, rarely are an independent or significant force in urban school politics. In the eleven-city study, as Stone reports, school boards generally were nonplayers, except on the few occasions when a coalition mobilized to elect school board members as a means of advancing a particular cause. The case of Charlotte-Mecklenburg County illustrates how the school board can be, at least temporarily, the focal point for contests over educational policy. Normally, however, urban school boards are relegated to peripheral roles such as servicing constituents and ratifying policy decisions made by superintendents.

In all policy arenas autonomy advantages insiders who know and benefit from the system and who are adept at erecting obstacles to effective involvement by outsiders. But this autonomy is more of a problem in the field of education than in other arenas because the very characteristics of education that contribute to autonomy—the importance and sensitivity of education—also increase outsiders' demands for a voice in school policy. Similarly, the sheer size of the public invest-ment in elementary and secondary education—about one-tenth of public spend-ing and over one-third of all local expenditures—both makes autonomy easier to maintain and increases the urgency of holding school officials accountable.

It is possible that this characterization of schools may soon sound outdated: during the 1990s the demands for accountability have gained ascendance over the structural and normative drive toward autonomy. Schools are not, after all, her-metically sealed. Elected officials have always been connected to schools through patronage, the awarding of contracts, the role of employees (and more recently teachers' unions) in elections, and the fact that voters occasionally punish mayors for scandals or undesired reforms such as mandatory desegregation. The fact that public education has so singularly failed to accomplish its tasks for so many chil-dren, most strikingly in cities like New York, Chicago, and Baltimore, has further increased the clamor from a widening range of outsiders. Citizens and leaders alike are increasingly realizing that education is both too important and too prob-lematic to leave to insiders and hope for the best.

The contributors to this volume demonstrate, however, that despite growing outside involvement, up to this point at least insiders retain substantial advantages in school politics. Along with professional expertise, formal autonomy, and the norm of nonpartisanship in schooling, insiders have staying power. Administra-tors and teachers are essential to the continuous process of education; other major actors matter little except in what have historically been relatively brief periods of outside intervention. These reasons for insiders' advantage are reinforced by the rhythms of fostering and implementing educational reform. Politics, including the politics of school reform, is driven by bursts of activity, short-term changes, and claims of sweeping improvement resulting from this or that restructuring or refinancing. But the outcomes of reform seldom show up for several years, if then, and they inevitably are heavily influenced by the people who stay around the longest—that is, the teachers and administrators who were in place before the reform ever got off the ground.

School politics and prospects for reform are further distinguished from other policy arenas by the unusual kind of organizations produced by professionaliza-tion and internal control. Large school districts, whether in cities like New York or big suburban systems like Montgomery County, spawn hierarchical institu-tions that seldom encourage decentralization or innovation. They operate under detailed sets of rules that codify local policies and practices, state and federal regulations, and in many cases, state or federal court orders. Collective bargaining agreements add to the complexity, setting policies for everything from important matters such as deployment of teachers and class size to trivial matters such as the scheduling of lunch breaks. These rules frame the perspectives and prospects of participants in school politics, usually to the disadvantage of outsiders (or insiders) who want change.

Moreover, school politics is critically and distinctively affected by the labor intensity of education. Most resources go to pay staff salaries and benefits; recipients make strong claims for incremental additional resources and often have enough influence to shield themselves from budget cuts. Thus relatively little funding is available to underwrite substantial reforms without changing the personnel system, as Cheryl Jones and Connie Hill emphasize in their examination of Montgomery County. Since such changes are rare, innovations typically require new sources of funding from local or state government, federal agencies, foundations, court-ordered tax increases, or the private sector. Teachers also derive political influence from their numbers, particularly in large jurisdictions like those examined here. School employees often live in the district in which they work and thus vote and otherwise influence local political outcomes. In Baltimore, as Marion Orr emphasizes, teachers and administrators have developed a web of relationships with influentials in local churches, firms, and community organizations. That web reinforces internal control of the schools and makes inevitably disruptive reforms extremely hard to sustain.

Teachers, of course, are more than claimants and consumers of educational resources; they are the principal players in the actual education of children. Despite the bureaucracies, regulations, and contractual requirements, the essential core of service delivery in education is microlocal. Teachers typically work alone in classrooms, isolated from each other and outside the reach of administrative controls and external pressures. Unfortunately, educational politics usually deals with process reforms of one kind or another that do not connect easily—or at all—with the microcontexts in which most teachers work. And yet it is these contexts that are critical to substantive change in the way children learn. Many education policy experts are converging on an argument that is almost embarrassingly straightforward yet generally ignored: the main determinants of educational achievement are time on task and teaching that actively engages students at a skill level just beyond their current abilities. And yet even these points are surprisingly hard to demonstrate and to instantiate in the hundreds of thousands of classrooms across the nation.

Large school systems, then, are connected with but distinct from other local policy arenas. They are relatively autonomous and highly labor intensive as well as being the locus of huge budgetary outlays and major employment in big cities. They are the carriers of citizens' greatest hopes and deepest values. They are also rule-bound, politically convoluted, and too often substantively disastrous. Thus they are increasingly the focus of reform efforts, although so far reformers have only isolated victories to show for their pains. This complexity is played out in locations with singular contexts, histories, cultures, and personalities. But this context is only the beginning of understanding the complexity of schools; we turn now to another way of mapping the forest while remaining alert to the variations among the trees.

RACE AND SCHOOLS

Race and class, and their interaction, have more impact on education than on any other major public function. With a few celebrated exceptions, the quality and effectiveness of public schools are strongly related to the class (and therefore usually to the race) of the students in a particular school or district. Race and class are intermixed and their effects difficult to disaggregate, but race is in the political forefront even when class is the underlying explanatory factor. The pursuit of racial equality is the primary reason for courts' deep entanglement in public education, particularly in cities. Federal courts have not, in contrast, addressed class-based educational differences, despite the considerable evidence that city-suburban differences in schools derive less from race per se than from the socioeconomic status of students and the wealth of districts. Racial concerns spur the most vehement public involvement in public education. And because race is entangled in almost every issue concerning urban education, racial anxieties and animosities permeate school politics.

With the end of de jure segregation, racial separation in public schools results primarily from the interplay of racially structured housing markets and school district boundaries. School districting, along with land-use policies and locational policies for subsidized housing, bolster market forces and individuals' social choices. De facto school segregation, in turn, reinforces housing choices based on racial considerations. These patterns are pervasive because they serve the desires of most whites, who want to be separated from blacks, especially from lower-income African Americans, and who do not want to live in places where blacks, regardless of their incomes, are the predominant group.

Municipal and school district boundaries frame the organization of school systems and their racial composition. Schools in the city typically are in a separate school district from schools in suburban areas, as in the case of all the cities we studied except Charlotte and Yonkers. City schools enroll most of the African American students in a metropolitan area because blacks are concentrated in cities. City schools also have disproportionate shares of Latino, Asian American, and immigrant students as well as a larger share of students from low-income families, regardless of race or ethnicity. The prevalence of poor and minority students in city schools has accelerated the exodus of white and better-off families with children, who exit either to the suburbs or to private schools. The result, as Stone points out and the other case studies implicitly demonstrate, is that city

schools have larger minority and low-income proportions than the city population as a whole and much larger minority and low-income proportions than the
surrounding suburbs. These developments combine to make race a pervasive and
explosive element in the politics of education in big cities.

Concentration of African Americans in the urban core has made city schools
the primary battleground over de facto school segregation. And confining integration efforts to city schools — the outcome of political resistance to more inclusive
approaches and judicial unwillingness to move beyond existing school district
boundaries in addressing school segregation — has exacerbated rather than alleviated racial separation. For most of the school systems in this study, as across the
nation, the possibilities of integrating black and white students have been undermined by the availability of exit options for middle-income whites, particularly
school districts beyond the city limits that offer safe haven from court orders. For
places like Chicago and Baltimore, desegregation has become virtually irrelevant.

As Kathryn McDermott shows in New Haven, African Americans as well
as whites increasingly question efforts that can yield only token integration in
city districts that contain few white children. Even in places such as Charlotte
and Yonkers, where integration is demographically feasible (in Charlotte because
of a countywide school district and in Yonkers as a result of district boundaries
that encompass substantial amounts of suburban development), many blacks have
lost faith in desegregation schemes. Their reasons are various. Some African
Americans see themselves as short-changed by efforts to retain whites, which involve pouring resources into schools in white neighborhoods and shielding these
schools from inner-city children. Others see any desegregation effort as inevitably paying insufficient attention to the distinctive educational needs of black
children in a white-dominated society. Still others (a small minority of citizens
but an important segment of political activists) are ideologically committed to
race-based nationalism and black control of black institutions. Surveys indicate
that most African Americans would still prefer integrated schools to any other
alternative; but with a few notable exceptions, the energy and initiative have left
the desegregation movement.

Blacks (and other nonwhite groups) do not constitute a monolithic interest
in urban schools, an underappreciated fact that makes the interplay of race and
school politics even more complex. In cities like Atlanta and Baltimore, African Americans are both influential insiders who benefit from the system *and*
marginalized outsiders with no voice in schools that fail their children, and in
places like Chicago and New York, Latinos as well as blacks play both roles. City
schools that do not work hasten the exodus of black and brown, as well as white,
middle-class families and thus increase the concentration of disadvantaged minority children in city schools. Growing numbers of Latino and Asian American
students further change (and complicate) the racial complexion of school politics. African Americans and other ethnic groups are frequently more divided than
united; a good example is San Francisco, where Latinos and Asian Americans are

contesting their lack of representation in the process that oversees court-ordered desegregation efforts.

CITIES AND SCHOOLS

School district boundaries, of course, frame more than racial boundaries among students. Urban schools, encompassing the same political space as cities, face the same demographic, economic, and financial constraints as those cities themselves. They serve most of the poor as well as the minority students in the metropolis; they rest on a declining economic base; and they depend on a severely pressured tax base. City schools have relatively little control over these contextual factors. They do not fix city and school district boundaries; they do not determine the local taxable resources that can be tapped to finance schools; they have no control over who lives and works in the city and who does not. Working within these givens loads the deck against success for city schools. And their frequent failure to function effectively in this environment, though hardly surprising, sharpens the substantive and political contrasts between public education inside and outside the city limits.

Our case studies underscore the importance of the political separation of city and suburban schools. What are the critical differences between a tragically ineffective school district such as Baltimore and a largely successful one such as Montgomery County? Large bureaucracies and powerful teachers' unions often are accused of causing urban school failure. But both Baltimore and Montgomery are large districts, organized along standard hierarchical lines, run by education professionals who have mostly internalized control and teachers who collectively have considerable influence on outcomes. What Montgomery has that Baltimore does not is the good fortune of a largely affluent population base, a burgeoning economy, and a political boundary that separates it from the District of Columbia.

Within cities, the social and economic changes that have compounded the schools' problems have also increased their importance as sources of employment, contracts, and other rewards. Marion Orr documents the significance of public schools as major employers in older cities, and school jobs loom ever larger as private firms continue to leave the city. Tim Ross shows similarly that jobs are one of the prime attractions of New York City's community school districts in poor areas like East Brooklyn and that jobholders will fight fiercely to hold onto the little they have, even at the expense of children's education. These cases are not unusual; in a number of big cities, African Americans hold many if not most school jobs, from the lowest service to the highest administrative positions.

Thus the economic implications of public schooling increase minority stakes in existing institutional arrangements in cities that are otherwise hemorrhaging jobs and infrastructure. Reform threatens both black school employees and black control over a key economic and political resource, adding racial and material dimensions to already-tense negotiations over school boards, superintendents, principals, and teachers. Excessive bureaucratization, in short, does not in itself cause the educational failures of inner-city schools—after all, Montgomery County is also topheavy. But too many placeholders interact with too little money and severe social problems both to worsen the problems that already exist and to make possible solutions much harder to attempt.

Black control of city schools brings substantial risks as well as rewards for city residents. In Atlanta, blacks traded off desegregation for control of the schools, which were seen by African Americans as a great prize—a source of pride, jobs, and contracts. But the price was high. Black control was unable to stem the established dynamic of growing corruption, falling test scores, increasing public dissatisfaction, and widespread disgust with the board of education. White and black middle-class flight accelerated, and Atlanta's influential business elite turned its back on the public school system. Critics, including African Americans who wanted schools that worked, joined forces in 1993 to oust the school board and to reorganize school finances. But education continues to have low salience for business leaders and elected politicians in Atlanta, in contrast to some cities discussed in this book where political and economic elites are leading efforts to overhaul the schools.

It is important to emphasize the recency, and therefore the indeterminacy as yet, of these elite-led reform efforts. Mayors have typically preferred to avoid entanglement in schools, emphasizing city hall's lack of authority over education. A good example here is New Haven, where McDermott shows how the mayor carefully avoided engaging with the Regional Forum to plan for desegregation despite the statutory requirement for his, or his delegate's, participation. But in other cities mayors are changing their tune, concluding that they cannot afford to stand on the sidelines as school problems worsen and public dissatisfaction grows. After all, political foes, the media, and the public increasingly blame mayors for the multiplying woes of their city's schools, regardless of their formal authority. Mayors also cannot ignore the costs of public education for fiscally hard-pressed city governments, which typically are responsible for the local share of school funds. As a result, education has moved to center stage in some cities, most notably Chicago, where Mayor Richard Daley now has direct responsibility for the schools, and New York, where Mayor Rudolph Giuliani has effected substantial change even though the legislature denied him the direct powers he requested. Executive control in Cleveland, Boston, Philadelphia, and Washington, DC, is not far behind. As Clarence Stone emphasizes, these are major changes in urban politics, and they will dramatically change the politics of education in at least some big cities.

Mayors, however, were not major players in most of the cities examined in this book—showing once again the importance of context in determining various interests' engagement with school politics. Business executives, in contrast, were increasingly involved in our cases, as they have been more generally in recent years, especially in large cities. Business leaders play a major role in reform efforts in Charlotte and, according to Dorothy Shipps, were at base responsible both for the decentralization of school management in 1988 in Chicago and for the even greater centralization than ever before in 1995. In Houston too, as Thomas Longoria shows, corporations have moved into the schools on a number of fronts.

In Longoria's view, a goal of these unusual forays is to heighten business influence in education policy and curriculum; and economic elites' influence on the content and the structure of public education is certainly growing. This dynamic occurs for several reasons. City schools are increasingly dependent on businesses to provide resources. Businesses increasingly perceive that they cannot lure the workers they want to their city if the schools in that location have a poor reputation. Most important, citizens and policy actors alike increasingly think of schools, and especially of school reform, in terms of economic development. Reformers argue that the economy, national and local, needs workers with technological and interpersonal skills, and the schools are the appropriate place to begin inculcating these skills. But, continues the argument, urban (and rural) schools are failing in that task, so they must be reformed to make them more productive.

These rationales based on the desire for economic development may be powerful levers for change in reified educational establishments, especially if they bring with them powerful external actors such as mayors and corporate vice-presidents. But our studies suggest wide variations in the levels of economic elites' engagement rather than a steadfast pursuit of control over schools. Corporate elites get involved in some places but not others, stay involved in some reform efforts but bail out elsewhere after a few years, and range from influential to marginal participants in school politics. At most, these studies provide uneven evidence of schooling structures analogous to those regimes that control economic development and downtown revitalization in many cities; after all, the latter concerns not only are more important to business, but they also offer better prospects for favorable outcomes than the seemingly intractably failing public schools.

Most striking, and most disheartening, in almost all of these cities is the virtual absence of involved parents and the thin presence of community groups. If any set of people ought to have the interests of children's education at heart, it should be parents in a local school; even if parents care only about their own child, they can be expected to recognize that their child cannot be taught effectively if other children in the same classroom are not. But parents' concerns usually get lost as better-positioned actors pursue their particular interests, in which children's learning often comes second to job security, electoral prospects, or simply making it through the day. Community school boards, parental advisory groups, and other devices designed to enhance grassroots access have had little sustained impact, and they have mostly failed to increase either the amount of involvement or the effectiveness of poor and minority parents whose children are at greatest risk in city schools.

Sometimes groups lack impact because they do not try very hard, are internally fragmented, or lack staying power. Sometimes, as in Chicago, the effects of parental control vary enormously, depending on subtle factors such as the personal interactions of particular principals and particular parents. But too often community groups struggle vigorously for paltry results, as Timothy Ross shows in East Brooklyn, because school personnel bitterly resist not only their specific suggestions for reform but also the very idea that the community has any right to be involved in what happens in the purportedly public schools. That may be the saddest commentary on the deterioration of urban public education.

CIVIC CAPACITY

Clarence Stone responds to this depressing portrait with the concept of civic capacity. He sees engagement by mayors, business leaders, parents, community interests, and other outsiders with city schools as enhancing the collective ability to undertake and sustain desired changes, which in turn increases the likelihood that educational reform efforts will take root. Perhaps. But among the eleven cities that Stone examines, only Pittsburgh demonstrates a strong link between civic capacity and substantial change in educational policy. The case of Charlotte indicates further that even when civic capacity is mobilized in support of educational reform, that mobilization is difficult to sustain over time. Although Stephen Smith shows how a high level of civic capacity was essential in initiating both Charlotte's desegregation plans and its later neighborhood-based educational reforms, he also shows how fragile both coalitions have proved in the face of demographic and political changes. (The role of business in the Charlotte coalition is particularly interesting because corporate involvement was neither short term nor focused on goals specific to business. The economic elite steadfastly supported a new school superintendent and his reform efforts, and this strong backing was critical to his initial success. But even business commitment did not suffice to sustain civic capacity for reform.) Whether the exceptionally long-standing involvement of Chicago's business community will show greater effects in the next decade than it has shown in the past few remains to be seen. Shipps shows that at this point business leaders seem determined, the mayor is in accord, and some other components of a civic coalition are in place. Even that ever-receding goal, enhanced educational achievement, seems closer at hand, given that both reading and math scores improved during the 1996–1997 academic year in many Chicago schools.

Part of the appeal of civic capacity is the notion that broad-scale involvement in educational politics will produce not only better test scores but also a deeper commitment to fostering the public interest through more equitable public schooling. But the evidence on this score is at best mixed, both in these studies and more generally. Wide involvement usually has not fostered racial integration; to the contrary, participation by concerned citizens and elected officials continually and effectually undermined local, state, and judicial efforts to desegregate

Yonkers's schools or to disperse subsidized housing in order to lessen racial concentration in the schools. The case of New Haven also underscores the limits of participatory processes in resolving racial issues or promoting racial equality and integration. Kathryn McDermott suggests that increasing civic capacity through widespread participation in Connecticut's reform process might have worked had the law that established the process been stronger. But we doubt that the legislature would have passed a stronger law under most plausibly imaginable circumstances — and even if it had, we see few grounds for believing that any politically feasible participatory process would have produced a different outcome.

We are not arguing that participation in school politics is unimportant or undesirable. We claim instead that, at a minimum, inclusive processes do not necessarily advance educational reforms and that, at a maximum, additional participants make progress even more difficult than it otherwise would be, given the variety of interests, priorities, and stakes of different players, particularly in the beleaguered realm of city schools. But this is hardly an argument for leaving city schools to the entrenched insiders and inert bureaucracies. The cases of Baltimore, Chicago, New York City, and elsewhere provide stark evidence that circumstances are likely to get even worse in the absence of multiple stakeholders. Schools in these cities were left alone to rot, and they did.

BEYOND THE CITIES

School district boundaries, particularly between city and suburb, create separate political worlds that preoccupy almost all local participants in school politics. We see essentially no shared interests in education among cities or across city/suburban lines lacking boundaries that encompass both units. Among the many possible examples in our cases, McDermott's analysis of New Haven vividly illustrates how local boundaries are reified. District lines set constraints on finances, educational planning, issue definition, potential political alliances, and logistical possibilities for school desegregation — creating what even participants in educational reform efforts deem to be an immutable prior condition rather than a politically manipulable institution like any other. Similarly, the only shared goal in many metropolitan areas is economic development; other matters (such as education) that also affect everyone in the region are marginalized or ignored.

Ironically, although district boundaries inhibit the search for solutions, they offer little resistance to the social and economic forces that substantially create the problems of urban school systems to begin with. We have already discussed the implications of the fact that firms' and families' movement across these boundaries has increased the concentration of poor and minority students in city schools. But movement out of cities has also resulted in growing minority populations in some suburbs. Thus suburban school systems are increasingly wrestling with racial issues — which vary, as does everything in school politics, depending

on the particular context. In many metropolitan areas, the concentration of minority students in small portions of suburbia combines with a multiplicity of suburban school districts to confine racial issues to a few particular school districts.
Large suburban jurisdictions, however, engage substantial portions of suburbia in
racial issues, thereby providing a setting in which school integration is more feasible than in cities or in small suburban districts.

As Cheryl Jones and Connie Hill demonstrate in chapter 7 on Montgomery
County, the trajectory of racial issues in a large suburban system reflects the political dynamics of the particular school district. (This point should sound familiar
by now.) Minorities in Montgomery County see a school system whose center of
gravity is its large enrollment of white, middle-class students. Not surprisingly,
schools in the more affluent, predominantly white areas, are the most successful. Their continued success is essential to sustaining the county's reputation for
an excellent school system, a central concern of economic and political elites as
well as of top school officials. Parents in the favored areas have experience with
and influence on the school system, and their interests largely concur with those
of the insiders who control the system. More precisely, the schools' primary goal
in dealing with racial issues was to accommodate the dominant interests; thus the
centerpiece of Montgomery's desegregation effort was a magnet plan designed
to minimize opposition from whites while foreclosing intervention by the courts.
On both counts the plan succeeded (although Montgomery's magnets, located in
minority areas, have not attracted many white students).

The importance of context is further underscored by the willingness of most
minority interests in Montgomery to trade off influence in the schools for a better
education. After all, their main comparison group is African American and other
non-Anglo students across the school district line in Washington, who are in
much worse educational circumstances than their own children are. Thus even
though minority students do not do as well as whites in Montgomery County and
are disproportionately taught in older schools and classrooms largely populated
by other minority students, African American and Latino parents have offered
only a limited challenge to the inequities of their system.

Stephen Smith's study of Charlotte provides a window on a different kind of
metropolitan setting, which joins city and suburbia in a single countywide school
system encompassing 530 square miles. The presence of white suburbs within
the school district made metropolitan catchment areas—which many reformers
prefer as a way to ensure racial integration, provide an economic mix among students, involve a wide range of interests, and secure more equitable financing—
possible. And the busing plan backed by the business community and other interests was, in fact, unusually successful in promoting desegregation for several
decades. But metropolitan-based student assignments have not been sustained
in this highly dynamic setting. Interests that favored metropolitan desegregation
have lost political energy and resources. The African American community developed internal splits, similar to those in major cities, over whether resources

should be allocated primarily to neighborhood (racially separate) or districtwide (racially desegregated) schools. Newcomers to the rapidly growing region, particularly in the burgeoning white areas along the periphery, had little or no commitment to desegregation and no knowledge of Charlotte's unusual history on this score. To be sure, Charlotte-Mecklenburg County continues to provide a metropolitan institutional and financial base for the schools, which yields important benefits for schools and children in black areas; and, as Smith reports, the latest change in school leadership has bolstered the prospects for desegregation in the district. These ups and downs underscore the political obstacles to lasting desegregation of the schools even in a favorable setting.

A district's financial base also has important implications for school politics, and here too suburban and urban districts typically differ. All school districts face growing resource constraints in an era of less government, lower taxes, and dissatisfied citizens. Thus demands on the schools are perhaps becoming more difficult to satisfy, even while they are increasing in scope and intensity. Nevertheless, school officials in districts with relatively abundant resources, such as suburban counties like Montgomery, are better equipped to incorporate critics into a mutually accommodating benefit coalition that supports the existing system than are officials in poor districts. The politics of plenty are always easier than the politics of scarcity—teachers are more easily satisfied, programs added, and facilities upgraded. And once again, context is the determining factor, since at the margin resources are determined by the boundaries of a school district.

FEDERAL AND STATE INTERVENTION

Several of our cases underscore the critical impact that judges and court rulings can have on educational politics and policy. We have already discussed court-ordered desegregation in Charlotte. In San Francisco, court decrees established a parallel and often superior set of policymakers to the regular system of school governance, in the process creating more and less privileged players in educational politics. Court intervention in Yonkers broke an impasse over school desegregation, leading to substantial changes in education and housing policies (if not always to changes in practices). The threat of court intervention also can be a powerful stimulus to local education policymakers, as illustrated by Montgomery County's desegregation plan. The effort to head off court intervention generated the abortive process of participatory desegregation planning in New Haven; had the planning been more effective, the ruling in *Sheff v. O'Neill* might have been different.

Courts, however, like other outsiders in the world of educational politics, are at a disadvantage in their efforts to create and sustain reform. They intend to be temporary rather than permanent participants (although they retain jurisdiction in some school desegregation cases like San Francisco for decades). They necessarily rely on local school administrators for implementation of their decrees and usually for information about the success of that implementation. Most parents, community groups, and educational professionals agree with each other in seeing the court as an interloper, even if they agree on little else. Thus courts can be effective agents for desegregating schools and changing funding formulas, but their effectiveness even here is by no means guaranteed and in general is limited to the form rather than the substance of schooling.

This generalization does have at least one exception. San Francisco's consent decree created an unusually effective process of court-supervised reform that, as Luis Fraga, Bari Anhalt Erlichson, and Sandy Lee point out, led to substantial and persistent changes both within the schools and in educational politics. Two factors enabled this success: the creation of a parallel policy process and a decree that was detailed with respect to goals but sufficiently vague on the means to permit flexibility and generate acquiescence or even support from administrators and teachers. Still, the path to school reform has not been smooth. Opposition to the consent decree led the school board to dismiss one superintendent, and his two successors did little to implement the decree; only recently has there been a new superintendent committed to the process. (And, since this case was completed, the teachers' union's resistance to full-fledged reconstitution is again threatening to halt the process.)

This history suggests that even where court intervention has great impact and longevity, the long-term viability of court-ordered changes depends on developing local constituency support. And, as Fraga and his coauthors note, this is the most tenuous aspect of reform in San Francisco. No leader has sought to create such popular support; and an increasingly vocal Chinese American constituency, as well as the teachers' union, opposes the consent decree.

Perhaps state governments are the solution; after all, in many respects, states are more potent sources of outside intervention into immobilized school districts than are the federal courts. Local school systems derive their authority, structure, and boundaries from state governments as well as a growing portion of their finances. Thus states have the formal power to change the way schools are organized, financed, staffed; they can also dictate curricula, standards, and testing for various grade levels.

In our studies, however, the states are notable mainly for their low profile. This observation may reflect the particular cases and the timing of these studies; after all, state financing of local schools, often in response to state court rulings, clearly has had a significant impact on many urban school systems. Further, states have begun recently to stir from hibernation and to exercise their power, as new laws on school governance in Illinois, New York, and Ohio, and the active involvement of Maryland in restructuring Baltimore's schools, suggest. Nonetheless, in most cases presented in this book, governors and state legislatures are largely absent, and state education departments made little difference to school or district policies.

State intervention, moreover, is not guaranteed to make much headway in reforming schools. When states do intervene, as the Yonkers and New Haven cases show, their actions are likely to be shaped by the same kind of political forces that influence local school policy. Plans of the New York state Education Department for fostering school integration in Yonkers, for example, foundered on the same legislative and constituency resistance to desegregation that had halted local superintendents' plans to integrate. Ditto in New Haven.

The ideology of local control over education has also historically constrained federal and state involvement in school district policymaking. Few participants in school politics deny that school systems should reflect local interests, values, and needs; even strong supporters of national standards, state financing, or metropolitan desegregation typically pay homage to local control. For our purposes, the merits of local control matter less than the political consequences; the specter of centralization produces a context that discourages direct intervention by politically sensitive players in state capitals and in Washington and provides a rallying point against court-ordered desegregation that sidesteps race. It remains to be seen whether the new efforts by states to get control of foundering urban districts can be sustained in the face of so many pressures against them.

DISSATISFACTION AND DISSONANCE

What can be said about the prospects for reform? We start with the widespread demand for change in education. Kathy Doherty's review of survey data underscores strong support for national educational standards and increased school funding and high levels of dissatisfaction with the schools (at least in other people's districts). But it also shows wide variance in recommendations for specific changes. Demands reflect agendas ranging from (more or less) sex education and creation science to a focus on good work habits and the three Rs (or, alternatively, a focus on open classrooms and extensive extracurricular activities). Interested parties always identify another set of players as the problem: everyone but school administrators cites bureaucracy as an obstacle to reform; all but teachers cite teachers' unions as a barrier to change. Parents blame teachers, who return the compliment even more forcefully. The result, as Doherty notes, is that all actors dislike the current system, but no majority coalesces around support for any particular set of changes. As with all other problems of school reform, this outcome occurs most often and most virulently in cities.

Confusion, low expectations, and cynicism about education reform are understandable, given the endless wave of contradictory reforms that roil through the schools. Underlying all the froth are two central problems. One is the lack of really trustworthy evaluations of the many well-meaning programs to educate children more effectively (although this problem too may be partly solved by the forthcoming Rand evaluations of the New Schools Corporation). Perhaps a more severe problem is the demonstrated difficulty in bringing even successful programs on one site up to scale. There are many reasons for the barriers to systemwide success: the apparent success of an individual program may have been exaggerated; contextual differences are crucially important in schooling; children learn in different ways and thus respond differently to various treatments; almost no reform has much impact on a resistant teacher in his or her own classroom.

One possible conclusion is that educational policy change is not worth the effort; certainly evidence from studies of desegregation, funding equalization, decentralization, and vouchers fuels skepticism about substantial connections between process and performance. Nevertheless, activists seeking to change the organization, content, or financing of education seem little affected by doubts about the efficacy of their preferred reforms. In other words, educational politics is not going to go away just because who wins or loses the next round may not have much impact on what children learn.

Rising dissatisfaction clearly complicates this already convoluted dynamic of reform and retrenchment. More interests demanding a voice increase the number of stakeholders with claims on the educational system. The diversity of those interests and claims means less consensus and more conflict. Without severe external pressures and profound budget cuts as in New York City, insiders, ironically, find it easier to deflect pressures for change, despite the growing number of participants. Divergent visions of what needs to change, how to create those changes, and what would count as "success" neutralize one another in most cases, permitting school officials to maintain their preferred course with relatively minor accommodations.

Here too, the politics of education reform is moving so swiftly that it is possible that our cases will soon be outdated and these cautions outworn. But we doubt it. The reasons for stasis are strong, and we predict that without cohesive and sustained demands for reform, insiders are likely to protect their core interests. Even with cohesive and sustained external demands, change is not possible without the active involvement of insiders. These case studies teach us, over and over, that the people who operate the educational system will not be reorganized, decentralized, priced, privatized, or otherwise reformed out of the picture. Someone has to run whatever system operates public education, and lots of someones have to teach our children every day, starting tomorrow. There are no others to do these things.

The political lesson here is that the existing policy system will necessarily be a central part of any change, which in turn means that change has to accommodate at least some of the interests of the key existing players. Equally clear from these and many other studies of educational politics is the low probability of insiders implementing significant changes without substantial external pressures. Change, therefore, requires outsiders as well as insiders, particularly outsiders with the talent and sustained commitment to bridge the multiple interests and goals that accompany rising demands for change. No particular type of outside intervention is necessary or sufficient to produce educational change. But whether the key outside actors are local (mayors and business elites are the usual suspects) or nonlocal (courts and state education commissioners), their prospects for reform will improve if civic capacity is enhanced through the creation of broad reform coalitions that include but are not dominated by insiders.

CAUTION BUT NOT DESPAIR

Much of what emerges from this volume is not very encouraging for the larger issues of democracy, representation, accountability, and equal opportunity. Schools are supposed to be a democratizing institution, but public education is an uninspiring role model for young minds. School boards are presumably the instruments of democracy, but they seldom fostered citizen participation or attended to the educational interests of the community. Instead, they typically were captured by insiders, focused on constituency service or patronage, and had little influence on significant school policies. Only in opposition to desegregation did school boards' representative role usually come to the forefront, as responsive boards dampened integration efforts in Charlotte, Yonkers, and San Francisco.

The ironies continue: local control is supposed to empower parents and community residents who have the interests of children at heart, but it is mostly a fiasco for the poor and minority communities who are among its intended beneficiaries. Fewer than 10 percent of residents bother to vote in local school board elections in cities that have experimented with decentralization. School-based management committees in Chicago and elsewhere have often been captured by small cliques—sometimes committed parents and community activists, more often school insiders or predators eager to exploit the schools for their own benefit. Teachers' unions, products of a labor movement that once offered a progressive counterforce to powerful and reactionary business interests, have become powerful and largely reactionary defenders of their own interests. Business, conversely, in these cases is typically more progressive than labor and shows greater concern for educational achievement than do teachers' unions, or for that matter, education bureaucrats or school boards. The consequence of these failures of democratic representation, political accountability, community activism, and labor organization is painfully clear in most urban school systems—there is very little education going on and no equality of opportunity.

What has gone wrong? In the final irony, democratically based demands, as well as most authoritative external intervention, have been muffled by the desire to keep politics out of education. Parents often do not think of themselves as legitimate interveners in the professional realm of education, and school insiders do their utmost to limit parental involvement to bake sales and checking homework. Mayors generally have steered clear of education, rarely been punished electorally for ignoring failing city schools, and get involved primarily to advance their political interests. State and federal elected officials are inhibited by the ideology of local control of the schools and by their need for cooperative local officials to carry out their mandates. Courts, the least democratic institution, are the most focused on attaining equality in the schools; but they are poorly positioned to engage in the detailed actions needed to secure equitable educational opportunities for all children.

In this political world, no reform proposals—about either educational practices or processes—are so persuasive that they are likely to create broad-based coalitions committed to massive change. And without such a coalition or central direction, educational policymakers are unlikely to agree—even within a district, never mind across districts—on revolutionary new strategies or paths of action. Thus piecemeal incrementalism appears inevitable, with the pace and direction of change strongly influenced by the particular context. Many will continue to do a bit of this or that, or switch course before the previous reform has had much of a test—responses that will themselves be encouraged by the endless succession of reform proposals, most of which neither produce the promised results nor are persuasively evaluated. We are sorry to conclude, therefore, that the most powerful message emerging from these studies is that given the configuration of local political forces, there are no clear rules about how to create, sustain, or motivate either educational reform from below or the pursuit of national goals from above.

Some observers may find this conclusion a cause for celebration; for them, local autonomy and variation are the saving virtues of public education in the United States. In a diverse society where people are spatially differentiated by income, class, ethnicity, race, and religion, particular school districts and individual schools inevitably march to different drummers. Despite the general failures of urban school systems, some city schools do a much better job of educating disadvantaged children than others. Within most schools, some teachers are strikingly more effective than others. And some children learn, graduate, and succeed in even the most dismal city classrooms. Parents and community groups connect with each other and educators far more productively in some places than in others; and involvement by business and political elites has changed the dynamics of public education in some cities. Education, moreover, is an inherently decentralized function with respect to the most important transactions, those involving teaching and learning. Finally, the lack of widespread consensus on what kinds of change are needed—more equitable financing, less class and racial separation, greater choice, smaller classes, more emphasis on basics, or standards for this or that—should give pause to advocates of systemic reform.

Still, we question whether the answer lies in reaffirming the virtues of local autonomy. Like most of the authors in this volume, we find the benefits of decentralization come with heavy costs rooted in disparities in financial resources, school facilities, effective teachers, responsive administration, educational practices, and community inputs. Our nation's history shows that systemic changes are necessary, if not sufficient, to generate more equitable outcomes for poor children and children of disfavored races. Should Americans concur that every child must be enabled to reach some minimal level of educational accomplishment, then national standards and a new set of nationally shared educational practices will be needed. In the end, practices are more important than standards, since the goal is to improve education rather than to provide a national scorecard that presumably will underscore what we already know — that city school districts, schools, and students perform poorly in contrast to most other schools. Improving the substance of urban education requires systematic efforts to identify what seems to work in particular contexts, to evaluate promising practices, and to make this information widely available to school districts, political leaders, economic and community interests, and citizens. Both scorecards and workable models should strengthen the hand of those who seek better educational outcomes in cities, the performance regimes that Clarence Stone discusses in the introduction. The studies in the volume suggest both the potential of such groupings and the need for more supportive frameworks for change. The need is to marry the reality of a diverse and decentralized system with the promise of systemic change dedicated to narrowing the gap between what we are doing and what we need to do for our children's sake, particularly those children whose life chances are unfairly constrained by the failure of so many urban schools.

NOTE

1. We would like to thank Kathryn McDermott, Tim Ross, Dorothy Shipps, Stephen Smith, Clarence Stone, and two anonymous reviewers for their help in revisions of this chapter.

Contributors

Michael N. Danielson is the B. C. Forbes Professor of Public Affairs and professor of politics and public affairs at Princeton University. He has written widely on urban politics, with most of his work focusing on the interplay of urban and political development. His books include *Home Team: Professional Sports and the American Metropolis; Profits and Politics in Paradise: The Development of Hilton Head Island; The Politics of Rapid Urbanization; New York: The Politics of Urban Regional Development;* and *The Politics of Exclusion.* With Jennifer Hochschild, he is currently engaged in a study of New York state's ill-fated involvement in Yonkers and its implications for politics and policy involving race, education, and housing, which is supported in part by the Spencer Foundation.

Kathryn M. Doherty is a doctoral candidate in the Department of Government and Politics at the University of Maryland, College Park, working on a dissertation on citizenship, community, and private homeowner associations.

Bari Anhalt Erlichson is assistant professor of political science in the Edward J. Bloustein School of Planning and Public Policy at Rutgers University. She received a B.A. degree (1991) from Dartmouth College in government, an M.A. degree (1994) from the School of Education at Stanford University in administration and policy analysis, and a Ph.D. degree (1997) in political science from Stanford University.

Luis Ricardo Fraga is an associate professor in the Department of Political Science at Stanford University. He received his A.B. from Harvard University and his Ph.D. from Rice University. In 1989–1990 he was a fellow at the Center for Advanced Study in the Behavioral Sciences. He has published widely in scholarly journals, including *Journal of Politics, Urban Affairs Review, Political Research Quarterly,* and *West European Politics* as well as in a number of edited volumes.

He is a coeditor of *Ethnic and Racial Minorities in Advanced Industrial Democracies* (Greenwood Press, 1992). He is also coeditor of a book series, "Race and Ethnicity in American Politics," with the University Press of Virginia.

Connie Hill is a doctoral candidate in the Department of Government and Politics at the University of Maryland. Her research focuses on community support for public schools. She is currently studying community support in Alabama.

Jennifer L. Hochschild is a professor of politics and public affairs at Princeton University with a joint appointment in the department of politics and the Woodrow Wilson School of Public and International Affairs. She is the author of *Facing Up to the American Dream: Race, Class and the Soul of the Nation, The New American Dilemma: Liberal Democracy and School Desegregation,* and *What's Fair: American Beliefs about Distributive Justice.*

Cheryl L. Jones is a doctoral candidate in the Department of Political Science at the University of Maryland. She is currently working on her dissertation, a comparative study of education politics in two Maryland counties.

Sandy S. Lee is a second-year student at Boalt Hall School of Law, University of California, Berkeley. She received her B.A. in public policy, with honors, from Stanford University in 1996.

Thomas Longoria Jr. received his Ph.D. from Texas A&M University and is currently assistant professor of political science at the University of Wisconsin–Milwaukee. He is the author of recent articles in *Social Science Quarterly* and *Urban Affairs Review.* He is also coauthor with J. P. Polinard, Robert Wrinkle, and Norman Binder of *Electoral Structure and Urban Policy: The Impact on Mexican American Communities* (M. E. Sharpe, 1994).

Kathryn A. McDermott is a public policy consultant in New Haven, Connecticut. Her current project is a proposal for integration and interdistrict school choice in the Hartford metropolitan area. She has also taught political science at Yale University, where she earned her Ph.D.

Marion Orr is an assistant professor of political science at Duke University. He earned his Ph.D. from the University of Maryland. In 1991 and 1992 he was a research fellow at the Brookings Institution. His research interests are in the areas of urban politics and urban public policy. His work has appeared in *Journal of Urban Affairs, Urban Review, Urban Affairs Review, Politics and Society,* and other publications.

Timothy A. Ross is a senior research associate at the Center for Urban Research in New York City. His research interests include community organizing, urban policy analysis, and minority political incorporation. He lives in the Park Slope section of Brooklyn, New York.

Dorothy Shipps is a research associate at the University of Chicago studying the relationships among urban schools, districts, and state governance. Currently, she is writing a historical study of corporate involvement in Chicago school reform. Shipps is also a director of the Consortium on Chicago School Research, where she has managed the three-year study *Cross-Site Analysis of School System Decentralization* and the institutional analysis of the *Chicago Annenberg Challenge*.

Stephen Samuel Smith is associate professor of political science at Winthrop University in Rock Hill, South Carolina. He is currently working on a book about the political economy of school reform in Charlotte.

Clarence N. Stone is professor of government and politics at the University of Maryland. He is the author of *Regime Politics: Governing Atlanta, 1946–1988,* winner of the American Political Science Association's Ralph Bunche Award and of the Urban Politics Section's Best Book Award. Stone is currently engaged in a multicity study of urban education.

Index